Cuban Sugar in the Age of Mass Production

A l a n   D y e

Cuban Sugar in the Age of Mass Production

Technology and the Economics of the Sugar Central, *1899–1929*

Stanford University Press
Stanford, California   1998

Stanford University Press
Stanford, California
© 1998 by the Board of Trustees of the
Leland Stanford Junior University
Printed in the United States of America
CIP data are at the end of the book

A c k n o w l e d g m e n t s

MUCH OF THE RESEARCH for this book has depended on the extensive material contained in the Braga Brothers Collection in the University Archives at the University of Florida at Gainesville. I would like to express my appreciation to the archive staff there and, in particular, to Carl Van Ness. The time and energy he took to discuss with me the contents of the collection and to make the resources of the archives available to me went well beyond the call of duty. I would also like to express my gratitude to the Fanjul family, who made the Braga Brothers Collection available for public use.

Two of these chapters have appeared elsewhere in different forms. Chapter 6 appeared as "Avoiding Holdup: Asset Specificity and Technical Change in the Cuban Sugar Industry, 1899–1929," *Journal of Economic History* 54 (1994): 628–53; copyright the Economic History Association, reprinted with the permission of Cambridge University Press. The work presented in Chapter 7 appeared as "Cane Contracting and Renegotiation: A Fixed Effects Analysis of the Adoption of New Technologies in the Cuban Sugar Industry, 1899–1929," *Explorations in Economic History* 31 (1994): 141–75; reprinted with the permission of Academic Press. The Schoff Fund of Columbia University Seminars provided funding to aid the final manuscript preparation.

Many people have contributed in one way or another to the completion of this book. The research represented here began with my work on a Ph.D. dissertation at the University of Illinois at Urbana-Champaign under the direction and mentorship of Larry Neal. I wish to thank him for the numerous hours spent reading and criticizing repeated drafts of these chapters. His suggestions were often critical to the development of the ideas herein. Also very important to the research of this book has been the contribution of Jeremy Atack, whose input has been key to the direction that the empirical examination has taken. I also wish to thank Steve Haber, who in the later stages of the work was instrumental in helping me envision the conversion of what was initially purely a cliometric work into one with broader appeal. Further, I would like to thank Stanley Engerman for two careful readings of the manuscript, one in its earlier, one in its final form, and James Simpson for a very thorough reading of the final manuscript. I would also like to thank Werner Baer for comments on the research and for encouragement to continue with the work. His devotion to the study of Latin America has been an inspiration to me, as it has to many others.

Besides these it gives me pleasure to acknowledge a long list of people whose comments and suggestions have aided me greatly, either through readings of various preliminary versions of the chapters or through participation in seminars and workshops. Different parts of the book have benefited from the participants in economic history workshops at the University of Illinois, the University of Michigan, the Universidad Carlos III de Madrid, Columbia University, the Universidad de la Habana, the Universidad Autónoma de Barcelona, Northwestern University, the University of Chicago, and the Fundación Ortega y Gasset in Madrid, and from conferences of the Economic History Association, the Cliometric Society, and the Instituto de Historia Cubano. I would also like to emphasize the important influence of my former colleagues at the Universidad Carlos III de Madrid. The active academic environment of the economic history group there in 1991–93 acted as a greenhouse for my research as it entered its second phase. I benefited repeatedly from discussions with my colleagues: Leandro Prados de la Escosura, Pedro Fraile, Francesco Galassi, Carlos Newland, Zacarías Moutoukias, Antonio Tena, Daniel Díaz Fuentes, Antonio Santamaría, Stefan Houpt, Pedro Lains, Andrés Hoyo, and Juan Carmona. Thanks also to my research assistants, Juan Balán and Judy Berenthal. Numerous other persons should also receive recognition for helpful comments, suggestions, and discussions at various stages of the work. Many thanks to Arnab Acharya, Lee Alston, César Ayala, Laird Bergad, Lou Cain, Greg Clark, Jim Conklin, Michael Edelstein, Shane Greenstein, Knick Harley, Fe Iglesias, Sumner LaCroix, Francine LaFontaine, Maggie Levenstein, Jordi Maluquer, Scott Masten, Joel Mokyr, Steven Quinn, Chris Schmidt-Nowara, Rebecca Scott, Rich Sicotte, Ken Sokoloff, Ross Thomson, David Weiman, Warren Whatley, and Oscar Zanetti.

Much of the research also depended on the efficient operation of the libraries of the various institutions where I have worked. In particular, the interlibrary loan staff at the University of Illinois deserves considerable recognition. At the early stages of research, their expertise at locating obscure documents was essential to my collection of some of the quantitative materials. I also wish to extend my appreciation for the archive staff at the Cuban National Archive and at the National Library José Martí in Havana. Because of their devotion to learning, they continue to provide cheerfully the services essential to research, even under the extremely adverse economic conditions of the 1990s in Havana. They have my greatest admiration.

Finally, I would like to thank my wife, Linda Barrington, who has read sections of the work, given me many useful comments on content and style, endured my incessant discussion, and performed thankless tasks that aided either in putting the materials together or in completing the manuscript. My deepest appreciation goes to her.

A.D.D.

Contents

Figures and Tables

Figures

Tables

Cuban Sugar in the Age of Mass Production

Chapter 1

Introduction

IN THE LATE NINETEENTH CENTURY, a wave of innovation in industrial processes brought about a profound change in the size and structure of business enterprises across the world. In most instances, the industries affected by the technical changes of the second industrial revolution and the organizational innovations of the accompanying managerial revolution centered in Europe and the United States. In one industry they did not — sugar. Unlike most other tropical commodities, sugarcane could not be traded internationally in crude form to be processed in the industrial countries. The economic value of sugarcane deteriorates if it is not processed immediately. This fact imposed a different regimen on the industrialization and modernization of the cane sugar industry. Modern sugar manufacturing technology was a product of this period. It emerged after 1880 on the wave of innovations in industrial chemicals, becoming most noticeable first in the rising European beet sugar industry. Its application to sugarcane was more promising, however, and it swiftly spread throughout the tropical world, settling where conditions proved to be best. One of these places was Cuba, the largest island in the Caribbean, already famous for its fertile cane soils and propitious climate.

In this new technical regime, Cuba occupied the position as both the largest and the lowest-cost sugar producer in the world. Cuba produced between 25 and 30 percent of the world's sugar from the 1840s to the 1870s. After 1875, however, internal social unrest had caused the Cuban industry to stagnate and decline just as technical advances in European beet sugar challenged all major cane sugar producers. Recovery for Cuba came on the wings of technical progress. By 1913, it was again producing more than 20 percent of the world's sugar and about 30 percent of the world's cane sugar. In the North American trading system it contributed a greater weight. As the principal supplier of sugar to the United States, in some years it contributed over 60 percent of all sugar consumed in that rising economic power.[1] Less well-known is the importance of Cuban commerce to certain sectors of the United States. For example, from 1922 to 1926, Cuba was the United States's major customer for rail freight cars and the second major customer, next to Japan, for steel rails — a demand that reflects the extensive private railroad construction on the island. The remarkable expansion of the industry was also reflected in a voracious demand for materials and equipment used in industrial construction. Cuba was the major importer of materials such as structural iron and steel and steam boiler plant. Also, and perhaps not as surprising, Cuba absorbed about two-thirds of all U.S. exports of sugar manufacturing machinery, which had become very sophisticated industrial apparatus by that time. If not as prominent, Cuba was also a principal destination for U.S. exports of numerous other modern durable goods and equipment. Also, along with Canada and Mexico, Cuba was among the top three principal destinations of U.S. foreign capital in the Western Hemisphere.[2]

The relations between Cuba and the United States were narrow but complicated. Besides the close economic ties, there were also tricky diplomatic and political relations. Since its foundation, the United States had seen Cuba as important for strategic reasons because of its geographical position in the shipping lanes between the east coast and the Gulf of Mexico and as a logical extension of U.S. boundaries.[3] The economics and politics were closely intertwined. Although the attitudes of policymakers in the United States included elements of exploitation and benevolence, the interventionist policy toward Cuba was defended on moral grounds. It was widely held that the relationship was mutually beneficial, both enhancing U.S. interests and orienting Cuban society in a proper direction. Moreover, private North American cultural and economic influences played a significant role in the process of orientation.[4] Reciprocally, just as

North American leaders understood the strategic importance of Cuba, Cuban leaders understood the economic importance of the United States, both public and private. The context of economic relations was established as Cuban interests gravitated inevitably toward the North American trading system.

Broad generalizations about the relationship between the United States and Cuba have led to some misconceptions about the Cuban economy. First, there is a myth that Cuba's technological advances were actually the doing of North American expertise. After the Spanish-American War (which coincided with the Cuban War of Independence), North American entrepreneurs are said to have moved in to set up the modern sugar enterprise, replacing backward plantations with the latest technology. This characterization of Cuban industrialization in sugar has been shown to be unequivocally incorrect.[5] Cuba had obtained and held preeminence in the world sugar industry largely on the basis of domestic capital and expertise long before North American investors began to cast their eyes in Cuba's direction. When the achievements of the second industrial revolution appeared on the scene, Cuban producers were well prepared to adapt the new methods to their environment and industrial needs. As the industrial techniques became more capital-intensive after the turn of the twentieth century, however, North American capital markets and technical institutions became indispensable to the progress of the sugar industry.

A second obverse myth is the predatory image that the United States converted Cuba into an area of sugar monoculture and led the island into a relationship of dependency on the U.S. market for sugar.[6] Cuba's dependence on the U.S. market for sugar is certain, but the notion that monoculture was caused by the United States is misleading if taken literally. Whereas Cuban monoculture did come about through the rising demand for sugar in the United States, Cuba's dependence on the North American market did not originate through coercion on the part of the United States. Rather, it was well established by the middle of the nineteenth century, and it came about as Cubans sought a market for their sugar in a world market particularly prone to protectionist legislation. The United States's interest and the European opposition to imports of Cuban sugar led to the "inevitable gravitation" of Spain's *siempre fiel* colony to the economic sphere of the United States.[7] Later, aggressive U.S. actions became more important. After 1898, when occupation of the island by the U.S. military began, North American capitalists entered in a big way. As they did, the shape and character of the sugar industry were transformed by new technology. It is a common belief that U.S. intervention, in its various forms, was responsible. My proposition is that the principal forces behind these structural changes were neither the political intervention nor the arrival of North American capital as predator. Rather, they were manifestations of the second industrial revolution, which heralded the rise of mass production in Cuban sugar.

As a sugar producer, after the turn of the twentieth century, Cuba had a reputation for being both highly advanced and backward. On the one hand, in sugar manufacture, Cuban firms occupied positions of technical and organizational leadership in the world industry. On the other hand, many thought the organization of cane cultivation on the island to be an anachronism. In some cases, it seemed to preserve a less progressive element of society—a deeply rooted sugar aristocracy that harked back to the days of the slave plantation, not that distant because slavery had not ended in Cuba until 1886. In other cases, it set up share contracting and tenancy arrangements for large quantities of the cane produced on the island, even though economists of that time universally considered sharecropping and similar arrangements to be economically inefficient. Yet contemporary studies (and the market) showed that Cuba produced sugar at a lower cost than any other place in the world.[8] Some features of the Cuban sugar economy seemed to reflect current tendencies in modern business organization; others did not. In this exotic land filled with the sweet smells of cane and wafting with the romanticism of the world's most legendary tobacco, people abroad did not perceive that Cuba was participating directly in the second industrial revolution, which at the time was sweeping the industrial world.

This book probes the economic developments that led to a profound transformation of the Cuban sugar industry from 1899 to 1929. Proponents of the dependency view have stressed the importance of the economic transformation for later social developments, pointing to far-reaching effects of the resulting inequitable distribution of land and the industrial concentration of the national economy. Despite emphasis on these structural features, exactly what economic forces underlay them has not been examined carefully or understood. The following chapters seek more careful explanations of the economic forces and will identify them to have been specific outcomes of the adoption of mass production techniques in sugar. Milling and cane cultivation were tightly integrated by means of internal organization and contractual arrangements. The rational interaction of the economic interests reflected by these two activities had much influence on the structure that arose in the industry and its regional differences.

The Years of *las Vacas Gordas*

This study traverses the period known as the second great sugar expansion in Cuba. It opens at the termination of the Cuban War of Independence (1895–98) when, shortly after, the Cuban sugar industry took off into a period of rapid growth which led the economy into three decades of export-led prosperity. This was also the period of greatest U.S. influence and intervention. Closer ties to the U.S. market improved trade relations with the United States, contributed to greater political stability, and stimulated a huge inflow of North American capital. The period of study ends with the coming of the depression of the 1930s, at which time Cuban sugar exports fell abruptly to a quarter of their former level. But before the world crisis Cuba experienced one of the most dynamic periods of economic growth in its history. Annual sugar production from 1860 to 1937, presented in Figure 1.1, shows both the collapse in the level of production during the war and the rapid recovery and expansion after the war. Production peaked in 1925 and remained at comparable levels until 1930, when the next severe contraction took place.

As Figure 1.1 reflects, the War of Independence led Cuba into the greatest economic crisis it had ever seen. Stagnation had beset the economy since the mid-1870s, affected by an earlier unsuccessful war for independence, known as the Ten Years' War (1868–78). The period after the Ten Years' War was a time of recurrent civil strife and economic uncertainty. It culminated in the horrifying and disastrous second War of Independence, sometimes referred to nowadays as the Spanish-Cuban-American War. Direct strategic attacks on the sugar industry by both sides resulted in a remarkable three-quarter decline in the level of sugar production during the years of the war. The rural economy was left devastated by these actions and by the Spanish policy of forced evacuation of the rural population from the countryside.[9]

After the War of Independence, the sugar industry was left in drastic need of an injection of capital from abroad to rebuild inoperative mills and torched cane fields. At the same time, closer business links began to be established between North American and Cuban interests. Some arose out of the U.S. military occupation, which lasted from 1898 until 1902. But

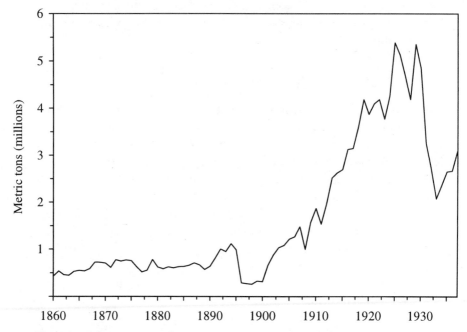

Fig. 1.1. Cuban sugar production, 1860–1937. Source: Moreno Fraginals, *El ingenio*, 3: 35–40.

improved optimism among foreign investors probably relied more on the opportunities opened up by the dismantling of the burdensome Spanish mercantilist regulations, which had interfered with U.S.-Cuban trade relations during the colonial period, and by the U.S. Congress's granting Cuba preferential access to the U.S. sugar market. This second factor was an outcome of the passage of the Reciprocity Treaty of 1903, in which Cuba received a 20 percent discount on the full U.S. duty on sugar imports. The treaty gave Cubans preferential access to the U.S. market vis-à-vis most other sugar producers worldwide, but they still had to compete unequally with U.S. mainland cane and beet sugar producers and with Hawaii, Puerto Rico, and the Philippines, all of which enjoyed duty-free status.[10]

Nonetheless, between 1903 and 1929, Cuban producers came to be the major supplier of the U.S. market, as seen in Figure 1.2. Figure 1.2 shows the importance that Cuban sugar imports came to have in the American market. The consumption of sugar in the United States grew at an annual rate of 4 percent, but growth of purchases from Cuba grew at 8.5 percent annually. During World War I, Cuba's capacity increased considerably.

The Cuban share of the U.S. market thus rose from 15 percent in 1900 to about 65 percent at its peak in 1922. Favorable trade relations with the United States lasted until 1930, when the Hawley-Smoot Act was passed, which included an increase of the sugar tariff. Cuban sugar production then dropped by two-thirds between 1930 and 1933, but before that time, Cuba's close ties with the United States attracted substantial quantities of North American capital used for rebuilding, updating, and expanding the sugar industry, railroads, and other sectors of the economy.[11]

The rise in exports of sugar contributed considerably to the prosperity of the age. (Almost all of the output shown in Figure 1.1 was exported.) In Cuba these times were known as the years of *las vacas gordas*, or "fat cows," which connoted opulence as well as an end to the lean years that had prevailed since the Ten Years' War. Adequate national income statistics are not available to track the impact of the volume of exports on per capita national income, but estimates of per capita gross domestic product

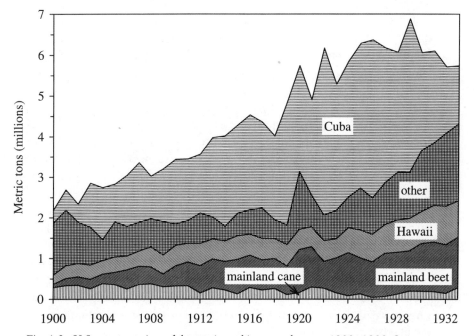

Fig. 1.2. U.S. consumption of domestic and imported sugar, 1900–1933. Source: U.S. Congressional Committee on Agriculture, *History and Operations of the U.S. Sugar Program*, p. 3.

used by Angus Maddison for 1929, at the end of the period, rank Cuba second, along with Chile, among all Latin American countries.[12] Likewise, Henry Wallich remarked around mid-century that it was "safe to say among all tropical countries Cuba had the highest per capita national income."[13] In a similar vein, like Argentina and Chile, contemporaries placed Cuba among emerging nations such as Canada and Australia, rather than among the "poor" or underdeveloped countries. Although Cuba was not characteristically similar to the core industrial economies of the world, many economic and social indicators separated it from poor or backward countries such as Bolivia, Mexico, or Thailand.[14] By 1930, life expectancy at birth was more than 40 years, which among Latin American countries was exceeded only by Argentina. Also by 1930, census figures reported a literacy rate of over 70 percent of the population.[15] This export-led growth gave rise to many characteristics of a prosperous and growing settlement economy — massive immigration, the development and improvement of much underutilized land, the inflow of capital from abroad, and a rising national income.

Notwithstanding this stimulus, a perusal of the literature of the last couple of decades on Cuban social history will demonstrate that these events are seen most commonly in a pejorative light. The technical advance in the sugar industry, particularly after the turn of the century, is spoken of darkly despite the advantages that Cuba's outstanding success in the technical arena gave it in the sphere of international competition. This period of growth is not portrayed as an age of progress but, rather, as the age in which a sociopolitical storm brewed, whose culmination was to be the Cuban Revolution of 1959. In a large segment of the literature, progress in sugar is seen as Cuba's greatest enemy.[16] The problem was that the sugar boom intensified some undesirable features of the economy. Modernization of the sugar industry imposed a structural transformation on the rest of the economy that led it into inadequate sectorial diversification and inordinate concentration of industry. The list of structural features used to characterize the early twentieth-century Cuban economy has become almost canonical: sugar *latifundismo*, monoexportation, and the subordination of the economy to North American capitalists. These features of the Cuban economy led the country into the severe economic and social crisis of the 1930s.

These features are reflected in quantitative trends of the period. Between 1899 and 1929 the amount of land in sugarcane increased dramatically. The area of land owned or controlled by sugar mills is estimated to have increased by about 2.5 times from 7 to 17 percent of the total land mass from 1860 to 1925. Besides these lands, additional acreage, unaccounted for in the above estimate, was brought into production by the gradual increase in participation of outside cane growers, known as *colonos*. A conservative (downwardly biased) estimate suggests that the acreage planted in cane increased by 3.5 times from 1860 to 1929.[17] This estimate accounts for the land of both mills and colonos planted in cane. Lands used complementarily as pastures for the oxen and lands in fallow probably increased less than proportionately. But the fivefold estimated increase does not account for increases in lands held in reserve for planned increases in milling capacity, which were considerable after 1899.

Specialization in sugar seemed to crowd out many of the socially healthy aspects of Cuban agrarian society. By the measures mentioned above, the agricultural specialization in sugar began in the early nineteenth century, and although with some fluctuation, it continued into the twentieth century. In sheer acreage in cane, however, its presence became considerably more imposing as sugar expanded in the twentieth century into the eastern provinces of the island and as more and more of the unutilized, or underutilized, arable land of the island was taken over by sugarcane. It seemed irreversibly to eliminate the dream that many held of a diversified regional agrarian economy consisting of a middle class of small farmers in the yet underpopulated areas of the island. Sugar was inimical to this dream because of the large-scale structure it imposed on the sugar enterprise, which made it financially inaccessible to independent small farmers. Yet the arrival of modern sugar mills in remote areas was welcomed by those who saw an opportunity for a standard of living beyond subsistence, either through obtaining a cane *colonia* or through trade with the mill and its workers. Especially in the early years, becoming a colono was lucrative and commercial activities boomed. Similarly, wage laborers, foreign and native, flocked into these new regions seeking what they considered to be the high wages offered by the modern sugar mills.[18]

After independence from Spain and the establishment of a well-defined political and commercial relationship between the United States and Cuba, North Americans had greater interest in business ventures on the island. This resulted in an injection of badly needed capital, but it also resulted in many foreign companies investing directly, moving in and buying up land and other assets. U.S. foreign investment, estimated at $50 million before 1894, increased to about $200 million by 1906 and around $1,150 million by 1928.[19] At first, the presence of North American investors was widely welcomed. But in the aftermath of World War I, many became alarmed at the degree of concentration of the island's resources in the hands of foreign companies.[20] The concentration was most prevalent in sugar, railroads, and banking. Leland Jenks estimates that in 1927 about 62 percent of the Cuban sugar crop was produced by mills that could "be identified as wholly American."[21] And virtually the entire public service railroad system — about 4,300 kilometers by 1929 — was consolidated in the 1920s under British- and American-controlled companies, with the exception of the Guantánamo and Western, a small railroad in eastern Cuba, which earned only about 2 percent of the total revenues of the industry in 1927.[22] In banking, a financial crisis associated with the readjustment from a controlled wartime sugar price to an uncontrolled peacetime price in 1920 resulted in the closures of most of the domestic banks and their replacement by North American banks. The share of deposits in U.S. and Canadian banks suddenly went from about 25 percent in 1919 to about 75 percent in 1923, where it remained until the 1930s.[23] These trends alarmed many Cubans as they watched the ownership and control of key sectors of the economy slip into the hands of foreigners.

Technological Change and the Reorganization of Sugar

An underlying theme of this book is the close connection between the technical and organizational changes in the Cuban sugar industry and the technological changes behind the managerial revolution in industrial countries. The technical changes in the sugar industry, derived from high-throughput, continuous-process technologies, were characteristic of most progressive industries of that time. Alfred Chandler has shown how application of these new high-throughput, mass production technologies heralded the transition from proprietorships to modern hierarchical and corporate forms of business organization in the United States, Germany, and Great Britain.[24] This book links the developments in the Cuban sugar industry to the global movement in business organization and technology that Chandler has referred to as the rise of managerial capitalism.

Nationally focused studies have emphasized the rise of the corporate form of organization in Cuban sugar as characteristic of the industrial transformation of this period, but they have generally criticized it as an instrument of oligarchical capitalism and North American imperialist domination—an institution carried in by the wave of North American imperialism rather than by the wave of mass production technologies.[25] Studies of the United States and European countries, following Chandler's approach, indicate that the new forms of corporate organization contributed to the productivity, organizational capabilities, and international competitiveness of the innovating countries.[26] As this study links the developments in Cuba and its rivals to the global technological developments, it becomes clear that the new forms of business organization had the same function in the Cuban context. The relative performance and competitiveness of Cuba and its rivals depended greatly on the adoption of mass production technologies and the firm structures that most efficiently supported them.

Few have understood the implications of the revolution in sugar manufacturing technology that was under way during this period. This technical revolution was behind many of the structural changes in the Cuban sugar industry, in the scale of production of sugar mills, in the reorganization of contractual relations with cane growers, and in land concentration. The revolution, as it was adopted in Cuba, advanced technical capabilities on the island, but it did not extend the set of technical choices available to domestic sugar producers. The progress of the technical revolution among Cuba's international rivals acted as an ever-tightening constraint on the freedom of Cuban sugar producers to neglect the wave of technical innovation—if they had wished to do so. Survival in these times depended on the producer's responsiveness to competition in the technical arena.

In the context of global technological revolution, it should not be surprising that the sugar industry underwent a complete reorganization. The introduction of modern equipment into the factories accelerated in the 1870s. Initially pieces of more sophisticated machinery were introduced to augment the existing equipment and style of mill organization. As each stage of production in the mill received a major innovation, however, the mills became highly mechanized. A repercussion of this mechanization was the remarkable increase in the scale of the production unit. The number of mills in operation from 1877 to 1891 fell from 1,190 to 850. By 1929 the number had fallen to 163. Meanwhile, the size of the sugar crop on the island increased from 0.5 million to more than 5 million tons. Table 1.1 presents the average mill capacity in Cuba from 1860 to 1929. Remarkably, output of sugar per mill increased fourteen times from 1877 to

Table 1.1
Sugar Production per Mill, 1860–1929

Year	Mills grinding (no.)	Sugar produced by all mills (000s of bags of 325 lbs.)	Sugar produced per mill (000s of bags of 325 lbs.)
1860	1,365	2,968	2.2
1877	1,190	3,574	3.0
1904	174	7,253	41.7
1916	189	21,063	111.4
1929	163	35,540	218.0

SOURCES: Taken from Dye, "Tropical Technology and Mass Production," p. 3, using Cuba, Secretaría de Hacienda, *Industria azucarera*; Cuba, Secretaría de Agricultura, Comercio, y Trabajo, *Portfolio azucarero*; Cuba, Secretaría de Agricultura, Comercio, y Trabajo, *Industria azucarera*; Ferrara, p. 96; Pezuela, 1:67.

1904; from 1904 to 1929, output per mill increased another five times. Taking the long view from 1860, before the first glimpses of this technical revolution had begun, until 1929 the average capacity of mills in Cuba had increased a hundredfold.[27]

The larger mill capacities at the turn of the century represented only the beginning of a continual process of technical change. Modifications in the machinery and improvements of the factory continued to make important changes. The application of mass production technology came in repeated, more or less minor modifications in machinery, factory design, and the logistics of factory and field organization. The contrast between the traditional and modern mill was striking. By World War I the new mill hardly resembled those of the earlier plantations. The mid-nineteenth-century mill, driven by a steam engine or a team of oxen, produced a few hundred tons of sugar annually. The twentieth-century mill was a massive factory, dependent on a power plant combining steam, gasoline, and electric power, that produced thousands and even tens of thousands of tons of sugar annually. Altogether, the sugar factory underwent a remarkable transformation.[28]

By the first years of the twentieth century, the technology had revolutionized the mill, and the internal organization of sugar manufacturing in Cuba had been transformed by the new optimal scale of production. The replacement of the traditional plantation by the central factory began in the 1880s. Once completely self-contained, mills now broke with tradition to enlist outside cane growers to cultivate cane under contract. As mills grew larger, they contracted out to obtain the additional supplies of cane needed to keep them running at capacity. In the long run, this division of labor proved to be economically advantageous to the sugar mill. The number of outside growers, known as colonos, grew. By 1929 they supplied over 80 percent of the industry's raw material.

The innovations behind centralization were not limited to mechanical solutions to the problems of sugar manufacturing; they also involved a fundamental restructuring of the sugar enterprise.[29] The restructuring took place at many levels. Greater capital requirements resulted in a reorganization of ownership. More and more mills adopted a corporate structure and sold shares both to nationals and to foreigners to cover higher capital requirements. The division of labor between central mills and colonos also reflected changes in firm structure. Mills now had much larger cane requirements, and vast quantities of land were needed to satisfy them. Cane field layout, internal transportation infrastructure, and cane handling at the factory had to be reconfigured to fit the new technology. The trend toward contracting with colonos was a part of this reconfiguration. It represented the restructuring of cane land management. Sometimes misleadingly characterized in the historiography as simple farmers or peasants, colonos actually provided a different function than the one implied in the usual description. They were the managers of the vast cane fields or, rather, contractors set up by mutual agreement to manage cane lands, sometimes owned by the mill, sometimes by the colono. As the technology of sugar manufacturing became more complex, so did the organizational structure that supported it. Continual changes also determined that the relationships between colonos and mills would not remain unchanged. (This issue will be taken up further below.) Other innovations were complementary, ranging from the technical, such as use of scientific instruments for greater quality control, to the administrative, such as new methods of accounting for internal costs.

Cuba's technological successes have often been discredited as historians focus on the political or social disruptions they created. This is at times done, however, at the peril of neglecting the economic needs and limitations of the nation. The successful technological adaptations that sugar producers made during this period meant greater competitiveness internationally, greater ability to generate employment domestically, and greater ability to import industrial necessities that could not be produced at home. As one economist has pointed out, the successful application of new industrial technology in sugar production in such places as Cuba, Java, and Hawaii gave those countries a decided advantage over other once very successful sugar-producing countries that failed to make the adaptation, such as Jamaica and Mauritius.[30] Despite the inequities that seemed to be exacerbated by sugar-induced prosperity, the average person was probably much better off than he or she would have been without the injection of foreign capital, the industrial renovation, and the market competitiveness it made possible.

Uneven Regional Development

A salient feature of the great economic transformation of this period was the rapid expansion of the sugar industry into the frontier eastern provinces. Indeed, after the turn of the century, the transformation of the sugar industry was greatest in the east. The western provinces of Havana, Matanzas, and Santa Clara, the bastions of the plantation system of the nineteenth century, adapted relatively gradually to the new technology. In the 1880s and 1890s, mass production technologies had been introduced

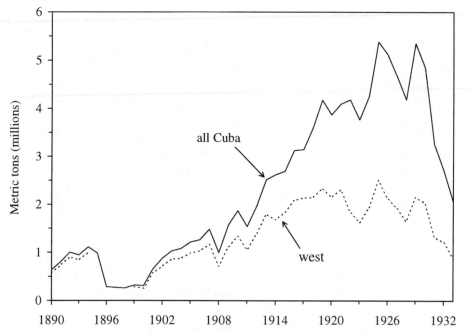

Fig. 1.3. Regional production of Cuban sugar, 1890–1933. The west includes the provinces Pinar del Rio, Havana, Matanzas, and Santa Clara. Source: Calculated from Moreno Fraginals, *El ingenio*, 3: 35–40, 60–62.

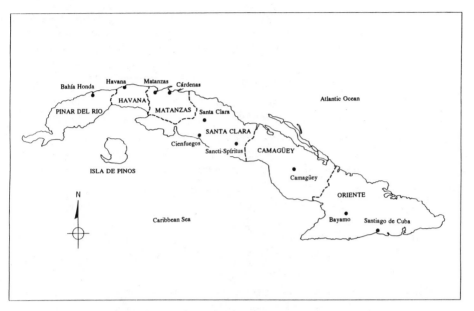

Fig. 1.4. Map of Cuba showing provinces and major cities.

in these provinces, and although the war discontinuously acted to clear out many old mills—a sort of Schumpeterian creative destruction—the modernization of the western industry did not overturn the society there. By contrast, the transformation in the east was, as Robert Hoernel put it, "deeper and more painful."[31] At the turn of the century, the eastern provinces of Camagüey and Oriente were known principally for their extensive open cattle ranges and small subsistence farming. The preexisting regional sugar industry was backward and of unimportant size, confined to a small area near Guantánamo.[32] Then after the turn of the century, the east served as the industry's fertile frontier. In the remote areas of this region the largest mills on the island were erected on new sites yet unknown to cane cultivation. Land was quickly absorbed and put into cane. Private company railroad systems were being extended throughout the surrounding cane zones for hauling cane. Throughout the period, the center of gravity of the sugar industry shifted farther and farther eastward, as Figure 1.3 illustrates, showing how eastern sugar production levels overtook western levels. (Figure 1.4 gives a map showing the provinces.) The contribution of the eastern provinces to the total sugar crop went from less than 10 percent at the beginning of the century to about 60 percent.

Not only did the center of gravity of production levels shift eastward but so did the technical dynamism of the industry. Before the turn of the century, the renowned technical expertise and innovativeness of Cuban producers referred to the western producers. When the large-scale technologies that would sweep the country appeared in the late nineteenth century, only the western producers responded (Santa Clara included). But after the turn of the century, when the political turmoil, which had been more intensive in the east, had died down, a number of sugar entrepreneurs backed by North American capital moved into remote areas there and built some of the most advanced sugar mills and organizations known to date. Notable among these were American companies such as the Boston-based United Fruit Company, but also represented were figures such as the Rionda family, cosmopolitan immigrants from Spain who had settled both in New York and in Cuba. As the central mills, or *centrales*, of these entrepreneurs became established and profitable, others followed. The east came to be the more frequent destination of inflowing North American capital. The greater abundance of capital lubricated the process of technical adaptation. As new technologies became available in this period of dynamic technological innovation, they spread to centrales throughout the island, but the greatest concentration of mills operating with the latest technology was in the east.

Related to these developments, a sharp distinction arose in the social systems of the eastern and western provinces, associated with land tenure and contractual arrangements.[33] Outside cane growers in the eastern provinces more often were tenants occupying land owned by the central. Western cane growers, by contrast, were often from the planter class and often owned the land they farmed. The distinction was related to the historical development of the two regions. The cane lands of the western provinces, the sites of the earlier plantation economy, were already possessed by a well-established class knowledgeable of the sugar industry. As new mass production technology entered Cuban sugar, the existing plantations in the west had to consolidate to accommodate the greater capacities of mills using the new technology. As some planters converted their mills to the larger production units, other planters ceased grinding their own cane, instead converting their plantations to colonias and contracting to sell their cane to the new large-scale mills. Consequently, a pattern of cane contracting grew up in the west based on independent landowning colonos, many of whom were former planters, who supplied the greater part of the cane ground by the mills. Cane farming also became the common means of organizing the cane supplies in the eastern mills, but under entirely different circumstances. Eastern centrales established themselves on lands previously unoccupied by the planter class by purchasing vast tracts of land in relatively remote areas of the country.[34] Large portions of these lands were contracted out to tenant colonos, who would supply the main part of the mills' cane needs.

The distinction in land tenure between independent landholding colonos of the creole aristocracy in the west and small tenant colonos in the east was not absolute, but as a matter of degree it resulted in substantial differences in the colono arrangements of the east and west. The contemporary historian and reformist Ramiro Guerra y Sánchez saw the independent colono, predominant in the west, as having been the basis of a Cuban rural middle class, but he argued that the independent western colono was a dying breed in Cuba. In his view, the arrival of North American capitalists threatened the existence of the landowning independent colono. The evidence he offered for this was the relative absence of landowning colonos in the east, which was dominated by American-owned centrales, and the declining percentage of cane all over the island coming from landowning colonos. Of course, this was one manifestation of the trend toward land concentration in the hands of sugar centrales. But Guerra identified another factor which he attributed to North American capitalist dominance. In the east, the largest centrales were actively building private company railroads that effectively monopolized the transportation systems of local cane zones. He argued that by controlling the transportation system of an area, centrales monopsonized the purchases of cane in that area and subordinated the landowning colono to the central. In time, he predicted, it meant the demise of the Cuban colono as centrales would eventually convert their landholdings to administration (internally produced) cane. This practice was more commonly found in the east, where the public access railroad system was less developed.[35]

Others have pointed to the power of landowning colonos in affecting the terms at which mills had to deal with them. In contrast to Guerra's arguments, César Ayala remarks that centrales in the west had difficulties consolidating land areas, particularly in the west, because of the power of existing landowning colonos and the difficulty of keeping the prices demanded by colonos under control.[36] At the end of World War I, the auditors of the Cuba Cane Sugar Corporation, the largest sugar company on the island, commented that "considerable doubt has been expressed by those familiar with the Cuba situation whether the mills in the west will be able to make any profit after the resumption of world competition, unless the price of cane is materially reduced. It may compel centrals to consider seriously the growing of more administration cane."[37] Consequently, North American corporations followed a strategy of land acquisition, which gave rise to Guerra's observations. But Ayala points out that their attempts to gain control of the land were often frustrated in the west because of the power of landowning colonos.[38]

Why did the problems between the contracting parties become so intractable when the cane transaction seemed potentially so mutually beneficial? Land acquisition trends show that centrales were gradually reducing the influence of landowning colonos, although much of it was owing to the incorporation of new central-owned colonias in the east.[39] Ultimately, in the 1930s, landowning colonos gained a political upper hand by obtaining regulatory legislation that effectively blocked reductions in the shares of cane they supplied to the mills.[40] But the conflictive nature of the bargaining relationship always seemed to threaten the existence of one side or the other.

A natural question that the economist would ask is why no spot market for cane arose that would have given greater flexibility both to the cane farmer and to the central mill. Instead, cane was traded in long-term contracts which often suffered from the bargaining conflicts described above. The reason, to be explained in Chapter 6, is that investments in cane fields and railroads acted as specific assets to the transaction that exposed the central to opportunistic threats of landowning colonos and often left it with little choice but to accept their demands for higher shares of the sugar output. (Colonos were paid in sugar at a ratio fixed by contract per weight of cane delivered.) Centrales responded by attempting to preempt the opportunism through unified ownership of the land. To some readers the proposition that colonos had more power than the giant centrales may seem doubtful. The point to be made is that the "power" was derived not from the colono but from the constraints that the biology of cane imposed on the transaction plus certain other conditions to be explained later.

Chapter 6 will show that this intractable bargaining problem explains many features of the uneven pattern of sugar industry development between the east and the west. This problem was greater in the west, where most self-reliant landowning colonos were concentrated. Other factors also worked to the advantage of the colonos in the west. Therefore, the movement of sugar entrepreneurs into the eastern provinces after the turn of the century can be seen as an attempt to escape the demands of colonos in the west. Furthermore, the geographical shift of the technically dynamic center of the industry to the east was a related outcome. Not only mill owners but also potential (foreign or national) investors saw the opportunism that landowning colonos tended to resort to. As a mill sought funds for updating its equipment, eastern mills offered a more attractive option from the point of view of investors; consequently, the eastern centrales found credit for technical improvements to be more readily available. The contemporary association of the eastern provinces with North American capital, better technology, local cane monopsonies, and lower cane prices were all outcomes of the structure of the transaction costs and the potential for opportunism in the cane transaction.

The Sugar Latifundium

The language and content of the above description departs considerably from other descriptions of the central-colono relationship. Prevailing interpretations of the socioeconomic developments of twentieth-century Cuba suggest that the root cause of the colono's demise — and many of the nation's other social ills — was the rise of sugar latifundismo in the early republican period. In general, the concentration of landholdings into enormous latifundia was characteristic of all Spanish America. Reference to the "sugar latifundia" conventionally in Cuban historiography, however, is intended to evoke an image quite different from the traditional latifundium. Although the legacy of Spanish land grants had left Cuba with a heavy concentration of land ownership, the sugar latifundium was a product of modern capitalism.[41] By the standards of the day, many of the nineteenth-century sugar estates were quite large; however, the greatest sugar centrales of the twentieth century occupied lands of an entirely different order of magnitude. Up to 1878, the largest *ingenios* (the nineteenth-century sugar estates) typically owned 3,000 acres or more. But the largest sugar centrales of the 1920s controlled (owned or leased) 100,000 to 200,000 acres of land.[42] This development in landholding was not a structural feature left by early colonization of the island; it was a product of the early republican era associated with the leading enterprises in the key growth sector of the economy.

The classic study of the rise of the sugar latifundium is Ramiro Guerra y Sánchez's *Azúcar y población en las Antillas*. The prevailing conventional view is derived from his provocative work. First published in 1927, it has remained for some time the best historical analysis on the subject. Many authors who make reference to the rise of the sugar latifundia simply summarize aspects of Guerra's arguments. But unquestioned use of the work as an authority is not entirely satisfactory; the purpose for its writing was not entirely objective. The author wrote the book as an analysis of contemporary events with a decidedly nationalist focus and certain clear political objectives. Its contribution to the understanding of the economic organization of the modern sugar industry at the time was very significant, but given recent advances in economic history and theory, many of his arguments could stand refinement.

This book reexamines some of the questions Guerra addressed as well as additional questions related to the internal economic workings of the early twentieth-century sugar industry in Cuba, using more recent tools of economic analysis. Like Guerra, the book focuses on the mill, or the central, as the unit of analysis. But its focus is somewhat different in that much attention is given to exploring the costs of production to understand what influenced the mill owners' decisions regarding technical innovation and firm organization. Other questions could be raised at the firm level rather than at the factory level — say, regarding the degree of industrial concentration — but this issue has been left aside here. Some of the conclusions of this study support Guerra's analysis, but others differ considerably either from Guerra or from what has become the conventional view of the rise of the giant sugar centrales.

Guerra argued that the use of the railroad, beginning in the 1880s, for hauling cane to the mills caused the increase in the size of sugar properties. Consolidation began modestly before the end of Spanish rule. But when powerful North American companies with more access to capital entered the picture after the turn of the century, they financed enormous railroad construction projects and adopted a strategy of land capture by monopolizing local transportation with private railroad systems. This story has been attractive in the historiography because of a key piece of evidence. The timing of this change is supported by a fall in the price of steel rails in 1878, which stimulated private railroad construction.[43] The substantial fall in the price of the principal material input to their construction supports the story. The problem with the story is that it only provides an explanation for the increased size of landholdings. It offers no explanation for the rise in the capacities and complexity of the modern mills and no motive for the extensive organizational changes that took place internally in the sugar enterprise.

Emphasizing a different set of features than does Guerra, I propose that technically determined economies of scale were the driving force of change in the sugar mill. More precisely, as the adoption and adaptation of continuous-process technologies in the sugar mill developed, the optimal scale of production increased. From time to time, as mills renovated their equipment and factory designs, they adopted larger and larger mill capacities. The frequent intransigence of the mill-colono bargaining relationship provided an incentive for centrales to pursue a policy of land acquisition in conjunction with their expansion of mill capacity. An implication of the economies of scale hypothesis is that the *latifundización* of the countryside in sugar regions was a secondary development derived from the adoption of mass production technologies in the sugar mill and driven by the changing economies of scale.

The question of why there was no spot market that permitted cane to be traded competitively by independent growers in a nationwide market is key to understanding the rise of the latifundium as a by-product of mass production. The root of the problem is in the biological characteristics of sugarcane as a raw material. It recalls the point made in the first paragraph of this chapter. Just as modern industrial technology had to pursue the cane plant to the tropics, within tropical countries such as Cuba, the industrial plant used to process cane was fettered to the fields where the cane grew. This technical requirement created a unique industry and a unique set of social relations, of which Guerra has provided an evocative picture. An implication of this observation for analyses of political or social behavior is that these features came as a set. Any contemplation of alternative social relations was feasible only if it took into account the constraints that cane imposed on the organization of production.

An Economic and Institutional Analysis

A growing body of literature has developed in the last decade that represents a joint effort between economic historians and some economists to explore why the form of economic organization or institutions differs from one activity to another. This literature combines the tools of analysis of mainstream economics with the concepts of transaction costs, agency, and the analysis of explicit or implicit contractual relationships. Founded on the work of Ronald Coase, it has been furthered by others. A major contributor is Oliver Williamson, who pioneered the concept of asset specificity and has demonstrated its broad usefulness for understanding firm organization in the context of large capitalist business organizations.[44] A recent awareness has also developed of the close interaction between the organizational and technical features of firms, reflected in the works of Nathan Rosenberg and Alfred Chandler. Alfred Chandler in particular, influenced in recent years by theorists of firm organization such as Williamson and David Teece, has incorporated the concepts of economies of scale and scope in firms into a far-reaching historical analysis of the rise of industrial capitalism. He argues that these microeconomic influences, which arise from specific technical characteristics of modern industries, go far to explain many features of the modern hierarchical enterprise in the major industrial economies of the world.[45]

Making use of this literature, the analysis of this book combines mainstream economics, the concept of transaction costs, and an examination of specific technical features to understand the economics of the rise of the giant sugar centrales in Cuba. The combination of these three analytical elements reveals that many features of economies once explained only by resort to a vague notion of monopoly power can be shown to have root causes in the specific features of the prevailing technology, the endowments of resources and infrastructure, and market and nonmarket institutions. The analysis has two intentions. First, it examines the rise of the central to clarify many issues regarding why the sugar industry developed this industrial structure at this particular time. This examination attempts to shed light on the issue as well by bringing the industrial developments in Cuba into the broader context of global technical change. Second, it contributes to the literature mentioned above. Until now these issues have been examined most carefully only for the core industrial economies of the world. This examination of Cuba provides a case study of how the dynamics of industrial capitalism have affected countries on the periphery of the international trading systems. Although this book does not attempt to address them directly, its conclusions open up many questions regarding the interaction of the influences of private capitalist institutions and institutions of international politics and diplomacy.

The organization of the book is as follows. To set the stage, Chapter 2 surveys the long-term economic development of the Cuban sugar economy to point out many relevant economic, social, and political features of the Cuban economy, which should be kept in mind for the subsequent analysis. Chapter 3 describes the rise of mass production technology in the global context and then examines its introduction into Cuba made manifest in the rise of the great sugar centrales. Chapters 4 through 7 are of more rigorous analytical content. In Chapters 4 and 5, the pattern of expansion of Cuban sugar mills is examined closely in an effort to understand the incentives for the rise of large-scale production units. Chapters 6 and 7 look more carefully into the uneven pattern of regional development described above to ascertain its causes. Conventional explanations of this phenomenon have been more political than economic in nature; however, what we find is that technical and institutional features specific to the Cuban sugar industry created economic incentives that explain part of this pattern. Yet an important role for international factors, including imperialism, is not refuted by the evidence. Chapter 8 discusses the technical choices made in the Cuban sugar industry in a comparative context in an attempt to understand why certain features of the Cuban sugar industry were specific to Cuba and were not found universally among Cuba's major competitors.

Of interest is the persistence of a wide variety in the levels of technical advance in mills. Since the most advanced mills were most frequently associated with North American capital, in the historiography of Cuba many authors have asserted or implied the technical superiority of the "North American technology," so to speak, over the "Cuban technology." A premise of this analysis, supported by historical evidence, is that the technology was not North American but essentially global in character. Therefore, it is of interest to examine the statistical association of advanced mills and their North American orientation for alternative explanations. We find that explanations of a purely economic nature go far toward explaining features of the Cuban economy long thought to have been political. We also gain insight into the dynamics of the Cuban sugar industry in the 1920s which led to the alarm and concern for the economic future of Cuban nationals.

Chapter 2

A Long-Term View of the Sugar Economy in Cuba

TO UNDERSTAND the point at which the Cuban sugar economy had arrived at the beginning of the twentieth century, it is useful to sketch out a brief history of the sugar industry in Cuba to concentrate on some of its most important features. Sugar rose into prominence during the nineteenth century. By mid-century both Cuba's leadership and dependence on sugar had been well established. In the latter half of the century, the world sugar industry was challenged by the end of the slave-based labor regimes, and it resulted in the downfall of a number of formerly prosperous sugar colonies. Cuba's transition to a wage-labor economy, however, was relatively smooth. The rise of a racially heterogeneous voluntary labor force after 1880 provided the labor basis for expansion and the preservation of Cuba's concentration in sugar. To serve as background for the arguments in later chapters, this chapter discusses the trends in sugar production and exports, demography, and labor organization through the nineteenth century to 1930.

The Ascendance of Sugar

Sugar became an important industry only late in Cuba's colonial history, but once it did, it almost immediately dominated the industrial structure of the island. Even though the Caribbean was the production center for European sugar throughout the seventeenth and eighteenth centuries, the Spanish West Indies were not an important participant, nor did they become one until the beginning of the nineteenth century. Until this time, Spain, unwilling to adopt policies that encouraged a plantation economy, stifled the development of the industry. Once reforms were implemented, however, the sugar industry grew and rapidly became the most important of Cuba's export industries. Early in the nineteenth century, Cuba displaced the French and British West Indian colonies as the major provider of sugar to international markets. When the sugar industry took off in the nineteenth century, Cuba would be recognized as one of the best natural environments in the world for the cultivation of cane.[1]

Production statistics indicate two periods during which the Cuban sugar industry underwent remarkable and sustained rates of growth. One occurred in the first two-thirds of the nineteenth century and the next in the first quarter or so of the twentieth century. Data that illustrate the nineteenth-century expansion are presented graphically in Figure 2.1. They show a steady upward trend of sugar production from 1790 and a vigorous expansion that began no later than 1826. Estimates show that by 1862 sugar contributed half of the value of agricultural produce on the island.[2] The expansion continued in a sustained manner until about 1875. Eight decades lapsed, from 1791 to 1875, before the steady advance of Cuban sugar was halted. This expansion of a single primary export led the Cuban economy into a truly remarkable period of growth. Sugar had indeed become "king" in this island economy. By the end of this period, sugar production had grown from just over 15,000 tons in 1790 to over 750,000 tons in 1875. The growth rate had averaged 3.9 percent annually, with no significant interruptions, for these eight decades.

Growing demands for sugar in the North Atlantic economy were in part responsible for the high rates of growth. Cuba's fertile plains offered room for expansion and an attractive investment relative to other potential sugar-producing countries.[3] Consequently, Cuban producers gradually captured a larger and larger share of the market. From a negligible share in the eighteenth century Cuba captured 27 percent of the global market by 1850. Table 2.1 gives a comparative illustration of Cuba's rise to prominence in the world sugar market. Panel A gives decennial estimates of tonnage produced by selected major producers from 1770 to 1930. Panel B gives shares in world production contributed by each of these countries, based on Noel Deerr's estimates of world sugar production from 1840 to 1930. A couple of observations are noteworthy. First, the rise of Cuban sugar production coincided with the decline of the sugar industry of the French West Indian colony of St. Domingue. Second, production in the rest of the Caribbean continued to grow, but in relative terms it was gradually displaced by newcomers. Cuba and several producers in the Pacific Ocean came onto the scene in the nineteenth century to claim a considerable portion of the market. Cuba, the earliest of these newcomers, had become the largest producer of cane sugar by mid-century. Java was the next most important newcomer and by 1890 it had become the second largest cane sugar producer worldwide.

After 1875, the Cuban sugar industry entered a period of apprehension and decline. War erupted on the island in 1868, initiated by a separatist insurgency. It lasted until 1878, but conflict and disorder continued until the struggle for independence led to a renewal of war in 1895. To add to the chaotic conditions, Spain adopted a policy of imposing all the costs of the 1868–78 war on the Cuban Treasury and simultaneously

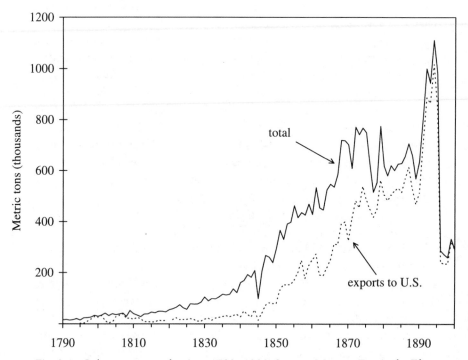

Fig. 2.1. Cuban sugar production, 1790–1900. Source: Moreno Fraginals, *El ingenio*, 3: 35–44.

Table 2.1
Output and Market Shares of Selected Sugar Producers, 1770–1930

Year	St. Domingue[a]	British W. Indies	Other W. Indies[a]	Cuba	Brazil	Java	Australia	Hawaii	Sum[b]	Beet	World
			A. Production Levels of Selected Producers (000 metric tons)								
1770	60	82	13	7	—	—	—	—	—	—	—
1780	68	73	15	7	—	—	—	—	—	—	—
1790	75	85	22	15	—	—	—	—	—	—	—
1800	9	110	33	29	12	—	—	—	192	—	—
1810	6	135	48	39	5	—	—	—	233	—	—
1820	1	166	54	55	11	—	—	—	287	—	—
1830	0	189	67	105	21	6	—	—	389	—	—
1840	—	107	69	161	37	47	—	—	421	44	753
1850	—	123	44	295	52	87	—	—	600	145	1,091
1860	—	163	78	429	84	136	—	1	891	319	1,567
1870	—	207	84	703	68	153	—	8	1,222	852	2,360
1880	—	225	90	619	160	216	14	26	1,349	1,685	3,393
1890	—	258	88	636	148	400	63	105	1,699	3,338	5,694
1900	—	204	72	309	167	744	84	234	1,814	5,448	10,214
1910	—	217	94	1,869	192	1,278	205	420	4,275	7,863	15,262
1920	5	241	51	3,872	252	1,544	163	450	6,578	4,451	15,269
1930	19	295	71	4,849	334	2,969	487	749	9,772	10,805	25,268
			B. Shares of World Market (percent)								
1840	0	14	9	21	5	6	0	0	56	6	100
1850	0	11	4	27	5	8	0	0	55	13	100
1860	0	10	5	27	5	9	0	0	57	20	100
1870	0	9	4	30	3	6	0	0	52	36	100
1880	0	7	3	18	5	6	0	1	40	50	100
1890	0	5	2	11	3	7	1	2	30	59	100
1900	0	2	1	3	2	7	1	2	18	53	100
1910	0	1	1	12	1	8	1	3	28	52	100
1920	0	2	0	25	2	10	1	3	43	29	100
1930	0	1	0	19	1	12	2	3	39	43	100

SOURCES: Cuban data are from Moreno Fraginals, *El ingenio*, 3: Table 1. Brazilian data, 1800–1910, are from Denslow, pp. 8–10; and 1920–30 from FAO, Table 1. All other data are from Deerr, *History of Sugar*, 1: 193–204, 211, 224–26, 235–40, 258, 2: 490–91.

[a] "Other W. Indies" includes estimates for Martinique, Guadeloupe, and Surinam. Approximations have been made for missing years in the French West Indian statistics. For St. Domingue, the figure reported for 1770 is actually from 1768; the 1780 figure is an interpolation of 1776 and 1783; the 1790 figure is an interpolation of 1789 and 1791; the figure reported for 1800 is from 1801; the 1810 figure is an interpolation of 1801 and 1818. For inclusion in the estimates for "other W. Indies," the figure reported for 1770 for Guadeloupe and Martinique is from 1767. The figure used for Martinique 1790 is from 1789. No figure for Guadeloupe in 1780 is available, but it has been plausibly assumed to be the same as for Martinique. Approximations for missing years in the British West Indian statistics are as follows: the figures reported for 1790 are from 1792, and the figure used for Tobago 1810 is from 1809.

[b] Sums may not appear exact due to round-off error.

announced the end of slavery in 1880. The fluctuation in the level of sugar production, observable in Figure 2.1, reflects the uncertainties of these times. A dip in production after 1875 was followed by a more prolonged fall in 1880. An abrupt recovery occurred in 1890, when the United States briefly placed sugar imports on the free list. Throughout the century,

Cuban producers had faced stiff barriers in virtually all major markets. The liberalization of the American market had been long sought after, but it was terminated in 1894, almost as soon as it had started. The following year, war erupted on the island, and the sugar industry in Cuba collapsed as the armies of both sides ravaged the countryside. By 1896, production had fallen to a quarter of the 1894 level.[4]

The second period of expansion was launched only after the chaotic conditions of war were superseded by a radical political change. Cuba had obtained independence from Spain but ended up under the tutelage of the United States. This period of expansion is illustrated in Figure 1.1. Optimism among North American businessmen toward Cuban sugar encouraged a massive inflow of capital. The prostrate sugar industry recovered and resumed a path of rapid growth not seen since the 1870s. Production quickly achieved levels far exceeding anything known in the nineteenth century. The peak level of 1.1 million tons had been reached in 1894. In three decades, by 1925, that level had been multiplied by five. The period of greatest expansion was driven by the demands of World War I. Immediately after the war, the Cuban sugar and banking industries suffered from disruptions related to the relaxation of wartime price controls, but expansion continued and peaked in 1925. The Cuban government, under President Gerardo Machado, became concerned about overproduction in the sugar market and unilaterally adopted a policy to restrict the Cuban sugar crop. The policy remained in force for the crops of 1927 and 1928, but it had little effect on the world production level and was discontinued for the 1929 crop.[5] Correspondingly, in 1927 and 1928 a decline in production is visible in Figure 1.1, but in 1929 the former peak level resumed. The Hawley-Smoot Act of 1930 had a devastating effect on Cuban sugar production. In two years, production fell to one-third of capacity. Although for different reasons, the relative magnitude of the collapse was comparable to the one experienced during the War of Independence.

Table 2.1 shows a peak of 30 percent in Cuba's share of the world market in 1870, but during the subsequent years of conflict the Cuban share diminished. Expansion was renewed after 1900, and Cuba regained its former share of the market by the 1920s. But the policy of crop restrictions and the rise of protectionism prevented that level from being maintained after 1927.

Cuba's swift ascendance into prominence in the world sugar industry is an indication of its unusually good natural conditions for growing cane. The late start in sugar production in the eighteenth century was an outcome of Spanish mercantilist regulation. Immigration and commercial policy discouraged any trade not perceived to be organic to the Spanish imperial system. Trade policy centered on the extraction and shipment of precious metals from the mainland American colonies to the Iberian peninsula. Havana was early on established as the principal naval station for the passage of fleets carrying silver to the peninsula and as a principal military outpost for controlling the Caribbean waters for Spanish commerce. Policy, dominated by questions of security in the Cuban port, discouraged the early development of industries that did not directly service the transit of precious metals. Most important, officials attempted to restrict immigration and settlement to persons who directly served the Crown's purposes and to block settlement of "undesirables" who might have contributed an element of instability. This policy included restrictions on the importation of slaves to reduce the threat of slave uprisings. This restrictive policy limited sugarcane planters' access to coerced labor, which was commonly used by competitors in other West Indian colonies. Heavy taxation and further restrictions on shipments of sugar further limited expansion and ensured that the sugar industry remained a minor component of the Cuban economy.[6]

Two key events of the eighteenth century changed Spanish policy toward sugar production in the Caribbean and stimulated the initial rise in the Cuban sugar industry. First, the taking of Havana in 1762 by the English (during the Seven Years' War) gave sugar producers in Cuba a taste of more liberal policies. Creole planters thereafter made greater political demands. Spain responded by liberalizing the slave trade in 1789 and implementing trade reforms that released the industry from many existing barriers. The second event was the slave revolt in the French colony of St. Domingue — the Haitian revolution — in 1791. The revolution caused a complete collapse of the sugar industry in St. Domingue, leaving a huge gap in sugar supplies on the world market. That vacuum resulted in high prices and presented a timely opportunity for Cuban sugar producers to enter the market.[7]

Several factors contributed to the nineteenth-century expansion. To explain the timing, Manuel Moreno Fraginals emphasizes the role of shocks to the global sugar supply. The nineteenth-century challenges to slavery and colonialism in other New World colonies permitted Cuba, continuing to use slave labor, to expand easily into existing markets.[8] In the 1830s, emancipation of slaves in the British colonies opened more

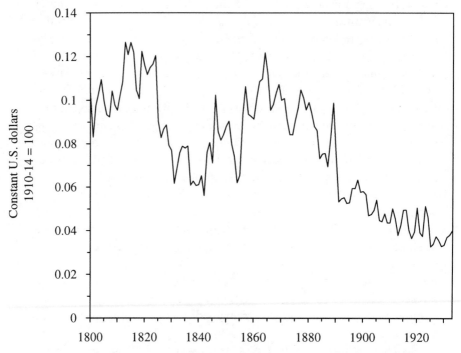

Fig. 2.2. Price of sugar in New York, 1800–1933. Prices are deflated using the
Warren and Pearson wholesale price index, 1910–14 = 100. Source: U.S.
Department of Commerce, *Historical Statistics of the United States*, Series E-40,
p. 200.

opportunities for Cuban sugar. Stricter enforcement of slave trade pro-
hibitions in the 1840s and 1850s disadvantaged planters in other European colonies, but simultaneously Cuban planters accelerated their involvement in the slave trade and took over a greater share of the market,
using an accumulation of slaves as the labor basis for expansion.[9] Later, in
the 1860s, another disruption of world sugar production and high prices
during the Civil War in the United States gave further stimulus to Cuba
(see Figure 2.2).

   Despite the series of blows to competitors, factor endowments underlay Cuba's swift overtaking of the market. Through these secular opportunities for expansion, it was discovered that the Cuban climate and soils
were among the most favorable to cane cultivation in the world. Sparsely
populated and little exploited, the Cuban plains offered both quality and
abundance. Cane cultivation could be extended easily into rich virgin

soils, and a nearby abundance of forested land could provide fuel for boiling the cane juices. It would be difficult to explain the extent of the expansion without such an endowment.[10] If natural conditions had not been so favorable, the stimulus that Cuban producers received would have spread more evenly to other competitors as well. But its factor endowments — climate, soils, and other natural resources — gave Cuba a clear natural advantage over many existing sugar-producing countries. Once this was discovered, its sugar industry rose to prominence very quickly.

Given the continual mechanization of sugar plantations throughout the nineteenth century, however, the expansion would likely not have reached the same magnitude without the technical and organizational innovativeness of Cuban producers. Innovation kept Cuba on the technical forefront of the industry. The mechanization involved more than power technology, but the adoption of steam power is a key indicator. Cuban producers became leaders in the application of steam power to sugar. According to Noel Deerr, steam power in sugar was introduced in 1768 in Jamaica, but the steam engine was first successfully applied on a sugar plantation in Cuba in 1797. By 1808, 25 sugar mills in Cuba were being driven by steam power. By 1860, 72 percent of the sugar mills were steam-powered, and they produced 90 percent of the Cuban sugar crop. Improvements in other mechanical and nonmechanical devices of the mill showed similar trends, and Cuban producers were major contributors in developing and perfecting new ideas within the industry.[11]

Demographic Trends

Growth in sugar production required comparable additions to the population and the labor force. In the first expansion these additions were accomplished by a massive increase in the slave labor force, an involuntary immigration. Similarly, the second expansion, in the early republic, was accomplished through a massive immigration of whites, this time voluntarily.

Indeed, the policy incentives responsible for the initial sugar expansion were largely related to the liberalization of the slave trade in Cuba. The Royal Decree of 1789 relaxed the restrictions on importing slaves, and a massive inflow of Africans began that lasted until 1867. David Eltis estimates that 739,000 slaves were imported between those years, most of whom were destined for labor on the sugar plantations. This first sugar expansion happened, however, at a time when slavery was under attack internationally. Spain had signed a treaty with Great Britain prohibiting the slave trade in Cuba as early as 1817, but it was not enforced in Cuba. British confiscation of slave ships and the complications of dealing in contraband did, nonetheless, raise the risks and costs incurred by slave traders. Higher prices eventually made slavery less attractive relative to other labor sources.[12] As the middle of the nineteenth century approached, one of the unique characteristics of the Cuban plantation economy was the diversity of its labor force. As slaves became scarcer and prices rose, Asian contract workers and free laborers, both of color and white, joined the slave labor force on plantations.

As one would expect, the massive introduction of slaves at the beginning of the century had a substantial compositional impact on the island's population, raising the percentage of blacks and mulattoes. Unlike other West Indian colonies, however, the population of African descent never reached an overwhelming majority on the island. Offsetting the African stream, a substantial stream of white immigrants had the effect of preserving a certain racial balance among the inhabitants of the island. Since the liberalization of the slave trade, many Cubans of high standing had advocated white immigration programs, pointing to the Haitian slave rebellion as an example of what could happen if a racial balance in the population were not preserved.[13] Table 2.2 indicates that the share of the population of color was in the majority only in the first half of the nineteenth century, as shown in the censuses of 1817, 1827, and 1841. The pattern indicates both a rise in the relative numbers of slaves in the initial stages of sugar expansion and then a decline after 1841. The rise brought the African population into the majority by 1817, but by 1862 it was no longer in the majority, and the share of the African population fell gradually to less than 30 percent by 1919.

The oscillation in the relative shares of the two segments of the population reflects the net effects of two principal factors — the level of activity of the slave trade and the incentives for Spanish emigration to Cuba. According to Eltis's estimates, the highest rates of importation of slaves occurred in the periods 1810–20 and 1825–45. After the effective ending of the slave trade in 1867, immigration of blacks was largely prohibited until after the turn of the century, and rates of population growth depended on natural increases alone.[14]

Table 2.2 also indicates consistently high rates of growth in the white population. Immigrants from Spain were by far the largest contributors. After 1817, annual rates of growth of the white population were compa-

Table 2.2
Population of Cuba by Race, 1791–1931

Year	Inhabitants in thousands (percent in parentheses)			Average annual rates of growth (percent)			
	Total	White	Of color	Total	White	Of color	Sugar production
1791	272	154 (56)	119 (44)	2.7	2.7	2.7	—
1817	553	240 (43)	313 (57)	2.7	1.7	3.7	4.1
1827	704	311 (44)	393 (56)	2.4	2.6	2.3	4.5
1841	1,008	418 (42)	589 (58)	2.6	2.1	2.9	5.7
1862	1,359	765 (56)	594 (44)	1.4	2.9	0.0	4.7
1877	1,522	1,032 (68)	489 (32)	0.8	2.0	−1.3	0.9
1887	1,632	1,103 (68)	529 (32)	0.7	0.7	0.8	3.2
1899	1,573	1,052 (67)	520 (33)	−0.3	−0.4	−0.1	−6.3
1907	2,049	1,428 (70)	621 (30)	3.3	3.8	2.2	18.7
1919	2,889	2,088 (72)	801 (28)	2.9	3.2	2.1	8.7
1931	3,962	2,857 (72)	1,105 (28)	2.6	2.6	2.7	−2.1

Peak-to-peak sugar production growth rates

Period	Rate of growth
1791–1872	4.7
1872–1894	1.7
1894–1925	5.1

SOURCES: Census data taken from Maluquer de Motes; *Nación e inmigración*, p. 15; sugar production data from Moreno Fraginals, *El ingenio*, 3: Table 1, pp. 35–40.

rable to those of the population of color until 1841. Afterward, rates of white population growth remained steady, even as the rates of growth of the African population stagnated or declined. Gross immigration rates were high after 1887, although the rates of population increase, shown in Table 2.2, fail to reveal them. High rates of gross immigration were offset by high rates of return to Spain. Many migrated to Cuba only temporarily, as merchants, seasonal workers, or soldiers, and others returned to the homeland or emigrated elsewhere because of troubled political conditions.[15]

Similar to the British colonies' importation of Asian contract laborers, Cuba imported Chinese laborers under long-term contracts between 1847 and 1874. In Table 2.2, the Chinese residents are included in the figures for the white population.[16] Their contribution to the overall "white" growth rate was small. In 1841–62 the Chinese contributed only 0.2 of a percentage point to the 2.9 percent rate of growth in the white population. And in 1862–77 their contribution was only 0.3 of a point to the overall rate of 2.0 percent. The Chinese, however, did play an important role in the years of adjustment to a diminished supply of slaves. Most of the Chinese seem to have been employed in the sugar plantations where slavery was most concentrated.[17]

The highest rates of white population growth were registered in the republican period, after 1903. As in earlier periods, these high rates reflect immigration largely from Spain. It might seem paradoxical that severance of political ties with Spain led to increased flows of Spanish immigrants; however, cultural and economic ties remained very strong. Also, the highest rates of general emigration from Spain to the Americas occurred between 1903 and 1924 (although they were interrupted by World War I). Argentina was the first destination of choice and Cuba the second during these years. In the early republic, the rate of growth in the black and mulatto population was renewed after 1906. Immigration of Africans had been restricted since the ending of the slave trade. This restriction was relaxed gradually after 1906 to permit contract laborers, mostly from Jamaica and Haiti, to be introduced for work in the sugar industry. Approximately 300,000 West Indian immigrants (gross) were recorded between 1907 and 1929.[18]

There was a high correlation between long-run rates of population growth and growth in the sugar industry, as can be seen by comparing the growth rates of population and of the sugar industry given in Table 2.2. The two periods of sustained population growth between 1774 and 1931 were also periods of rapid growth in the sugar industry. From 1791 to 1862, the average annual rate of population growth was 2.4 percent, and the average annual rate of growth of sugar production was 4.7 percent. From 1862 to 1899, the average annual rate of population growth had slowed to 0.4 percent. Sugar production growth saw a net average annual decline of 0.9 percent, if we use the census date as the end point of the period.[19] Sustained population growth picked up again after 1899, at the time of the second sustained wave of sugar expansion. From 1899 to 1931, annual growth rates of the population and sugar production averaged 2.9 and 7.1 percent, respectively.

Export Concentration

The success of the sugar industry in Cuba resulted in an extreme specialization of the economy. The rise of monoculture and export concentration
in sugar has been considered one of the central issues in the long-term
economic development of Cuba. The long-term progression of this structural feature is often discussed as occurring in two stages. First, the initial
specialization in sugar came about in the first wave of expansion of the
sugar industry in the early nineteenth century. Second, an intensification
of export concentration and monoculture is said to have occurred with the
second wave of expansion in the first three decades of the twentieth century, when North American influence increased.[20] Export concentration
ratios show, however, that there was no increase in concentration after
1900 over the peak levels found in the nineteenth century. There was,
nonetheless, a greater degree of concentration of purchasers because of
the growing isolation of Cuban producers from continental European
markets, which made Cuba more dependent on the U.S. market and the
oligopoly of refiners in the United States.

Peak levels of concentration were reached first in the mid-nineteenth
century, lost during the economically depressed years of the 1870s and
1880s, and regained during World War I. Figure 2.3 demonstrates these
trends, giving shares of Cuba's principal export commodities — sugar, tobacco, and coffee — from 1821 to 1933. It shows, first, that by 1821,
exports of sugar and the derivative product, molasses, had concentrated
sufficiently to contribute over 50 percent of all export earnings. From the
1830s through the 1860s, there was steady movement toward further
concentration to the point that around 90 percent of all export earnings
were from sugar. The steady ascension of sugar reflects a latent comparative advantage that, once discovered, resulted in a rapid shift of resources
into that sector of the economy. The concentration of productive resources into this single activity might have resulted in greater aggregate
instability if the market for Cuban sugar had not been so robust.

Figure 2.3 also indicates that a long-run intensification of export concentration in the second stage did not occur. During the medium run, from
1901 into the 1920s, there was an increase in the degree of concentration
of export earnings in sugar, but this is a phenomenon related to the long-
term cycle of the sugar industry. Comparing peak-to-peak export concentration ratios (likewise in sugar tonnage) shows that concentration in

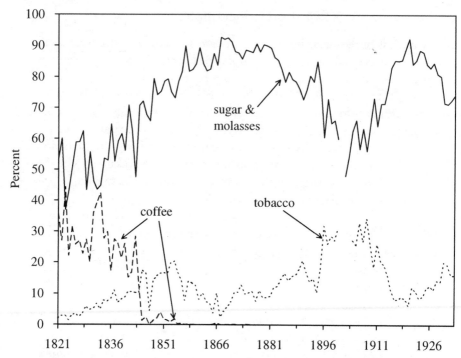

Fig. 2.3. Major Cuban exports as shares in total exports, 1821–1933. Source: Moreno Fraginals, *El ingenio*, 3: 88–89.

sugar was similar in the colonial and the republican periods. Sugar declined in importance from 1883 to 1901, reflecting both depression in sugar production and a bit of expansion in the tobacco industry. The decline in the share of tobacco in total exports after 1908 did not indicate that the recovery of the sugar industry was drawing resources from the tobacco industry (to the point of displacing it) to feed the sugar industry. In fact, tobacco as well as sugar exports were at record levels during this period of integration into the U.S. economy, and tobacco export earnings continued to increase until 1925.

On the one hand, export concentration in sugar came about as a result of success in the sugar industry. On the other hand, in part, it reflected problems faced by Cuba's other principal export industries. From the beginning of the century until 1843, Cuba's exports were concentrated in both sugar and coffee, which together constituted between 75 and 80 percent of total exports. But Cuban coffee suffered a complete collapse in

1843–45. The advance of the Brazilian coffee industry had driven the price of coffee down. Then a severe drought hit Cuban coffee growers in 1843, and a disastrous hurricane struck in 1844, which reportedly left the stock of coffee trees damaged and coffee growers in ruins. The coffee industry in Cuba never recovered.[21]

Tobacco, which had a long-standing tradition in Cuba, had declined in importance with the rise of the sugar and coffee industries around the turn of the nineteenth century. Afterward, it remained an important industry but was plagued by uncertain trade cycles. Its contribution to total export earnings fluctuated. Export booms of greater or lesser degree occurred in 1829–37, 1848–59, 1867–73, and 1882–93; however, the effects of these booms on the economy were shadowed by the dynamic growth of the sugar industry. The contribution of the tobacco industry to earnings became more important at the end of the nineteenth century, reaching 30 percent. But this came about when cane fields and sugar mills were deliberately destroyed and sugar production was halted during the War of Independence.[22] In any case, sugar monoculture in Cuba was well established in the nineteenth century. The apparent intensification of concentration in sugar between 1899 and World War I was in a sense a return to "business as usual."

Another issue in Cuba's long-term economic development had been its growing isolation in international markets, which left it dependent on the United States for selling its sugars. This geographical concentration of export destinations was unstable. At times the United States proved to be willing to allow Cuban imports to take over a large share of the market, but at other times it became politically advantageous to close them off. The long-term progression toward dependency on the U.S. market has been said to have occurred in two stages. In the first wave of expansion, Cuba found a diverse group of countries in which its sugar could be marketed. Later, however, many of these markets closed, and by the end of the nineteenth century, the United States came to be Cuba's principal customer. While Cuba remained a colony of Spain, it fell naturally into the geographical sphere of influence of the United States. As the U.S. economy developed, Cuban producers were in a prime location for supplying its markets with sugar. The sugar refining industry on the northeastern seaboard of the United States expanded and reorganized in part in response to the available supplies of raw sugar in Cuba.[23] The trend of exports to the United States shown in Figure 2.1 indicates the increasing relative weight of sales to the United States in Cuban aggregate sugar production. Sugar exports to the United States were important early on; however, after about 1850, the yearly increments in Cuban sugar output went almost entirely to the United States. Cuba's export orientation steadily gravitated away from Spain toward the growing economic power to the north.

Manuel Moreno Fraginals underscores the inability of Spain both to control and to complement Cuba's economic activities. As Cuba's metropolis, Spain was incapable of providing an adequate market for Cuban sugar. A glance at the export shares going to different destinations, presented in Table 2.3, supports this conclusion. The Spanish economy remained stagnant throughout the nineteenth century, and per capita consumption of sugar in Spain showed only negligible growth until 1890. Even by 1860, Spain absorbed less than 10 percent of the Cuban sugar crop, and that share continued to fall. Nevertheless, Cuba enjoyed a diversified market for its sugar during the first half of the century. Western European nations and the United States, where sugar consumption per capita was growing rapidly, provided ample markets for Cuban sugar.[24]

This diversification diminished by the end of the nineteenth century as a result of two important factors. First, the progress and policy in the European beet sugar industry made it difficult for Cuban sugar to compete. France and Germany, once importers of Cuban sugar, closed their doors to the sugar trade and promoted their domestic industries with generous export subsidies. The combination of technical improvements in the beet sugar industry, protectionism, and aggressive European export promotion closed Cuban sugars out of continental markets.[25] The rise in the importance of beet sugar in world supplies is seen in Figure 2.4.

Table 2.3
Cuban Sugar Exports: Shares to Principal Destinations, 1830–1900
(percent)

Year	U.S.	Spain	Great Britain	Western Europe	Other
1830	17	19	6	4	54
1840	23	14	6	25	31
1850	35	10	11	17	27
1860	48	8	20	11	13
1870	57	5	21	8	9
1880	80	3	8	3	7
1890	84	6	1	—	9
1900	96	2	0	—	2

SOURCE: Data from Moreno Fraginals, *El ingenio*, 3: Table 4, pp. 43–46.
NOTE: Percentages calculated from five-year averages of exports centered on years shown in the table.

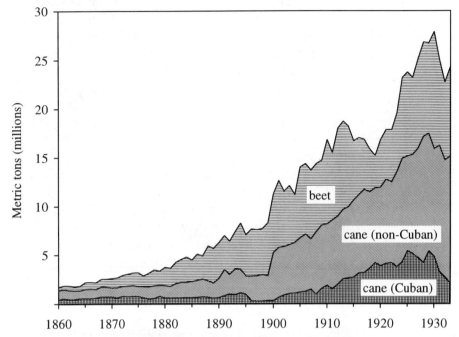

Fig. 2.4. World cane and beet sugar production, 1860–1933. Sources: Moreno Fraginals, *El ingenio*, 3: 35–41; Deerr, *History of Sugar*, 2: 490–91.

Second, by the end of the century, the demand for sugar in the United States had grown sufficiently to absorb almost the entire annual crop, which by 1892 had reached a million tons (see Figure 2.1). Nonetheless, conditions in the U.S. market were not unambiguously favorable. The Louisiana cane sugar industry continued to thrive under protective tariffs. A nascent beet sugar industry was developing in the United States behind the same protectionist walls (it would become an interest group with considerable political influence by World War I), and the notorious Sugar Trust rose in the 1880s and exercised monopsony power over the prices of raw sugar entering the United States.[26] In the meantime, the United States incorporated the Hawaiian Islands into its duty-free sugar zone with a reciprocity treaty in 1876, adding another element to the unequal competition that Cuban producers faced. Also, Cuba's locational advantage became less significant as the costs of shipping from more distant locations fell. Cuba's share of the U.S. sugar market consequently declined from 1870 to 1897.[27] But despite the adverse events and policies, the United

States remained the best option for placing Cuban sugars, and an increasing share of the Cuban crop was being marketed there. Elsewhere, Cuba's options had diminished, except in Britain, and as a consequence, Cuban sugar exporters were largely dependent on conditions in the North American market and U.S. trade policy.

These circumstances led to a political movement in Cuba within the island's principal economic associations, which materialized in 1884, to pressure Spain to open negotiations with the United States to permit liberalization of the trade between the United States and Cuba. The McKinley tariff of 1890 resulted in a brief four years of duty-free exports of sugar to the United States, but then there was a return to protection on both sides.[28] A more prolonged favorable policy to the sugar trade with the United States came in 1903, when Cubans were granted a 20 percent preferential discount on the full sugar duty. After that point, the share of the U.S. market provided by Cuba began to increase again until the 1920s (see Figure 1.2).

The Years of Revolution: Technology and Labor

The first prolonged expansion of the sugar industry ended in the late 1870s, after eight decades of steady growth. Cuba would not again see a sustained expansion of the sugar industry until after 1898, when it had achieved independence from Spain and saw itself a protectorate of the United States. In the interim was a period of relative stagnation in economic activity. Though suffering wide swings in its level, the expected sugar crop remained roughly constant, or in a slight downward trend, after 1875. Then in 1891, the sugar industry seemed to take off again on an upward trajectory, but four years later it was interrupted by a continuation of fighting between the Spanish authorities and Cuban separatists that had plagued the island since 1868. These years were a complicated time for Cuba's history because the social order of the plantation economy was ruptured. A series of political events reflects the degree of reorganization going on in Cuban society and the economy. Political and social unrest in the relations between metropolis and colony were behind the Ten Years' War (1868–78), the Guerra Chiquita (1879), and the (second) War of Independence (1895–98). Slave resistance was increasing as were other pressures for abolition. Slaves were declared free both by the rebel forces and the Crown during the Ten Years' War. Though complete abolition was not implemented at that time, the legal actions of emancipation were set in motion, and emancipation proceeded gradually until it was achieved in 1886. A successful transition to free labor prepared the way for recovery of the sugar industry.

Two revolutionary events had profound and long-lasting impacts on economic relations in the sugar industry. The first was the abolition of slavery and the establishment of a free labor force. The second was a revolution in both the manufacturing technology and the organization of the firm in the sugar industry. Both of these events reflect global trends associated with the evolution of Western capitalism. The reorientation of the labor force began with the suppression of the slave trade in Cuba, which was accomplished because of pressure on Spain by the international movement for abolition and diplomatic pressure from Britain.[29] The technological revolution was also global. The recent advances were part of a more general movement in technology, which involved the application of science to industry and the fundamental reorganization of factories and machinery that would revolutionize all leading industries — not only sugar. This technological movement in other contexts also stimulated the formation of large business organizations capable of efficiently managing extensive operations, sometimes multinational, in production and distribution. This dynamism was centered in Europe and the United States.[30] That Cuba was so deeply affected is one indicator of the advanced technological state of the sugar industry in Cuba at this time.

Although there has been much interest in showing a causal connection between abolition and the technological advances in sugar manufacture, empirical results show that they were largely independent events.[31] They did, however, have complementary effects on institutional developments, particularly in rural labor and land tenure. Emancipation permitted almost 30 percent of the country's inhabitants to escape the labor of the plantations, if they wished, and to settle independently in areas remote from the toil of the cane fields.[32] Technology had as profound an impact on the land tenure (or integration) of sugar estates as abolition did on plantation labor. The new technology promoted a consolidation of mills into much larger units of production but, simultaneously, a disintegration of the sugar estate as a self-contained unit of production. The organizational innovations developed for supplying cane to these enormous mills involved the formation of the cane farming institution. As the numbers of cane farmers grew over the course of these decades, they formed what has been considered the basis of a new rural middle class — the colonos. Some political thinkers had hoped that these men and their families would build the foundation of a more stable rural society, the Cuban counterpart to the Jeffersonian concept of the small grain farmer in the United States.[33] But the institution did not fit that ideal. A more thorough discussion of the formation of this new institution and the implications it had for Cuba's economic transition must wait until Chapter 3. But it is important that its origins are found in both the introduction of the new technology and the transition to free labor.

These revolutionary changes in the sugar industry came about despite the depressed condition of the economy. As Figure 2.1 illustrates, the sugar industry contracted during the Ten Years' War. Between 1875 and 1877, sugar production fell by more than 30 percent.[34] The war was ended formally in February 1878, but the economy and the level of sugar production remained stagnant until 1891. Three easily identifiable post-war events contributed to the contraction — the abolition of slavery, the emergence of the European beet sugar industry as a new competitor, and the Spanish authorities' refusal to acknowledge the needs and demands of the colony.

The abolition of slavery, the first of these contractionary influences, was an outcome of the Ten Years' War. Although emancipation had not been achieved during the war, the question of abolition had emerged as an issue that could no longer be neglected. Both sides had promised freedom of some sort to slaves during the war. The insurgents had promised a quali-fied version of freedom to attract the support of people of color, although enactment was to be postponed until after the war. Spain, as a coun-teroffensive, attempted to take the moral high ground by the passage of the Moret Law in 1870, which initiated a process of gradual emancipation. Slave resistance and massive desertions from the sugar estates led Spain in 1880 to declare legal freedom and to place the slaves under the *patronato*, an intermediate institution analogous to the British "apprenticeship." The patronato did away with slavery in name but did not grant freedom of action to the *patrocinados* — the former slaves. Patrocinados remained under the supervision of their former owners and under the obligation to work for them for provisions and a stipulated below-market wage. Begin-ning in 1884, however, the patronato called for a graduated emancipation in which slave owners were required each year to grant freedom to a fraction of their patrocinados. The gradual process of legal emancipation was completed when the patronato was terminated in 1886.[35]

As a consequence of these legal actions, the number of laborers bound to the plantations diminished steadily until all were freed in 1886. As the number of coerced laborers diminished, planters had to make adjustments to attract and make use of free labor. Judging by the previous experiences of adjustment to emancipation in other European colonies, the long-term damage to the Cuban sugar economy caused by the elimination of property rights over its labor force could have been much worse. Sugar production stagnated, but it was not as deeply depressed as it was in other colonies after emancipation.

The principal threat to the profitability of plantations was the potential shock to the supply of labor. Liberated slaves left the plantation labor force, refusing to work in their former occupations even as free laborers. When they had freedom of choice, the arduousness of cutting cane, the bitterness of gang labor on large plantations, or the lure of independence drove former slaves away from the plantations. Many migrated and settled as squatters in undeveloped areas of the eastern provinces, setting up subsistence plots for their families. The experiences of British planters had forewarned that the labor force would flee. After the British emancipation in 1838, planters complained that they were unable to attract former slaves at wages they could afford to pay, given the price of sugar. Cuban planters made similar claims of labor shortage, calling on the government for immigration subsidies or laws to restrict labor mobility.[36]

It is interesting to compare the postemancipation responses of the Cuban sugar industry with those in other sugar economies. In light of the other experiences, it is remarkable that Cuban producers enjoyed a burst of recovery just five years after the last patrocinados were released from bondage. Cuba's response was nothing like the collapses that occurred in Louisiana and some of the British colonies. The Louisiana industry collapsed completely during the Civil War; for a few years production levels were at 5 to 15 percent of prewar levels. Though not as severe, production in Jamaica fell by more than 50 percent after emancipation in 1838. Still, it was a substantial reduction, and previous levels of production had not been recovered even by World War I. A more favorable adjustment was experienced by British Guiana, which suffered a drop of about 40 percent after emancipation in 1838 but restored previous levels of production in about 30 years. Cuba's reduction was yet milder. The drop in production after 1875 was about 30 percent, and recovery of previous levels came within about 25 years. But not only was it milder, the timing was different. In the British colonies, collapse in the sugar industry came immediately after and in direct response to the release of the slave labor force from legal obligation to work on the plantations. This was not true of Cuba.

The passage of the Moret Law had a visible negative direct impact on the level of production for only one year. The gradual release of the patrocinados from 1884 to 1886 was accompanied by a small but positive average annual rate of growth of sugar production of 2.5 percent.[37]

Stanley Engerman, in another context, has shown that successful adjustment to free labor following emancipation was a function of population densities and success in finding alternative sources of plantation labor. In his comparative study of the British West Indies, he identifies three types of response in the post-1838 adjustment to emancipation. In the first type, islands with high land-to-labor ratios failed to make the adjustment because planters had to compete with attractive conditions for subsistence farming and the economic independence of former slaves. In Jamaica, for example, when slaves received their freedom, they fled the estates to unoccupied lands unsuited to cane cultivation. Planters were not generally able to induce them to return, and the sugar industry there declined. In the second type of response, by contrast, islands with low land-to-labor ratios made successful adjustments because they offered few alternatives to plantation labor. Planters could more easily induce former slaves to work as wage laborers on the plantations because fewer alternatives were available to former slaves. Barbados, the prime example of this type, seemed to suffer almost no employment shock because the arable lands were already occupied and former slaves had no means other than wage labor for making a living. In the third type of response, some islands with high land-to-labor ratios avoided Jamaica's fate by tapping new sources of migrant labor from Asia. The best examples of this type, British Guianese and Trinidadian planters, financed a steady importation of Indian contract workers to work for low wages at sites determined by their employers. Greater soil fertility in these colonies relative to Jamaica, and hence higher profitability, seems to explain the success of this strategy.[38]

The high land-to-labor ratio in Cuba was comparable to that of British Guiana or Jamaica, and former slaves had similar access to land.[39] Therefore, it is interesting that there was no direct shock to production caused by the enactment of emancipation and no long-term dependence on indentured labor. Even though planters there made claims of economic distress caused by labor shortages, other observers noted an abundance of unemployed laborers seeking wage work during the economically depressed period after the Ten Years' War.[40] The depressed state of the economy kept labor demands down, making the potential labor constraints of emancipation less binding.

But in addition, unlike the British colonies, the Cuban labor force had begun its transition to free labor well before the process of abolition had been completed because the growing scarcity of slaves had caused planters to seek alternative sources of labor. The gradualist policy toward emancipation also ameliorated the employment shock to the system.

The Transition to Free Labor

After the outbreak of the Ten Years' War, planters and other slaveholders realized that the decline of slavery was inevitable. Spanish officials who debated social reform sought the support and cooperation of sugar interests in Cuba. Planters warned of the complete ruin of the economy if workers could not be found to replace the freed slaves. The key to the policy established in the Moret Law, then, was to permit time for adjustment. This law has been described as the "slaveholders' version of abolition" because such care was taken to ease the economy out of its dependency on slavery.[41]

Meanwhile, Cuban liberals were calling for reform in the plantation labor system. Some planters sought the replacement of the slave-based cane plantation with independent cane farms to be operated by white immigrant laborers. The earliest reformist notions of the cane farm were linked directly to the movement to "whiten" the population. As early as 1837, proposals were made to settle Canary Islander families to farm cane independently. By 1857, one of Cuba's leading liberals and an expert in sugar production, the Conde de Pozos Dulces, began to advise the adoption of cane farms as a viable mode of organizing the sugar enterprise. He argued that this would be the only effective way to attract European immigrants to replace black laborers in the cane fields. His motives, like those of many others who advocated this reform, were to reduce the island's dependency on African labor and reduce the proportion of blacks. But the programs that were devised directly to promote white immigration by offering land for settlement proved to be limited in scope and effectiveness.[42]

The somewhat later adoption of cane farms came about more pragmatically and without the direct racist objective of the earlier reformists. As the slave population declined, planters saw cane farming as a practical way to attract additional laborers. In the 1870s, there were scattered cases in which planters arranged for nearby landowners or tenants to cultivate cane to supplement their own crops. Sometimes plots on the edges of plantations were given or leased to slaves or former slaves; in other cases they were leased to white immigrants, but not all of these early small-holders were white, nor were they necessarily immigrants. Initially, these experiments reflected a wide range of social and land tenure arrangements.[43] As experience was accumulated, these scattered attempts at establishing outside growers increased in number, the practices became more standardized, and the contractual arrangements converged to form the institution known as the colono system.

Other measures were also taken to alleviate dependency on slave labor. Imitating the importation of Indians by the British, Cubans imported Chinese under long-term contracts from 1847 to 1874. Initially, the importation of Chinese was promoted under the auspices of the white immigration programs, but the trade in Chinese indentured laborers turned out to be little different from the slave trade.[44] From the planters' point of view the program of importing Chinese had achieved limited success. But Chinese immigration ended even before the patronato had begun. In place of these long-term (eight-year) contractual arrangements, the formation of *cuadrillas*, or work gangs, became common among the resident Chinese population. Planters would arrange to employ a cuadrilla through a contractor to provide work during a specified season. Payment would be made directly to the contractor, who would provide food and wages to the workers. This practice gradually became common among other segments of the free laboring population. Similarly, former slaves formed cuadrillas to gain independence from their former estates yet remain in plantation work.[45]

After the Ten Years' War, the principal new source of free laborers came as a result of the late nineteenth-century wave of emigration from Spain. Almost 300,000 Spanish immigrants entered Cuba (gross immigration) between 1882 and 1894 — about 23,000 per year on average. The rate of immigration picked up considerably after 1886, when the Spanish government decided to pay the passage from Spanish ports of those able to work in agriculture who wished to migrate to Cuba with their families. It picked up even more after the turn of the century, as is evident in Table 2.2, when recovery in the sugar and tobacco industries brought renewed prosperity to the island and even greater economic opportunity to immigrant Spaniards. On average 27,000 Spaniards migrated annually (gross) between 1902 and 1929.[46]

The links between Spanish immigration and the sugar industry were clear. There was a high correlation between the price of sugar and the annual rate of immigration from Spain. Among the high number of entrants and returnees were many seasonal migrants who would arrive in Cuba from Spain (mostly from the Canary Islands and Galicia) at the beginning of the grinding season and return when it was over. They came to take advantage either of high harvest-time wages or of the greater commercial activity during the same peak season. This "migration of *golondrinas* (swallows)," as it was called, was interrupted during the War of Independence, but its renewal afterward followed the recovery of the sugar industry until it leveled off in the 1920s.[47]

When Spanish immigration tapered off, West Indian seasonal migrants supplied a new source for expanding the labor force. After 1906, there was a partial reversal in the racial bias of Cuban immigration policy. The Cuban government lifted a restriction to permit the entrance of a new migratory stream — West Indian seasonal migrant workers (under seasonal contracts), mostly from Haiti and Jamaica — at the request of eastern-based North American sugar producers. The volume of this stream increased in the 1920s as sugar production in the east expanded and as a substitute for Spanish migration. On average there were about 12,000 official West Indian immigrants (gross) per year from 1907 to 1929 and an unknown number of illegal entrants as well. There was a strong reaction in Cuba against West Indian immigration, especially against the Haitians. Recalling the white immigration movement, objections related to the illiteracy and poor health of many entrants but also to racist fears. There were also complaints that West Indians were detrimental to labor conditions because they were willing to accept lower wages than Cuban laborers were, yet their absence may have been more detrimental to economic activity and employment. Before employment of West Indians had become widespread in the east, mill owners reportedly made decisions to limit otherwise advisable additions to mill capacity because of the insecurity of obtaining enough field labor.[48]

In summary, the replacement of slave labor with alternative forms of voluntary contractual arrangements and wage labor proceeded with relative ease for various reasons. First, the transformation of the labor force had begun much earlier than the process of emancipation set in motion by the Moret Law. The formation of colonias as one of the first steps became significant no later than the 1870s. It provided a means both for keeping former slaves on the plantations and for attracting whites to plantation work. The trade in Chinese contract workers perhaps represented an attempt to retain a system of coerced labor, but the rise of independently contracted work gangs, or cuadrillas, seems to have been an innovation (within the Cuban context) of resident Chinese who had served out their terms of indenture. Their experience led to imitation by free people of color and Spanish immigrants. The sugar industry in a land-abundant country had always depended on high rates of immigration to sustain a high rate of growth. High rates of immigration from Spain replaced the earlier stream from Africa and the relatively less important stream from China. After the turn of the century, the Spanish stream continued to flourish, supplemented by a new stream of seasonal workers from Haiti and Jamaica. Further, the participation of white Spanish immigrants in plantation work also led to a racially mixed labor force in the cane fields — no small accomplishment given other countries' experiences. Changes in rural employment practices also suggest a move in rural labor conditions toward the impersonal forces of the market that led to greater independence of choice for workers of all races relative to what they had had before. By the turn of the century, with the euphoria of emancipation ending and the recovery in the sugar industry beginning, many were attracted by the more secure earnings that cane field work offered, relative to subsistence, in a time of industrial expansion.[49] By the end of the 1880s, slavery had ended, but the pool of labor had widened considerably. Elastic labor supplies awaited the next great sugar expansion.

The Sugar Crisis

The adjustment to free labor might have gone less smoothly in the 1880s had the sugar industry not entered into a crisis of international scope at the same time that emancipation was reaching its completion. In the 1880s and later, the landscape of the global sugar industry was transformed as subsidized exports from European beet sugar producers expanded. The expansion is demonstrated in Figure 2.4 and Table 2.1, which show the steady rise in beet sugar production, which by the 1880s had taken over a substantial share of the world market. By means of export drawbacks, direct subsidies, and legalized cartels, European producers (German, Austro-Hungarian, French, Belgian, and Russian) closed their markets to competition and promoted domestic exports. The influx of cheap wheat from the United States into western Europe from the 1870s also seems to have had an important influence as governments promoted the expansion of sugar beets on "wheat soils" to alleviate the agricultural crisis there.[50] Earlier in the century, these countries had been important destinations for Cuban exports. In the transformation, Cuba was hit with the loss of a major market. Table 2.3 shows the steady decline and ultimate elimination of western European demand for Cuban sugar between 1860 and 1890.

The price of sugar on the world market collapsed as former European markets for cane sugar were taken over by beet sugar. The price of sugar, which had been on the rise since the 1840s and relatively high during the Civil War in the United States, had shown signs of weakness since the 1870s, as is observed in Figure 2.2. The plummeting price in 1882–84 came as a blow to many producers. H. C. Prinsen Geerligs, the renowned Dutch sugar technician, in his technical work *Cane Sugar and Its Manufacture* in 1924, recalled 1883 as a landmark in cane sugar history in which an international sugar financial crisis alerted cane sugar producers of the emerging beet sugar threat. For the next several years, the Círculo de Hacendados (Sugar Planters' Club) in Cuba referred to 1884 as the initial year of crisis of Cuban sugar that would endure until the effects of the McKinley Act were felt in 1891.[51] Producers worldwide were well aware by this time that the steady fall in prices represented a structural change in the sugar market caused by new technology. Decades of scientific research on the extraction of sugar from beets in Europe had reached fruition. But new methods of extraction in cane sugar were rapidly displacing those used in the traditional plantation.[52] The impact on unit costs of production was revolutionary. Competitors on the forefront of this technology were permanently driving the price of sugar down. As Figure 2.2 reveals, after 1890 the price of sugar would never again reach previous levels.

The response of Cuban sugar producers to the challenge of new competition and technological upgrading was seriously inhibited by the internal postwar condition of the sugar industry. Besides the effects of emancipation and fiscal and monetary disarray, shortsighted Spanish authorities left sugar producers unable to finance improvements to their mills. First, the budgetary adjustments that planters needed to make so they could pay wages were complicated by inflationary uncertainty and a war-related credit crisis in the 1880s.[53] Growing demands on operating capital exacerbated the crisis.[54] Wage labor required greater liquidity to cover expenses during the grinding season, in contrast with slave labor, which had a large fixed-cost component. Because of this and other new credit needs, planters were taking out mortgages on their estates at high interest rates. American diplomatic personnel, using hindsight, suggested that many of these mortgages were taken out imprudently. But there had been many surprises that caused an unforeseen delay in economic recovery. Extraordinary increases in taxes, falling sugar prices, and prolonged drought in 1883 made the difficulties of the amortization of planters' debts unexpected. The American consul in Havana noted in 1884 that "out of twelve or thirteen hundred planters on the island not a dozen are said to be solvent." Under these conditions, only a few could afford the complete revamping of the factory required by the new technology. The remainder of planter families were either in financial ruin or were unable to obtain the credit to finance repairs plus six months of wages, fuel, and other operating expenses.[55]

Second, the imperial tax burden became even more onerous. During the Ten Years' War and its aftermath, Madrid transferred much of the burden of the war debt onto Cuba. A complex of tax increases and tax surcharges was imposed from 1867 to 1883 on property, production, trade, and transport despite depressed economic conditions and reduced ability to pay. For example, under legislation of 1880, sugar producers claimed to suffer a tax burden of over 32 percent of the value of their crops. Spanish policies preserved a high-cost trade zone in Cuba by maintaining the highly protective barriers for Spanish goods. At the same time, they raised walls of protection for the inefficient cane and beet sugar industries in peninsular Spain — all at the expense of the colony's more efficient sugar producers. Most planters had remained loyal to Spain during the Ten Years' War, but they paid dearly in the war's aftermath, and many were alienated by the time fighting broke out again in 1895.[56]

Mistaken Recovery

The interwar conditions in the sugar industry improved considerably when, in the United States, the passage of the McKinley Act in 1890 placed Cuban raw sugars on the free list. The liberal treatment of sugar proved very short-lived, however. Duties were reimposed on sugar imports four years later. By 1894, the sugar tariff decision of 1890 was overturned in Congress, and the Wilson-Gorman Tariff Act imposed a 40 percent ad valorem tariff on all sugar entering the United States. Not foreseeing the brevity of these propitious conditions, sugar producers responded with alacrity to the new incentives in the sugar trade. Sugar exports rose by nearly 60 percent to reach more than one million tons in just two years' time — between 1890 and 1892 — and investments to build modern continuous-process sugar mills accelerated (see Figure 2.1).

Spain responded to the U.S. reversal of the liberal tariff policy in 1894 by canceling the concessions it had made to the United States in 1890. The highly protectionist regime returned, and the Cuban economy was hit again with high prices of imported inputs.[57] These events led to an upsetting of colonial relations. Facing a continuation of depressed economic conditions and fearing a disastrous trade war, Cuban interest groups opposed the removal of trade concessions to the United States and tried to force Spanish authorities to admit that the closure of the European and Spanish markets for Cuban goods required a conciliatory attitude toward U.S. trade policy. Powerless and unable to influence policy decisions in Madrid, the increasingly disaffected privileged classes contributed to a prevailing current of social turmoil.

Meanwhile, dissatisfaction with Spanish policies had grown at all levels of society. The political outcome of the Ten Years' War had left many disillusioned. The depressed state of the economy since then and since emancipation had left many displaced and with limited economic opportunities, and colonial authorities lost control of much of the countryside to bandits.[58] Under these social conditions, the movement for independence resurfaced, and the second War of Independence erupted in 1895.

North American Intervention

Independence brought an unexpected degree of control by the United States and the military occupation of the country, which lasted until 1902.[59] The shift in U.S. policy toward imperialist "dollar diplomacy" with Cuba resulted in a more favorable business and trade environment from the standpoint of foreign investors. Vigorous economic growth was one of the consequences, driven largely by the expansion of the sugar industry. Some scholars have dismissed this economic growth as having accrued to imperialist investors and as a temporary prelude to the crises of the 1930s and 1940s. It did, nonetheless, promote economic development to the point that social indicators in Cuba, such as life expectancy and literacy rates, were some of the best in Latin America even during the years of crisis.[60]

The recovery began around 1901, after which the sugar industry expanded at a rate previously unknown. From 1901 to 1925 sugar production grew at an average annual rate of 8.8 percent, compared with the average rate of 4.7 percent during the first period of expansion, 1791–1872. This dynamism remained relatively intact until the late 1920s, although economic turbulence associated with the adjustment to peacetime after World War I introduced a greater element of uncertainty after 1919.[61]

The rejuvenation of sugar was boosted by two important acts of the United States in establishing the new economic relationship. First was the Platt Amendment, passed by the U.S. Congress in 1901 and amended to the Cuban constitution in the same year, which defined U.S.-Cuban treaty relations. Second was the Reciprocity Treaty of 1903, which lowered tariff barriers preferentially between the two countries. The Platt Amendment gave the United States broad powers to intervene in the affairs of Cuba to maintain political stability and protect private property rights, and it ensured that the sweeping bureaucratic reforms of the provisional government would be retained by any future Cuban administration. The first two articles established U.S. control over aspects of Cuban fiscal policy and foreign relations. Article I limited Cuba's authority to sign treaties that might impede its independence or permit another power to challenge the United States as the dominant power in the region. Article II limited Cuban fiscal policy by prohibiting the government from contracting any public debt that could not be covered by the "ordinary revenues" of the island. Outstanding among the provisions were Articles III and IV, which established the broadest powers of intervention:

III. That the government of Cuba consents that the United States may exercise the right to intervene for the preservation of Cuban independence, the maintenance of a government adequate for the protection of life, property, and individual liberty, and for discharging the obligations with respect to Cuba imposed by the Treaty of Paris on the United States, now to be assumed and undertaken by the government of Cuba.

IV. That all Acts of the United States in Cuba during its military occupancy thereof are ratified and validated, and all lawful rights acquired thereunder shall be maintained and protected.[62]

This amendment was highly controversial in the United States, and it provoked widespread protests in Cuba. Even those Cubans who favored strong U.S. involvement suggested modifications. But the U.S. State Department made clear that this attenuation of sovereignty was a condition of the establishment of a Cuban republic. Before its acceptance, it was made clear to the Cuban Constitutional Convention that the occupational government would not be withdrawn without the acceptance of the Platt Amendment as a formal treaty between the United States and Cuba and its inclusion in the constitution of the new republic.[63]

Once the Platt Amendment was accepted, the United States ended occupation in 1902. But occupation was renewed in 1906–9 and U.S. marines were stationed in various cities and ports and certain sugar mills in 1912, 1917, and at other times before the amendment was abrogated in 1934.[64] Many military orders made by General Leonard Wood remained in force under the auspices of Article IV of the amendment. Not all Cubans would have disagreed with this interference in the sovereignty of the Cuban legislature. But the military orders were not always made with complete impartiality, and this treaty regulation tended to skew the legislative outcome in favor of those whose interests were served by the military orders. The outcomes were sometimes completely irrational. One blatant example, which I will discuss in Chapter 6, was the regulation of private railroad construction, which tended to discourage rather than encourage the integration of the private and public service railroad systems.

The Reciprocity Treaty of 1903 was granted as a reward for Cuba's conformity to U.S. demands. Unlike the Hawaiian treaty of reciprocity of 1876, which had granted Hawaiian sugar duty-free status, the treaty with Cuba granted a 20 percent discount on the full duty for sugar in the United States (as well as for Cuba's other principal export, tobacco). In exchange, the United States received reductions on the tariffs applied to its exports to Cuba ranging from 20 to 40 percent. Many Cubans argued that this was not reciprocity, but exporters proclaimed it a generous offer on the part of the United States and of great benefit to Cuban industry. For sugar producers, it opened up and secured the large U.S. market and stimulated the boom in Cuban sugar production. Despite the unequal competition they faced from domestic cane and beet sugar interests and from Hawaii, Puerto Rico, and the Philippines (all of which had received duty-free status), Cuban sugar producers were competitive enough to supply a considerable portion of the U.S. market. From less than 15 percent in 1900, the share grew to fluctuate between 50 and 70 percent during most of the 1920s (see Figure 1.2). The period of reciprocity represented an era of trade prosperity and market security for Cuban exporters unlike anything experienced in the surrounding years.[65]

Labor and Immigration Policy

Cuban labor policy during the early republican period was based primarily on the contention that labor was scarce and needed to be augmented by immigration. The result was an open-door policy toward immigration. Without such a policy, early republican economic growth would likely have been much less pronounced. Foreign investors would have been reluctant to sink funds into the Cuban economy if they had perceived Cuba as offering only restricted supplies of labor and the risk of rising wages. At the turn of the century, even before economic recovery had begun to take shape, American bureaucrats in Cuba were asked to assess the postwar economic outlook of the country, and they reported that the existing labor sources in the country were "inadequate" to satisfy even immediate demands.[66]

Despite the political strength of sugar producers on the island, the immigration policy of the early republic did not solely reflect their interests in increasing the labor supply. Immediately after the war, the open-door policy applied only to white immigration, whereas restrictions were placed on immigrants of color. Thus the racial question weighed heavily in directing national policy, and the long-standing movement to "whiten" the island remained deeply entrenched.[67] The transition to a racially more inclusive open-door policy came gradually, as eastern sugar interests attempted to break down the restriction against importing laborers under contract. As sugar production spread into the eastern provinces, eastern producers found they had less access to the labor pool. The population was densest in the west, and Spanish immigrants disembarked in Havana. Separated from Havana by more than 700 miles, eastern mills had greater difficulty attracting laborers. Since 1902, the Cuba Company railroad connected the east and west, and normal travel time had been reduced from 10 days to 24 hours.[68] But the eastern mills found themselves at the end of the queue as Spanish seasonal migrants moved eastward from Havana in search of employment.

The first steps at breaking down the contract labor restriction were taken by North American sugar interests in 1906 and 1910. At the request of the manager of the Nipe Bay Company (subsidiary of the United Fruit Company), legislation was passed that permitted Nipe Bay to import Spaniards from the Canary Islands as contract laborers under the guise of a white settlement program. A few years later, in 1913, the Nipe Bay Company succeeded further in relaxing the restriction on black contract labor by obtaining permission to bring a thousand West Indian contract laborers to work in the cane fields on the condition that they would be returned to their countries after the grinding season was over.[69]

Shortages of field laborers in the east became more and more acute during the years following 1913. The construction boom of new sugar mills in the eastern provinces during World War I heightened competition

Table 2.4
*Average Annual Growth Rates of Sugar Production and
Prime-Age Population, 1903–31*
(percent)

	1903–7	1907–19	1919–31
Sugar production	9.1	8.7	2.5
Prime-age population[a]	3.3	2.0	3.5

SOURCE: Luzón, p. 76.

[a] Prime-age population is defined as ages 14 to 64.

for the local labor supply. To prevent labor shortages from hindering the expansion of sugar production (considered Cuba's contribution to the war effort), Cuban authorities passed special legislation permitting West Indian contract workers to enter and remain until two years after the conclusion of the war. Once the war was over, other provisions were made to permit a continuation of West Indian immigration.[70]

Comparing growth rates of the prime-age population and sugar production gives some idea of the relative growth of demand and supply of the labor force. This simple comparison is not without its weaknesses. It does not account for movements of domestic labor into sugar employment from other sectors of the economy, and it does not account for the contributions of nonresident seasonal migrants, which were substantial. Nonetheless, the comparison provides a sense of how additions to the resident labor pool matched the demands of the sugar industry. Table 2.4 gives average annual growth rates for sugar production and the prime-age population between 1903 and 1931. The table shows that annual growth of sugar production was more than three times that of the prime-age population between 1903 and 1919. After 1919, average annual growth rates of sugar production and the population were about the same. The average annual growth rate of sugar production from 1919 to 1925 was 4.2 percent. Spanish immigration dropped considerably in 1925, but West Indian immigration remained steady until 1928.[71]

As time passed, it appears that the open-door policy was crucial to the continued growth of the republican sugar economy before 1929. Expansion depended on additions to the labor force. As the economy grew, the need for foreign additions to the labor supply was even more pronounced. In the eastern provinces, where sugar was expanding most rapidly, labor shortages were a recurring problem. Sugar producers in these more remote areas had to pay considerable attention to the problem of recruiting laborers from Havana and other population centers.[72] Since new large mills were constantly appearing in these areas, the demand for labor increased and new participants competed for local labor supplies. Furthermore, the timing of the two migratory streams suggests that the West Indian stream acted as a substitute as Spanish immigration tapered off and yearly additions to the labor force became less reliable. After 1913, the yearly number of Spanish entrants became erratic, just as the West Indian stream was mounting.[73]

Foreign Investment and Enterprise

North American and British investments in Cuba rose in the years following independence and injected foreign capital into the economy left destitute by the war. The increase in foreign investments after the war came most frequently in the form of direct investments and the establishment of foreign enterprises. These typically involved varying degrees of participation of both Cuban and foreign entrepreneurs and financiers, though normally they involved close links between Cuban and foreign firms.[74] As the political status of Cuba stabilized over the first decade of the century and the policies of the United States toward Cuba were clarified, North American enterprises became more firmly established, and the weight of North American direct investments in the economy grew, driven largely by the profitability of sugar. World War I stimulated an unprecedented rate of construction of new mills. The financial crisis of 1920–21 ended in the collapse of the domestic banking system and its replacement by large North American banks. The catastrophe resulted as well in a large number of mills changing abruptly from domestic to North American hands. Alarm over growing control of the sugar industry by large North Ameri-

Table 2.5
Direct Foreign Investment in Cuba, 1913, 1929
(millions of U.S. constant dollars, 1926 = 100)

Origin	1913	1929
Great Britain	309	318
United States	308	1,195
France	19	—
Germany	7	—
Other	—	—
TOTAL	643	1,513

SOURCES: Lewis, *America's Stake in International Investment*, pp. 615–16; U.S. Department of Commerce, *Investment in Cuba*, p. 11; Pino Santos, *El asalto a Cuba*, p. 37.

Table 2.6
U.S. Foreign Investment in Cuba, 1896–1929
(percent in parentheses)

	1896	1906	1911	1927
Direct Investments (millions of constant dollars, 1926 = 100)				
Sugar	—	49	100	629
		(15.3)	(31.7)	(52.6)
Tobacco	—	49	—	21
		(15.3)		(1.8)
Other agriculture	—	58	15	26
		(18.3)	(4.9)	(2.2)
Railways	—	63	39	126
		(19.8)	(12.2)	(10.5)
Telephones	—	4	31	121
		(1.3)	(9.8)	(10.1)
Mercantile	—	—	—	31
				(2.6)
Mining	32	5	—[a]	52
	(29.8)	(1.5)		(4.4)
Government debt	—	60	46	105
		(18.8)	(14.6)	(8.8)
Other	—	31	85	84
		(9.7)	(26.8)	(7.0)
TOTAL	108	318	316	1,195

1908	1914	1919	1924	1929
Securities				
24.3	51.4	23.5	77.8	99.5

SOURCES: Lewis, *America's Stake in International Investment*, pp. 615–16, 655; Jenks, pp. 36–37, 162–65, 294–300. Deflated using the U.S. Bureau of Labor Statistics wholesale price index.
[a] Mining was not itemized in the estimates for 1911.

can companies and the sentiment that they were exploitative provoked reactions among Cuban nationalists that intensified in the 1920s.[75]

The magnitude of foreign assets in Cuba can be observed in Tables 2.5 and 2.6.[76] The participation of North American capital in the Cuban economy did increase significantly. As Table 2.6 shows, real assets directly held by persons in the United States increased about threefold from 1896 to 1906. Nonetheless, throughout the first decade of the twentieth century, British capital flows rivaled North American flows and may have outweighed them (see Table 2.5). By 1913 North American direct investments roughly equaled British direct investments. British participation remained the same after 1913 until 1927, but North American capital transfers accelerated during and after World War I until U.S. assets were about ten times what they had been before Cuban independence. By that time, U.S. assets in Cuba were overwhelmingly in the form of direct investments. Table 2.6 shows that portfolio investments also increased, although at a considerably slower rate. There was also substantial domestic investment. An estimate of 1913 suggests that domestic assets on the island consisted of at least a billion dollars evaluated in 1926 U.S. prices. Cubans also invested considerable sums abroad, and it is highly likely that some of the assets in Cuba classified as owned by North Americans were actually owned by Cubans participating in the New York capital market. There are no available data to suggest how great this channeling of Cuban assets through New York was, but estimates of overall Cuban ownership of U.S. assets were quite high.[77]

As is shown in Table 2.6, North American direct investments were concentrated consistently in two sectors — sugar and railroads. Before the 1880s, foreign investment in Cuba had been limited. Commercial credit advanced to planters and other agriculturalists, usually on a twelve-month basis, was supplied largely by Spanish immigrant merchant houses. North American, British, French, and German merchant firms were also present, but they supplied only a small share of commercial credit even into the next century. Most North American investments were made either by settlers or by merchants advancing credit. The first important North American investment in a sugar estate was acquired by E. Atkins and Co., the Central Soledad, in 1883 as part of the settlement of defaulted commercial debt. Forecasts of prosperity in sugar in the 1890s attracted further foreign direct investment in the sugar industry. A handful of new modern sugar mills were built by North Americans during this period. Still, until 1898 there were few direct foreign investments in sugar. Long-term investment in the sugar industry had been financed largely by domestic capital. Although many mills were being retired during the 1880s and 1890s, those being updated remained in the hands of families that had been involved in sugar production and export since mid-century. By 1896, North American direct investments in Cuba were estimated at around $108 million evaluated in 1926 prices ($50 million current), concentrated primarily in sugar, mining, and tobacco.[78]

These conditions changed somewhat during the military occupation between 1898 and 1902. An influx of North American capital went to finance the reconstruction of a number of Cuban mills. Also, North American investors built new mills or acquired old ones. Among these were investments that set precedents for building sugar mills in the eastern provinces. The Central Francisco was founded in 1901 by the Rionda family in a remote location in southern Camagüey, backed by capital from

New York and Philadelphia. The Central Boston was founded by Andrew Preston and Minor Keith, of the United Fruit Company, in a remote location in the province of Oriente. J. B. Hawley, congressman from Texas, working jointly with Mario Menocal, founded two mills, one in a remote location on the northern coast of Oriente and the other in the province of Havana. In each case huge outlays of capital were expended to build large modern mills. The eastern establishments also involved vast purchases of land in remote areas. The initial investment by United Fruit included an estate of 170,000 acres that subsequently was expanded. The investments by Rionda and Hawley included land purchases of 80,000 and 66,000 acres, respectively. Each involved collaboration between Cuban or Spanish entrepreneurship and North American capital. In the case of the Central Boston, Preston and Keith collaborated with two brothers, Hipólito and Simón Dumois; Hawley worked with Mario Menocal; and the Rionda investment was a joint effort of brothers Manuel and Francisco who had emigrated from Spain, one to New York and the other to Cuba.[79]

North American investments continued to expand in the years to come. Hawley had acquired six mills by 1913, consolidated by the Cuban-American Sugar Company, which was organized in 1906. The United Fruit Company founded a second mill, the Central Preston. The Rionda family invested in a third mill, the Central Manatí, in 1912. Even though North American capital played an important role, in most cases it supplemented Cuban entrepreneurship or experience. Before 1913, another fifteen new mills were built, and many existing mills were expanded. Although the North American capital market contributed capital to finance improvements in most mills, many of the mills remained in the control of domestic proprietors or companies.[80]

By 1913, the Cuban Secretaría de Agricultura, Comercio, y Trabajo classified 39 out of 172 active mills as of U.S. ownership. Another 12 were classified as British or French. Table 2.7 shows the breakdown in mills and in the percentage of crop that each nationality group represented in 1913. Determining the nationality of ownership of sugar properties is not straightforward, however. There were two sources of ambiguity. One was that ownership of shares in corporations involved people of different nationalities. Another was that sometimes the nationality of persons was either ambiguous or difficult to determine. Some Cubans had become naturalized U.S. citizens during the latter colonial years hoping to obtain U.S. representation in dealing with Spanish actions toward private economic interests. Immigration also tended to confuse lines of nationality.

Table 2.7
Sugar Mills by Nationality of Ownership, 1913

Nationality	Mills		Sugar production		
	N	Pct.	000 tons	Pct.	000 tons per mill
Cuban	67	39	918	33	14
Spanish	41	24	510	18	12
U.S.	39	23	1,013	37	26
British	7	4	106	4	15
French	5	3	67	2	13
Unknown	13	7	151	5	12
TOTAL	172		2,765		

SOURCE: Ayala, pp. 108–9. The data, compiled by Ayala, are from Cuba, Secretaría de Agricultura, Comercio, y Trabajo, *Portfolio azucarero.*

The Rionda family of three brothers, for example, migrated from Spain (Asturias) and lived at times both in Cuba and in New York. The family investments in sugar transcended national dimensions, and Manuel Rionda, who became the patriarch, prepared a line of nephews in both places to manage the family business. Another example is Edwin Atkins, who was an American, but his family had been involved in Cuba for decades, and he had intimate familial ties there. By many accounts, his economic interests in Cuba were also domestic interests. Yet when mills are listed by nationality, both the Atkins and Rionda interests are listed as North American. By contrast, the properties of the United Fruit Company represent interests with few domestic ties. Mills classified as North American often involved considerable domestic interests as well. Alejandro García Alvarez suggests that there were three categories of sugar enterprise: those financed inherently by domestic capital and economic interests, those financed principally by foreign capital and interests, and those financed by "mixed entities, formed by businessmen and capital from both sources." He suggests that the third category was the most common.[81]

Many of these new investments reflected the wave of vertical mergers going on at this time in the United States. Edwin Atkins and Henry Havemeyer were both major shareholders in the American Sugar Refining Company, the Sugar Trust. Manuel Rionda was a major figure in the New York operations of the London-based sugar agency Czarnikow-MacDougall, and he became president of the New York operation, reorganized in 1912 into the Czarnikow-Rionda Company, which at its height handled some 60 percent of Cuban sugar sales in the United States. The most outstanding venture was the formation of the Cuba Cane Sugar Corporation, which in 1916 purchased seventeen existing mills, making it the largest sugar company in Cuba and the largest permanent investment of North American capital in Cuba. Cuba Cane was organized by a combination of New York investors, including the Rionda group, J. and W. Seligman, and J. P. Morgan. Besides Cuba Cane, the Rionda family investments included at various times three or more other mills and collaboration with the McCahan refinery of Philadelphia. The National Refining Company held interests in J. B. Hawley's Cuban-American Sugar Company as well as several other companies. United Fruit had sugar properties in Cuba, and Atlantic Fruit, Hershey Chocolate, and Charles E. Hires Company bought sugar properties in Cuba between 1919 and 1923.[82]

In the years following independence, considerable investment was made in extending and consolidating the public service railroad system on the island. British and North American enterprises dominated railroads from the first years after independence. The participation of British capital in Cuban railways increased after the Ten Years' War through loans to the Cuban- and Spanish-owned enterprises. The first direct British investment in a railroad came about in 1889, when a group of Spanish railroad entrepreneurs and the merchant banking house J. H. Schröder of London collaborated to merge two major Havana railroads into the United Railways of Havana. In 1898, control of the United Railways of Havana was transferred to Schröder, and in 1899 two other important western railroads were acquired by British railroad investors. In 1901, William Van Horne, who had recently completed the construction of the Canadian Pacific Railroad, undertook the building of a railroad that would run the length of the island connecting the western system to the eastern end of the island. This established the major eastern railroad company before World War I, the Cuba Railroad, financed largely by North American capital. Between 1905 and 1913 there was a wave of mergers of railway companies in the western provinces until most of the western public service system was consolidated into the British-controlled United Railways of Havana. Most of the remaining smaller railroads came under the control of British or North American companies. The only exception was the Guantánamo and Western Railroad, which had only 3.5 percent of total trackage in the public service system by 1925 and only about 2 percent of total revenues. Overall mileage of track in the public service rail system increased from 1,792 kilometers in 1900 to 4,276 kilometers in 1929, fed by these foreign investments. Railroad investments represented about 60 percent of British and 12 percent of North American direct investments by 1913.[83]

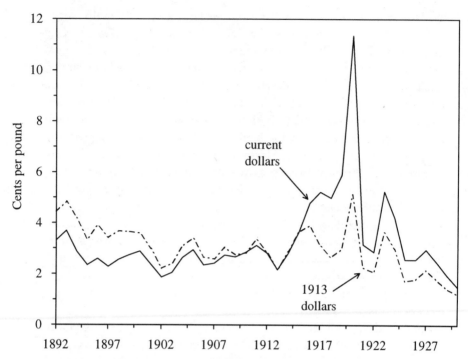

Fig. 2.5. Price of Cuban sugar in New York, cost and freight, 1892–1933. The real price is displayed in constant U.S. dollars of 1913 deflated by the U.S. Bureau of Labor Statistics wholesale price index. Sources: *Willett and Gray's Weekly Statistical Journal,* Jan. 5, 1911, p. 8, Jan. 9, 1930, p. 26, Jan. 18, 1940, p. 24; *Czarnikow-Rionda Annual Sugar Review.*

   The tempo of foreign investment in sugar changed during World War I. The price of sugar rose in 1915 in response to the fall in supplies from Europe. As is apparent in Figure 2.5, from 1900 to 1914 the price paid for Cuban sugar in New York fluctuated between 2 and 3 cents per pound, c.i.f. net of duty. In 1915 it increased to 3.6 cents and continued to rise.[84] The high prices stimulated a sudden jump in investment activity. Thirty-nine mills were newly built or reconstructed between 1916 and 1918. Cubans of all classes either invested in sugar or sought the privilege of becoming a colono for these new centrales. North Americans also built new mills and bought up existing mills, but Jenks comments that at least 25 of these were domestic enterprises. The chief contribution of North Americans was capital and in some cases organization.[85]

   World War I brought immediate prosperity but eventual disaster.[86] Although the price ceiling was binding, prices were high and sugar producers, colonos, and the economy in general prospered. The price of sugar was put under international controls in 1918 and 1919 to prevent further increases. When price controls were released during the 1920 crop, uncertainty over what the prevailing market price would be led to a wild speculation in sugar, known in Cuba as "the dance of the millions." From March through June the price soared, peaking at above 20 cents for several weeks. The average price for the year was over 11 cents per pound (see Figure 2.5). Mills changed hands, and the rights to yet uncut cane were bought and sold at prices based on the two-digit sugar prices. The major domestic and foreign banks also participated in the frenzy, taking on increasingly risky assets and building portfolios that were too dependent on sugar. Then the price began to collapse in July, and by December it had fallen to 3.75 cents — the lowest since 1914. Many who had borrowed on credit to purchase sugar and cane were unable to repay their debts. On October 6, 1920, a run started on the Banco Español, one of the major domestic banks. An emergency bank moratorium was called on October 11, but when it was lifted in the spring of 1921, eleven domestic banks closed, including all the largest banks. In the vacuum, the National City Bank, which had first set up branches in the country in 1914, and the Royal Bank of Canada, which had first entered Cuba in 1899, became the leading banks on the island. The Bank of Nova Scotia and subsidiaries of Chase National, Guaranty Trust, and J. and W. Seligman were also present and expanded their assets. Foreign banks went from having 20 percent of the deposits and making 30 percent of the loans in 1920 to having 79 percent of the deposits and making 84 percent of the loans in 1922.[87]

In the reorganization after the crisis of 1920–21, North American banks found themselves in possession not only of the major share of the banking system but also with considerable equity in sugar mills that had run into difficulties, most of them formerly under domestic control. National City Bank consolidated 10 mills under a subsidiary, the General Sugar Corporation, to manage them, and in 1925 it had interests in 22 other mills.[88] Banking groups came to have a large representation in most of the major sugar companies. Jenks lists seventeen dominant North American companies, producing two-thirds of the Cuban crop, which were controlled largely by big sugar companies in combination with large financial groups including National City Bank, the Royal Bank of Canada, J. and W. Seligman, Chase National Bank, and Guaranty Trust Company. By 1927, North American companies controlled about three-quarters of the Cuban sugar crop, North American banks held three-quarters of deposits, and British and American-owned companies received 98 percent of railroad revenues. Additionally, North Americans dominated mining, oil distribution, and public utilities. The major domestic banks, which in the first two decades of the century had supplied the greater part of bank credit, were no longer in existence, and powerful North American banking interests had taken over the control of a large number of mills once in domestic hands. The rate of expansion of average mill capacity as well as the aggregate milling capacity on the island continued to rise after the 1920–21 crisis. Indeed, Jenks comments that investments in the sugar industry quickly pulled the economy into recovery. By 1923 the economy had returned to its former prosperity.[89]

Protection and the Market for Cuban Sugar

It is important to recognize how little the sugar market could be characterized as a free market and how much sugar producers depended on secur-

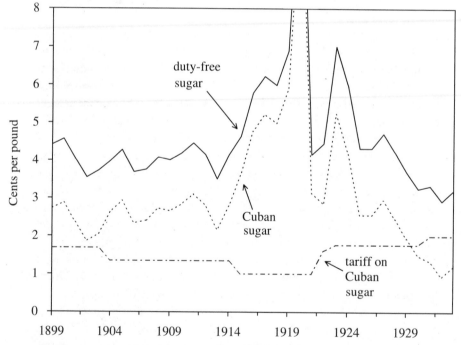

Fig. 2.6. Tariff rates for Cuban sugar and prices quoted in New York for duty-free and Cuban sugars, 1899–1933. Sources: See Fig. 2.5.

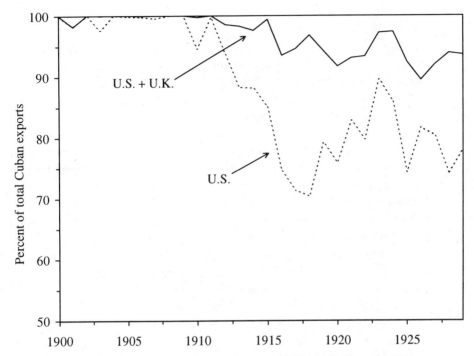

Fig. 2.7. Percent of Cuban sugar exports going to the United States and Britain, 1900–1929. Source: República de Cuba, Secretaría de Hacienda, *Industria azucarera y sus derivados.*

ing favorable trade agreements with the nations of at least one major market. Intervention through subsidies and tariff protection had been the rule for centuries and had changed little even in the so-called free trade era. The complex system of bounties that protected the European beet sugar industries had been reformed at the Brussels Convention of 1902. It made trade conditions somewhat better for cane sugar producers, but it did not eliminate dependence on protective policies. The only major free market during this period was Great Britain, and even Britain raised protective barriers beginning in 1914. During and after World War I Britain adopted a policy of reducing dependency on Europe. The free trade policy in sugar was abandoned and replaced with policies of colonial preference for cane sugar and promotion of a domestic beet sugar industry.[90] Otherwise, all major markets were protected, and marketing arrangements were characterized by more or less bilateral relationships. If Cuba had not succeeded in gaining preferential treatment in the United States, it would have faced exclusion from the international market because there was virtually no free market for sugar.

Cane sugar interests in the United States were vocal in expressing to Congress their concerns or desires for a reciprocal trade agreement between the United States and Cuba. But differences in regional interests and partisan political battles between cane and beet sugar interests created uncertainty about the trade policies that would be maintained between the United States and Cuba. The fluctuation in the U.S. sugar tariff in the early twentieth century reflects a shift of the political winds at the termination of World War I. Figure 2.6 shows the sugar tariff that Cubans paid from 1899 to 1933. The tariff declined from the end of the Cuban War of Independence to 1920.

In 1921, beet sugar interests began to obtain greater favors from Congress, and the tariff began a period of increase (see Figure 2.6). The 1921 Emergency Tariff Act was passed while Cuba was recovering from the worst financial crisis of its history. These changes meant that in the late 1920s, Cuba sought other markets, but the attempt enjoyed only limited success. The United States remained the major market for Cuban sugar throughout the period, as is seen in Figure 2.7.[91] F. W. Taussig comments that the rates set in 1921 and 1922 followed an underlying principle of "equalization of competitive conditions," based on relative costs of production. The 1921 and 1922 legislation might be interpreted as an adjustment in U.S. sugar policy to the great expansion of aggregate sugar milling capacity in Cuba during World War I. The Smoot-Hawley legislation abandoned any such principle. Cost calculations would not have justified the increase in the tariff. Although costs had fallen, there was likely little change in the cost differential between U.S. domestic and Cuban sugars since 1922. The rate established in 1930 was an outcome of political bargaining alone, backed by widespread populist sentiment in the United States that something had to be done for American beet farmers.[92] Cuban sugar producers continued to hope that they would be rewarded with new tariff concessions after the world war for their cooperation in the sugar price controls of the Allied war effort, but the hope was misguided.[93] In 1930, the three decades of growth of the demand for and production of sugar in Cuba ended.

Chapter 3

Mass Production
and the Sugar Industry

THE SUGAR TECHNICIAN H. C. Prinsen Geerligs marked the year 1883 as the beginning of a fervor among cane sugar producers to improve the methods of extraction to compete with the looming presence of the European beet sugar industry.[1] By the 1880s, the European beet sugar industry had taken over a large share of the world market for sugar, and a collapse in the sugar price caused a worldwide financial crisis in 1883–86 among cane sugar producers (see Figures 2.2 and 2.4). If the cane sugar industry were to survive, it would have to adjust to the technological advances that had been made in the beet sugar industry in recent decades. In the decades that followed, cane sugar responded to the challenge. Numerous successful improvements were made in cane sugar manufacturing technology that fundamentally altered the world cane sugar industry. It soon bore little resemblance to the plantation-based technology of the nineteenth century. These decades saw the construction of the modern, highly capital-intensive sugar mills that more resembled the physical plant of petroleum refineries or massive food-processing facilities than the rudimentary apparatus of traditional plantation technology. The improvements took on this character as they exploited the concept of continuous processing to a much greater extent than before.

Early in the nineteenth century, Cuba had developed one of the more innovative and advanced sugar industries in the world, becoming a leader in the adoption of both steam power and vacuum-heating technologies. In the latter decades of the nineteenth century, Cuba's international position of leadership slipped as the country fell into conflict and sugar producers became victims of oppressive Spanish colonial policies. The period of most severe crisis came in the 1880s. In 1890, the Círculo de Hacendados (Sugar Planters' Club) of Cuba addressed the Spanish Ministerio de Ultramar to call attention to the 1884 crisis of the sugar industry. The Círculo pleaded to the colonial authority for legislation that would relieve the situation. In its written appeal, it listed five problems that contributed to the difficulties of the Cuban planters: the severity of the crisis, the weight of the tax burden imposed on planters by the Spanish state attempting to retrieve the costs of the Ten Years' War, the lack of capital and credit, the scarcity of labor, and the slow introduction of recent innovations in cane sugar technology.[2] By the 1890s, immediately before the Spanish-Cuban-American War, there were indications of recovery, though it proved a false start as war returned in 1895. In any case, when stability came after the war, sugar producers in Cuba were not inexperienced or ignorant of the modern technology as applied to the sugar industry.

To the contrary, Cuban producers saw the newfound stability and the influx of North American capital as an opportunity to regain their former status as a leader in international competitiveness and the application of sugar manufacturing technology — this time with closer political ties to their major market, the United States. Though not by all Cubans, American hegemony was actually sought as a means of achieving recovery from the economic devastation of the war. In 1902, there was alarm among Cuban leaders when word went out that the U.S. Congress was hesitating in signing the Treaty of Reciprocity for commerce between the two nations. Some of the most influential representatives of the Cuban economy — lawyers, politicians, and businessmen — met at the Tacón Theater in Havana and urgently demanded that the treaty be signed. One spokesman commented: "With this treaty we would save national production, and with national production our existence; for once Cuba is under American hegemony; having solved the economic problem, all her other problems are secondary."[3]

In 1890 the Círculo de Hacendados had pointed to the ultimate source of the producers' difficulties — scarcity of capital that prevented the adoption of the latest technological advances. It also acknowledged the inevitable gravitation toward the North American product and capital markets, and even before independence the Círculo had sought greater access to those markets. The hope and vision of Cuban sugar producers was that greater economic integration with the United States could prove to be beneficial to industry on the island, despite their neighbor's economic and political strength. They believed that the global transformation of industrial technology that had made the older sugar manufacturing methods obsolete was a greater threat to the economic wealth of the island. If the economic problems in Cuba could be solved, there would be much reason for optimism. Cuban producers had succeeded in the past at competition in the technical arena, and they would succeed again. But Cuban elites continued to argue, as they had for some time, that it could not be accomplished without reciprocity and American capital.[4]

Sugar as a Tropical Agricultural Commodity

Within the world trading system, sugar was the only major tropical agricultural commodity to experience such a change in technology. Coffee, tea, tobacco, cocoa, and other tropical commodities received only minor processing before they were sold and shipped to the industrial countries as intermediate goods. Only for sugar was there substantial industrial development within tropical countries themselves.[5] Dependency advocates have made much of this typical international division of labor in which the tropical countries were assigned the task of cultivation and the industrial countries the task of processing crude materials. Industrial countries benefited both from trade in goods that they could not produce and from the industrial development stimulated by the demands for the processing of imported raw materials. Transferable new technology tended to be mechanical and applicable mostly to manufacturing rather than agricultural activities. New technology in agriculture in Europe or the United States tended to be location specific.[6] Therefore, the effects of technical advances on tropical countries, even for tropical products, was limited — with the exception of sugar.

W. Arthur Lewis argues that, in contrast with events in temperate countries, technological change in tropical agriculture could not take place because the incentives for developing labor-saving technologies similar to those developed for agriculture in temperate climates did not exist. The argument goes as follows. Migrants from Asia provided an essentially endless supply of cheap labor at the prevailing low wages of tropical countries. For various reasons, including the cost of passage and immigration restrictions that cheap labor faced in industrial countries, Asians were prevented from migrating to the most attractive temperate countries. But in tropical countries, favorable immigration policies and contracting arrangements for financing the migrants' passage encouraged an endless stream of Asian migrant workers. The apparent perfect elasticity of labor supplies in tropical countries kept labor cheap and prevented innovation in agriculture.[7]

Lewis's theory is elegant and provocative, and it has had a very strong influence on theories of economic development and dependency. In certain respects, however, the theory lacks generality and accuracy. It seems to fit best those British colonies that were recipients of massive migration from India. The Cuban case stands out as one that did not fit the descriptive elements of Lewis's theory quite as well. The importation of cheap labor from Asia was attempted, but it failed to be of much significance. The British would not permit Indians to be brought there, and even when the official doors from China were open, the number of Chinese immigrants did not have a large effect on the size of the labor force. Those doors were closed in 1874, and immigrant labor had to be obtained from elsewhere.[8] Nonetheless, aside from such details, the emphasis on the elasticity of labor supplies deserves attention. It is clear that the expansion of sugar in Cuba was dependent on a massive inflow of migrants to work the growing acreage in cane on the island.

But, the elasticity of labor supplies did not prevent technical change in the sugar industry, as Lewis predicted. Lewis reasoned that an abundance of cheap labor provided a disincentive in tropical countries for the adoption of labor-saving mechanical techniques of production. But the sugar industry defied this reasoning. In fact, Lewis's model is misleading because it considers only two factors of production — labor and capital — and an aggregate production function, with no consideration of complementarities between the agricultural and the processing phases of sugar production. If we confine attention to the agricultural phase, Lewis's general observation seems more directly applicable to Cuba. There was no significant technical change in Cuban cane cultivation. Planting and harvesting continued to be performed much as they had been for centuries, making use only of simple tools such as the hoe and the machete. Cane yields per acre fell as high differential rents of virgin soils were diminished.[9] Abundant cane lands ensured high labor productivity using simple techniques.

In other sugar-producing countries, such as Java and Hawaii, land was less abundant. There was greater economic incentive to develop higher-yielding varieties of cane, and as they were developed, they were readily adopted. But although high-yielding cane varieties were land-saving, they were also more intensive users of other inputs such as fertilizers, irrigation, or labor. In Cuba abundant fertile cane lands provided little incentive to incur those additional costs.[10]

Where the sugar industry defied Lewis's reasoning was in the processing phase. To someone familiar with the technical requirements of sugar production, it should not be surprising that sugar producers actively adopted advanced industrial technology, despite the lack of strong incentives for saving labor. There were several reasons. First, the innovations were cane-saving and fuel-saving, and they offered economies of scale far beyond that offered by the older technology. The innovations that appeared reflected solutions to problems that arose in one sugar-producing country or another, such as the depletion of forest reserves for fuel wood or the diminishing marginal productivities of existing scarce cane lands. Second, they also reflected the technological interdependence between beet and cane sugar. Cane manufacturing technology reaped windfalls as research to improve the productivity of both raw sugar refining and beet sugar production in Europe advanced. Heavy financial backing of research in beet sugar manufacturing had begun early in the nineteenth century in Prussia, France, the Low Countries, and Italy. Over the long trajectory of technical advances, most of the methods developed were straightforwardly transferable to cane sugar production.[11] Third, both cane and beet sugar reaped windfalls from the technological interdependence between sugar manufacture and other industrial chemical processes. These were years of revolution in chemical engineering and chemicals industries. Chemicals-related improvements operated as a source of innovation for numerous industries just as the machine tools industry had affected the general trend of technological change in earlier decades.[12] Quality improvements and cost reductions in steel production were not the least important of these. For example, in grinding the use of steel improved capabilities for handling stress induced by crushing the cane. The improvements were derived not only from the adoption of steel as a construction material but also from design alterations to take advantage of the capabilities of the new construction material. Other important improvements based on learning in chemical engineering were the successive new designs in cane juice evaporators and other apparatus for economizing on heat and fuel consumption.[13] Consequently, total factor productivity was improved in processing, but not growing, cane.[14]

Sugar as an Industrial Commodity

Sugar was unlike other tropical agricultural commodities. For coffee, tea, rubber, cocoa, and other tropical products, only limited processing was performed on the raw material before it was shipped to the industrial countries. The biological characteristics of cane did not permit the same in sugar production. Cane deteriorated rapidly after being cut, forcing producers to perform most of the processing of cane into sugar on site. Whereas typically the international division of labor allocated the processing of tropical commodities to the industrial centers, technical constraints on handling cane prevented that pattern from ruling in the sugar enterprise. Neither the cane nor the cane juice could be shipped unprocessed. Without immediate processing cane suffered substantial losses of sucrose, and the cane juice would spoil in shipment. Consequently, raw sugar was processed on site. The nature of cane determined that to adopt modern technology in sugar, industrial plant would have to be built in relatively remote locations where the climate and soils were suitable but where investments of international capital were less easily monitored. The rise of beet sugar in Europe circumvented this pattern of industrial development to some degree, but the application of modern sugar manufacturing technologies in cane sugar was potentially much more productive. If the new technologies and continuous-processing methods were to be adopted in the manufacture of cane sugar, the technical characteristics of cane dictated that it be done in the tropics.[15]

The sensitivity of cane — or its rapid deterioration — had a great influence on the formation of the modern sugar industry. Indeed, industrial plant had been part of sugar plantations from the early stages of the industrial revolution. A complex of grinding mills and boiling and curing houses had been a characteristic of cane sugar plantations since their inception. Historically, manufacturing equipment on plantations did not tend to remain primitive. The steam engine was first introduced in sugar production in 1768 in Jamaica, but the first economically successful application, according to Deerr, was in Cuba in 1797. The first railroad in Latin America was also built in Cuba, constructed in 1834–37 to transport sugar from inland to the port of Havana.[16] Both uses of steam power diffused into more general use on the island at a steady pace. Technical advances were made in other areas, too. Significant new designs in the pans for boiling cane juices were introduced to economize on the use of fuel. The introduction of vacuum heating technology later revolutionized the boiling process, and the introduction of the centrifugal machine likewise revolutionized the curing process. Upon introduction, these mechanical innovations were attached as appendages to augment the traditional plant and the traditional concept of the mill complex. Eventually, however, the combination of mechanical processes and interfaces resulted in a complete and unmistakable transformation of the design of the sugar factory.[17]

At the end of the nineteenth and the beginning of the twentieth century, when processing industries in general became more capital-intensive, huge facilities for sugar manufacture embodying new continuous-process technologies were constructed in Cuba and other sugar-producing countries worldwide. New opportunities to build factories that could produce raw sugar at low cost and high quality attracted the attention of investors in the industrial centers and stimulated the formation of business and financial links between the tropical producers and their markets. Likewise, connections developed, in inventive activities, between the users and the developers of sugar manufacturing technologies, which facilitated the exchange of new discoveries and knowledge gained by production experience and learning by using.[18] Technical change in this context was not a question simply of the transfer of a completed technological system from the United States or Europe to the tropics. Its development was being carried out simultaneously in the industrial countries and the tropical countries, and the exchange of ideas went in both directions.

Technology and Slavery

In other respects, until the late nineteenth century, the sugar industry had been organized along lines that were very traditional and seemingly backward. Throughout its history the sugar industry had been associated with slavery and plantation economies. Gradually in the nineteenth century the emancipation of slaves in the European colonies progressed. Cuba was a holdout — one of the last two countries in the Western Hemisphere to abolish slavery.[19]

A predominant view of the dynamics of technology in sugar states that the continuation of slavery in Cuba until 1886 acted as an obstacle to technical change. One of the most influential proponents of this view is Manuel Moreno Fraginals, who argues that slavery and modern technologies were incompatible. In his argument, a growing contradiction between slavery and mechanization in sugar manufacture in the latter half of the nineteenth century caused the economic attractiveness of slavery to decay.[20] Under such circumstances, the sugar trade crisis of 1884 in Cuba has been seen as a result of the continued adherence to slavery. This interpretation, of course, ignores the international scope of the 1884 crisis.

A number of studies have refuted this incompatibility hypothesis. Some have placed greater weight on the political origins of emancipation and the contributions of antislavery movements.[21] Others have shown convincing evidence that supports the notion that slavery continued to be viable economically even as legal emancipation was completed in Cuba. Examining production and price data, Laird Bergad has shown that slave-based production continued to be profitable on sugar estates. Using sugar estate census returns in jurisdictions of Matanzas from 1859 to 1878, he shows that the expected stream of plantation income per worker compared favorably with slave prices. He also shows that the costs of slave labor compared favorably to the costs of employing wage labor in those years.[22] Additional light on the incompatibility hypothesis has been shed in an analysis by Rebecca Scott which focuses on the geographical patterns of abolition and technical adoption. If mechanization and slavery were indeed incompatible, one would expect that the technically most advanced regions would have been the first to abandon slavery. Nevertheless, as abolition proceeded gradually, the opposite occurred. The advanced sugar areas were the most heavily concentrated in slaves, while the least advanced regions in the east were the ones where the most significant declines in slaveholding occurred before general emancipation. Similar evidence is found at the mill level. Advanced mills in the 1870s tended to hold onto their slaves, and some of the most advanced mills used almost no free wage laborers.[23]

In sum, there is ample evidence to reject the hypothesis that slavery acted as an obstacle to technical change or that technical change meant slavery's demise. The best evidence suggests that these two transitions in the sugar industry, although coincident, had independent causes. But in one sense, slaveholding may not have been conducive to making the technical transition. Since both slave labor and the new technology contributed substantially to the fixed-cost component of production costs, they competed as investments in physical assets that would tie up financial resources. But offsetting this effect, if it had not been for abolition, planters' assets in slaves would have been more liquid and more easily sold to invest in machinery.[24]

Regardless of its cause, the final abolition of slavery was destined to have a great impact globally on the organization of the cane sugar industry. As discussed in the previous chapter, one might not have expected the sugar industry to have recovered so quickly from the shock of emancipation to become such a technologically progressive industry. But the recovery was accompanied by a major shift in the geographical distribution of the industry. Most former slaveholding sugar-producing countries lost market shares to newcomer producers without histories of chattel slavery. The prominence of British and French colonies in the sugar industry disappeared.[25] Cuba, Java, Hawaii, and Australia became new centers of sugar production. In fact, by the 1920s, the two major producers, Cuba and Java, alone produced 50 percent of all cane sugar supplied to the world market, which represented 35 percent of all sugar supplied, both cane and beet[26] (see Table 2.1).

Comparison of Cuba, Java, and Hawaii

The three sugar-producing countries that would have to be included in any list of the most technically advanced are Java, the Hawaiian Islands, and Cuba.[27] Producers were conscious of the degree of competition in the technological sphere. It began, as Prinsen Geerligs commented, with the threat of substantial cost reductions in beet sugar manufacture; but once cane sugar producers became successful at applying the new principles to cane sugar manufacture, an environment of technical competition was created among cane sugar producers. Java, Cuba, and the Hawaiian Islands were the most successful at adopting and improving the new milling technology, but in other respects — in their agricultural technologies, their cane supply institutions, and their business organization — they did not employ identical technologies. Different climatic and institutional circumstances and different resource availabilities dictated that they choose different techniques of production and emphasize different factors of production.

The unique feature of the Cuban industry was that mills were significantly larger there than in any other sugar-producing country. In 1924, the average mill capacity in Cuba was 50 percent higher than the average mill capacity of any other producer; the next highest was Hawaii (see

Table 3.1
Sugar Production in Selected Countries, 1924

Country	Number of mills	Annual production (000 tons)	Average annual output per mill (000 tons)
Cuba	200	5,255	26.3
Java	183	2,250	12.3
Hawaii	43	756	17.6
Puerto Rico	40	628	15.7
Philippines	30	518	17.3
Mauritius	45	250	5.6

SOURCE: Maxwell, chap. 8.

Table 3.1). Contemporary sugar technicians often noted the distinction and sometimes discussed it as indicative of a contrast in the function of the sugar mill in Cuba relative to Hawaii or some other sugar-producing region. Francis Maxwell remarked that, peculiarly, in Cuba the capacity of the mill was commonly used as a measure of its success. Noel Deerr contrasted the techniques of Cuban and Hawaiian mills: "Capacity and not extraction is the object of the Cuban mill. Whereas Hawaiian practice regards the milling plant as a means of extracting sugar, that of Cuba looks upon it as a means of grinding cane."[28] How can the economic historian interpret this contrast in the perceived function of the sugar mill?

Can the difference be explained by different access to technology? The openness of the professional sugar community prevented any such barriers. The technical findings of the period were published and widely distributed, and there was plenty of correspondence between the sugar producers of various regions. Equipment producers and engineering consultants were international in scope and accessible. The relationships between users and producers of technology were instrumental in the dispersion of information. Long-distance communication was frequent and active. As an example, throughout the first two decades of the twentieth century, Manuel Rionda maintained regular correspondence with Carl Hedemann of the Honolulu Iron Works, who at times acted as a consultant of mill operations on the Rionda estates. Hedemann also reported discoveries and improvements in all aspects of production in Hawaii to Rionda, which were of no direct concern to him or the consultancy but were of interest to Rionda simply to keep abreast of the latest developments in that part of the world. His reports included notices of new discoveries regarding the operation of the mills, irrigation systems, cane varieties, and pest and disease control. As a further avenue of information, the channels were also open for the transfer of technical personnel from one part of the world to another. As an example, a chemist, A. C. Van

Neemskerch Duker, who was working in Nukuihaele, Hawaii, contacted Manuel Rionda in search of employment in the Cuban or Puerto Rican industries. He was recommended by the sugar technician H. C. Prinsen Geerligs of Amsterdam, who was well-known for his scientific work at the Javanese Experiment Station.[29] Such global linkages between sugar technicians suggest that information about new discoveries and users' experiences with them flowed freely and that differences in technique, for those countries not strapped by capital constraints, were freely chosen.

There is no doubt that the abundance of fertile cane lands in Cuba was a major factor influencing its choice of technique. In contrast with Cuba, the lands in the Hawaiian Islands suited to cane cultivation were scarce and hilly. Cooler ocean currents around the Hawaiian Islands created a cooler climate so the cane was slower to mature. Therefore, not only was there a relative scarcity of cane acreage in Hawaii, but the land had to be occupied by each crop longer to allow cane to reach maturity. The growing period in Cuba was about 12 to 15 months, while in Hawaii it was about 18 to 24 months.[30] Conditions in Java also created a relative scarcity of land available for cane. In Java there was much land, but there was also a very dense population. Since food was not generally imported, much of the land was devoted to food production. The sugar industry was strictly regulated to ensure that enough good land and irrigation water were left available for the native population to grow food crops. A maximum planting area was fixed for every sugar factory, and a system was established by which the good lands were rotated between the sugar companies and the peasants.[31]

Because of Java's dense population, its sugar industry did not depend on labor-saving techniques. Instead, it became known as the most innovative in agricultural techniques, excelling in the breeding of new specialized varieties of cane. The Hawaiian industry, characterized by scarce land but with the strongest connection to U.S. capital markets, came to be known as one that was extremely capital-intensive, employing not only large-scale milling technologies but also extensive irrigation systems. The cane lands in Hawaii received little rainfall so irrigation was employed in the cane fields. And Hawaii tended to be the most skilled at internal milling activities — extracting the sucrose from the cane. Cuba, in contrast, was known for the enormity of its mills and the extensive private cane railroad networks. Techniques were extremely land-intensive. The massive organizations of Cuban mills were established to exploit as much as possible the fertile, abundant Cuban soils. Irrigation was rare. Furthermore, Cuba was the only one of the three that had an organizationally decentralized cane

Table 3.2
Comparative Internal Cane Productivities: Cuba, Java, and Hawaii, 1927

	Productivity rates			
	Purity of cane juice	Extraction	Recovery	Overall
Cuba	83.8	93.3	91.8	85.6
Java	84.0	93.9	90.5	85.0
Hawaii	84.5	97.3	91.2	88.7

SOURCE: Maxwell, chap. 8.
NOTE: See text for definitions of each productivity rate.

supply system. Cane cultivation both in Hawaii and in Java was vertically integrated with the mill, but in Cuba cane was contracted out to semi-independent cane farmers, or colonos.

Table 3.2 presents comparative indicators of average productivities of mill activities for Cuba, Java, and Hawaii. The extraction rate in the table represents the percentage of sucrose in the cane which is extracted from the cane in the form of cane juice (an intermediate product). The recovery rate is the percentage of the sucrose in the extracted cane juice which is successfully converted into crystallized sugar. The overall rate is the product of the extraction and recovery rates. It indicates the percentage of sucrose in the cane which was successfully converted into sugar. The remainder is thus the manufacturing losses of sucrose. The table shows that there were higher rates of extraction in the Hawaiian mills but similar rates of recovery among the three countries. But more generally, it shows that the internal cane productivities of Java, Cuba, and Hawaii were roughly similar even though mill capacities and other features of the mills differed.

The abundant and rich endowment of virgin cane lands in Cuba would lead us to expect a larger array of cane fields to support a given mill capacity. But would this have contributed to the difference in mill capacities in Cuba relative to other places? This question is investigated in the following chapters by focusing on the wide diversity in the capacities of mills within Cuba.

Mass Production Technologies

New mechanical and chemical technologies developed during the second half of the nineteenth century had a pervasive influence on industry. Greater use of power, greater understanding of the composition and properties of metals, and greater scientific understanding of heat transfer were applied to economize on the use of labor and materials in processing industries. The new technologies required capital intensification of production processes, but the qualitative changes in the machinery were more fundamental than simple quantitative relative increases in capital inputs. There were relatively few basic innovations, but they spread to numerous processing industries. Alfred Chandler notes that it was primarily in processing and refining industries that the initial innovations in continuous processing took place. Processing and refining industries of all types were transformed by these developments — petroleum refining, metalworking, distillation and brewing, grain processing, papermaking, and sugar processing. Many benefited from new developments in roller-milling technologies. The cheapening of the production of steel allowed structural improvements in the roller mills to endure greater stress; therefore, rolling machinery could be used to apply greater pressure to the cane without breaking down as frequently.[32] The same techniques were important in their application to the milling of metals and food processing. Industries also benefited from the application of vacuum boiling and superheated steam in distillation. These were especially important in petroleum and in sugar processing and refining. More intensive use of energy and mechanical power was applied to drive the larger-scale machinery. The designs of the engine and power plants were improved. The Corliss (automatic variable cutoff) engine, developed in the second half of the nineteenth century, reduced the irregularity of the velocity of steam engines, which was important for coordinating a steady flow of materials and reducing the frequency of machinery breakdowns. Further improvements to regulate and maintain constant steam pressure were made in water-tube boilers and furnaces and in the choice of fuels.[33]

Furthermore, many new mechanical devices were introduced to increase the continuity of flow of the materials in the factories; they also displaced manual labor in transferring materials from one station to another. Devices such as conveyor belts, elevators, and pumps were adopted more extensively, and factory layouts were redesigned to accommodate the new methods of transferring materials. These new devices were initially driven off the factory's main power source by belts, but it was eventually found that separate control of these smaller devices could simplify the organization and improve the continuity of production. Auxiliary power sources in the form of electric and gasoline motors became common to drive smaller devices to increase control over their services to the production system.[34]

Some control innovations arose from human capital specialized for the sugar industry. Much improvement was made by using newly invented instruments and scientific techniques for measuring the chemical components of the cane juice or the conditions under which they were put. Their usefulness also depended on the employment of formally trained chemists at the factories. In Cuba the most innovative mills were beginning to hire chemists in the 1880s. By 1914 most Cuban mills had at least one chemist and many had three or four. Manuel Rionda wrote to his partner, Caesar Czarnikow, in London in 1909 that it was "not well to dispose with chemical advice." Even the superintendent who knows the workings of his mill thoroughly cannot "afford to work the house blindly." The trend in employment of chemists in the Cuban sugar industry at this time reflected the chemical basis of the new general wave of industrial innovations, but it reflected more. Their formal training and scientific orientation were also a manifestation, for the sugar industry, of the increased professionalization of technical personnel and a reflection of a general increase in the employment of professional scientists and engineers in industry, particularly in the United States.[35]

New continuous-processing technologies tended to have much higher minimum efficient scales of operation than the technologies they replaced. Chandler describes the fundamental change that took place in processing industries as based on a radical increase in the amount of throughput, the amount of materials handled per worker. The increased throughput resulted in an increase in the minimum volume of materials which could be handled economically; therefore, plants had much higher optimal scales of operation. But Chandler emphasizes that to realize the cost advantages of larger scales of production, improvements in the coordination and synchronization of the flow of materials within the plant were necessary. The greater capital intensification of the production processes implied a much higher proportion of fixed costs in total outlays. If the volume of output of the capital facilities was reduced significantly or interrupted, substantially higher unit fixed costs would result. Therefore, careful coordination of inputs and intermediate materials between the various activities in the production process was essential for the efficient operation of continuous-process plants. As Chandler has demonstrated, as a response to these problems of organization, economies of scale were instrumental in stimulating the development of modern business practices and the formation of the modern industrial enterprise.[36]

These general trends are evident in the technical developments in the sugar industry. Steam was already a common source of power in sugar

mills; however, after 1890 and more so after 1900, power plants were enlarged greatly to drive the larger facilities being employed. Steam vacuum technologies were also already being used to increase efficiency in boiling the juices, but new means of capturing the latent energy in exhaust steam introduced much greater sophistication into their application at the sugar mills. Also, new laboratory instruments for measuring the components of the cane, the juices, and the sugar added an element of precision to the control of factory operations which had not existed before.[37] In reference to industrial development in the United States, Chandler has underlined the importance of the removal of constraints on factors of production for opening the possibilities for increasing the scale of operation in factory production. The opening up of the anthracite coal fields in eastern Pennsylvania lifted the constraint on fuel consumption. Similarly, in Cuba, fuel constraints were lifted in the late nineteenth century. Bagasse furnaces were developed in the 1870s and 1880s that made it feasible to run mills off green bagasse. Bagasse, the trash from cane that has been crushed, had been used as fuel in sugar making for centuries, but only after it had been dried; and previously it was used only as a supplement to wood. In the last decade of the nineteenth century, some mills began to be operated entirely by burning green bagasse.[38] Also, mills began to substitute imported coal and, later, fuel oil for wood.

It is helpful to have some knowledge of the processes of cane sugar manufacture to understand how the innovations were applied. In sugar manufacture, cane was brought to the mill, where it was first ground using roller mills (three-roll *trapiches*) to press the juice out of the cane. Then the cane juice was purified and evaporated, and the sucrose contained in the juice was crystallized. This process of evaporation was carried out in a series of stages referred to as defecation, clarification, and concentration. The resulting substance, referred to as "massacuite," contained both crystallized sucrose, or sugar, and molasses. In the final stage, the crystallized sucrose and molasses were separated in a process referred to as curing or, in Cuba, purging. Then the sugar was dried and packaged and the molasses sold as a by-product, distilled or used in some other fashion, or thrown away. It is convenient for our purposes to refer to three principal milling stages in the production of raw sugar—the grinding process, the evaporation process, and the separation process. These divisions of sugar manufacture existed both in the old and new technologies, but each of these processes underwent major technical changes either in the late nineteenth or early twentieth century.

The grinding process, which had otherwise not changed much since the early nineteenth century, underwent a radical improvement in the early twentieth century with the introduction of multiple milling. This innovation involved the better application of roller-mill technology for grinding cane. Improvements in filtration devices allowed an increase in the number of times each cane was squeezed to extract the juice. To accomplish this, a sequence of three-roll mills were lined up in tandem, and the cane was passed directly from one into the next. The cane thus received repeated bites of pressure to extract the juice. Then, the introduction of cane preparation devices (crushers and shredders) allowed greater and more uniform application of pressure to the cane. And adoption of maceration used compositional properties of cane to facilitate the flow of liquids from the cell walls of the cane. These interrelated innovations resulted in much greater extraction rates than had been obtained previously. Thus they used the improved capabilities of steel-framed roller mills to endure greater stress. Another innovation in mill design—hydraulic regulatory mechanisms—increased the elasticity of the rollers so as to apply greater constancy of pressure to the cane and to cut down on the frequency of mill breakage. Multiple milling is described in greater detail in Chapter 4.[39]

The evaporation process was radically changed in the late nineteenth century by the introduction of multiple-effect evaporators. In the mid-nineteenth century, vacuum pans were introduced to replace open pans for boiling the cane juice. Multiple-effect evaporators were a further innovation to vacuum pan technology, which used exhaust steam from the power plant to create the vacuum in the pans and to heat the liquid in the successive stages of the crystallization process. They resulted in a great reduction in fuel and clean water requirements, both of which were of importance for the sugar industries in remote areas or in the periphery where fuel was costly, if it had to be imported, and infrastructure for supplying clean water was scarce.[40]

The introduction of the centrifugal machine to separate the molasses from the crystallized sugar was a landmark for product innovation in the sugar industry. Before the centrifugal machine, the curing process was achieved primarily by setting the massacuite aside in numerous conical molds and allowing the molasses to drain by force of gravity. Sugars obtained using this procedure varied greatly in quality—they were caked products that varied in color from brown to yellow to "white" because of the high quantities of molasses remaining in the sugar. The most common varieties used only gravity to accomplish the task of separating the molasses from the sugar. Not only was the process slow, but it required a large storage area where the draining sugar would be protected from the weather. In the slave-based ingenio about 10 percent of the labor force of the estate was employed to attend to the thousands of draining molds of sugar.[41] The introduction of the centrifugal machine accomplished the task of separation both more quickly and more thoroughly and with less labor.

In fact, the raw sugar became a much purer and drier product. The sugars obtained using multiple-effect evaporation and centrifugal machines were of such a different character from earlier sugars that they were given a new marketing name—"centrifugal sugars" or "centrifugals." Shipping costs of centrifugal sugars were lower than for the older varieties of raw sugar for several reasons. There was less spoilage or drainage during transit with centrifugals, the newer product being shipped required less space for shipment, and it weighed less because it contained less liquid and was shipped in lighter packages. The old sugars required bulky, heavy containers—hogsheads or boxes. They continued to drain even while they were being shipped and spoiled or broke up more easily. The hogsheads could only be stacked three high or they would burst.[42] The jute bags that the centrifugals were shipped in were relatively inexpensive, lightweight, and could be easily stacked. They drained very little; indeed, they would sometimes gain weight by absorbing moisture during the journey.

Another improvement in the raw sugar product was accomplished with the development of the polariscope, a laboratory instrument used to grade the purity of raw sugar. Since the eighteenth century the imprecise grading system known as the Dutch Standard was used. The system consisted of up to 21 different grades of sugar, which were based on color and appearance. In the late nineteenth century, sugar began to be graded by the polariscope, which measures the refraction of light through sugar crystals to determine their purity. In the early twentieth century, the standard raw grade of sugar being produced was 96° pol. (The degrees of polarity roughly indicate the percentage of purity of the sucrose in sugar.) Because of the capabilities of the centrifugal machines and laboratory instruments for greater precision and control of the product, raw sugar reached a much greater level of standardization. By the 1890s, *Willett and Gray's Weekly Statistical Sugar Trade Journal* quoted prices for only two grades of sugar, 96° and 89° pol.[43] Market prices for any sugars that varied from these two grades were adjusted by formula according to the number of degrees of deviation from these two standard polarity readings.[44] By 1917 over 99 percent of the sugar produced in Cuba was graded at 96° pol. or purer.[45] In contrast, the sugars of the mid-nineteenth century were much less standardized. The polarities of the highest grades — intended for final consumption — were around 96° pol. or lower. And the polarities of muscovadoes or other marketed products may have ranged as low as, or lower than, 75° pol.[46]

This standardization of the product was of great importance to the commercialization of raw sugars. With a standard raw material input, refiners were able to maintain control over the chemical processes with greater precision and lower cost. Similarly, in buying raw sugars, they were able to confirm the stated grades of purchased sugars more straightforwardly. Consequently, there were fewer agency problems associated with purchasing sugar from a distance. It became common to make purchases without prior direct inspection of traders. The trading centers for Cuban sugars, consequently, shifted from Havana to New York and London, and futures markets for sugar developed.[47]

Creative Destruction

The War of Independence left Cuba in complete and utter economic disaster. The degree of destruction of wealth on the island during the war was unparalleled. Once the hostilities were over, Cubans were faced with the task of revitalizing the economy. An unintended consequence of the war was the elimination of most of what remained of old machinery and old sugar mills. Once the reconstruction of mills after the war was under way, the old yielded to the new. Most mills closed down at some point during the war. The oldest and least efficient of those mills were never reopened.[48] Instead, as recovery demanded more mill capacity, it was created by the construction of new mills using the latest technology. For four years, investment and the updating of the sugar industry that had begun in the 1880s was interrupted by the hostilities; but afterward, the ground had been laid for a rather sudden replacement of the existing physical capital in the industry.

The war broke out in February 1895 at the initiation of separatists in the eastern part of the island. Both sides engaged in ruthless destruction, laying waste to the countryside and destroying the rural wealth. Upon the declaration of war, the insurgent forces adopted a policy of attacking the economic base of the colonial government so as to avoid direct engagement with the Spanish army. In February 1895, the insurgent General Máximo Gómez proclaimed a moratorium on all economic activity and threatened to set fire to the estates of any violators, knowing full well that suspension of production would have a disastrous effect. Planters in the western provinces were the prime targets. The market conditions since the Ten Years' War had made the situation for most planters tight and their staying power weak. With their properties mortgaged and with prices at half their level since the early 1880s, planters were struggling and threatened with bankruptcy. The separatists thus adopted a policy of setting fire to cane fields and all other forms of rural property as part of a strategy for destroying the economic base of the loyalists.[49]

The Spanish forces answered with an even more heavy-handed and destructive strategy of striking at the economic base of the insurgents. At his inauguration in 1896, General Valeriano Weyler, the commander of the Spanish forces, pursued a policy of complete decimation of the countryside and the removal and reconcentration of the rural population into the municipalities. Plantations and other agricultural establishments were systematically burned, structures were demolished, and cattle slaughtered. Through the policy of reconcentration Spanish forces rounded up an estimated 300,000 rural inhabitants and confined them in resettlement camps. Conditions in these camps and in the municipalities brought demographic disaster, as epidemics and malnutrition claimed the lives of a horrifying number of civilians. In Matanzas, for example, it has been estimated that 24 to 30 percent of the rural population died between 1895 and 1898 as a result of these conditions, in addition to casualties suffered in combat. In the western and central provinces, it was reported that the populations declined during the war by about 30 percent. Not only was the economic basis of the insurgent army destroyed but so was the basis for production and subsistence. Ranchers were ordered to drive their cattle to the cities, and all unauthorized commerce was banned. Starvation was the most common form of death, especially in the areas of the country where blacks and mulattoes made up a large portion of the rural population.[50]

Destruction of such magnitude had a devastating effect on the physical capital stock of the country. The severity of the economic crisis is visible in the level of sugar production shown in Figures 1.1 and 2.1. In 1900, the status of 570 mills was reported in a provisional military government report. Of those 570 mills, 364 (or 64 percent) were classified as "destroyed" or "demolished." Another 84 (15 percent) were "not destroyed" but also not active, 11 (2 percent) were "in reconstruction," leaving only 7 mills (or 1 percent) "in production." Burned cane fields also represented a loss of physical capital. A single planting of cane in Cuba could be harvested annually for at least six to ten years. Producers frequently took on debt to finance the plantings, and when they were destroyed, the means of generating the returns to repay those debts went up in smoke. Besides mills and cane fields, every type of agricultural establishment was destroyed or looted. Bergad reports estimates of Mantanzas, one of the principal sugar-producing provinces, that more than 95 percent of the small farms were devastated—houses, huts, fields, and fences torched or trampled. Of the 50,000 estimated yoke of oxen before the war, only 5,500 were available in mid-1899, and this was after imports from the United States had arrived. Only 3 percent of the horned cattle and 4 percent of the horses remained of the stocks that had existed before the war.[51] Furthermore, the transportation infrastructure was left in ruins— highways and railroad tracks were torn up, ties burned for fuel, and cars destroyed. Much of the capital stock in the rural sector was destroyed.

Restoration of the sugar industry was, nonetheless, rapid once peace had been regained. By 1902, stocks of cattle, horses, and mules were double what they were in 1894, and the 1894 level of sugar production was restored by 1903.[52]

This degree of destruction had an enormous effect on the restructuring of the industry. A process of Schumpeterian creative destruction had been under way since the end of the Ten Years' War, clearing out many of the older ingenios and making way for the mills with larger capacities brought in with the new technology. The war acted to accelerate this process. The reconstruction after the war would make the transition complete.[53] Moreno Fraginals comments that out of the largest 50 mills, 39 remained standing, although many could not immediately take up production because of the need for replanting.[54] Most of the existing modern centrales at the end of the war returned to production soon afterward, but the general experience was quite different. The rate of displacement of older mills had accelerated during the 1890s, but the war facilitated the process of displacement. At the end of the war, the older ingenios had largely been eliminated from production, if not directly by destruction, by the need to incur fixed costs to return to production. Many older mills were so technologically outmoded before the war that they could not justify any capital expenditures unless sufficient capital could be raised for a complete overhaul and updating. When faced with necessary capital expenditures to replace the draft animals, replant, and repair the machinery, many of these mill owners chose to cease grinding.[55] Those mills that did survive and renew their operations tended to be the larger mills that had already undergone renovation in the 1890s. For all of its tragedy, the destruction of the war paved the way for an immediate restructuring and updating of the sugar industry. The devastation acted as a catalyst to the technological transition.[56]

The Central Factory

The transition in sugar manufacture had been going on since the 1880s; however, the turn of the century marked a new phase for the development of the sugar enterprise in Cuba. The devastation of the War of Independence and the influx of North American capital stimulated not only growth in the industry but also a restructuring of the industrial organization of Cuban sugar. Two fundamental changes in the industry are noteworthy. First, there was an enormous change in the optimal scale of production, as occurred in other industries when continuous-process technologies were adopted. The capacities of new mills being constructed reflected the new optimum (see Table 1.1). Second, the self-contained, or vertically integrated, structure of the sugar mill/plantation complex was abandoned in favor of the disintegrated firm structure in which the large mill became a processing center and cane was obtained from outside growers, or colonos.[57] The older mills, known as ingenios, were dismantled and replaced by modern, large-scale central factories, known in Cuba as centrales. Characteristic of these centrales was a central mill site, an array of colonias surrounding the mill, and a hub-and-spoke rail system to connect the colonias to the mill. For an illustration of one such central, see Figure 3.1.

The conversion to this organizational structure began in the 1880s and accelerated after 1890. But around the turn of the century the conversion to the central was completed, and the last of the nineteenth-century, self-contained ingenios disappeared. The rise of the central factory was not unique to Cuba. It was making its appearance in numerous other sugar-producing countries as well. The institutions that were set up to support outside growers differed considerably from one country to the next. Some countries (notably Hawaii and Java) did not adopt such a structure, opting instead for a vertical integration of their cane cultivation and milling operations.[58] Nonetheless, though differences in factor endowments and regulatory environments affected its formation in different places, the centralization of milling was driven globally by the same forces — technological capabilities, which made the large scale advantageous, and the fall

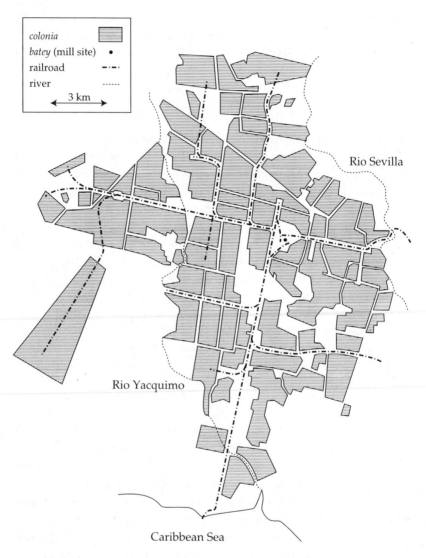

Fig. 3.1. Layout of the mill site and colonias of the Central Francisco, 1921.
Source: Braga Brothers Collection, Record Group 4, ser. 96.

in the cost of railroad construction (or other transportation infrastructure), which reduced internal costs of hauling cane to the factories.

Even though a limited use of colonos in Cuba is known to have existed
before this time, historians who have investigated the beginnings of the
central have placed its origins roughly between 1875 and 1880.[59] In the

decade and a half between the Ten Years' War and the War of Independence, radical technological changes at every stage of sugar production transformed the best-practice sugar mill. During these years, a few local sugar regions were transformed as local entrepreneurs financed complete makeovers of their mills. The results of these ventures were widely discussed in the press and recommended as the remedy needed for the industry to meet the challenge of European beet sugar.[60] A wave of imitation followed as other centrales were erected, but in general, the diffusion of the central proceeded at a slow pace until the expansionary 1890s, when it was interrupted by the outbreak of war in 1895. Consequently, the new mill did not immediately displace the older mills. Into the War of Independence, ingenios organized along lines similar to the days of slavery had continued to exist, harking back to the mid-nineteenth century and to a tradition in sugar making of more than a century.

This is not to suggest that the technology of the ingenio had been primitive. The application and adoption of new machinery in ingenios had been under way since before mid-century. There was always an array of old and new techniques in use in different mills. By 1860, the diffusion of the steam engine was almost complete; 91 percent of the sugar crop was produced using steam power.[61] Also by 1860, diffusion of the mechanical evaporation processes was under way. About 5 percent of the 1,318 active mills, representing 15 percent of the sugar produced, had installed the first generation of vacuum evaporators.[62] Nonetheless, most mills continued in the evaporation processes to boil sugar in "trains" (sequences) of open pans. The basic technique of using open pans was ancient, but the technology even in these apparently traditional implements was not static. In the mid-nineteenth century, Cuban sugar producers were in the process of adopting the Jamaica train, a modified train designed to economize on fuel consumption. The adoption of the Jamaica train for a time paralleled the early adoption of vacuum evaporation.[63] In curing, the first centrifugal machine for purging sugar in Cuba had been acquired in 1840, but centrifuges did not replace simple drainage until the 1880s. When replacement did occur, it happened quickly. The spread of the centrifuge was accelerated by the demands of refineries that paid a premium for the cleaner and more uniform qualities of centrifugal raw sugars.[64]

Fe Iglesias García has illuminated an important feature of the late nineteenth-century sugar mill. Not only did old and new mills coexist, but many mills juxtaposed elements of the old and new systems, creating a mixture of the traditional and the modern. For example, steam-powered grinding was often combined with open pans for boiling. Also, animal traction was sometimes used next to vacuum evaporators, and centrifugal machines were used to purge sugars that had been concentrated using Jamaica trains. Indeed, according to Iglesias, it was not uncommon to find mills using Jamaica trains for the first phase of evaporation combined with a vacuum pan as the final "strike" pan.[65]

The real technical revolution and transformation of the sugar mill came only as all of the new methods were adopted, the old ones displaced, and the new factory systemically redesigned according to the logic of continuous processing. The continuity in the flow of processing was enhanced piecemeal by mechanization at each stage of production. The next step in redesigning the factory was the further removal of the human factor in the conveyance of materials from one stage to the next. Feeders that automatically fed cane into the grinding mill were already common in 1860. The replacement of Jamaica trains with vacuum evaporators mechanized the transference of material through the successive stages of the boiling house. With the open pan system, material was transferred from one pan to another manually, using a large dipper, or *bombón*.[66] But when vacuum evaporators were adopted, mechanical pumps were used to transfer material from one vacuum pan to the next. Similarly, the replacement of the *casa de purga* with centrifugal machines sped up the curing process and eliminated the need for storing and tending to the draining molds of sugar, which could take 30 to 50 days to drain.[67] Complementarily, automatization was amplified when moving belts were introduced, first to carry the dried sugar to be bagged and then in other parts of the factories.[68] Implicit in many of these changes is a rearrangement of the factory and an enhancement of coordination between stages of production. In each stage of production, the demands for manual labor were reduced; but more important, the flow of processing was made more continuous and faster. There were fewer nodes in the system where the pace of work could be set by human participants. Technically, the changes meant that a given establishment of plant and equipment had a larger daily capacity. Economically, it meant that better use was being made of the existing plant and equipment. Plant and equipment involved fixed costs. Greater speed led to a greater overall volume of production, for given sizes of equipment, which meant lower fixed costs per unit of sugar. The great transformation of the sugar mill came at the point when this logic began to rule the design of new factories.[69]

Diffusion of continuous processing was evident in certain quantitative aspects of production from the 1880s. The capacities of mills, which on average had not changed greatly between 1860 and 1881, began to show signs of the dramatic changes in scale that would soon follow. In a study of Remedios, an early progressive sugar region in the province of Santa Clara, Hernán Venegas Delgado shows that its transformation occurred between 1878 and 1894. In 1878, none of the sugar produced in Remedios was classified as centrifugal sugar; by 1888, 73 percent of the region's sugar was centrifugal.[70] Nevertheless, the average capacity of Remedios's mills increased in that period by only 50 percent. Afterward, the average mill capacity was increased substantially by the construction of several modern mills. From 1888 to 1894, the average mill capacity in Remedios increased to more than four times its 1888 scale, reaching nearly 6,500 metric tons by 1894. This scale increase was only a hint of the changes to come after the turn of the century. As an illustration, the Central Narcisa, one of the most advanced of the Remedian mills which Venegas Delgado examines, had reached an output of almost 62,000 bags (of 325 pounds) in 1890. By 1925, the Narcisa produced 337,000 bags annually.[71]

The increase in mill capacity implied an inverse movement between the number of mills and the aggregate capacity of the industry resulting from the consolidation of former ingenios. There is some disagreement as to how many mills were actively grinding immediately before the war, but the most reliable figures suggest that the number of active mills fell from 1,190 in 1877 to about 850 in 1891, then probably fell to around 450 by 1894.[72] But by 1899, only 207 mills were in operation. In the next decade, the number of active mills was just under 200; by 1926 it had fallen to below 180. The process of diffusion of the central factory proceeded on two fronts. Financially strong mills underwent a complete dismantling and renovation of their equipment. Less technically or financially robust mills were retired, and their cane zones were dedicated to supply the larger capacities of the renovated mills. The process of retirement, on the second front, was largely completed by the end of the war. It acted to speed up the process of Schumpeterian creative destruction that had been under way since 1880.[73]

Many historians imply that the technological formation of the Cuban central factory stopped in the 1890s. There is a conventional view of Cuban economic development, harking back to Guerra y Sánchez, which evokes a sequence of two formalized stages.[74] In the first, the process of adoption of new technology and centralization was completed between 1870 and 1895 largely under the influence of Cuban capital and expertise.

The second stage came after the war, under U.S. economic influence, when the process of concentration of the existing centrales into large properties proceeded. Because land concentration was characteristic of this period, it is often referred to as the period of *latifundización*. Although this formulaic stage model of Cuban development is useful for some interpretive purposes, it is not accurate in its depiction of the path of technical change in Cuban sugar. The 1880s were the beginning, but only the beginning, of a trajectory of technical transformation that would last half a century. After 1899, accompanying the continued transformation of the central were institutional and social changes that historians of this period have been more inclined to emphasize. Behind these broader societal changes, however, was a continuation of the mill's technical transformation with modifications as radical as any introduced before the turn of the century.

Continual improvements were made in the roller mills, evaporators, filtration devices, and other apparatus into the 1920s. Indeed, a major technical barrier was crossed at the turn of the century with the innovation of multiple milling in Hawaii in 1900. This technique very quickly migrated to Cuba and resulted ultimately in another radical change in the grinding process. The first twelve-roll tandem (consisting of four three-roll mills), according to Jenks, began grinding in 1902, a joint venture of J. B. Hawley and Mario Menocal. As improvements in multiple milling were developed, one of the landmark innovations was first introduced in 1914 at the Central Amistad, in the province of Havana, an estate owned and operated by the Gómez Mena family.[75] This innovation, which involved the repeated application of pressure to squeeze more juice out of the cane, increased the efficiency of grinding considerably. The yields of the best mills of the late nineteenth century ranged around eight pounds of sugar per hundred pounds of cane, whereas yields achieved by World War I, after widespread diffusion of multiple milling, ranged between eleven and thirteen pounds of sugar per hundred pounds of cane.[76] It had been understood for some time that repeated application of pressure would improve grinding efficiency, but before the turn-of-the-century innovation, problems were encountered further down the line of processing because of added impurities that repeated pressure introduced in the cane juice. To accompany the new grinding method, a number of mechanical devices were introduced that refined or modified the mechanically performed tasks. Pregrinding crushers and shredders became more widespread. Noel Deerr, documenting in detail the patents for three-roller mills (trapiches), observes that active invention occurred up to the turn of the century.[77] The adoption of such new designs in the roller mill headstock and hydraulic regulators, with some modifications, continued well into the following decades. Besides these innovations, numerous modifications and refinements were introduced in filter presses, evaporators, vacuum pan crystallizers, and other devices.[78]

A comparison of inventories of equipment between a leading 1890s mill and a leading 1920s mill shows a considerable increase in the number of evaporators, vacuum pans, and centrifugals and a considerable increase in complexity in detail and specifications of these devices, indicating numerous additional features and options that were available through modifications and amendments to the original technical concepts. Qualitatively, the greatest differences are noticed in the grinding machinery, which in the 1920s was more massive and consisted of more components. Furthermore, the quantity of additional auxiliary devices, such as cane elevators, bagasse carriers, pumps, scales, and bag handling equipment, increased considerably. The horsepower of the main boiler plants increased, in the best-practice mills examined, from about 1,700 horsepower to over 7,000 horsepower. In addition, in the 1920s, inventories of small electric motors, gasoline-powered internal combustion engines, and auxiliary steam plant were maintained to power much of the auxiliary machinery.[79] These innovations, to be discussed in further detail in Chapter 4, represented a trajectory of continuous technical improvement that lasted through the first three decades of the twentieth century.

The optimal mill capacity continued to increase considerably, driven in part by multiple milling and in part by enterprise design and organizational innovations. The dramatic decline in the number of active mills in the period 1877–94 did not accelerate after the turn of the century only because the level of production rose considerably. In 1877, 1,190 mills produced half a million tons. By 1894 only 450 mills produced over a million tons. But by 1929, 163 mills produced 5 million tons — five times the 1894 level using a third the number of mills (see Table 1.1).

The adoption of private cane railroad networks to haul cane into the central factory from vast distances became an essential component of the central factory system as the capacities of mills grew. Because of the extensiveness of cane agricultural practices in Cuba, the cane fields serviced by a single central stretched over considerable areas. By the 1920s, centrales on average gathered cane from land areas of around 20,000 to 30,000 acres, not all of which would be in cane. Indeed, on the larger properties, that area extended to over 150,000 acres.[80] Rapid transportation of cane was essential to successful sugar production because it deteriorated rapidly after being cut.[81] As a rule of thumb, cut cane needed to be ground within 24 hours to avoid substantial losses of sucrose. Therefore, obviously, distance was an obstacle that at times imposed serious demands on the activity of transporting harvested cane to the mill. Speed of delivery was required, but also the railroad provided the physical link in the coordination between harvest and grinding activities. In the early twentieth century, the practice in Cuba came to be to combine the use of private (company-owned) railroads with public railroads (privately owned but open for service to the public). Public service railroads were commonly referred to as "public" railroads, even though they were privately owned, in distinction from those owned privately for exclusive use by sugar companies, the latter of which became quite extensive after the turn of the century.[82] The ubiquitous presence of private company railroads came only with the U.S. occupational government of 1899–1902, when the railroad regulations were revised to favor private over public service railroads.[83]

In his writings, Guerra y Sánchez criticized the relaxed regulations toward private railroads as inhibiting the construction of the public service railroad network.[84] Private plantation railroads were first built in Cuba in the 1870s. Mill owners seeking alternatives to the traditional oxcart for hauling cane imported portable railroads. Some mill owners also invested in fixed railroads for their exclusive use, but their construction was initially limited. After 1881, a number of public service railway companies began to offer for the first time the service of hauling cane to mills to facilitate the rising needs of colonos. The demands for those services quickly outstripped the capacity as railroads became congested with traffic.[85] According to Guerra, however, because of unfavorable colonial regulations, the rise in the use of private railroads awaited the regulatory reforms enacted by the U.S. occupational government in 1902.[86]

In contradiction to Guerra's criticism, the right to exclusive use of the railroad by private companies may have had the net effect of encouraging more overall railroad construction. Even though many of them did not offer public service, the extensive network of private railroads was the vehicle by which much of the coordination of production between central and colono was accomplished. The congestion on public service railroads, which was often heavy, was an obstacle to that coordination. Therefore, the companies often reserved the private railroads for their own production to enhance internal coordination. As will be discussed in Chapter 4, the strategic use of these private railroad networks became important, especially as the areas they covered became larger. Guerra has emphasized that railroads were often used to establish local monopolies over the transportation of cane.[87] This was another facet of their application. Control over the traffic on the railroad was sought to assist in the coordination between factory and field, but that form of control permitted other forms. When possible, centrales built their railroads so as to control their cane lands. As I show in Chapter 6, this is a strategy that was sometimes, but not always, possible. The conditions in the eastern provinces were more favorable to both objectives because there the layout of cane fields and railroads was drawn out along with the central from an initial plan. It did not evolve out of the arrangement of preexisting railroads and fields laid out initially for the smaller ingenio.

The Colono System

Accompanying the centralization of milling was the establishment of a set of arrangements by which outside growers supplied cane to the centrales. The result was the institution for cane farming known as the colono system.[88] For Cuban producers, the new division of labor represented a radical break with tradition, a highly innovative approach to the business organization of the sugar-producing enterprise. In former times, both the agricultural and manufacturing activities were conducted by the owner of the ingenio and his staff. Production decisions at all levels, up to the point of selling the sugar, were internal to the ingenio, and the physical capital necessary to bring the processes of production to completion were under the control of this single organizational entity. The centralization of production created new problems associated with the externalization of some of the decisions of production, that is, the opening of the cane transaction to market forces. In the early years of its formation, there was uncertainty among producers and repeated discussion about how the transaction should be done, or how the arrangements for purchasing cane from colonos should be made.

At its earliest appearance, the colono system arose when owners of ingenios attempted to attract labor (both white and black) for cane cultivation as the slave trade was ending. As laborers became scarcer, the owners of ingenios partitioned land on the perimeters of their plantations and leased it to colonos who agreed to supply cane to the owner's mill. Similar arrangements were made with landowners with property adjacent to the ingenio. As the optimal capacities of mills increased, it was convenient to arrange for local growers to add to the ingenio's internal cane supplies. Evidence for such arrangements exists as early as 1867.[89] The Ten Years' War and the subsequent economic stagnation further stimulated use of similar contractual arrangements. Many former planters holding mortgates and in arrears after the Ten Years' War sought a means to recover. Unable to raise capital to grind their cane, some could obtain contracts and advances to supply cane to neighboring incipient centrales.[90] In the late 1880s and 1890s Cuban sugar producers frequently emphasized the function of the colono system as a means of division of labor between the industrial and agricultural sectors that permitted the mill owner to concentrate his financial resources on the modernization of the mill. Colonos in these early years were often expected to find their own source of funds for financing the cane crop. Later in the twentieth century, the central was often the colonos' creditor as well.[91] In the meantime, technological improvements dictated increases in the optimal capacities of mills and an ultimate reduction in the number of mills needed to process a given amount of cane. The process of consolidation of existing ingenios was accomplished through the formation of colono arrangements. The spread of the institution of the *colonato* became inseparable from the rise of the central factory.

Often historians have interpreted the appearance of the colono system as a response to these difficulties. For most sugar producers, the years between the Ten Years' War and 1890 were lean ones. In this interim, the abolition of slavery, the fiscal policy of Spain, and the fall of the sugar price had hurled most planters into a crisis. The colono system offered advantages for sugar producers attempting to deal with these challenges. First, setting up small colonos on the perimeters of the plantations provided a new source of labor to aid in the transition to free labor. Not all the colonos were white, but many advocates of "whitening" settlement thought that this institution was needed to attract white immigrants to cane cultivation.[92] Second, the colono system was seen as a means of relaxing some of the credit problems of those mill owners who were trying to modernize their mills. Many sought the division of labor and the dispersal of financial liability as a means of concentrating their capital and entrepreneurial resources on renovating the mill, permitting others to manage its cane supplies. These circumstances obviously weighed heavily in the decisions of the mill owners and colonos to establish contractual relationships in these years, but they do not explain the permanence of the institution. The needs just described were transitional. By the end of the 1880s alternative sources of labor had been found, and the recuperation from the Ten Years' War had to give way to long-term concerns. Those mill owners who had recovered would have established cane supply arrangements that were efficient and reliable in the long run. Yet by the 1890s it became clear that the colono system was going to be a permanent feature of the emerging sugar industry in Cuba. The long-term arrangements being established were the refinement of the colono contract. Leland Jenks comments that by 1887 it was believed that about 35 to 40 percent of the cane in Cuba was being cultivated by colonos. By 1905 it was the most common arrangement for supplying cane to the mills — 70 percent of the Cuban cane crop was supplied by colonos, and the trend was rising.[93]

As time passed, the role of the colono as a laborer diminished, and his role as manager of a portion of the mill's cane supplies became the principal one. This meant that his main tasks were tending the fields and employing and supervising wage-earning field laborers, especially during harvest and planting time, to perform the manual labor.[94] It also involved the management of procedures and precautions for preventing cane fires or other problems that might threaten the cane crop.[95] The smallest colonos' families performed a larger portion of the labor themselves, especially during the dead season, but virtually all became managers of wage labor during the harvest. More important, not all colonos were smallholders. Many were either former planters or wealthy businessmen with large estates. Often they were absentee owners, involved in other businesses at the same time — agricultural or commercial establishments. In any case, it is clear that by the 1890s, most participants discussed the establishment of a colonia as a business venture.[96] Debates on the proper function of the colonia in the 1880s and 1890s emphasized it as an agricultural business rather than an institution for obtaining labor.[97] In 1888, when Juan Bautista Jiménez, author of a manual for colonos, argued in favor of the colono arrangement, he emphasized the colono's managerial function — supervision, vigilance, and counsel.[98]

The contractual relationship between the colono and the mill and the function of the colono in the sugar enterprise evolved as well. In earlier years, the means of payment, length of contract, and other arrangements varied. But by the twentieth century, these aspects of the contract became more standardized as the needs of the central were better understood and as experience with various payment schemes and stipulations or clauses in the contract had been accumulated.[99] The payment to the colono came to be a share payment or, more precisely, a payment in sugar for every 100 *arrobas* of cane delivered to the mill (1 arroba = 25 pounds). The contracts were of long-term duration, lasting from about six to ten years. In the contract, the colono typically was obligated to sell the cane produced on the colonia (the plot of land specified in the contract) exclusively to the central that was party to the contract, although some large colonos had separate contracts with more than one central. Many have noted that these contracts tended to tie the colonos to a single central. The long-term contractual arrangements established a bilateral economic relationship between colono and central. In many cases, where the means of transportation other than the central's railroad were limited, the bilateral nature of these relationships was effectively much stronger and unalterable.

A question that one might naturally ask is, Given the breakdown of the traditional slave-based plantation structure of the sugar enterprise, why did an intermediate market for cane not develop on a national or regional level? Theoretically, centrales might have obtained the cane they needed, at market prices, from a commodities market for cane, whose supplies were provided by a mass of cane farmers who entered the market anonymously in response to the price stimulus, similar to markets for wheat or other staples. But this kind of spot market did not form in any country where sugar was produced. The reason was technical — harvested cane deteriorated too rapidly. This technical requirement imposed serious problems of coordination of the harvest and the grinding activities, and its solution required continual communication between the central and the grower to synchronize the harvest and the grinding. Because of the coordination requirements, complete independence of the outside growers would not have been economically viable. Consequently, transacting cane in spot markets was technically prohibitive, or because of lost cane quality, the transaction costs were prohibitively high. Each central had its own "hinterland" of cane fields in colonias located in the lands surrounding the mill, and the rail connection between the mill and the fields formed something of a hub-and-spoke system of cane supply.

Therefore, whereas the observation that colonos were tied to the centrales — obligated contractually to sell to a single mill — there was a corresponding obverse bond. In many cases the centrales were equally tied to the colonias — dependent on the supplies of cane that colonos controlled.

Since cane had to be obtained from nearby fields and delivered promptly to minimize deterioration, central managers also had limited options for procuring adequate cane supplies. Guerra y Sánchez's arguments suggest that greater independence would have been a natural development had it not been for the inordinate power of North American financiers imposing what he called a collar of feudalism on them. From a comparative perspective, however, the emphasis on the unique Cuban-American relationship does not seem justified. In no country were cane farmers contractually independent of the mills, and in at least half the sugar-producing countries worldwide, cane cultivation was directly managed in vertically integrated mill organizations. Indeed, to many contemporary sugar specialists it seemed peculiar that mills in Cuba did not integrate the cane and sugar operations vertically. Unlike its principal rivals, however, the decentralized system was the most common form of organization.[100]

Conclusion

Chandler argues that the general technological trend toward continuous processing and high throughput, which was so important for developments in the sugar industry, was also the critical stimulus for the development of modern methods of business management. The organizational innovations of the early twentieth century developed simultaneously with the technological innovations because of internal factory requirements to improve the coordination and control of the line of production. Often the organizational response to larger-scale, continuous-process production and new capabilities in transportation involved vertical integration either forward into distribution or backward into supply industries. Chandler noted, however, that in processing and refining industries, the machine-induced control required by factory design was often sufficient to synchronize the activities in the production process; consequently, these industries were not particularly innovative in the area of factory management. In contrast, he found that for metal-making and metalworking industries — especially the automobile industry and also railroads — coordination problems of an organizational or management nature were much more critical. Therefore, the latter industries tended to be the originators of the organizational innovations that were the pillars of modern business organization.[101] Nonetheless, continuous processing in sugar manufacture led to organizational innovation, perhaps most notable in adoption of the modern line and staff form, the primary significance of which was the separation of the responsibilities of those performing the individual tasks of production from those who supervised the logical working of the entire system of production.[102]

Change in the vertical structure of the sugar enterprise was less apparent than in other industries because sugar plantations had traditionally been vertically integrated. Nevertheless, with the larger scale of production, the problems of coordination were greater and produced more bottlenecks in the flow of production in the fields. Organization was critical in the interface between cane field and factory. The machine-induced factory control did not extend into the activities of the harvest or the operation of the plantation railroads. These activities required more organization-based coordination to ensure the continuous arrival of cane at the mills, and in many parts of the world, even though the scale of production had changed greatly, a vertically integrated structure between cane cultivation and processing had been retained. Underlying that apparent continuity was a restructuring as modern sugar enterprises divided their operations into greater internal specialization and organizational departments with the corresponding line and staff to manage them. Consequently, the tendency which Chandler identifies for modern enterprises to adopt more intensive managerial structures is seen as well in the sugar industry.

The pattern of replacement of the invisible hand of market mechanisms with the visible hand of management, which Chandler describes in other industries, was not so explicitly found everywhere in the sugar industry. In some countries, vertical integration of cane cultivation and processing was the rule; however, half of the cane grown worldwide was grown in countries where outside cane growers supplied a significant amount. Indeed, there was great variation in the institutions that developed around the world for managing and coordinating the cultivation of cane with milling activities.[103] The reliance in Cuba on the colono system was in this regard seen as unique by contemporaries. This was not simply because it existed but because it was so successful. "Scientific" cultivation of cane, of the kind adopted generally in Java and Hawaii, was not found among Cuban colonos, yet the colonos managed to produce cane at lower costs than the central administrations in Cuba, Hawaii, and Java with more knowledge of modern cultivation techniques.[104] This seemed rather inconsistent with the strict coordination required of the cane field and milling management, which introduced incentives for vertical integration.

Institute of Latin American Studies

31 Tavistock Square

London WC1H 9HA

(The coordination requirements and their implications for the development of the Cuban industry will be discussed further in Chapters 4 and 6.)

Although its function changed over the decades, the colono system remained a basic constituent of the organization of the Cuban sugar industry even though other major sugar producers in the world did not find it advantageous. The centrales generally formed separate departments to handle the management of machinery, labor, laboratories, and transportation. Colonos were an integral part of this managerial division of labor.[105] Many view the continued existence of the colono system as a historically specific path-dependent phenomenon, derived from Cuba's history as one of the last remaining colonies of Spain in the West Indies.[106] Moreno Fraginals suggests that the separation of mill and cane field management preserved the backwardness of cane cultivation and created a technical gap and a dual industry in Cuban sugar with segmented backward agricultural and progressive industrial sectors.[107] The abundance of land in Cuba, however, implies that the efficient agricultural techniques would be less intensive in the use of other inputs and technology relative to other countries. In other words, the observation that colonos did not use the latest scientific techniques developed in Java and Hawaii is perfectly consistent with plausible expectations of the efficient allocation of resources. In either case, the links between the adoption of modern business organization methods, the transformation of the sugar mill, and the evolution and preservation of the colono system in Cuba were undeniable.

Chapter 4

Coordination and Scale Economies

THE NEAR hundredfold increase in the average mill capacity in Cuba in 52 years is remarkable, but it was not out of line with the experience of other processing industries. Petroleum refineries, distilleries, breweries, and food-processing industries all saw enormous increases in their optimal scales of production in brief spans of time. These industries had in common the adoption of high-throughput, continuous-process machinery and factory design that formed the technological basis of modern mass production. So the transformation of the cane sugar industry was not unique for its time. Rather, it was linked to a wave of global technological change that exhibited not only general reductions in unit costs but also substantial increases in scales of production in a wide variety of industries.

The arrival of the new technology and the expansion of mill capacities nonetheless provoked an alarmed reaction among many Cubans because it was not equally distributed among the existing sugar producers. The presence of North American companies in key sectors of the economy had increased substantially since independence. Opposition to the imperialist pretensions of the United States government toward Cuba reflected in the Platt Amendment and the North American control of the banking system increased after the crisis of 1920–21. To make sense of the distribution of technical and organizational changes taking place in the industry, the notion of imperialist intervention was also projected into the technical dimension. The newcomer North American enterprises (and some well-established domestic producers) seemed to enjoy an advantage because they adopted larger-scale technologies more quickly and easily. The association between the latest technology, the largest mills, and foreign ownership of sugar mills led many observers to explain the large-scale sugar factories as arising from the power and domination (both economic and political) of North American financiers who funded the massive investments. The evident technical superiority of North American mills seemed to corroborate these criticisms; and the concentration of that technology in the east, which was the center of most North American direct investment, reinforced them. The distribution of coexisting old and new mills seems to have been the principal statistical motivation for this claim.

Other research leads one to believe that Cuban businessmen and industrialists were neither as economically powerless nor as disconnected with modern technology as this image appears to suggest. To understand the cause of the foreign bias in the distribution of new technology in the sugar enterprise, one should examine more carefully how the process of investment in new technology affects the distribution of techniques. A problem with the above power-based assessment of the foreign bias is that it does not consider the distribution that would otherwise have existed if the ownership of mills by North Americans had not been a factor. Association is not sufficient to determine causation. One also needs an understanding of what might have happened if the proposed causal factor were hypothetically eliminated. In this context, the following question should be addressed: If one supposes that Cuban and North American producers had the same access to technical inputs and capital, what would the resulting distribution of techniques between Cuban and North American mills have been? The economics of technical change has shown that it is common for producers with the same *access* to technology to differ willingly in their *decisions* regarding their desired levels of investment in new technology (or the scale of production) depending on their own needs and circumstances. This implies for the early republican Cuban sugar industry that a wide range of mill capacities and technical levels between domestic and foreign mills could easily have existed for purely economic reasons. If so, the politically based explanation of the differences in scales of production or technology employed may not be justified. At least it should be questioned more carefully in the face of alternative explanations.

The claim that North American imperialist domination had a technical dimension builds from the belief that equal opportunities would have generated a more or less uniform pattern of adoption between nationality groups. That belief notwithstanding, the distributions of both technology and nationality might be explained by a third factor. For example, an alternative explanation might be related more to the age of the equipment in the mills. As the industry modernized, a large number of the older producers seemed always to be lagging in the adoption of the latest methods or machinery. Perhaps a historical correlation between the age of a mill's equipment and the nationality of ownership explains why the existing Cuban and Spanish sugar producers fell behind in the contest for reducing unit operating costs.

As an alternative to a nationality-based explanation, this chapter investigates the proposition that producers rationally chose when to adopt new milling technology based on the particular needs and profit potential of individual mills. The persistent range of variation in the levels of technology at different mills is thus explained as an outcome of the choices of mill owners to maximize profits. Evidence implicit in the patterns of mill-level investment in new capacity supports this proposition, although it does not exclude the possibility of nationality-based factors as well. The evidence turns on a concept in the theory of investment known as "vintage capital." In the context of Cuban sugar, the effect was as follows. Existing producers, given the opportunity to purchase and install the new technology at the same prices and under the same conditions as North American newcomers, would often have chosen freely to postpone investment in the new technology because it was in their best economic interest to do so. Despite the lower unit operating costs the new technology provided, the high fixed costs of adopting it presented existing producers with a trade-off rather than a clear-cut decision to update their technology. Sometimes returns to the existing producer were higher when the older, outmoded equipment was retained rather than updated because costly investment expenditures could be deferred. Of course, this choice was not available to the newcomers. (This divergence of investment behavior is referred to as the "vintage-capital effect.") This effect combined with the timing of capital flows originating from different national sources explains the foreign bias in the distribution of techniques. Because the majority of existing mill owners at the beginning of the technical transition were Cuban or Spanish and the newcomers were often North American, the distribution of mills using older techniques and machinery was skewed toward the Cuban and Spanish mills.

As we shall see, the patterns of investment in mill capacity support the vintage-capital explanation for the distribution of mill capacities on the island. The results represent a step toward understanding the historical process that led to wide differences in the techniques used between one mill and the next. They dispel the notion that differences in technology were the result of a political process and support the notion that the appearance of large-scale factories was the result of an evolutionary process of technical adaptation. Why Cuban and Spanish mills tended to be smaller and retained intermediate degrees of technical adaptation as innovations became available is a question that is best addressed within the framework of this evolutionary economic process of change.

It will also become clear that the relationship between the scale of production of mills and their technological "vintage" was not a simple one. Evidence shows the presence of substantial economies of scale. But oddly, mill-level investment patterns show unexpectedly that newly founded mills, which one would expect to have adopted the latest technology, regularly did not initially adopt the large optimal scale. Reconciling this anomaly leads us to recognize the importance of costs of adjustment in the process of adoption of the latest technology. High adjustment costs, as we shall see, provide considerable insight into a number of events in the economic history of this period.

Implications of the analysis are revisionary to the economic historiography of early republican Cuba. First, large-scale production, which previously has been seen as a political outcome of large private economic entities, is understood, rather, to be an outcome of the peculiar technical characteristics of sugar manufacture. Just as the rapid deterioration of cane had an impact on the international division of labor in the global sugar industry, it also had a profound impact on the internal industrial organization of sugar in Cuba. The structure of the sugar industry that emerged in early twentieth-century Cuba was driven largely by technical factors related to the optimal procedures for grinding cane. The economies of scale usually present in mechanical aspects of continuous-process technologies were accentuated by additional economies of extremely large-scale agriculture that entered the cost structures of sugar firms as organizational solutions that were developed to deal with the problem of rapid cane deterioration.

Second, the adjustment costs of investment in sugar mills introduced an inertia in the rate of increase in the capacities of individual mills which was projected into the rate of increase in the aggregate milling capacity of the island. This inertia was of particular significance for understanding the investment episode of the post-1921 Cuban sugar economy. The continued expansion of capacities of many mills after the crisis of 1920–21 has attracted considerable attention and criticism by economists interested in these events.[1] In contrast with the steady expansion of the 1899–1919 period, the continued investment in mill capacity after 1921 took place during a period of an initially uncertain and then falling price of sugar. The continued high rate of expansion in these less propitious conditions was peculiar. The contemporary economist Leland Jenks felt he needed to explain why, "despite the grave warning of the crisis," the aggregate milling capacity on the island continued to increase until in the 1925 crop year more than 5 million tons were produced. To Jenks "the expansion policy seemed suicidal" because it clearly led to aggregate overproduction of sugar. The explanation Jenks offered for the expansion of capacity was that since the industry had come into the hands of North American banks they channeled capital into their own mills to reduce unit production costs, accomplished by expansion in the volume of production.[2] But Jenks does not explain why these investments to reduce unit costs were not made earlier by the former owners. This chapter and Chapter 5 present evidence that the optimal procedure for investment in the new technology involved a process of adjustment to a large optimal scale of production that took several years to complete. The investment in the post-1921 period was a continuation of investment programs begun during the war. For the mills either founded or rebuilt during World War I, the process of adjustment to the desired scale was still not completed. When mills changed hands in 1920 and 1921, the new owners had the same incentives as the old ones to complete the investments needed for individual mills to reach their optimal capacities. Those mills taken over by the banks may have faced fewer capital constraints, but the reason for the continued expansion was the remaining midproject potential for lowering unit costs. Thus it was a continuation of the process of modernization that had been under way since the beginning of the century and even earlier.

The logic of vintage capital also clarifies that the increase in aggregate capacity was the consequence of two types of decisions—the decision to build a new mill with new technology and the decision not to shut down an old mill with an outmoded technology. Besides the capacity added to new or rebuilt mills, the expansion of capacity after World War I was in part attributable to market conditions that discouraged outmoded mills from closing. Once those conditions changed, a large number of domestic mills became unprofitable and were forced to shut down. By this time, the market incentives for building new mills or rebuilding had worsened and, as a consequence, the domestic share of ownership in the industry declined considerably.

Vintage-Capital Effects in the Growth of Mill Capacities

To understand the economic relationship between technical change and the growth and variation of mill capacities in Cuba, we need to examine the mechanism by which investment decisions were made. The technologies being adopted were capital-embodied (that is, new technology was embodied in new equipment that had to be purchased), and therefore, the adoption of new technologies was by necessity tied to investment in physical capital. The concept of vintage capital is useful for understanding this mechanism. Vintage capital is defined as physical capital equipment that embodies a state of technology determined by the year in which the equipment was built. The metaphor "vintage" is used to indicate the analogy between a "vintage" of wine, whose qualities at a given point in time are determined by the year it was produced, and the "vintage" of technology inherent in any existing piece of equipment, also determined by the year it was produced. Vintages in capital also have the added unidirectional characteristic that each year's vintage is by definition at least as good as the previous year's because each year's vintage is determined by the existing stock of technological knowledge, which, of course, includes the previous stock of knowledge. In this chapter, I will examine the notion of vintage capital and demonstrate that it offers a plausible explanation for the persistence of the wide array of technologies and mill capacities that existed in Cuban sugar.

However, the standard vintage-capital model, often conceived in theoretical models of investment in new technology, is not consistent with all investment behavior we observe. It turns out that in addition to the vintage-capital effects, the effects of the costs of adjustment to the optimal capacity were also important. In this chapter and the next, I demonstrate that new mills were not built initially at their optimal capacities. Rather, they were built at suboptimal capacities with explicit investment plans to expand capacity steadily to reach the optimal capacity within a few years' time. Taking the gradual approach to arrive at the most efficient capacity was advantageous to the investor because the overall costs of erecting the mill were lower than they would have been with the immediate construction of the optimal capacity. In summary, the process of adoption of new technology proceeded in a gradual but deliberate manner for two reasons — the effects of vintage capital and the effects of adjustment costs. There were two important ramifications of this for broader developments in the sugar industry. First, at any point in time during the years of expansion, the aggregate optimal capacity of the industry was larger than the existing capacity. Thus even when the perceived market stopped expanding sometime in the 1920s, an incentive to build more capacity continued to exist for some mills as they continued to approach their optimal capacities. Second, if a mill was started but its access to capital was interrupted before it reached its optimal capacity, the mill would be left unviably inefficient. Casual observation of the evidence suggests that this happened more frequently with Cuban than with North American mills.

The focus of the quantitative investigation is on the period 1917–29 because the data are richer for this period; however, the process identified was present much earlier, in the years after the end of the Cuban War of Independence, when the boom in the Cuban sugar industry began.

Mill Capacities

The increase in the capacities of sugar mills in these early years of the Cuban republic was remarkable. The average production of mills increased by over 400 percent from 1904 to 1929. Table 1.1 shows this change to have been most rapid in the twentieth century between 1904 and 1916; the average production of mills rose by an annual average of 8.2 percent in these twelve years. The scale increase of the next thirteen years was less rapid, but it was still a remarkable 5.2 percent per year on average.

The change in the distribution of mill capacities in this period is also interesting. Table 4.1 shows that there was a steady shift of the entire distribution of mill capacities. One can see that the statistical mode of the distribution increased from 100–199 to 200–399 thousand bag capacity from 1917 to 1929. If we were to think of the mode of the distribution as representing the "preferred" mill size, then the preferred mill size changed, say, from 100–199 to 100–399 (either 100–199 or 200–399) thousand bag capacity. Also, both the minimum and maximum rose with time. Mills

Table 4.1
Frequency of Mills by Production Capacity, 1917–29
(capacity in 000s of bags of sugar, bag = 325 lbs.)

	0–24	25–49	50–99	100–199	200–399	400–799	800+	Row total	Total no. mills grinding
			Absolute Frequency of All Mills Reporting Their Capacities						
1917	2	10	53	86	37	9	0	197	199
1918	2	6	45	89	44	12	0	198	198
1919	2	4	36	94	43	15	1	195	198
1920	3	4	35	91	45	15	1	194	194
1921	2	4	32	97	47	15	1	198	198
1922	1	2	26	91	50	17	2	189	189
1923	0	1	27	83	51	19	2	183	183
1924	2	0	21	85	50	21	2	181	181
1925	0	0	19	83	54	26	1	183	183
1926	0	0	10	77	58	27	4	176	176
1927	0	0	14	70	61	26	6	177	177
1928	0	1	10	65	63	25	8	172	172
1929	0	1	9	57	60	27	9	163	163
AVG.	1.1	2.5	25.9	82.2	51.0	19.5	2.8	185.1	185.3
			Relative Frequency (percentage)						
1917	1	5	27	44	19	5	0		
1918	1	3	23	45	22	6	0		
1919	1	2	18	48	22	8	1		
1920	2	2	18	47	23	8	1		
1921	1	2	16	49	24	8	1		
1922	1	1	14	48	26	9	1		
1923	0	1	15	45	28	10	1		
1924	1	0	12	47	28	12	1		
1925	0	0	10	45	30	14	1		
1926	0	0	6	44	33	15	2		
1927	0	0	8	40	34	15	3		
1928	0	1	6	38	37	15	5		
1929	0	1	6	35	37	17	6		
AVG.	0.6	1.3	13.7	44.2	27.9	10.8	1.6		

SOURCE: Author's calculations. Data are from Cuba, Secretaría de Agricultura, Comercio, y Trabajo, *Industria azucarera*, 1916/17–1929; Cuba, Secretaría de Hacienda, *Industria azucarera*, 1916/17–1929.

of below 100,000 bag capacity diminished greatly, and mills of 800,000 or greater appeared for the first time. The regularity of this pattern of change over the entire range of the distribution is also noteworthy. The average, the minimum, and the maximum of the distribution all roughly doubled between 1917 and 1929. A question that needs to be asked is, What explains the regularities we observe within these changes? Why was there such a regular pattern of change of the entire distribution?

The steady rise in the mean capacity could be construed as the adjustment to a disequilibrium in sugar mill capacities. World War I had created a shortage of cane sugar production facilities supplying the world market.

Devastation in Europe harmed the European beet sugar industry, and it resulted in the cane sugar industry regaining a greater share of the market both during and after the war. From 1914 to 1924 sugar prices remained high relative to what they were in the decade before the war, and they provided an incentive for investment in the sugar industry. The market conditions also created a certain amount of slack in supplies that kept old mills from closing even as new mills entered for a time. If the increase in the mean mill capacity is explained as an adjustment to a change in the optimal scale of production, however, the conventional view of the dynamics of adjustment would predict a convergence of the distribution of mill capacities to the new optimal scale over time. It does not explain the prolonged coexistence of outmoded techniques with the latest techniques of production that we observe.

Alternatively, a vintage-capital model predicts the persistence of heterogeneous technologies as long as the new techniques were capital-embodied — embodied in the physical equipment. If, in addition, the technological improvements increased the optimal scale of production over time, vintage capital, furthermore, provides an explanation both for the persistent range of mill capacities and for the shift upward of the entire range of mill capacities over time. The vintage-capital model nicely illustrates the process behind the changing distribution of mill capacities we observe as a "moving equilibrium," that is, it predicts that the equilibrium for the distribution of techniques is a range rather than a single technique. It also predicts that the equilibrium range of techniques would naturally move driven by a continuous flow of technological improvements.[3] (An explanation of this moving equilibrium is given in the section beginning on page 121.)

Multiple Milling

To consider the basic assumption of the model, the capital embodiment of the technology is certainly appropriate for the heavily mechanized cane sugar industry of the twentieth century. The most important innovation in the sugar mill in the twentieth century combined advances made in roller milling, filtering, and hydraulics technologies called "multiple milling." Multiple milling was, at least at intermediate scales of production, an important reason for the growth of the optimal scale in milling equipment. This innovation in the grinding process involved increasing the number of rollers in the grinding mill, that is, increasing the number of "bites" the cane received from the rollers to improve the rate of extraction of juice. Before its introduction, grinding mills generally consisted of three to six rollers, but with multiple milling, the number of rollers increased ultimately to more than eighteen rollers (six three-roll mills). Adding more three-roll mills to the tandem increased substantially the grinding capacity of a tandem.[4]

Since early in the nineteenth century, grinding machinery had become standardized in three-roller units. The standard three-roll mill was arranged with the three rollers placed horizontally in a triangular fashion, with two rollers below and one above. These standardized three-roller units were purchased individually and placed end to end to form the tandem.[5] The innovation of multiple milling consisted of lining up in tandem several standard three-roller units connected by conveyors to subject the cane to repeated pressure to extract the juice from the cane fibers more thoroughly. Figure 4.1 is a diagram of a typical three-roller unit (three-roll grinding mill) used to form these tandems. In Panel A of the diagram, the three circles arranged in a triangular fashion represent an end view of the three rollers. The cane is fed into the gap between the rollers labeled "a" and "b" in the diagram, where it receives its first "bite" (of pressure), then it is turned by a metal plate (called the trash turner) and sent out again through the gap between the rollers labeled "a" and "c" to receive its second bite. In the old ingenios of the nineteenth century, the grinding process was accomplished with only these two bites to the cane. (Toward the end of the century, some mills were using tandems of two three-roll units.) In multiple milling, after the cane passed out of the first of these three-roller units, it was carried by a conveyor belt to a third, fourth, up to a sixth three-roller unit.

Sugar producers found that lengthening the tandem allowed considerable refinement of the grinding process. With repeated bites, the canes were crushed much more thoroughly. But in addition, alteration of the width of the gaps between the rollers improved the smoothness with which the process operated and cut down the number of mill breakages. Canes are not a smooth material to crush. The fibrous nodes offered much more resistance to pressure than the fleshy internodal part of the cane. If only a few bites were applied to extract the cane juice, the gaps had to be set at a width that made jamming of the cane likely, and it made the mills prone to breakdowns. Lengthening the tandem and increasing the number of bites in the grinding process allowed producers to widen the gap between the roller of the first three-roll mill such that the first unit was used

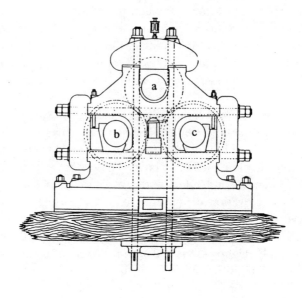

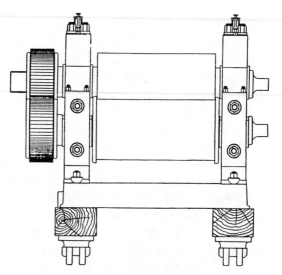

Fig. 4.1. Side and frontal views (top and bottom, respectively) of a three-roll mill. Reproduced from Deerr, *Cane Sugar*, pp. 172–73.

for breaking down the cane nodes and fibers so that they would pass more easily through the subsequent mill bites. By experience, mill managers learned to set the successive roller gaps such that they decreased in width at each bite. Tandems of lengths of eighteen rollers (six three-roll mills connected with conveyor belts) were the most common in Cuba by the late 1920s.

Multiple milling was first attempted in the mid-nineteenth century, and though it was successful in increasing the extraction of juice, it was not economically beneficial before 1900 because it created problems for the purification of the cane juice. A brief description of the history of the innovation will explain the initial problems of lengthening the grinding mill. It was known by the middle of the nineteenth century that repeated crushing of the bagasse (the crushed cane stalks) would give a better rate of extraction of the juice. It was also understood that maceration (the application of water to the bagasse) could improve the flow of sucrose from the fibers into the juice, but this required at least two sets of three-roller units because there was no use in macerating the uncrushed cane stalks. But it was not successful before 1900 because the grinding process interacted with the purification process. Repeated crushing of the cane caused tiny pieces of fiber (called *bagacillo*) that were difficult to remove to enter the cane juice. The bagacillo made purification of the juice so much more costly that the efficiency gains made in grinding were offset by the increased costs of purification. The problem was finally solved by the invention of a fine copper strainer that was cleared automatically. The mechanical clearing of the strainer was a crucial feature of this device. Without it the fine holes of the strainer became clogged with bagacillo.

Once this technical problem was solved, not only could the tandems be lengthened but also maceration could be applied more thoroughly. Maceration combined mechanical and chemical processes of extracting sucrose from the canes; it became a crucial element in the grinding process for obtaining high extraction rates. Its application on a significant scale required additional complementary inputs. Maceration required large amounts of clean water, which was scarce in the generally isolated sites of the sugar mills in Cuba; therefore, additional capitalization was required to extend the water supply infrastructure. Other innovations also improved the multiple milling process. In general, they involved the invention or refinement of devices that could be added to the tandems. These included (pregrinding) cane preparation devices, improvements in the grinding mills themselves, filter presses, and loading and feeding devices, all of which were capital-embodied improvements.[6]

Economies of Scale in Milling

According to Alfred Chandler, the scale economies of continuous-process technologies were the impetus for the development of the modern form of business organization which internalizes activities to resolve coordination problems. He argues that it was primarily in the processing and refining industries that the initial innovations of this sort in manufacturing took place. The industries he examined most carefully were petroleum refining, metalworking, distillation, and grain processing,[7] but the technological developments in sugar production were actually as closely related to the general technological trends that played such an important role in Chandler's story. Many of the innovations in sugar mills were also important in the other processing industries. To illustrate, some of the more important innovations in the sugar mill had to do precisely with the refinement of continuous processing: improvements in the quality and design of roller mills that improved their resistance to stress, the development of hydraulic mechanisms to regulate the pressure applied to the cane and avoid mill jamming and breakage, improvements in the chemical process of cane juice filtering and vacuum evaporation, and increased application of moving belts, pumps, and other devices for the automatic conveyance of materials from station to station within the mill and of auxiliary gasoline or electric motors to drive these mechanisms. These were clearly the same improvements being adopted in other processing industries — improvements in roller-mill technologies, vacuum heating technologies, and conveyance mechanisms.[8] One suspects that they involved the same kinds of scale economies that Chandler recognized in other processing industries.

The scale economies that could be obtained in continuous-processing industries are easy to understand. The principle behind continuous processing was to cut down on the time that resources were idle as materials passed from one stage of production to the next. Introducing new technologies to improve the continuity of flow of raw materials wherever possible in the production line achieved this reduction in idle time, but the degree to which each activity of the production process could be made continuous varied. Some activities thus had the potential to form bottlenecks in the line of production, and they imposed constraints on the degree of continuity that could be achieved. The statements of managers reveal a preoccupation with preventing or quickly eliminating any bottle-necks that arose.[9] For example, in the production of sugar, physical and chemical properties of cane juice evaporation introduced indivisibilities because evaporation required a certain amount of time to be accom-plished. Further, there was a minimum scale required to perform the task economically. So if the scale of operation was small enough to allow only one evaporator, it had the potential to form a bottleneck in the produc-tion process. One way to increase the continuity of flow was to increase the scale of production so that two or more evaporators could be operated at once in a staggered fashion. This tended to reduce bottlenecks in evaporation.[10]

Although this example of the evaporation process in sugar manufacturing suggests the principle behind the economies of scale in sugar milling, the bottlenecks were most likely to form elsewhere in the production process. Evidence suggests that the problem of coordinating the grinding process at the mill with the cutting of cane in the fields was the most important bottleneck to be alleviated. Therefore, the benefits from improving coor-dination in the delivery of cane to the mill would likely have had the greatest effect in reducing idle time. The yields of sugar from the cane would also have improved.

Reliability of cane deliveries to the mill was of great concern to sugar factory managers. Unreliable deliveries were costly for two principal rea-sons. First, the quality of the cut cane deteriorated rapidly. As soon as cane is cut, the sucrose content declines steadily. Since the sole objective of sugar producers was to extract sucrose from the cane, any deterioration was monitored carefully and avoided.[11] A rule of thumb often mentioned was that it had to be ground within 24 hours of being cut. Otherwise the yield would have been unsatisfactory. Therefore, any delay in transporting cane that was already cut increased costs of production because the other inputs in the process were being applied to an inferior raw material. Sec-ond, if the mill was stopped because of a delay in cane delivery, boiler pressure was lost, and extra fuel and time had to be spent to build it up again whenever grinding was resumed. The standard practice was to run the mill 24 hours a day from the commencement of the grinding season and stop it intentionally only once a week for cleaning. The grinding season in Cuba was generally treated as a race to grind as much cane as possible from the time the first canes began to ripen, in December or January, to the first torrents of the wet season, in May or June. These were the months when the cane had the highest sucrose content.[12] So not only the fuel costs but also the time lost imposed serious costs to production if the mill had to be stopped unintentionally.

Records of mill stops suggest that delays in cane deliveries were by far the most important reason for unintentional interruptions in grinding. Oscar Zanetti Lecuona and Alejandro García Alvarez find that in their first decade of production, the Centrales Boston and Preston, owned by the United Fruit Company, lost 32 and 39 percent of the time available during the grinding seasons to interruptions in the flow of production. Moreover, 80 percent of the time lost at these mills was caused by delays in the delivery of cane.[13] They attribute this loss to poor organization of the centrales but note that the characteristics of these mills were not substantially different from those of other mills on the island.

The organization of grinding at one of the Rionda mills, the Central Francisco, shows a comparable set of problems. Managers' reports of the Central Francisco in Camagüey province, covering the grinding seasons of 1918 to 1922, record the number of hours stopped and the reason for each time the mill was stopped during the grinding season. The reports, summarized in Table 4.2, reveal that 68 percent of all the hours the mill was stopped during the grinding at the Francisco were caused by delays in the deliveries of cane to the mill. Another 16 percent of the total hours stopped were intentional — for routine cleaning or holidays. If we exclude the intentional stoppages from the total hours in the grinding season, 81 percent of the unintentional hours the Francisco mill was stopped between 1918 and 1922 was caused by the failure of coordination in some way between the cane fields and the mill.[14] The coordination problems of the Central Francisco may not be representative of other centrales. If not, the Francisco likely had fewer delays on average because it operated its own private cane rail network, and its railroad department was known for being successful. The importance of this was that none of its cane had to be carried over, or even cross, public service rail lines. Those centrales that did have to cross public service railroads to transport cane to their mills had additional coordination problems caused by negotiation costs and regulation of public railroad traffic that affected as well any traffic that crossed the public service railroad.[15] Centrales that had to deal with public railroad traffic considered it a serious relative disadvantage to their operations. Nonetheless, despite the potential advantages that might have accrued to a completely private cane rail network, a comment of a member of the Rionda family involved in the management of the Rionda family centrales suggests that the percentage of stops resulting from cane delays

Table 4.2
Mill Stops, Central Francisco, 1918–22

		Percentage Hour Stopped (tandems A and B combined) [a]				
	No cane at mill (percent of all stops)	Cleaning and holidays (percent of all stops)	Other (percent of all stops)		No cane at mills (percent of total hours grinding)	All stops (percent of total hours grinding)
1918	69	23	8		26	38
1919	62	21	17		15	25
1920	58	19	23		13	23
1921	77	12	11		27	35
1922	68	5	28		21	31
AVG.	68	16	16		21	30
		Hours Stopped (tandems A and B separate)				
	A	A	A	B	B	B
1918	1,568	339	2,063	369	306	743
1919	1,043	277	1,570	353	200	689
1920	823	178	1,224	139	134	426
1921	1,724	217	2,151	567	133	825
1922	971	66	1,426	654	50	981
AVG.	1,226	215	1,687	416	165	733
		Total Hours of Grinding Season				
			A			B
1918			3,696			3,698
1919			4,584			4,584
1920			3,623			3,624
1921			4,224			4,224
1922			3,863			3,864
AVG.			3,998			3,999

SOURCE: Author's compilation. Data from Braga Brothers Collection, Record Group 4, ser. 96.
[a] Each tandem is a single grinding production line.

at the Central Francisco was representative, at least of the eastern part of the island. He commented that "in the East the factories lose 20 percent of their time by reason of lack of cane." (He is referring to the percentage of time lost out of the total number of hours in the grinding season caused by delays of cane arriving at the mill.)[16]

A frequent cause of unreliability in cane delivery was heavy rains. Rain flooded the cane fields and halted the transport of cane out of the fields. Cane was transported to the mill in these centrales by rail networks, but the cane was loaded onto the rail cars at loading stations located strategically throughout the plantations. The cane was carried from the fields to these loading stations by oxcart, and heavy rains often made the fields impassable to the oxcarts.[17]

An important strategy could reduce the weather-imposed costs. Diversification of cane fields acted as insurance against the risks of heavy rainfall. The distances between the plantations of a central could be very great. A length of haul of 15 to 20 kilometers was not unusual, and for the largest centrales longer hauls were encountered.[18] Also, the plots of land controlled by the centrales were often not adjacent so that the weather conditions would vary widely from plantation to plantation within the area supporting the central. Managers could take advantage of the distances by altering their cane-cutting plans according to weather conditions. An additional factor that could be used to coordinate cutting with weather conditions was the soil types of distant fields. The soils suited to cane cultivation in Cuba differed in their permeability. More highly permeable soils, which drained more quickly, remained impassable by oxcart for a shorter period of time after a heavy rain so that cultivation could proceed in these fields sooner after the rain.[19] Therefore, more flexibility could be had for coordinating the harvest with weather contingencies by reserving the more permeable fields to take up slack after heavy rains. Ordinarily, it is believed that costs of organizing larger scales of production increase with scale. If this is true, then expanding production capacity to reap these economies of scale would require extension of the organizational capabilities of the central.[20] The largest centrales, of course, offered the greatest scope for making these choices, and, therefore, coordination could be more thorough the greater the scale of production. The economies of scale achieved in this way were not the only possible sources of economies of scale associated with innovations that increased the continuity of production, but their existence indicates one source that might have influenced the growth in the size of mills.

Technical Diffusion

The literature on the economics of technology addresses two broad issues. One involves the economic causes of technological change, conceived generally as the extension of the body of technological knowledge and ability. The other is the impact of technological change on productivity, welfare, or other features of the economy. This chapter is concerned with the second of these questions. It has been observed that the rates of adoption of new technology differed by mill and region. These differential rates are of great interest if they had some systemic, rather than random, cause.

When examining the history of technical progress, historians have traditionally given too much attention to the first appearance of an invention or new method relative to its more general economic application. Similarly, historians of Cuba interested in the rise of technology in the sugar industry have often placed much emphasis on the first uses of mechanical inventions or the early instances of centralization.[21] Yet for understanding the impact of technology on the economy, questions of origination are of secondary importance, and questions related to the process of adoption and diffusion are primary. For the reader unfamiliar with this body of literature, two excellent reviews have been written by Nathan Rosenberg and Joel Mokyr.[22] I do not duplicate these reviews here, but a brief survey of some issues will be useful.

The rate of technical diffusion often is slow and variable. And the slowness of diffusion is itself intriguing. In the early development of this literature, it fell upon researchers to explain why superior techniques were not adopted immediately after they appeared.[23] A general finding has been that producers' decisions to adopt a new technique of production—quickly or slowly—are firmly grounded in economic incentives. Differences observed in the timing of adoption by different producers are explained by the differing incentives they face. Studies of these issues have proceeded along two lines of investigation. Some examine the rate of diffusion and develop models to explain either the nature of the diffusion process or the causes of slowness and variability in technical adoption. Others examine impediments to diffusion to understand why the process is sometimes curbed or halted altogether. The substantial body of work that has been developed has resulted in a long list of economic, legal, institutional, organizational, environmental, and other factors that can have strong effects on a firm's adoption of a new technology.

One finding of this literature is the overwhelming role of local factor endowments. A classic example is the work of Peter Temin, who has shown that the slow adoption of coke in American iron production, despite its centrality as an innovation of the industrial revolution, was caused by the scarcity of high-quality coking coal east of the Appalachians. As a result, American iron producers used charcoal in the blast furnaces long after it had been abandoned in Britain.[24] I have noted a similar effect in the choices of technique in Cuba and Java. An abundance of land in Cuba led Cuban producers to continue with age-old land-intensive cane cultivation techniques with simple tools and naturally occurring cane varieties even when methods with higher yields of cane per acre were being used in Java. The higher-yielding methods made economic sense only when the factor endowment involved a scarcity of land. Land-scarce Javanese producers were compelled to seek high-yielding methods to make the best use of their land, but land-abundant Cuban producers were compelled not to adopt the high-yielding agricultural techniques for similar economic reasons.

International differences in factor endowments are often used to explain technical differences between countries. Similar arguments of factor availability can be valid at lower levels of observation — at the regional or firm or plant level. An important example to illustrate the point is the classic work by Paul David on the adoption of the mechanical reaper for harvesting wheat in the midwestern United States.[25] David argues that the size of an individual farmer's land endowment affected whether he was willing to purchase a mechanical reaper. The purchase price of the reaper represented a fixed cost that would be compensated for by savings in the labor expenses of mechanical reaping relative to manual reaping. Because those savings were proportional to the size of the crop, whether the labor-cost savings were sufficient to compensate for the purchase price of the mechanical reaper depended on the size of the crop or of the farm. David's study identifies a threshold farm size beyond which the farmer was willing to purchase the reaper and shows that this threshold was dependent on the market wage for farm labor and the price of reapers. Consequently, all else equal, the mechanical reaper was adopted more quickly on larger farms, but intermediate-sized farms also adopted it as midwestern farm labor became relatively more scarce and wages rose, as the purchase price of the reaper fell, and as the size of farm plots in the Midwest increased. From the conceptual standpoint, an important contribution of this study is the demonstration that an apparently superior technology, even if its advantageous attributes were well-known by all, would not be perceived as advantageous (profit-enhancing) to all potential adopters. Correspondingly, the process of diffusion of a new technology may indeed be the process of movement in the adoption threshold to absorb more of the potential adopters.

An alternative model perceives technical diffusion as the process of spreading information and experience about a new technology with uncertain attributes. The most common model of this sort has been adapted from models of the spread of epidemics.[26] Potential users are seen to adopt a new technology, with some positive probability, whenever they come into contact with it. Diffusion proceeds slowly in the initial stages because contact is infrequent. As more users adopt it, however, nonusers more frequently come into contact with it, and adoption accelerates. In the later stages of diffusion, as the number of remaining nonusers diminishes, the frequency of contact between users and nonusers declines, and the diffusion decelerates. Others have attempted to refine the resulting S-shaped diffusion curve by considering more carefully the role of information, uncertainty, and expectations about the profitability of the new method relative to the more certain outcome of known techniques.

W. E. G. Salter, taking a different approach from these studies, has attempted an alternative to the epidemic analogy and to the threshold model — the vintage-capital model.[27] His model has come to be accepted as a common, but not exclusive, explanation for the slowness of diffusion. He observes that within a given industry, firms will not necessarily incorporate an improvement into their existing plant and equipment, especially if it involves replacing an old with a new piece of equipment. To explain this behavior, he demonstrates theoretically that, under certain circumstances, whether a firm acts to adopt a technical improvement will depend on the age of the older capital equipment in place and the difference between the market price of the good being produced and the price per unit produced of the new equipment being contemplated. Diffusion of a new technology proceeds along two fronts, both as continuous modifications improve the attributes of the new technology and as the existing equipment ages or the gap in attributes between the existing and new equipment increases. The result has been a powerful model for understanding investment behavior when a continuous stream of improvements and modifications incrementally transforms an industry such as was experienced in the Cuban sugar industry.

The Vintage-Capital Model

Salter referred to his model as "a model for the delay in the adoption of best-practice techniques." It has since become commonly known as the "vintage-capital model." The basic assumptions behind the model are as follows.[28]

1. Technology was capital-embodied, and capital equipment was fixed with regard to the technology that it embodied; therefore, the level of technological advance of each piece of equipment in use could be identified by the year in which it was built, referred to as its "vintage."

2. There was a continuous flow of improvements in the technology, and each year new equipment appeared that embodied the new improvements

and extended the technical frontier of the industry. Change in the distribution of techniques in use was driven by this continuous revision of the best-practice technique.

Some definitions may also be useful for the reader not familiar with the terminology. A "technique," in distinction from "technology," is a single combination of machinery and other factors of production that a producer may select for use from the existing set of available technology. A "best-practice technique" is a technique that lies on the frontier of the available set in the sense that it offers the lowest operating costs per unit produced.[29] Techniques inside the frontier are divided into two categories. An "outmoded technique" is one that is in use, although it is not best practice. An "obsolete technique" is one that is retired. The analysis also relies, in its treatment of costs, on the common economic distinction between fixed and operating (or variable) costs. "Fixed costs" (or "sunk costs") are those incurred, or committed to, in a lump sum at the outset of the investment. An important fixed cost is the purchase of machinery, the price of which may not be recovered should the producer decide to replace it down the road with new machinery. "Operating costs" are those incurred to purchase variable factors of production — materials, fuel, and labor services — to operate the mill month by month, and they can be reduced or increased in proportion to the employment of those variable factors of production. In a decision at the margin, a user of outmoded equipment will compare the expected price (of sugar) with the operating costs per unit alone. If the price is lower than unit operating costs, purchasing the variable factors of production would not be economically justified.

Applied to the Cuban sugar industry, the model explains when producers would find it preferable to continue to use an outmoded technique rather than to adopt a new technique. Whereas new investments would be made to obtain the latest best-practice techniques, old techniques would remain in use. Even though the older techniques were technically inferior, they were able to compete with the best-practice techniques because the decision to continue producing with outmoded equipment was made ignoring any fixed costs of investment. The decision to invest in the best practice involved the willingness of producers to incur all the costs of production, including the fixed costs of purchasing and installing the new equipment, while the decision to continue producing with existing outmoded equipment involved only the ability to cover the operating (variable) costs. The fixed costs of the outmoded capital, having already been sunk, gave the outmoded equipment a means of competition with the latest techniques of production.

This model is employed to understand why decisions would be made either to adopt new technology, to continue to use an outmoded plant, or to close down an outmoded plant, recognizing it to be obsolete. Careful reasoning can explain why there was always a range of techniques in use at any time. It can also reveal features of the industry that affected how wide that range would be. Answers to these questions lead to more historically motivated questions, such as why during World War I there were so many apparently backward active sugar mills in Cuba, and why this changed after the war.

The range of techniques in use at any time was described by the decisions of those producers who were constructing new plants or closing old plants. The decision to build a new plant was made if the expected returns to the investment were positive. The expected returns were positive if the present value of all expected net operating profits (defined as the difference between the expected revenues and expected operating costs) over the life of the equipment was greater than the price and installation cost of the new equipment itself. Or put simply, the decision to purchase new machinery would be made if

$$\Pi_i^N - G_i^N \geq 0 \tag{4.1}$$

where Π_i^N is the present value of the expected stream of operating profits for mill i when using the new equipment, and G_i^N is the investment cost of the installation of the new equipment. Otherwise, it would not be purchased.[30]

An owner of an existing mill would have a slightly different criterion. He would have the option of adopting the new technology by updating the existing equipment at the mill. The decision would be made if the expected stream of operating profits using the new technology exceeded the expected stream under the old technology enough to cover the additional fixed costs of purchasing the new equipment. That is, if

$$\Pi_i^N - G_i^N \geq \Pi_i^O \tag{4.2}$$

where Π_i^O is defined as the stream of operating profits that would be expected of mill i from continuing with the outmoded equipment. This distinction between the right-hand sides of inequalities (4.1) and (4.2) is highly significant. It illustrates that the owner of an existing mill had an option that the newcomer did not have. The owner of an existing mill had the option of continuing to work with outmoded equipment. At times, Π_i^O would have been greater than $\Pi_i^N - G_i^N$. Whenever it was, retaining the outmoded equipment was more profitable.[31]

The decision to shut down an old plant was made if unit revenues from producing with the outmoded equipment did not exceed the unit operating (variable) costs. This criterion was the following:

$$p_t - v_{it} \geq 0 \qquad\qquad (4.3)$$

where p_t is the price of sugar for a given year, t, and v_{it} is the operating costs for mill i in year t. This inequality (4.3) illustrates simply that the decision to operate with outmoded equipment (rather than shutting down) depended only on whether the mill could cover its operating costs. The fixed costs incurred when the outmoded equipment was installed were "sunk" and could not be escaped, even if the mill shut down; therefore, the decision of whether to shut down did not involve the fixed costs.

These three equations define the two margins of the range of the techniques in use at time t. The first two define the margins at which new equipment appeared in the industry, and the third defines the margin at which old equipment was retired. An equilibrium was achieved when there was no incentive to invest and when there was no plant in operation not covering its operating costs. The equilibrium of this model describes a process of technical evolution that nicely parallels the patterns of variation in mill capacities in Cuba presented in Table 4.1.

With a continuous flow of technical improvements, the equilibrium would have steadily moved as time passed and as improvements were introduced in the industry. This moving equilibrium can be described nicely in a diagram to illustrate its application to Cuban mill capacities. A few simplifying assumptions are helpful for the exposition of the diagram, although they are not necessary for any conclusions that are made.

S.1. Assume that the plant was indivisible. This implies that all investments entailed the construction of new, complete plants; no investment could be made to improve old existing plant. Therefore, the vintage of each plant is identified by the year in which the plant was built.

S.2. Also assume that plants operated at some normal capacity.

S.3. Finally, assume the improvements in the techniques in use showed up in the operating costs of production so that the newer vintages had lower operating costs.

Given these simplifying assumptions, Figures 4.2 and 4.3 illustrate the moving equilibrium. In Figure 4.2, on the vertical axis are unit operating costs, and on the horizontal axis is the production of sugar. The markers,

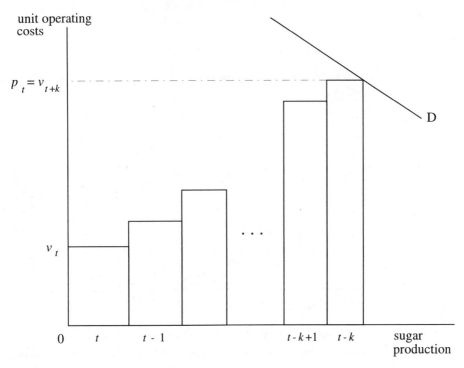

Fig. 4.2. Long-term equilibrium of an industry with vintage capital.

$t, t-1, \ldots, t-k$, represent the k techniques in use at time t, and the width of the corresponding blocks represents the amount of sugar produced using each technique. The demand, D, determines that the equilibrium price in the industry is p_t. The decisions to invest and shut down define the limits of the range of techniques. Looking at one end of the distribution, all vintages older than $t-k$ have stopped production because their unit operating costs exceed the current price. Looking at the other end of the distribution, at the best-practice technique, there must be an expected surplus of revenues over operating costs for a firm to be willing to invest in a new plant. In equilibrium, the gap between the unit operating costs and the price, $p_t - v_t$, is just sufficient to induce the investment in new equipment of vintage t.

Figure 4.3 demonstrates how the equilibrium will move over time as technical improvements extend the technical frontier in the industry. In Figure 4.3, a new technique is introduced with unit operating costs, $v_{t+1} < v_t$. Upon the introduction of the new vintage, $t + 1$, the range of already existing vintages is pushed to the right, as vintage t is displaced by vintage

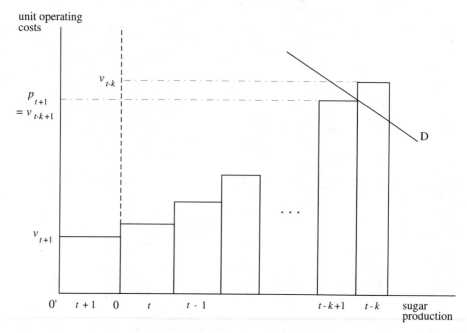

Fig. 4.3. Illustration of the moving equilibrium: The introduction of a new vintage. The origin of the diagram in year t is represented as 0. The current origin (for year $t + 1$) is 0'. The new vintage is $t + 1$. Its entrance increases the supply of sugar at each price such that the market price of sugar has fallen relative to its level in year t. Vintage $t - k$, which could continue operating in year t, has had to shut down in year $t + 1$ because it is no longer competitive with the more recent vintages given the demand. See Salter, chap. 5.

$t + 1$ as the low-cost technique. In the diagrams, the origin is 0 in Figure 4.2, but it is 0' in Figure 4.3. This shift of the distribution of vintages corresponds to an increase in the supply of sugar induced by the reduction in costs at the technical frontier. (The older origin, 0, is also shown in Figure 4.3.) If the demand remains unchanged, then the price falls from p_t to p_{t+1}. In response to the price reduction, the mills of vintage $t-k$ become obsolete, and they shut down. In this manner, if improvements in the technology are steadily being made, the entire range of techniques will steadily shift over time with a pattern similar to the one we observe in Cuban mill capacities. If we were to observe summary statistics of the unit operating costs of an industry that was innovating in this manner, we would see the mean unit operating cost of the industry decline steadily as well.

The problem with the standard vintage-capital explanation as it stands is seen by looking at the newly constructed mills in Cuba. The standard model predicts that new mills would enter the industry employing the best practice. Given a continuous increase in the optimal scale (which is investigated more carefully in the next section), this implies that new mills would generally have been larger than their predecessors, or at least as large. That was not the case with Cuban sugar mills. Figure 4.4 shows the capacities of each of the 26 mills that were newly established between 1917 and 1929 at the time of entry. Of these mills, 80 percent began small,

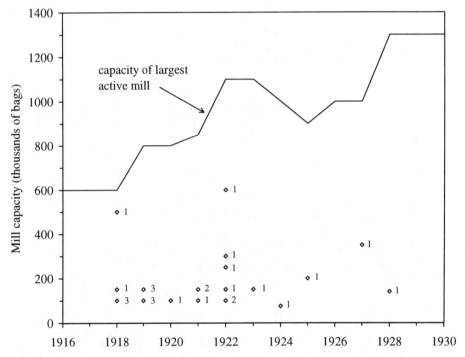

Fig. 4.4. Initial capacities of newly established mills, 1917–29. The capacities are given in thousands of bags of sugar, 1 bag = 325 pounds. All mills that were established in Cuba from 1917 to 1929 are included. The capacity given is the capacity of the mill in the first full season of grinding. There are many overlaid points on the diagram. To indicate the number of mills begun each year at each capacity, a numerical label has been placed beside each point to indicate the number of mills that entered in that year at the capacity indicated at that coordinate; e.g., three mills entered the industry in 1918 at a capacity of 100,000 bags. Source: República de Cuba, Secretaría de Agricultura, Comercio, y Trabajo, *Industria azucarera*, 1916/17–1929.

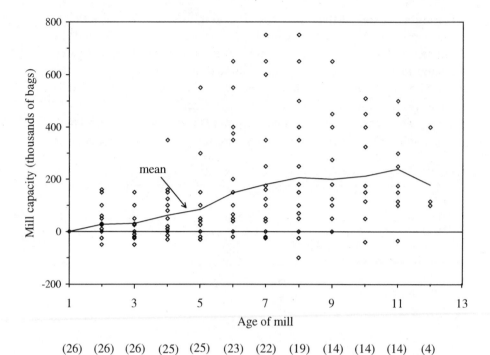

Fig. 4.5. Additions to capacities of mills established between 1917 and 1929. The y-axis indicates the sum of all additions made to the capacity of a mill after the first year of operation to the date indicated, exclusive of the initial capacity of the mill. In other terms, if x_1 is the initial capacity of the mill and x_t is the capacity of the mill at age t, then the quantity indicated by the y-coordinate of each point in the diagram is $x_t - x_1$. The x-axis indicates the age of the mill, or number of years the mill has been in operation. The initial year = 1. The numbers in parentheses below the x-axis indicate the number of new mills that reached each age during the years 1917–29. They thus indicate the "sample size" of new mills at each age. "New mills" are defined as mills established between 1917 and 1929. Source: See Fig. 4.4.

roughly between 100,000 and 200,000 bag capacity. The maximum capacities, in contrast, were between 800,000 and 1,300,000 bags. Furthermore, we observe that the majority of the new mills increased their capacities steadily after entry, as can be seen in Figure 4.5. The standard vintage-capital model does not explain why entering mills would consistently follow the pattern exhibited in Figures 4.4 and 4.5 — initially adopting apparently suboptimal capacities and increasing them steadily afterward. If there were economies of scale to be achieved at scales beyond 100,000 to 200,000 bags, why were new mills begun at suboptimal capacities? This question remains unanswered, so we will return to it below where we will recover the descriptive validity of the vintage-capital model for investment behavior in Cuban sugar mills. The steady but regular change in the distribution of mill sizes is explained by a gradual process of adjustment of entering mills to the optimal capacity.

Before doing this, we turn again to examine the economies of scale in milling. The predictions drawn above from the vintage-capital model depend on the assumption that the optimal scale of production was increasing steadily over time. A previous section of this chapter discussed how economies of scale were prevalent in continuous-processing technologies and some factors that explain them. Quantitative investigation of mill productivities also concludes that economies of scale were present in sugar mills in Cuba and shows that they were increasing over time during this period. The next two sections of the chapter develop and present an econometric model to demonstrate these conclusions.

Modeling the Sugar Manufacturing Processes

The production activities internal to the sugar mill consisted of several processes involving different departments within the mill — grinding, clarification, evaporation, and curing. The data available enable us to identify two processes — grinding (the process of extracting the cane juice by crushing) and recovery (the process of recovering the raw crystallized sugar from the cane juice, i.e., the combination of evaporation and curing).[32] These processes were performed sequentially, and their contributions to the product of the mill, raw sugar, are described in the following set of relationships.

$$y_{it} = \mu_{it}\xi_{it}c_{it} = \sigma_{it}c_{it}$$
$$y_{it} = \mu_{it}J_{it} \qquad\qquad (4.4)$$
$$J_{it} = \xi_{it}c_{it}$$

where y_{it} is the quantity of sugar produced by weight at mill i in year t, and c_{it} is the quantity of cane delivered and ground at the mill. J_{it} is the quantity of cane juice obtained from grinding the cane. The (juice) extraction rate, ξ_{it}, is the ratio of weight of cane juice obtained to the weight of cane ground, a measure of the productivity of the grinding process. The rate of (sucrose) recovery, μ_{it}, is the ratio of the weight of sugar obtained from the cane juice, a measure of the productivity of the recovery process. σ_{it} is known as the yield and is a measure of the joint productivities of these two activities in the mill.

Productivity measures. These measures of productivity are not those typically used to observe economies of scale because their increase can be caused by higher employment of alternative factors of production. An increase in the productivity of cane might be caused by a substitution of other factors. For the sugar mill, the most likely substitutes would have been labor and fuel. A lack of data for the labor use or fuel consumption of the mills in Cuba prevents us from observing directly whether substitution of this sort was occurring, but the prices of both mill labor and fuel behaved in such a way that there was no incentive for factory managers to substitute labor or fuel for cane. Figure 4.6 gives the wages of mill boiler workers relative to unit cane costs, and Figure 4.7 gives the relative price

Fig. 4.6. Wages of boiler workers relative to unit cane costs, 1919–28. Source: Braga Brothers Collection, Record Group 2, ser. 10a, box 7, f. 9; ser. 10c, box 27, ff. 27, 38; Record Group 4, ser. 96.

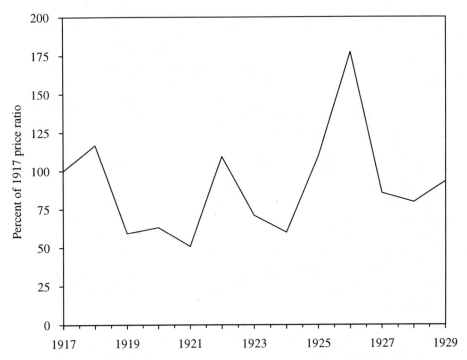

Fig. 4.7. Fuel oil prices relative to unit cane costs, 1917–29. Source: Braga Brothers Collection, Record Group 4, ser. 96; U.S. Bureau of Labor Statistics, 1917–30.

of fuel oil. Both rose over the period 1917 to 1929. They suggest that whatever increase is observed in either the yield or the extraction rate was not caused by changing factor price incentives that caused producers to substitute away from cane use toward greater relative intensity of other factors. Indeed, the relative price movements are consistent with the rapidly increased demand for all three inputs as the scale of output was increased but with lower supply elasticities for labor and fuel than for cane.

Price effects. The price data used for wages are the average wages paid to sugar boilers at the Central Francisco in Camagüey. The fuel price used is the average price of Oklahoma fuel oil, determined by the U.S. Bureau of Labor Statistics. The primary fuel used in the mills was the bagasse (or trash) from the cane. Historically, in Cuba the bagasse was supplemented with firewood, which was obtained from the forests surrounding the properties of the mill. Data for the costs of firewood collection are sketchy, but the labor used generally competed with labor either for planting or for harvesting cane because all these activities were conducted during the same season so the labor costs would likely be similar to the labor costs of harvesting. Another factor was the depletion of forests in Cuba, especially within proximity to sugar mills; this would have increased costs of collection. The factories were substituting fuel oil for wood to supplement the bagasse in the post–World War I period. The use of fuel oil gave greater control to maintain a constant level of steam pressure in the boilers. Constant steam pressure made operation of the mill proceed more smoothly, with fewer breakdowns.[33]

Cane quality. Accounting for the influences of weather is also important. Cuban sugar factories were without question subject to nontechnical influences that ensured differences in operating costs. The most obvious are the influences of soil and weather. The dependence of the Cuban sugar industry on its unusually favorable soils was well-known, and the varying soil qualities of the different regions were also well-known to have significant influence on the quality of the cane and on yields. Rain and sunshine also affected the quality of cane; these varied from year to year and introduced considerable uncertainty into manufacturing yields, σ_{it}.

For the quantitative analysis of the productivities of milling, it is essential to account for these influences; without effective measures of them, it would be difficult to attribute any variations in the productivities of mills to technical differences. Weather conditions and soil qualities affected the efficiency of production primarily through their effect on the quality of cane, so measuring the cane quality is a substitute for, and indeed is superior to, attempting to account directly for weather conditions. Fortunately, we have excellent measures of the qualities of the cane entering the mills, taken from the laboratories of each mill each year. Measurements describing several qualities of the cane are constructed from data reported by the mill managers to the Secretaría de Agricultura, Comercio, y Trabajo. The data were taken from the lab reports of each of the mills for each year from 1917 to 1929. The construction of the variables of cane qualities that enter into the regression model are made using chemical models of cane composition that employ the routine measurements taken in mill laboratories at that time.[34] The appendix to this chapter describes the data and procedure to construct the measures of cane quality used.

Correlation Between Mill Productivity and Capacity

In the historiography of Cuban sugar, the existence or effects of economies of scale have at times been ambiguous, even though there is little reason to doubt their existence or their effects on productivity. An example of such ambiguity is found in the writing of Julio Le Riverend, who, in discussing the appearances of the large centrales, argues that they were caused by the elimination of "deficient *ingenios*" and by "the drastic fall in prices."[35] Others have been unambiguous about recognizing the higher levels of productivity that larger mills offered producers.[36] To clarify, the downward trend in prices was a result of mills progressively reaping greater economies of scale. This on a global perspective represented an improvement in consumer welfare resulting from cost reductions enacted by new technology. But these improvements in welfare, as is usually the case in a competitive industry, accrued to the consuming rather than the producing countries.[37] For our analysis, changes in the degree of economies of scale are also of interest. Economies of scale exist when the optimal capacity of a mill is large so that there is a considerable range of capacities below the optimum which exhibits decreasing average costs or rising productivities in factors of production. Increases in the economies of scale were realized by an increase in the optimal scale, which extended the infraoptimal range over which productivities rose as the scale increased.

To examine the existence of economies of scale, the relationship between the productivities and the capacities of different mills is instructive. To examine changes in economies of scale over time, the average change in productivities as mill capacities increased needs to be examined. The following regression analysis of the statistical correlations between mill productivities and mill capacities captures the influences of capacity differences both between mills and over time by examining a panel of data that consists of a time series for each mill that ground cane between 1917 and 1929. Yearly observations of a number of useful variables were recorded for most active mills by the Secretaría de Agricultura, Comercio, y Trabajo.[38]

Four log-linear regression estimates are given in Table 4.3.[39] The four equations differ in two ways. Two dependent variables measuring productivities are examined. Columns A and B give estimates for which the yield (or sugar-to-cane ratio) is the dependent variable. Columns C and D give estimates for which the extraction rate (or the weight of the cane juice pressed from the weight of the cane) is the dependent variable. Linear and nonlinear relationships are considered. A strict linear relationship is estimated in columns A and C. Log-quadratic terms are added in columns B and D to test for nonlinearities in the relationships of the dependent variables with mill capacity. My primary interest is to discover whether the data reveal a positive relationship between the capacities of mills and their

Table 4.3

Regression of Mill Productivity Measures on Mill Capacity

Dependent variable:	Yield (sugar-to-cane ratio, by weight)				Extraction rate (cane juice-to-cane ratio, by weight)			
	A		B		C		D	
N	1,265		1,265		1,381		1,381	
F	77.210		55.027		21.626		16.600	
Prob > F	0.0001		0.0001		0.0001		0.0001	
R^2	0.481		0.491		0.171		0.195	
DW	1.970		1.961		1.787		1.832	
Explanatory variables:	Estimated coefficients	t-ratios	Estimated coefficients	t-ratios	Estimated coefficients	t-ratios	Estimated coefficients	t-ratios
A. Mill capacity interacted with provincial dummies								
Capacity, Pinar del Rio	0.045	1.755*	0.178	1.317**	0.033	2.346*	0.051	1.939*
Capacity, Havana	0.048	4.893**	0.087	0.561	0.021	3.795**	0.048	4.650**
Capacity, Matanzas	0.028	3.730**	0.112	1.635**	0.023	5.078**	0.024	2.672**
Capacity, Santa Clara	0.052	6.153**	0.047	0.922	0.027	5.663**	0.038	4.497**
Capacity, Camagüey	0.011	1.324	0.033	0.726	0.012	2.641**	0.027	3.222**
Capacity, Oriente	0.032	7.264**	0.038	1.458	0.012	4.916**	0.024	5.424**
Capacity², Pinar del Rio	—	—	0.026	1.179	—	—	-0.005	-0.787
Capacity², Havana	—	—	0.006	0.673	—	—	-0.008	-3.092**
Capacity², Matanzas	—	—	0.015	1.278	—	—	-0.000	-1.141
Capacity², Santa Clara	—	—	-0.001	-0.096	—	—	-0.003	-1.448
Capacity², Camagüey	—	—	0.004	0.518	—	—	-0.004	-1.863*
Capacity², Oriente	—	—	0.005	1.037	—	—	-0.003	-2.973**

			B. Cane quality control variables					
Sucrose in juice	0.813	15.823**	0.801	14.868**	—	—	—	—
Water in juice	−2.100	−1.795	−1.935	−1.589	—	—	—	—
Water in cane	3.136	11.100**	2.862	8.948**	0.488	4.869**	0.431	4.374**
C. Trend and constraints								
Year (1917 = 1)	0.003	4.634**	0.002	4.355**	0.003	7.501**	0.002	6.740**
Constant	−2.718	−1.889	−2.402	−1.564	1.800	14.751**	1.621	15.375**
Pinar del Rio	−0.033	−0.348	−0.291	−0.995	−0.048	−1.357	−0.056	−1.123
Havana	−0.065	−1.566	−0.178	−1.341	−0.023	−1.486	−0.045	−2.093*
Matanzas	0.015	0.447	−0.180	−1.190	−0.026	−2.018*	−0.010	−0.547
Santa Clara	−0.070	−1.951	−0.092	−0.766	−0.036	−2.623**	−0.034	−1.858
Oriente	0.093	2.396*	0.015	0.129	0.003	0.169	−0.002	−0.129

SOURCES: Author's calculations. Data are from Cuba, Secretaría de Hacienda, *Industria azucarera*, 1916/17–1929; Cuba, Secretaría de Agricultura, Comercio, y Trabajo, *Industria azucarera*, 1916/17–1929.

NOTE: All regressions were estimated in logarithmic form. The coefficients are GLS estimates that correct for first-order autocorrelation. * indicates significance at 0.05 and ** at 0.01.

productivities. To do this, I include several other independent variables, besides mill capacity, to control for other factors of influence. These include the quality of cane at each mill each year, accounted for by the measures developed in the appendix to this chapter—the sucrose content of the juice, the water content of the juice, and the water content of the cane. A control variable for the year is included to account for changes over time in productivity. One would expect this relationship to be positive in accordance with the effects on productivity of continual improvements to the available technology. Provincial differences are also accounted for by assigning dummy variables to each province and interacting them with the mill capacity variable. The reason for this is exploratory. The historiography of Cuba has placed considerable emphasis on the regional differences in the existence and productivities of large-scale mills. These dummy variables should capture quantitative differences that may have existed. When the estimated regression equations are examined, the consistency of those results with a priori expectations for the control variables lends confidence to the overall outcome of the regression.

The results yield a strong positive relationship between mill capacity and productivity. Columns A and C show that there was indeed a positive correlation between the productivities of the mills and their capacities. The estimated coefficients in Panel A of Table 4.3 are all positive, and all are significant at levels of 0.05 or better, except for the province of Camagüey in column A. These correlations in themselves are consistent with the existence of economies of scale over the existing range of mill capacities. When we consider in conjunction with these results our observations regarding the wage and fuel price trends relative to the cost of cane, the results of this regression give strong evidence of the existence of economies of scale over the entire range of existing capacities of mills.

Second, in columns A and C the estimated coefficient for the relationship between productivities and time (or the year) is significant at the 0.01 level. This shows that the trend in the mean productivity of the mills was increasing, as expected. One might interpret this result as an indication that the optimal scale of production was, in fact, increasing during this period. Third, the signs of the cane quality variables are consistent with the a priori expectations, and they are significant at the 0.01 level. This result lends confidence to the measures of cane quality and assurance that the influences of soil and weather have been adequately controlled for. Fourth, the estimated coefficients on the provincial dummy variables show no consistent statistically significant differences in productivities by provinces unaccounted for in the other independent variables.

Finally, observing the coefficients of columns B and D, the estimates do not corroborate the existence of nonlinearities in the relationship between productivities and mill capacities. The quadratic terms were added to test for the existence of a peak in the level of productivity at an intermediate capacity within the range of mill capacities in use during these years. The more inclusive test is the one represented in column B, where the yield (or sugar-to-cane ratio) is the dependent variable, given that it incorporates all the manufacturing processes. In column B, it is seen that the logarithmic terms were not statistically significant for any of the provinces. When the productivity measure is decomposed to consider the extraction rate, the results change only marginally. The coefficients for the quadratic terms on the extraction rate, in column D, are significant only for the provinces of Camagüey, Oriente, and Havana, where the absolute largest mill capacities were found. These results suggest that a limit to scale economies in the grinding process alone was reached in the few mills of greatest capacity found in the provinces of Oriente and Havana. But recalling the results of column B, the returns to scale of other activities in the production of sugar must have offset the optimal scale associated with the grinding process because quadratic terms for the overall sugar-to-cane ratio were statistically insignificant. Undoubtedly, the great majority of mills faced increasing economies of scale because of the high and temporally rising optimal scale of production.

Vintage-capital effects and adjustment costs prevented an immediate increase to the new optimal scales. Organizational barriers to large-scale operations may also have caused costs per unit to rise as the size of the mill organization increased, and this as well may have impeded the immediate assumption of the technically optimal scale. If so, the pattern of investment behavior suggests that the organizational problems were being solved over time to permit an efficient growth in the scale of production to reap the technical benefits of scale economies revealed in this quantitative exercise. Despite these frictions to the process of expansion, incentives of a purely technical nature did exist to encourage an increasing scale of production at virtually all mills over this period of time.

Newly Constructed Mills

Given the empirical support for both capital embodiment and economies of scale, the vintage-capital framework seems to be a good explanation for the pattern of change in mill capacities, except that the newest mills entered at suboptimal capacities, which is contradictory to the vintage-capital framework because the new mills appear not to have adopted the most efficient techniques of production. Why did newly constructed mills usually enter the industry at suboptimal capacities? It also happened that the new mills often increased in scale in the years following their first grinding seasons. Figure 4.5 gives the additions to the capacities of the new mills after the first year of their operation. It appears from these observations that there were some costs associated with the rate of investment, costs of adjustment, which prevented the immediate adoption of the optimal capacity. In the remainder of this chapter and in Chapter 5, I explore the evidence that supports this hypothesis.

An alternative hypothesis that must also be considered is that the restraints on new mills' initial adoption of the optimal capacity were related to imperfections in the capital markets. The capital available to Cuban sugar producers came primarily from three sources — Cuba, Spain, and North America. Cuban and Spanish credit was much less abundant, however; therefore, those mills that could gain access to North American credit were less likely to face capital restrictions, or at least faced less severe ones. Given imperfections in the flow of information between Cuba and New York, those mills that had greater orientation toward North America had an advantage in gaining access to North American credit.[40]

Evidence on the orientation of mills suggests, however, that the restraint on the initial size of the new mills was not related to inaccessibility of credit. A rough indicator of the orientation of the mill is the name of the sugar company that owned each mill. Most of the mills were incorporated either in the United States or in Cuba. Stockholders in any company, regardless of orientation, could have been of either nationality or Spanish or European. If the name of the company was in English, however, an orientation of the company toward the United States clearly existed, and should unequal access to credit explain the adoption of suboptimal capacities, the firms with English names would have been less likely to face those capital restrictions. The data show that firms with English names had no advantage. Of the eight new mills in firms with English names, only one was started at a capacity greater than 200,000 bags. And of the eighteen new mills in firms with Spanish names, four started with capacities greater than 200,000 bags. In other terms, 88 percent of the new mills with greater U.S. orientation began at small capacities, and 78 percent of the mills with less orientation toward the United States began at small capacities. The failure to adopt initially the optimal capacity appears not to have been related to any imperfections in the capital markets. It appears more

Table 4.4
Increase in Capacities of New Mills

	Capacity in first year of grinding (000s bags of 325 lbs.)	Capacity in 1929 (000s bags of 325 lbs.)	Increase in capacity to 1929 (percentage)	Year founded	Province[a]
Average, English-named firms	156.3	468.8	252.1		
Average, Spanish-named firms	193.6	321.7	68.7		
New mills in firms with English names[b]					
La Francia	100	200	100.0	1918	1
Hershey	100	600	500.0	1919	2
Velasco	200	300	50.0	1925	5
Violeta	150	600	300.0	1919	5
Macareño	150	300	100.0	1922	5
San German	100	750	650.0	1921	6
Miranda	150	550	266.7	1918	6
Tanamo	300	450	50.0	1922	6
New mills in firms with Spanish names[b]					
Niágara	100	100	0.0	1922	1
San Cristobal	150	200	33.3	1921	1
Lincoln	100	215	115.0	1918	1
María Luisa	100	150	50.0	1922	4
Agabama	75	140	86.7	1924	4
Santa Isabel	150	150	0.0	1921	4
Estrella	100	400	300.0	1919	5
Pilar	150	300	100.0	1919	5
Santa Marta	350	350	0.0	1927	5
Najasa	160	180	12.5	1921	5
Jaronu	600	1,100	83.3	1922	5
Cunagua	500	600	20.0	1918	5
Vertientes	250	1,000	300.0	1922	5
Estrada Palma	200	240	20.0	1925	6
Cacocum	100	65	−35.0	1918	6
Mabay	100	150	−50.0	1920	6
Maceo	150	125	−16.7	1923	6
Baguanos	150	325	116.7	1919	6

SOURCES: Author's compilation. Data are from Cuba, Secretaría de Hacienda, *Industria azucarera*, 1916/17–1929; Cuba, Secretaría de Agricultura, Comercio, y Trabajo, *Industria azucarera*, 1916/17–1929.

[a] Provinces are 1, Pinar del Rio; 2, Havana; 3, Matanzas; 4, Santa Clara; 5, Camagüey; 6, Oriente.

[b] The names in the table are of the centrales. The names of the firms are not given in the table.

to have been related to the costs of construction of plant and establishment of cane fields.

The lower likelihood, apparent in Table 4.4, that mills lacking U.S. orientation would succeed in expanding their capacities may be an indication of imperfections in capital markets or unequal access to capital. The

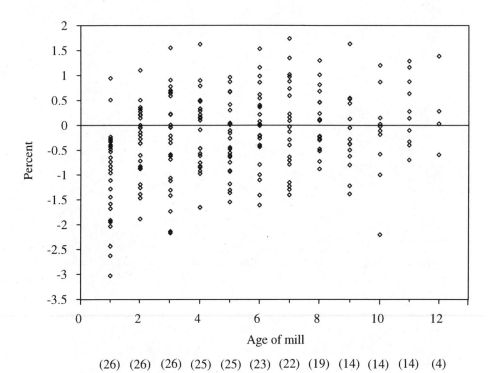

(26) (26) (26) (25) (25) (23) (22) (19) (14) (14) (14) (4)

Fig. 4.8. Difference of the percent annual yields of mills from the mean percent annual yield of all Cuban mills, 1917–29. The y-axis indicates the difference $\sigma_{it} - \overline{\sigma}_t$, where σ_{it} is the yield (the sugar-to-cane ratio by weight) of mill i in year t and $\overline{\sigma}_t$ is the mean yield in year t for all mills grinding in Cuba that year. The numbers in parentheses below the x-axis indicate the number of new mills that reached each age during the years 1917–29. They thus indicate the "sample size" of new mills at each age. Source: See Fig. 4.4.

mills with greater orientation toward the United States were more likely to expand their mills beyond their initial capacities once they were established. The mills with greater U.S. orientation increased their capacities on average by 252 percent. And the mills with less orientation toward the United States on average expanded their capacities by only 69 percent of their initial capacities. However, other factors may have created or contributed to the same effect. We return to this question in Chapters 6 and 7. It appears necessary to separate our investigation of the entry behavior and the postentry, expansion behavior of new mills.

Besides noting that new mills entered the industry at small initial capacities and then expanded their capacities after having been established, we also observe that the cane requirements of these new mills were high (or their yields were low) in their first few years of operation, suggesting that the costs of adjustment affected the cane requirement. Figure 4.8 plots the relative yields of new mills in their first few years of operation.[41] On the vertical axis is the difference between the yearly yield of the new mill and the average yield of all the mills operating in Cuba that year. On the horizontal axis is the age of the mill, that is, the number of years the mill had been in operation. The plot shows that the new mills generally achieved below average yields in, say, the first three years of operation. But after the first three years, their yields began to center on the overall mean yield achieved by all mills in Cuba.

The immediate impression of Figure 4.8 may be that there was a learning curve in sugar manufacturing. Upon entry into production, any new mill would have an initial few years of suboptimal productivity as the operators accumulated experience with skills as well as plant-specific and organization-specific characteristics of the newly constructed mill. Such learning behavior, referred to in the economic literature as "learning by using," would account for the initial rise and then the leveling off of the curve implicit in the scatter diagram of Figure 4.8; but it does not account for the patterns of mill entry at suboptimal capacities observed in Figures 4.4 and 4.5. However, considered as a subset of a more general phenomenon, learning along with other early problems of adjustment provides the most satisfactory explanation for the combined patterns observed in these graphs. The more general phenomenon is the existence of costs that act as friction to the process of capital accumulation. Whenever capacity was expanded, there were several input requirements, along with learning requirements, associated with the activity of expansion itself, classified as adjustment costs.

The investment costs a mill would incur when expanding its capacity consisted of the purchase prices of equipment, materials, and land and the labor and financing costs incurred for construction, installation, and land clearing. These costs varied roughly in a constant proportion to the proposed addition to capacity — an expenditure more or less fixed per unit of additional capacity. Adjustment costs were additional to these costs. They were not installation costs per se, which should be considered part of the total cost of a machinery purchase; rather, they were the increment in installation costs that would be required to *speed up* installation. Or in other words, they were associated with the *rate* at which all the services for setting up — construction, installation, and so on — were performed. If the additional capacity had to be built at an unusually fast pace, a premium over the "normal" cost of installation would have been incurred to accomplish it. These could be nonmonetary as well as monetary costs. For example, bounds on the learning capacity of the central's work force or organization would result in diminishing marginal learning by using as the rate of investment increased, acting as a nonmonetary adjustment cost.

The existence of appreciable adjustment costs explains the combined patterns of mill entry observed in Figures 4.4, 4.5, and 4.8. Costs that rose with the rate of investment in new capacity prohibited the immediate construction of a mill of considerable scale. They invoked a pattern, instead, of gradual investments, year by year, which began at a low capacity — both of machinery and cane supply — and approached a larger target optimal scale of production at a rate of investment that weighed the benefits and costs of the additions in capacity needed to reach that optimal scale.

If one accepts adjustment costs as the explanation for the anomalous low-capacity entry of mills, then the usefulness of the vintage-capital model to explain the variation in the rate of technical adoption between mills in the sugar industry is reaffirmed. There is considerable evidence that adjustment costs were indeed an important influence in the act of mill expansion. Chapter 5 will look more carefully at this evidence.

Conclusion

To summarize the findings of this chapter, first, we have found that correlations between yields and extraction rates of mills and their capacities corroborate the existence of economies of scale. This empirical support is useful because it permits the scale of production to be used as a rough indicator of technical advance mill by mill. Mill capacity, therefore, is used as the best available indicator to rank the level of technical advance and to identify mills operating with the best-practice technology. An important source of the economies of scale was organizational — related to the ability to diversify the effects of weather on the fields, which was a function of the land area from which cane supplies were drawn. Larger landholdings were associated with more efficient land use because there was less waste of sucrose as a result of unfavorable weather conditions. Diversification of cane fields permitted greater flexibility in adapting to unpredictable conditions.

Overall patterns of mill expansion corroborate the influence of vintage capital. Both the assumptions of the model (capital embodiment and continuity of technical change) and the observed pattern of variation in mill capacities support a strong vintage-capital effect on the rate of adoption of new technology. Yet there is an important anomaly in the observed pattern of expansion in mill capacity. Despite the economies of scale in milling and the increasing optimal scale of production, new mills almost always entered at a small initial scale. After their first years of operation, many of them expanded to a larger, long-run optimal scale, but the adoption of the large scale came only after they were initially founded. Furthermore, during their first years of operation, on average their productivities were initially low, and they rose only as time elapsed and as the capacities of the mills were increased. This observation suggests that high adjustment costs caused mills, as they entered the industry, initially to adopt suboptimal scales of operation from which they would expand gradually to their desired scale, to keep adjustment costs relatively small.

In Chapter 5, we find that the sources of the costs of adjustment were primarily costs of installing equipment and establishing cane fields. An examination of both technical features of production and empirical evidence shows that a major influence was the apparent inelasticity of skills in Cuba and in the United States for installing physical capital specific to sugar mills. Learning effects could also have contributed to the costs of adjustment. Another influence was likely the local inelasticity of labor supplies needed for construction and additional plantings. Because much of the construction was performed in the dead season, the labor constraint on construction may not have been binding. Nonetheless, the labor constraint on planting, because it coincided with the cane cutting season, likely was binding. These issues are discussed in detail in the next chapter.

In contradiction to the nationality-based explanation about differences in levels of technology at mills, we have seen that much of the heterogeneity of techniques is explained by the fact that producers faced different constraints vis-à-vis their fixed capital. Some producers received higher profits by delaying an investment in new equipment, rather than responding immediately. Whether or not they perceived updating their mills as a profit-increasing move depended on the vintage of their existing equipment. The vintage-capital effect does not exclude the possibility of barriers to access to new technologies, but it does invalidate the use of a simple observation of technical differences as evidence of such barriers. Admittedly, the unequal distribution of techniques between Cuban and

North American mills might still have been caused by differential access. The recognition of vintage-capital effects nonetheless clarifies a central issue. Absent any barriers to competition or access to technology, there would still have been a distribution in which newcomers to the industry disproportionately had both better technology and higher outlays to cover fixed costs.

Implications for the Post-1921 Adjustment

The foregoing analysis has broader implications that serve to clarify the reasons for some of the economic trends of this age of expansion of Cuban sugar. Nationality or politically based explanations of investment trends seem to connect only loosely to specific events of the period. The effects of the rising optimal scale, vintage capital, and adjustment costs revise an accepted view of the mechanisms of foreign influence on the Cuban economy. The investment trends once thought of as an outcome of foreign control of the industry are seen to have another explanation related to the transfer of mass production technology to Cuban sugar.

Table 4.4 shows that among the entering mills, the ones most likely to succeed at expanding after their start-up years were North American mills. One proposed explanation is that there may have been imperfections in the capital markets which gave North American mills (as well as some others with established credit connections or reputations) fewer barriers to obtaining credit needed for expansion. If this was true, then a number of mills may have failed to reach their optimal capacities, even after their initial start-ups, because unexpectedly they were unable to obtain credit. Under such circumstances, those mills in Table 4.4 that failed to increase their capacities might be seen as having faced some kind of market imperfection. The consequence of remaining at lower capacities was that they were left operating inefficiently. At the high prices of World War I, survival with a relatively inefficient technique was possible, and mills with a broad range of efficiencies — old and new — operated side by side. But in the declining price regime after 1920, many old mills and some relatively new ones had to close down.

Another ramification concerned the continued expansion of suboptimal mills even after the perceived aggregate capacity of the island was no longer expanding. Both the adjustment-cost and vintage-capital effects on individual mills had important implications for the rate of aggregate capacity creation.

The 1920s in Cuba are known as a period of an apparently irrational continued expansion of aggregate sugar mill capacity despite signs that pointed to a pending sugar crisis. As Figure 2.5 shows, the price of sugar was abnormally high during World War I. Investors in North America responded to the disruption of European beet sugar production by directing new resources toward the expansion of mill capacity in Cuba. Construction of new mills in Cuba had never been more active than during World War I. Thirty-five mills were founded between 1913 and 1919. This represented almost 20 percent of the number of mills in operation in Cuba by the end of the war.[42]

Mounting signs after the war suggested that the newly created global capacity for sugar production might not be viable. After the price bubble of 1920, it was clear that the high wartime prices would not be maintained. As European beet sugar recovered, there was talk of overproduction and a general glut in the market. The stocks of sugars in warehouses began to accumulate.[43]

Meanwhile, the tariff restrictions in Cuba's major market began to tighten. In 1913, the U.S. tariff on sugar had acted as an additional stimulus to the wartime expansion, having been reduced by about 6 percent. After the war, however, agricultural prices collapsed from a half to a third of their former levels, not only in sugar but also in wheat, corn, cotton, and meat. Farmers in the United States reacted by seeking and obtaining protection, first in the form of the Emergency Tariff Act of 1921, then by the Fordney-McCumber Tariff Act of 1922. The sugar tariff was raised by 75 percent over the 1913 tariff.[44]

But unexpectedly, existing mills continued to expand their capacities after the war.[45] Jenks and other scholars have associated this apparently irrational expansion as a manifestation of the transfer of much sugar property into the hands of North American banks after 1920. The following statement represents Jenks's attempt to explain these events.

The leading characteristic of this era has been a feverish attempt to reduce the unit cost of producing sugar by increasing mill efficiency, through more powerful machinery, more thorough extraction of the sucrose content of the cane, and an expansion of the volume of sugar produced at a mill. Hence, despite the grave warning of the crisis, the output of sugar in the island of Cuba went on increasing until in the crop year 1924–25, it amounted to 5,125,970 long tons, 30 percent more than in the crisis year, and in 1927 enough cane for 6,000,000 tons was grown. American mills took a leading part in this expansion. . . .

To many this expansion seemed suicidal. It was directly responsible for the critical condition of the sugar industry in Cuba for the last three years. Nevertheless, when it is recalled that the control of industrial and agricultural credit in Cuba had come chiefly into the hands of the North American banks, the logic of the policy becomes clear. As one of the wealthiest Americans in Havana summarized the situation for me, in 1926, " . . . [the banks] will lend money only to take care of the properties they are interested in."[46]

According to Harold van B. Cleveland and Thomas F. Huertas's study, from the 1926 crop National City Bank refused to advance capital to its own mills as well.[47] The other banks likely adopted the same policy. But even if this rationing of credit to the centrales in which the banks had direct interests did occur as the rate of growth in sugar slowed in 1926 and afterward, it does not explain why the mill owners or the controlling bank officials would want to expand mill capacities under such market conditions. At first glance, the expansion of aggregate milling capacity on the island — the tendency toward overproduction — does not seem consistent with the incentives of investors. If sugar market conditions warned of a general disaster for the Cuban industry, then continued investment in the industry would not have been advisable either for Cuban or for North American investors. Under circumstances of falling prices and rising stocks of sugar, how can one explain the investment in additional capacity?

The implied influences of adjustment costs and vintage-capital effects on individual mill investment behavior both provide elements of an explanation. First, from the entry behavior we have observed, the 35 mills built during the war had reason to continue expansion until they reached their optimal capacities. Each of these mills entered the industry with a capacity adjustment plan built into the original blueprints. Without the planned increase in capacity, the entering mill would have been left operating at a suboptimal capacity, which might have been profitable during the high wartime prices, but as the price of sugar fell, it would not have been viable in the long run.[48]

Second, the vintage-capital model reveals the mechanism by which the aggregate mill capacity was determined, and it points to the importance of considering both entering and exiting mills. Especially with such a dynamic technology, it was natural that obsolete mills were continually replaced with best-practice mills. Without this dynamic, the Cuban industry would not have remained competitive internationally. The vintage-capital model, and in particular the diagram of Figures 4.2 and 4.3, reveal how important the market price was as a determinant of this process. This is evident when one focuses on the margins of innovation and obsolescence in the diagrams, or the points at which mills decided to enter and to shut down. The high prices of World War I encouraged new mills to enter. Given best-practice unit operating costs, the gap between operating costs and revenues increased and rendered higher profits. The higher price also extended the margin of obsolescence. Outmoded mills that at a lower price would have shut down remained in operation at higher wartime prices because their higher operating costs were being covered by higher earnings. Once the war was over, however, marginal producers were forced to readjust to the lower prevailing price of sugar. Because the war had delayed the process of retiring outmoded mills, the aftermath of the war was cataclysmic for many older mills. Since most of these were domestically owned, the North American share of ownership of sugar mills increased after the war. Meanwhile, just inside the margin of innovation, the mills founded during the war had already sunk considerable investments into fixed capital, and it was in their interests both to remain in operation and to continue to expand capacity in line with their original adjustment-cost-constrained investment plans.

An important implication, apparent in the above paragraph, is that the decision at the obsolescence margin was largely independent of the entry of new mills at the best-practice margin. Recalling the criterion at the obsolescence margin, illustrated by inequality (4.3), it depended only on the price and the internal operating costs of the mill at the obsolescence margin. As long as the sugar price was fixed in international markets and relatively insensitive to capacity in Cuba, the decision to close down a mill at one margin was independent of the decision to build at the other.

In 1921 during the financial reorganization after the 1920 debacle, the major Cuban and Spanish banks had collapsed, and the New York banks suddenly dominated the Cuban banking industry. Furthermore, North American banks had foreclosed on many sugar properties and found themselves controlling a large portion of the industry. Investment in the sugar industry continued to flourish. Peak levels of production were reached in 1925, and the former growth or prosperity had returned. But many Cubans were alarmed by the recent change of ownership. Control of the industry had passed out of the hands of an old Cuban elite group into the hands of North American corporations and banks. Some well-placed Cubans were investors, directors, and managers of these corporate operations, along with other well-placed North Americans and Spaniards. But the transfer of directorships in these companies did appear to be a transfer of power from a conservative national elite group to a new managerial capitalist group with an alliance to North American big business.

The Cuban version of proprietary capitalism was giving way to the ongoing managerial revolution taking place in the sphere of North American capitalism. Accelerated by World War I, the long-term ramifications of this expansion were not truly seen until the 1920s, when the mills founded during the war reached their desired capacities and prices returning to normal levels forced many marginal Cuban producers out of business.

Appendix: Measuring Cane Quality to Account for Soil and Weather Influence

This appendix describes the data recorded from the lab reports and the procedure for converting them into useful measures of cane quality that are used to account for the effects of weather and soil quality on the yields, or sugar-to-cane ratios, in the regression estimations of Chapters 4, 5, and 7. These measures are constructed from lab data reported in the *Industria azucarero: Memoria de la zafra* of the Cuban Secretaría de Agricultura, Comercio, y Trabajo for the years 1917 to 1929. The raw data represent routine measurements taken in the laboratories at the factories. These data have been examined carefully for accuracy. There is an arithmetic relationship between some of the figures in the reports so that the internal consistency of the data for each mill could be tested. Also there are clear definitional limits to the values that these lab measurements could take. Any implausible values indicate errors in the data and have been discarded, but these were few in number. This section is concerned with the problem of making use of the raw data available by converting them into measures of cane quality useful for the quantitative analysis.[49]

The qualities that I use to capture the effects of cane quality are the percentage weight of water in the cane, the percentage weight of water in the cane juice, and the sucrose content in the cane juice. Cane is composed of water, dry substance (soluble), and fiber (insoluble). If W, D, and F are the weights of the water, dry substance, and fiber in the total weight of the cane (C), then

$$C = W + D + F \qquad \text{(A.4.1)}$$

In cane sugar manufacture, the grinding process was performed to separate $W + D$ from F. The cane juice is composed of sucrose (S), residual substances (R), and water.

$$J = S + R + W \qquad \text{(A.4.2)}$$

where $J = W + D$ and $D = S + R$. The recovery process was performed to separate S from $R + W$.

In the statistical analysis we control for the composition of the cane entering each mill. The quality that affected the grinding process which we account for is the water content of the cane, W/C. Qualities that affected recovery which we account for were the sucrose and water contents in the juice, S/J and W/J.

The reported data are the percentage of sucrose in the cane S/C, the percentage of sucrose in the cane juice S/J, and the Brix (B), or the specific gravity, of the cane juice, which was used to measure the percentage weight of dry substance in the cane juice.[50] The water contents of the cane and the juice are determined very simply. The juice is composed of water and dry substance. If J is the weight of the juice, W is the weight of the water in the juice, and D is the weight of the dry substance, then $W = J - D$. Therefore, since $B = D/J$,

$$\frac{W}{J} = 1 - B. \tag{A.4.3}$$

If we, further, make the assumption that all the water in the cane has been extracted, then, if C is the weight of the cane ground,

$$\frac{W}{C} = (1 - B)\left(\frac{S/C}{S/J}\right). \tag{A.4.4}$$

Using equations (4.7) and (4.8), we transform the factory data in the reports of the Secretaría de Agricultura, Comercio, y Trabajo into useful measures of cane quality. The measures used in the regressions of Chapters 4, 5, and 7 are the water in the cane and in the juice and the sucrose in the juice.

Chapter 5

Central Mill Expansion and Costs of Adjustment

THE 1920 FINANCIAL CRISIS had grave consequences for the domestic banking industry and the sugar industry. Uncertainty as to what was happening in the economy interrupted growth in production. Nonetheless, there was no lasting reduction in production. Recovery was swift with a high market price in 1923 and expanded production afterward. Jenks suggests that it was the continued health of the sugar industry that pulled the rest of the economy back into economic prosperity by 1923. The Fordney-McCumber Tariff Act did not have the injurious effect expected on Cuban sugar exports to the United States.[1] However, the distribution of ownership of sugar properties was deeply affected. The crisis was the critical point at which not only North American control of the industry increased substantially but the industry became more concentrated. Many mills in financial arrears were sold or taken over by creditors, and ownership fell into the hands of large commercial and banking houses.[2]

The aggregate processing capacity of Cuban sugar increased considerably during the early 1920s, largely as a result of attempts to improve the efficiency of mills founded during the war. At the end of World War I, many mills were at a suboptimal capacity and continued to expand. A large number of mill owners in danger of defaulting on bank loans could demonstrate that, although their estates at their present capacities were not profitable, investments in additional equipment and an increase in the scale of production would reduce unit costs sufficiently to make their operations profitable. New York banks, which in general were overexposed to Cuban sugar, were thus under pressure to advance additional loans to finance improvements in the hope that the borrowers could repay their debts. This pressure to make additional loans also came from the banks' own shares in many mills which they had acquired as a result of sales and foreclosures during the 1920 crisis. Whether they wished to keep them or sell them, they were advised to channel further investments into their mills to reap the potential economies of scale and boost their shares' values on the stock market.[3] Many of these mills were in such a suboptimal state after the war because of the effects of adjustment costs, as discussed at the end of Chapter 4. The effects of adjustment costs thus became a force of considerable historical significance in relation to the upward adjustment of mill capacities in the 1920s.

Adjustment costs are a feature of the cost structure of any capital-intensive production unit. They were not unique to the sugar industry. Nonetheless, their influence is sometimes overlooked. The concept has received considerable theoretical treatment, and a convincing case has been made for the significance of the effects of adjustment costs on investment behavior. But less attention has been given to their application. Because of a lack of general familiarity with them, I first look into their definition and intuition, then at the evidence to demonstrate that adjustment costs were an important — and large — component of the cost structures of Cuban sugar mills. The central sections of the chapter trace the sources of adjustment costs in the processes of sugar production. In the end, the reader will sense how they introduced an inertia into the expansion of mill capacities and how they were behind the so-called tendency toward overproduction. The final section presents lower bound estimates which indicate that the adjustment costs faced by entering mills were indeed substantial. Given their magnitude, the effect attributed to adjustment costs in stimulating expansion of mill capacities even under unfavorable market conditions is understandable.

The Concept of Adjustment Costs

In the economics literature, focus on adjustment costs came about with the development of the neoclassical theory of investment. It arose out of a debate over the existence of the investment function. The standard formal neoclassical theory of the firm inadvertently predicted that a finite level of investment for an individual firm could not exist—a conclusion that everyone knew did not conform with reality. Under competitive conditions, in the static neoclassical formal model, if the desired stock of capital should change, the firm would adjust instantaneously to that new desired stock. Distress over the incongruity of this theoretical result with common experience stimulated a series of papers dealing with investment as a dynamic optimization problem.[4] The principal contribution of this series of papers was to point out the crucial role that the hitherto neglected cost concept played in constructing a model of investment that exhibited more realistic (finite) rates of investment. This cost concept—adjustment costs—was the key element in intertemporal models of investment behavior that displayed a meaningful pattern of investment. To the practitioner, this meant that until this discovery a fundamental determinant of the rate of investment in firms had been overlooked. To date most of the analysis of adjustment costs has remained theoretical and highly abstract. Empirical identification and incorporation of adjustment costs into applied work is still at an early stage.[5] The theoretical literature has, nonetheless, made it clear that they are crucial for understanding how the investment behavior of firms works. I argued at the end of Chapter 4 that this cost concept seems to be useful for understanding empirical patterns in the foundation and subsequent expansion of new mills in Cuba. In this chapter, I examine evidence to support this claim. Although most theoretical treatments of adjustment costs have involved sophisticated analytical apparatus, the concept is not difficult or inaccessible.

A precise definition of adjustment costs is needed. Adjustment costs are the costs associated with increasing the *rate* of accumulation of some durable factor of production, as distinguished from the costs associated with either the *level* of use or the purchase of that factor. They might be thought of as a cost premium required to increase the rate of acquisition of physical capital. Intuitively, it is a straightforward concept when one considers the entire range of factors of production that might be purchased. Some factors, such as fuel or raw materials, are easily acquired from one month to the next. Others naturally face delays in acquisition. For instance, in the construction of a new building, time is needed to draw up the blueprints, to address the specific location, foundation, and functional requirements, to obtain financing, and to perform the construction. It can be built quickly or slowly. To build it quickly will likely cost more. Similar delays are natural in the acquisition of most major physical capital installations. These costs, which vary according to how quickly the construction or installation is to be completed, are the adjustment costs. Thus with adjustment costs, the acquisition of capital is treated distinctly from the acquisition of other factors of production by attributing costs not only to the level of employment of physical capital but also to the rate of increase in its level of employment.

An additional definitional feature of adjustment costs is their proposed shape. Adjustment costs rise as the rate of investment increases, and the rate of increase in adjustment costs increases with the rate of investment as well. In other words, their level accelerates as the accumulation of physical capital accelerates. Theoretically, the second feature is an essential characteristic necessary to obtain a meaningful, finite rate of investment. Intuitively, this shape for adjustment costs makes the most sense. For instance, suppose a piece of specialized machinery is being installed for a purchasing firm by the selling firm. If the seller is permitted to proceed at a pace most convenient for it, the cost of installation would be low, but if the purchasing firm wishes to rush the installation, the cost of installation would rise to compensate the seller for having to divert an abnormal amount of its resources to this particular installation. Furthermore, if the purchasing firm should insist that the machinery be installed instantly, the compensation to the seller might skyrocket to the point of being prohibitive. The point is that there is always a limit to how quickly the physical capital can be designed, produced, installed, and put in working order. That limit is transmitted to the purchaser through the adjustment costs of installation and other related costs, which beyond reasonable expectations begin to rise very quickly.

In the Cuban sugar industry there are a number of reasons to believe that the rate of investment was subject to adjustment costs with the proposed shape. I will focus on sources of adjustment costs that seem to have had the most important influences. All are related to the inelasticity of supplies of some inputs in the short run. All the sources are derived from the scarcity of some principal factors. The following sources of adjustment costs are discussed below: costs of installing new equipment, costs of developing new cane fields, and learning by using.

Installation Costs

The first and most obvious adjustment costs are those associated with the installation of the new plant. New equipment costs more to construct and install the shorter the time allowed to do it. It appears that, when the decision was reached to renovate the plant, most mills would embark on an investment plan that covered several years. Zanetti and García find that the United Fruit Company undertook investment programs for its mills that were to take several years — one covered the years 1917–20 and another began in 1926 but was cut short when expected returns to those investments degenerated.[6] A set of documents of the Central Francisco exemplifies this pattern. In 1917, the engineering consulting firm of Griggs and Myers of New York came to the Central Francisco to assess the condition of the Francisco mill, make suggestions for its improvement, and supervise the renovation. In their report, they made short-term suggestions, which could be carried out in one or two years, and long-term suggestions, which could be carried out by the end of the five-year project being initiated at that time. Over the next five years, unusually detailed accounts were kept of the performance of the mill, and at the end of the period, in 1922, a thorough inventory was taken to finalize the project and reassess the condition of the mill.[7] The objective of this project, in principle, could have been achieved much more quickly, but it would have been prohibitively costly.

The skills required of the consultants covered a large range of specialized knowledge. Numerous tests had to be run to isolate the problems of efficiency in each mill involving mechanical knowledge of the boilers, steam engines, grinding mills, vacuum apparatus for boiling, centrifuges, and electrical machinery both for power and generation of electricity (the mills operated their own electrical power plants). Knowledge of large-scale chemical processes using vacuum apparatus was also necessary. Furthermore, all recommendations had to be under the purview of the industrial engineer, who was aware of the economic problems of factory design and the volume and labor-saving requirements of continuous-processing technology.

The skilled personnel to perform this consulting were very scarce both in Cuba and in the United States. The emphasis on formal training and a scientific basis for the design and construction of industrial plant was new to all industries, so the demand for such training increased. The creation of institutions to support the training demanded took time and met with some resistance. Also, the knowledge required to design operative sugar mills was highly specialized. Modern sugar mills made extensive use of principles of mechanical and chemical engineering. The necessity of formal training in both mechanics and chemistry was recognized with the introduction of the modern sugar mills, but sugar technicians also recognized that general training in these areas was insufficient for a working knowledge of the sugar mill. Formally trained engineers or chemists also needed thorough practical knowledge of the sugar mill operation. Acknowledging the scarcity of men who were both formally and practically trained in special problems of engineering for sugar manufacture, John Dymond established the Audubon Sugar School in New Orleans in 1891 in an attempt to fill the need. Cuban technicians, or others who would get jobs in Cuba, were a major clientele of the school. Its graduates were hired as consultants or joined the staffs of sugar mills.[8] But training of this sort did not expand quickly to meet the demands of the market. In other words, the supply of skilled personnel remained inelastic.

The Audubon School discovered that formal instruction in classical chemistry was not suited to the needs of the sugar engineer because it lacked a program of study of the interaction of the machinery and the chemical processes. Emphasis was shifted from training in classical chemistry to the nascent field of chemical engineering, and at Tulane University and Louisiana State University new programs of sugar engineering were established. Instead of focusing on the study of chemical reactions, these programs studied "large-scale processes in the plant by introducing new designs of complex mechanical apparatus."[9] But the applied programs met with opposition from analytical chemists at Tulane, and because the decline of the sugar market at the turn of the twentieth century severely hurt the Louisiana sugar industry, private support for technical training declined.[10] The demands in Cuba, nonetheless, grew rapidly both for their own chemists and engineers and for consultants specialized in factory as well as plantation railroad design. In the 1920s, the technical personnel generally received their training in the United States (they were of both Cuban and North American nationalities), but the comments of sugar mill managers in Cuba suggest that those who came directly out of school were insufficiently acquainted with the practical workings of the mills. It was common practice to recruit men schooled in the United States to train them in the practical workings of the mills. One manager in Cuba, a Mr. Zell, became known for bringing young trainees directly out of college in the United States with technical schooling but no experience, whom he would prepare to be competent sugar technicians for mills in Cuba. This could not have been accomplished instantaneously. Supervision during on-the-job training was clearly important. The mill managers had to be involved in the training themselves. The Spanish mill owner Manuel

Rionda preferred training young technicians to recruiting experienced technicians. He remarked in 1921 that he had rarely seen men with experience recruited from other parts of the world be successful when they were introduced in the Cuban industry because they were not familiar with Cuban methods of cultivation and labor relations.[11]

Since the consulting firms were asked to give advice on very practical aspects of production, such as the proper application and even the organization of the machine operators, the engineering consultants also required such practical or specific human capital. Therefore, the supply of chemists and engineers could not have adjusted elastically to the market because of the requirements of formal training and experience. Because a principal input to the engineering firm was these inelastically supplied technical skills, the costs of installation would have risen at an increasing rate if mill owners demanded a faster rate of installation. For the reasons described, the number of technicians specialized in sugar mill design could only have responded slowly to the market incentives for training. Furthermore, a firm concerned with its reputation would have been concerned not to hire technical personnel too quickly and to set them on the job without first ascertaining the quality of their work. This means that in the short run engineering consulting firms, such as Griggs and Myers, were constrained to work with their existing staff. Lengthening the work hours of their staff would have required premiums or bonuses to offset the disutility of working longer hours. Because the engineering firm employed inputs that were inelastically supplied in the short run, it faced increasing marginal costs when it attempted to install machinery more quickly. These costs would have been passed on to the purchaser — the mill owner — in the form of adjustment costs.[12]

Costs of Cane Field Development

The next source of adjustment costs arose from the fact that expansion of mill capacity was very limited without also expanding the cane fields. Although some substitution of cane for capital existed, it was very limited and largely confined to the long run as the mill equipment was replaced.[13] In fact, it is a reasonable approximation to assume perfect complementarity between the cane supplies and mill capacities of the central. In other words, any increase in mill capacity could not be used unless there was a corresponding increase in cane fields dedicated to supply the additional cane needed. As a rough approximation, it is reasonable to think of these two complementary capital assets — mill capacity and cane field capacity — as having to increase in roughly fixed proportion if mill owners intended to make efficient use of them.[14]

The problems of cane field expansion were numerous because of the speed at which the cane had to be delivered to the mill once it was cut. The time requirement imposed strict coordination problems and caused producers to locate the cane fields close to the mill. The need to build railroads to deliver the cane to the mill also introduced an incentive to minimize distances so as to keep the costs of building the railroad to a minimum. Because of the complementarity and the strict coordination requirements, the planning for cane supplies was internalized by the mill. The mill often obtained its supplies of cane through its contracts with colonos. Nonetheless, the problem of procuring sufficient cane capacity was internalized by the mill as an additional facet of its investment decisions. The supply of cane was a function of the unskilled labor that went into cane cultivation and harvesting, but it was also a function of the development of the complex of cane fields (as an asset), connected by the transportation network, which was organized and contracted for by mill management. The railroad network was usually built and maintained by the mill rather than the colono; and because the location of the railroad was fixed once it was laid down, the mill management had an incentive to form long-term contracts to ensure the continued productivity of the railroad and to prolong their control over the cane supplies in the proximity of the mill.

The use of ratoons in the production process had the effect of increasing the fixed-capital component of cane production. Ratoons were cane plants that had sprouted from the roots of previously harvested cane. Cane is a perennial crop; therefore, besides the crop obtained from the initial planting (the plant cane), additional crops could be harvested from the sproutings of subsequent years (the ratoons). Across the world, ratooning was practiced only where land was abundant and fertile, and the agricultural methods adopted were extensive. The practice of ratooning was not only ubiquitous in Cuba, it was also extremely important to Cuban producers' strategy for remaining internationally competitive. The reason for the variation in the extent ratooning was practiced worldwide was that the bulk of the crop diminished with each ratoon (or each additional crop obtained from a single planting), and the rate of diminution varied with the fertility of the soil. In places where ratooning was practiced, usually only one or two ratoons would be obtained before replant-

Table 5.1

Cane Supply at the Central Francisco, 1919–23, and the Central Washington, 1913

Year	Ratoons		Plant cane		Total (000s of acres)
	000s of acres	pct. of all cane	000s of acres	pct. of all cane	
	Cane Supply at the Central Francisco, Camagüey				
1919	26.723	89.7	3.060	10.3	29.782
1920	29.381	96.9	0.947	3.1	30.328
1921	30.749	92.6	2.475	7.4	33.224
1922	31.051	85.9	5.117	14.1	36.168
1923	34.360	96.4	1.267	3.6	35.627
AVG.	37.314	93.1	2.620	6.9	39.934
	Cane Supply at the Central Washington, Santa Clara				
1913	10.458	90.1	1.150	9.9	11.608

SOURCES: Washington Sugar Co. Inventory of Cane, 1913, Braga Brothers Collection, Record Group 2, ser. 10a, box 7, f. 34, Francisco Sugar Co. manager's reports, Record Group 4, ser. 96.
NOTE: Total may not appear exact due to round-off error.

ing; but in Cuba typically six to ten ratoons were obtained, and in some extraordinary fields there were as many as twenty or thirty. It was sometimes described exaggeratedly as if the cane, once it was planted, simply continued to reproduce for ten years or so without any attention.[15] The use of ratoons thus greatly reduced the variable component of cane costs relative to what it would have been in the absence of ratoons. Planting records of the Centrales Francisco and Washington indicate that the proportion of the cane supply that came from ratoons, in a given year, would generally have been around 90 percent (see Table 5.1). Therefore, cane field development was an extremely important component of the capital costs of mills.

Because cane field development was internalized by the mill, its cost was a function of inputs employed by the mill. An addition to the "stock" of cane fields, then, can be described as a production function with labor, land, and railroad capital as the principal inputs, or $\Delta C = f(L, T, R)$, where ΔC represents the absolute increase in the available cane field acreage, T represents the land it occupied, R represents the railroad investment realized to make it accessible to the mill, and L represents the labor used to build and install these assets. Under normal circumstances, this function would have been subject to diminishing returns, and the corresponding rising marginal costs would have introduced an additional source of adjustment costs.

If cane field development had simply been a function of clearing land and planting cane with the use of unskilled labor, it might be reasonable to believe that the marginal costs of cane field development were constant.

But the essential features of the cane field in the central involved a considerable amount of infrastructure. In these centrales, the cane fields consisted of a complex of fields all connected to the mill by a network of railroads and cart roads which had to be capable of transporting cane quickly to the mill even from the most distant fields. As much as it required the agricultural preparation of the land, development of cane fields required the construction of the transportation network. Laying the railroads required a considerable amount of planning to maximize their value to the mill for many years to follow. It required surveying the land to locate points of potential problems during the rains. It required construction of bridges both for the railroad and for cart roads to link the fields to the railroad loading stations.[16] Some of the inputs for designing and building the transportation network were fixed in the short run. The management and technical personnel at the mill were likely to have been the major constraints. The mill would directly hire specialists to do some of the technical work, but the technical support was generally obtained through a consultant firm, and the costs to the mill for such services were similar to those described above for installation costs.

It may also have been that the additional labor requirement was satisfied only at increasing marginal costs. This would have been true, for example, if the management had to incur unusual search costs to attract the additional supplies of labor. When one considers the task of improving the lands, building the cart roads and bridges, laying down the railroad sufficient for one of the large-scale mills all at once, say in a single year, the labor requirements for field and railroad construction were enormously different from the ordinary labor requirements in the fields and railroad during the normal season of an already established mill. As Table 5.1 shows, plantings were not typically more than 10 percent of the total cane crop each season. Some of these plantings would have been replantings in already established fields, and therefore, they would have required labor only for maintenance, and not construction, of any necessary roads, railroads, or bridges. Consequently, attracting sufficient labor to set up the entire operation at once would require additional labor of an order of magnitude roughly nine times greater than the amount of field labor (including railroad construction crews) ordinarily demanded.

The investment patterns of the Central Francisco give an example of the actual rate of railroad construction of a mill. This central was one of the more successful mills on the island and property of the influential Rionda family. Therefore, it would not have encountered unusual barriers to credit access. Its railroad network was extensive relative to other mills because it had no outlet to the public rail system.[17] Table 5.2 shows that the capital expenditures on mill and railroad equipment remained roughly in the same proportion throughout 1917–30. Table 5.3 shows that the yearly extension of the length of the railroad at the Central Francisco typically represented less than a 9 percent increase of the total railroad length of the previous year. The large amount of railroad construction in 1922 may have been a response to a sudden change in the labor market. The wages paid to field labor at the Francisco dropped 32 percent in 1922 from the level of the previous year after a few years of historically high wages[18] (see Figure 5.1).

An additional factor was that much of the additional labor needed in the fields would have been required during the peak time for labor demand of the harvest. So that the cane would mature at the preferred time for milling, much of the planting was done in the springtime at the same time the harvest was going on. Therefore, additional labor demands for planting would have competed with peak season demands for cutting and hauling cane.

With a change in labor demand of this magnitude, managers could not depend on labor making itself available at a constant wage. The largest centrales were typically located away from the densely populated areas so they could not have drawn from local pools of unskilled labor. During the dead season, when much of the construction work was done, there may have been some slack in the local market, but it would not have been of the

Table 5.2
Capital Accounts of the Central Francisco, 1917–30
(millions of dollars)

Year	Mill plant	Railroad equipment	Lands	Property and plant
1917	1.242	1.169	1.350	3.761
1918	1.421	1.169	1.350	3.940
1919	1.911	1.219	1.350	4.480
1920	1.749	1.364	1.350	4.463
1921	2.748	1.631	1.350	5.730
1922	2.796	1.629	1.350	5.775
1923	2.912	1.629	1.350	5.891
1924	2.839	2.121	1.540	6.499
1925	2.965	2.284	1.540	6.789
1926	3.078	2.305	1.540	6.923
1927	2.794	2.369	1.540	6.702
1928	2.834	2.430	1.540	6.803
1929	2.860	2.509	1.540	6.909
1930	2.893	2.564	1.540	6.997

SOURCE: Annual Reports of the Central Francisco, Braga Brothers Collection, Record Group 4, ser. 96.

Table 5.3
Mill Capacity and Length of Railroad of the Central Francisco, 1916–30

Year	Length of railroad (miles)	Railroad extension (percent)	Mill capacity (000s bags)	Mill expansion (percent)
1916	38	—	350	—
1917	40	3.9	350	0.0
1918	44	11.4	350	0.0
1919	54	21.6	450	28.6
1920	57	6.5	450	0.0
1921	56	−1.3	450	0.0
1922	79	40.9	400	−11.1
1923	78	−1.1	400	0.0
1924	85	8.8	450	12.5
1925	92	8.1	450	0.0
1926	94	2.3	560	24.4
1927	99	4.7	500	−10.7
1928	103	4.2	600	20.0
1929	109	5.8	600	0.0
1930	109	0.1	600	0.0

SOURCE: Annual Reports of the Central Francisco, Braga Brothers Collection, Record Group 4, ser. 96.

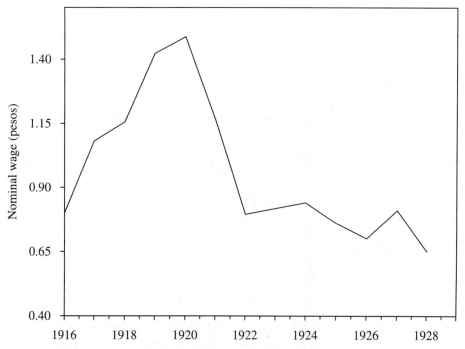

Fig. 5.1. Wages for cane cutting, 1916–28. Wages are given in pesos per 100 arrobas of cane cut. Source: Braga Brothers Collection, Record Group 2, ser. 10a, box 27, ff. 27, 38; Record Group 4, ser. 96.

magnitude suggested. To obtain so much additional labor, a large construction project would have incurred search costs in addition to the wage, and these would have raised the average outlay per field laborer.

Furthermore, the fact that the employment was temporary would have made a difference to laborers. The best, or most desired, jobs were assigned on the basis of the reputation, or personal relationship, of the worker with the local employer (i.e., the colono or the *mayordomo* at the colonia). Therefore, there was a disincentive for workers to change employers from season to season. In addition, laborers often received nonwage benefits on the colonias. The most important of these were the rights to dwellings and garden plots on the marginal lands of the colonia. But these were rationed such that those workers with good, long-standing relationships with the employer had better access to these benefits.[19]

Learning by Using

The sources of adjustment costs described so far depend on the relative fixity of capital expenditures, but they have nothing to do with the changing technological environment. The technical change going on in the sugar industry created an additional source of adjustment costs by introducing an element of uncertainty into the investment decision. Because of the interdependent nature of sugar manufacture, a way to reduce the uncertainty when several new pieces of equipment were to be adopted was to purchase the equipment in a stepwise manner. Once a new piece of equipment was installed, a certain amount of time had to be spent using it before the managerial and technical personnel had learned to use it with maximum efficiency. There would thus have been a learning curve associated with the installation of any new equipment. Likewise, if the new technologies altered the way the various activities interacted, there would have been a learning curve associated with any necessary change in the technical or personal interdependencies between activities as well as with changes in the routines devised for the operation of the mill.[20]

The Magnitude of Adjustment Costs

The foregoing discussion has given reasons for and evidence of the existence of costs that mill owners incurred as they expanded mill capacities that would be classified as adjustment costs. These arguments, however, have not provided a sense of how large or how important they were to mill owners. To get a sense of their magnitude, a quantitative analysis is performed in the next two sections which provides an estimate of the adjustment costs. As one might expect, any attempt to estimate adjustment costs is fraught with difficulties because adjustment costs are elusive to measurement. Any attempt at obtaining a single estimate would be subject to a very wide margin of error. An alternative method of estimation is to identify a range within which the estimate must logically fall, or in this exercise it is sufficient to identify a lower bound below which the adjustment costs could not have fallen. The next two sections confirm that this lower bound for the possible range of adjustment costs was indeed high, corroborating that adjustment costs must have had a significant impact on mill owners' investment decisions. The estimated lower bound may be thought of as a "conservative" estimate, but in fact, it is more rigorous. It actually defines the lower limit to the plausible range within which the actual adjustment costs must have fallen.

The interested reader will want to read the following section, which describes the procedure by which these lower bound estimates were obtained. Otherwise, the reader may wish to skip to the following section on the results of estimating the adjustment costs.

Estimation of Adjustment Costs — Analysis

The data show that new mills were initially established at small capacities of 100,000 to 200,000 bags of sugar per year and then were expanded in the following years to reap the economies of scale that could be had at larger capacities.[21] They thus give the appearance that producers were willing to operate for a time with lower profits because they often operated at a scale which the visible unit costs suggest was suboptimal. The apparent willingness of producers to operate at a suboptimal scale is only apparent, however. The presence of adjustment costs in the short run prevented the rapid rate of expansion necessary to build the mill at the optimal capacity in a single year. The adjustment costs required to establish a new mill at the optimal capacity were not visible because they did not involve actual outflows of cash, that is, because the option to build initially at the optimal scale was not chosen. The visible costs and the optimal scale would be better viewed as those which were achievable only in the long run. Direct estimation of the adjustment costs that sugar producers faced is, therefore, elusive, although it is possible to obtain a lower bound to the adjustment costs by estimating the profits that producers appear to have forgone (i.e., if we overlook the influence of adjustment costs). They appear to have been forgone when we observe the visible unit costs at different scales of production. If the mill owners were profit maximizers, they would not have been willing to forgo these profits unless they were facing additional costs at least as great as the profits forgone.

To clarify this notion of forgone profits that were not truly forgone, let us express it in slightly different terms. In the hypothetical world in which there were no adjustment costs, the producers would have forgone profits because they were initially building at a suboptimal scale. If the producers were profit maximizers, then this behavior could not have come about. If, on the other hand, adjustment costs did exist, then the apparent forgone profits were actually the adjustment costs unaccounted for. In short, these profits were only apparently forgone, and they appear so because we view only the visible costs of production. For lack of a better term, I will refer below to the apparent losses as "hypothetically forgone profits" or "hypothetical losses."

The exercise in this section provides lower bound estimates for the adjustment costs that would have been required to build the optimal-scale plant in a single year instead of the typical small-scale plant. It proceeds in two steps. First, a regression is estimated to infer the relationship between long-run unit costs and mill capacity. Previous sections have shown that the data are consistent with the claim that unit costs were lower at higher scales of production. These regression results give further support to this claim, and they also provide an estimate of the unit cost differential of operating alternately at large and small capacities. Second, the estimated rate of reduction in unit costs as mill capacity increased, obtained from the regression, is used to estimate the hypothetical losses from operating during the first year at a suboptimal scale. I show analytically that these hypothetical losses are a lower bound to the additional adjustment costs that would have been required to build the optimal-scale plant in a single year. Therefore, the estimated hypothetical losses provide a lower bound estimate of the opportunity costs facing the producers when they decided to build initially below the long-run optimal scale. The estimates of the hypothetically forgone profits reveal that the costs of building the optimal plant immediately, or equivalently the costs of not beginning at a small initial scale, may have been very high.

To estimate the rate of reduction in unit costs as the scale of production increased, consider a simple expression of the cost accounts of a mill.

$$C = v(x, z) + (g - \delta)u + h(u) \tag{5.1}$$

where: $v(x, z)$ is the yearly unit operating costs, x is the mill capacity (capacity is measured in thousands of bags of sugar, 325 pounds per bag); the variable, z, represents a vector of other factors of production; the variable, u, is the increment to the capacity of the mill added by the investments of the current year (in amounts of thousands of bags of sugar). The cost of the investment equipment required to increase the capacity of the mill by one unit is g (in units of 1,000 bags of sugar). The depreciation allowance given in the accounts for the new investments is δu. The cost of equipment and depreciation per unit of investment equipment, g and δ, are constants. The depreciation allowance is assumed to be proportional to the increase in capacity. The function, $h(u)$, is the adjustment costs to investment, a function of the degree of expansion of mill capacity in the fixed interval of time.

In a steady state, we imagine that $h(u) = 0$ such that the long-run yearly costs would be

$$C = v(x, z) + (g - \delta)u \tag{5.2}$$

In the steady state, all investment would go toward replacement of old equipment such that the level of investment was dependent on the mill capacity already in existence, and costs can be expressed as $C = v(x, z) = C(x, z)$.

Let us suppose that mills attempt to produce at full capacity, except that they are subject to the random influences of weather and soil quality. Assume that production can be expressed as $y(x, z, m) = Ey(x, z)f(m)e^{\epsilon}$, where the stochastic influences enter through ϵ, and m is a vector of variables that reflect the influences of weather and soil quality. Then the unit (average) cost, a, is

$$a = \frac{C(x, z)}{Ey(x, z)f(m)e^{\epsilon}} = \frac{a(x, z)}{f(m)}e^{-\epsilon} \tag{5.3}$$

Estimation of the rate of reduction in unit costs as the scale of production increased can proceed by estimating the log-linear relationship,

$$\ln a_i = \beta_0 + \beta_1 \ln x_i + \beta_2 \ln m_i + \beta_3 \ln z_i + \epsilon_i \tag{5.4}$$

The other factors of production, z, which would have been most influential were skilled and unskilled labor, fuel, and the cost of cane. Assume that the levels of employment of these factors were chosen to maximize profits given the capacity of the mill, x, and the vector of relative factor prices, w. Then $a = a[x, z(x, w)]$. Since the unit cost data are available for only three years, and since all mills faced the same market prices, it is econometrically feasible to include no more than two series of market prices to attempt to capture the effects of short-run market conditions.[22] Given the econometric limitations, an alternative is preferable to including prices directly in the model, that is, the short-run market conditions are treated as fixed effects on the average costs of mills.[23] To capture the fixed effects we replace z in equation (5.4) with dummies for the years 1916 (d_1) and 1918 (d_2), using 1917 as the base year. The coefficients of the dummies are interpreted as the changes in unit costs of production as a result of the different economic environments of the three years under observation. Consequently, we rewrite equation (5.4) as

$$\ln a_i = \beta_0 + \beta_1 \ln x_i + \beta_2 \ln m_i + \beta_3 d_{1i} + \beta_4 d_{2i} + \epsilon_i \qquad (5.5)$$

Equation (5.5) is estimated using data of various mills for the years 1916, 1917, and 1918. The unit costs (a_i) are taken from income and expenditure reports of the mills, and the mill capacities (x_i) are engineering estimates of production capacity, not production levels. Two measures of cane quality are included as explanatory variables — the sucrose content of the cane and the water content of the cane (m_i). As I argued in the previous chapter, the effects of weather and soil quality on the outcome of the production process were picked up through their influence on the quality of the cane. Therefore, these factors can be controlled for by using the sucrose and water contents of the cane (which measures were discussed in the appendix to Chapter 4). Also included are the dummy variables for 1916 (d_{1i}) and 1918 (d_{2i}).

The regression estimates are reported in Table 5.4. All the coefficients have the expected signs, and all are significant except for the coefficient for the water content of the cane. The coefficient of mill capacity estimates the rate of reduction in the unit cost of production as the size of facilities increases. Because of the logarithmic form of the regression equation, the rate at which unit costs are reduced depends on the initial mill capacity, so we resort to an illustration. If a mill's initial capacity is 100,000 bags and its capacity is increased to 400,000 bags — a plausible situation — then the estimated relationship predicts a 12.3 percent reduction in long-run unit costs or a 23 percent increase in long-run unit profits (i.e., omitting any adjustment costs).

A few additional comments about the regression results are warranted. The large relative magnitudes of the coefficients for the cane qualities —

Table 5.4
*Regression to Estimate the Rate of Reduction in Unit Costs
as Mill Capacity Increases*

Dependent variable: unit costs

N		65				
F		21.1978				
R²		0.6424				

Estimated coefficients:	Constant	Mill capacity	Sucrose content	Water content	Dummy 1916	Dummy 1918
Coefficient	1.75	−0.08	−0.45	0.26	−0.22	0.08
Standard error		0.02	0.20	0.21	0.03	0.03
t-ratio		−3.49	−2.21	1.19	−6.42	2.52

UNITS OF MEASUREMENT: Unit costs f.o.b. are recorded in cents per pound of sugar. Mill capacity is measured in thousands of bags (325 pounds each) of sugar. Sucrose and water content are recorded as percentages of the total weight of the cane ground.
SOURCES: Author's calculations. Data on unit costs are obtained from the Braga Brothers Collection, Record Group 2, ser. 10a, box 7, ff. 9–11. The other data are obtained from Cuba, Secretaría de Agricultura, Comercio, y Trabajo, *Industria azucarera*.

sucrose content and water content — indicate the great amount of local variation in cane quality and the high degree of uncertainty in the outcome of the cane crop each year. This is something we should expect in the regression results based on our experience with the regressions estimating the sources of variation of yields and extraction rates. This high degree of uncertainty was obviously of great concern to sugar producers, but it was also something they could not control. Therefore, they had to depend on recouping the losses of bad crops with the windfalls of good years. The relatively small magnitude of the coefficient for mill capacity in comparison does not suggest a diminished importance for it in the long-run cost strategy of the mill. It was a variable under the control of the management. The weather could not be controlled, but its effects would average out over time. That the magnitude of the coefficient in mill capacities was important is seen by observing the percentage change in unit costs or unit profits implied by the coefficients, as demonstrated in the preceding paragraph. Regarding the coefficients on the dummy variables for 1916 and 1918, their signs suggest a rising trend in long-run unit costs. The rising costs reflect the mounting scarcity of resources during World War I. There was a severe shortage of imported capital goods of all kinds, especially for railroad maintenance, so maintenance costs rose. Also, labor costs rose steeply during the war (see Figure 5.1). There was widespread dissatisfaction among labor organizations over the outcome of the international price control agreements. The occurrence of strikes and other labor-related interferences was very high, especially in 1917. It reached the point of creating local insurgencies that were suppressed by the Cuban military.

To understand the incentives facing sugar producers we must look not at costs but at profits. We have seen that new mills were usually established initially at capacities that were suboptimal from a long-run point of view. If the investors in these new projects were rational, the gains they apparently would have received by, instead, initially constructing the optimal long-run plant must have been offset by additional unaccounted costs. Therefore, the profits at the optimal long-run scale must have been smaller than they appear, offset by the additional adjustment costs that would have been required to build the optimal-scale plant all at once. The difference between expected profits at small and large mill capacities, predicted by equation (5.5), gives an estimate of the gains that might have been made by producing at the optimal scale initially instead of at a smaller scale. But these gains are hypothetical because they ignore the influence of the adjustment costs of building the large plant so quickly. It is useful to think of this difference as a comparison of the long-run profit potentials of mills of different capacities.

This hypothetical long-run profit differential is a lower bound estimate for the additional adjustment costs that would have been incurred to build the optimal sized plant initially. To see this, consider the expression of a mill's costs accounts in equation (5.1). In a steady state, $h(u) = 0$ such that the long-run yearly profits were

$$\pi(x_0, u) = px - v - (g - \delta)u \tag{5.6}$$

where p is the price of sugar. For simplicity, we ignore the stochastic influences in y and assume that the mill is producing at full capacity, $y = x$. The short-run profits are, therefore, $\pi(x_0, u) - h(u)$, such that the adjustment costs are also included. Let x_0 be the mill capacity of the previous year, then $x = x_0 + u$, and the long-run profits are a function of x_0 and u.

If u represents the increment in capacity necessary to expand to the initial capacity and u^* is the increment in capacity required to expand to the optimal scale, then the selection and establishment of a new mill at a small capacity, $u < u^*$ implies that initially

$$\pi(x_0, u) - h(u) \geq \pi(x_0, u^*) - h(u^*) \tag{5.7}$$

Since $x_0 + u^*$ is the optimal scale absent of adjustment costs, $\pi(x_0, u^*) \geq \pi(x_0, u)$, and

$$\pi(x_0, u^*) - \pi(x_0, u) \leq h(u^*) - h(u) \tag{5.8}$$

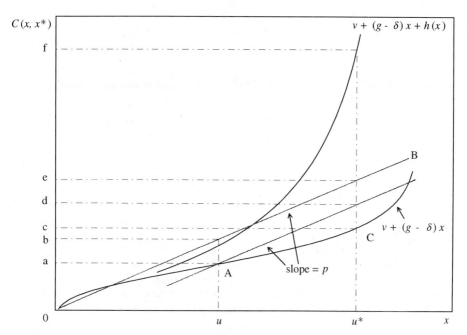

Fig. 5.2. Illustration of the lower bound estimate for the adjustment costs incurred in the first year of a mill's existence. In the diagram, it is assumed that the mill is in its first year of operation; therefore, the capacity of the mill, x, is equal to the new capacity added by investment incurred in that year, u. See the text for an explanation of the diagram.

The left-hand side of equation (5.8) is the hypothetical long-run profit differential. The right-hand side is the additional adjustment costs that would have been necessary to build the large-scale plant in the first year instead of the small-scale plant. Therefore, the long-term (total) profit differential is a lower bound to the opportunity cost of building the large-scale plant initially.

We can illustrate this lower bound for the case of a mill being established for the first time (see Figure 5.2). Then the amount of investment, u, is equal to the mill capacity being established, x. Suppose all variable factors, z, are chosen optimally ($z = z^*$). The two heavier curves represent the total costs $C(x, z^*)$, including and excluding the adjustment costs $h(x)$. The slope of line 0B is the price of sugar, p. (The slope of the straight line passing through point A is also p.) The points, u and u^*, on the x-axis are the small and large capacities in question. On the horizontal axis, u^* is the amount of new capacity needed to reach the optimal long-term capacity;

therefore, the slope of the tangent at point C is equal to the slope of 0B. The point, u, is determined as the first step (first year) on the optimal time path of x to reach the optimal capacity, $x^* = u^*$. The profits at u are $\pi(0, u) = b - a$. The profits at u^* are $\pi(0, u^*) = e - c$, and the profit differential is $\pi(0, u^*) - \pi(0, u) = d - c$. The additional adjustment costs which would have been necessary to build at capacity u^* rather than u are $h(u^*) - h(u) = (d - c) + (f - e)$, and the bias in our estimate of the adjustment costs is therefore equal to $e - f < 0$. So our estimates of the hypothetically forgone profits are lower bound estimates of adjustment costs.

Estimation of Adjustment Costs — Results

The previous section developed a framework with which a lower bound can be estimated for the adjustment costs that would have been incurred if the optimal-scale sugar mill were built in a single year rather than over several years.

Reviewing the empirical setting again, the data show that new mills were initially built at capacities that ranged from 100,000 to 200,000 bags of sugar per year. They were then expanded subsequently to reach the optimal scale of production. That expansion proceeded for several years, constrained by adjustment costs, until finally the optimal capacity was reached. Whereas the initial capacities of new mills are revealed in the data, the desired capacities are not directly revealed. We cannot ascertain precisely when a desired level was reached because of changing conditions that either hindered the rate of expansion or changed the desired capacity.[24] Table 4.1 shows that the largest mill capacities exceeded 800,000 bags. Among the active mills, by 1929, the modal range had shifted to the 200–400 category, and almost 40 percent of all mills were at 300,000 bags or more. It seems plausible that the desired range for any long-term viable mill would not have fallen short of a 300,000-bag capacity. As a matter of fact, given the range of mill capacities in operation in the 1920s, it appears that a conservative desired capacity would have been no smaller than 400,000 bags. The lower bound estimates to follow are based on these two conservatively chosen "desired" capacities.

Table 5.5 presents four cases of plausible investment plans, each specified by the mill's initial and desired capacities, and it provides estimates of the hypothetical long-run profit differential between the initial and desired mill capacities for each case. In Panel A of Table 5.5, initial and desired capacities are specified. Panel B shows the expected profits (in millions of

Table 5.5
Long-Run Cost and Profit Differentials Between Different Mill Capacities

	i	ii	iii	iv
A. Mill capacity (000s of bags) at:				
initial capacity	100	100	200	200
desired capacity	400	300	400	300
B. Expected long-run profit (millions of dollars) from operating at:				
initial capacity	0.265	0.265	0.664	0.664
desired capacity	1.580	1.107	1.580	1.107
difference	1.315	0.843	0.916	0.444
C. Percent profit differential:				
losses from operating at reduced capacity	83.2	76.1	58.0	40.1
D. Expected long-run unit cost (cents per lb.) at:				
initial capacity	3.66	3.66	3.46	3.46
desired capacity	3.26	3.34	3.26	3.34

NOTES:
B: The expected long-run profits are estimated by $\pi(x^j) = (p - \hat{a})x^j$, $j = I,D$, where p is the average price of sugar for 1917. The difference is $\pi(x^D) - \pi(x^I)$.
C: The percentage of hypothetical losses incurred from operating at the reduced capacity is calculated as
$$\frac{\pi(x^D) - \pi(x^I)}{\pi(x^D)}$$
Differences may appear inexact due to round-off error.
D: Using the notation of equation (5.5), the expected long-run unit costs are estimated as the exponent of $\hat{a} = b_0 + b_1 \ln x + b_2 \ln \bar{m}$ where x is either the initial capacity, x^I, or the desired capacity, x^D, as specified. The estimates b_i are the OLS regression estimates for β_i of equation (5.5), $i = 0, 1, 2$; $b_0 = 1.75$, $b_1 = -0.08$, and $b_2 = -0.45$ taken from Table 5.4. The predicted value for the estimated equation (5.5), $\hat{a}$, is calculated by treating $\bar{m}$ as the vector of sample means for the cane qualities, sucrose content, and water content.

dollars), given the 1917 average price of sugar (5 cents per pound). In Panel D the expected long-run unit costs at each capacity, as predicted by the regression model of Table 5.4, are given. In Panel C, the difference in expected long-run profits as a percentage of expected profits at the desired capacity is given.

To interpret the results, see, for example, Case (i), column i. Excluding the adjustment costs, a mill operating at 100,000 bags instead of at 400,000 bags would forgo $1.32 million in profits in a single year, or 83 percent of the profits it would make at the larger capacity. This difference in the hypothetical long-run profits, as we have seen, is a lower bound estimate of the additional adjustment costs that would have been required to build a mill of 400,000-bag capacity instead of 100,000-bag capacity.

The four investment plans represented in Table 5.5 are plausible. As we have seen in Figure 4.4, most newly constructed mills were built with initial capacities of between 100,000 and 200,000 bags. The desired scale, as the regression estimates support, was clearly larger. How large is a difficult question to answer, but if the desired capacity was 300,000 to 400,000 bags, then the estimated hypothetical long-run profit differentials in Table 5.5 give lower bound estimates of the opportunity costs of not building the optimal scale at the outset.[25]

I have presented the four plausible cases to give an indication of the range of possibilities, given how little we know of the specific investment plans of the mill owners. Cases (ii) and (iv) represent extremely conservative estimates of the desired mill capacities, but even in these conservative cases the expected long-run profits at the initial capacity are at least 40 percent lower than at the desired capacity. Therefore, one would conclude that the cost of building the desired (optimal) scale at the outset under ordinary circumstances was prohibitive. The additional adjustment costs that would have been required would have been at minimum 40 percent of the first year's profits, but it is likely that they were much higher.

Conclusion

In summary, adjustment costs were substantial as a component of the total investment costs of sugar mill expansion. Indeed, they were high enough that the founders of new mills considered it preferable to build gradually and in the meantime to grind for a few years at an inefficient suboptimal scale. The most obvious source of adjustment costs was associated with the costs of installation of new plant and equipment. The shorter the time allowed for installation, the greater the marginal costs of installation would be. One important reason was the scarcity of skilled personnel to provide the services needed for building a best-practice mill. Not only were skills deficient in Cuba, they were also scarce in the United States. Technicians with an understanding of chemical engineering or industrial chemistry were not abundant. So expansion depended on the abilities of the existing personnel, which could not be elastically supplied in the short run. The second source of adjustment costs arose from the strict complementarity between cane field and mill capacity. Even though centrales obtained most of their cane from colonos, the specificity of cane fields determined that the decision to expand cane capacity was made by the mills in conjunction with their decision to expand mill capacity. As in the case of mill installation, a shorter time allowed to clear land and plant cane fields resulted in higher costs because resources had to be drawn away from the harvest. Additional railroad lines also often had to be built. Finally, there were problems of adaptation and learning as new machinery was introduced that were more acute the faster the rate of introduction of new machinery and capacity expansion.

We have seen that because of these adjustment costs and vintage-capital effects, mills responded with a lag in adopting the optimal scales of production. The gradual process of diffusion of new large-scale technologies is important for understanding the changes in the structure of the Cuban sugar industry during this period. It shows that even though the process was gradual, it was largely a natural process of technical evolution. A persistent variation in the capacities of mills of Cuban and North American ownership was to be expected given the vintage-capital influence and the later entrance of North American direct investment into the sugar industry. Newcomers would more naturally have the latest technology. This economic argument, based on profit-maximizing behavior and constraints that differed according to the age of a mill's equipment, explains technical differences of mills without appeal to any inherent national differences.

Having established this, a question remains regarding the rates of mill expansion or the levels of investment. In examining the investment behavior of entering mills, we observed that there seemed to be few or no barriers to starting a mill, but continued expansion to the desired capacity was less likely to be successful if the mill did not have a North American orientation. Exactly how to interpret this observation remains unclear. An often advanced view simply takes for granted either an economic or political superiority of North American mills, attributed to the impact of capitalist imperialism. Attempting a bit more precision in identifying the economic mechanisms, one hypothesis that is consistent with this view is that capital markets were imperfect and that Cuban or Spanish mills faced barriers to competition for financial resources.[26] An alternative view is advanced in Chapter 6 in which it is argued that the observed differences in the rate of mill expansion were essentially caused by regional factors rather than national ones — or in addition to national ones. It is true that regions were distinguished by the nationality of mill ownership. North Americans tended to dominate the mills in the eastern part of the island whereas traditional Cuban and Spanish planter families tended to occupy the sugar estates in the western provinces. The reason for this distinction was in part related to their history — who were the established producers and who were the newcomers. But evidence presented in Chapter 6 shows that the slower rate of adoption of new technology in the traditional western region was also in part caused by east-west differences in transaction costs related to the different regional histories of sugar industry development. Chapter 7 conducts a quantitative analysis that concludes that both internal institutional factors and external capital market or informational imperfections, or related effects, were present.

Chapter 6

Holdup and Regional Diversity

IN THE MID-NINETEENTH CENTURY, Cuba had one of the more innovative and advanced sugar industries in the world. It was a leader in the adoption of both steam power and vacuum-heating technologies in sugar manufacture. As the further technological advances extending the concept of continuous processing to raw cane sugar manufacture after 1880 became available, Cuban producers were not in a good position to take advantage of them. The economy was in the throes of political and financial crises. After the War of Independence, when the economic environment had changed considerably, Cuban producers wanted to regain their status as a leader in the industry, this time with closer political ties to their major market, the United States. For the first time, North American direct investment was attracted in a big way to the Cuban sugar industry. But surprisingly, it did not seem to reinforce the once highly competitive establishment that had been located in the western provinces before the separatist insurrections had begun. Rather, foreign investment went more frequently to the east — away from the former center of dynamism. Since the Ten Years' War sugar producers in the east had remained small and backward. North American investors in sugar, showing less interest in the established industrial region, selected new sites and built new mills in remote locations. The objective apparently was not isolation because domestic interests were usually involved, especially in the earliest of the North American ventures. Ultimately, Cuban prominence in the sugar industry was regained, but the technologically dynamic center of the industry shifted to the east. As North American participation in the industry became important both through enterprise and as a source of capital, its influence both as an injection of resources and as a transfer of control over local resources was felt more in the east.

The east, particularly the province of Oriente, may not have been prepared for the revolution that overtook it after the turn of the century. The technical revolution in Cuban sugar, begun in the west in the 1870s and 1880s, did not reach the eastern provinces until the twentieth century, and when it did, it had the full backing of North American capital. By that time, a wide gap between the best-practice and existing sugar manufacturing techniques had also formed. As sugar expanded into the region, the traditional economy was completely overturned. The east went from providing an unimportant share of the Cuban sugar crop to producing over half of it in just over two decades, from 1901 to 1923. This sudden transformation had a profound effect on the regional economy and society — both constructive and destructive — as resources shifted from subsistence agriculture to the export-oriented agroindustrial sugar industry.

Robert Hoernel, in a critical study of the eastern expansion, points to the loss of a unique culture. Oriente, in particular, before the expansion was the province with the greatest concentration of small, independent subsistence farmers. In the latter half of the nineteenth century, it had been the last refuge of freed people of color seeking liberation from plantation society. It had been the region most responsible for the coffee boom in the early part of the nineteenth century, but the abrupt collapse of the coffee industry had ruined export agriculture there for the most part until sugar arrived. The sudden burst of growth in the economy disrupted the character of the society. Sugar and land companies moved in and bought up vast tracts of fertile land. In some cases the land was remote, but in others it was in areas where squatters had settled. So in some cases, sugar expansion meant that smallholders sold or lost their land. Even where smallholders were not displaced, the magnitude of investments being carried out changed the shape of the local economy. These investments created enormous opportunities, but Hoernel notes that they also disrupted the culture. Hoards of immigrants flooded into the once isolated region, attracted by the wages that plantation work offered, so the former isolation and identity of the region was broken.[1] The speed of the economic transition itself may have been enough to cause such disruption, but it is a common belief that the disruption was related more to the deeper penetration of North American capital and the position of economic dominance it occupied there relative to what happened in the west.[2]

Explanations of North American investors' attraction to the east have been indirect or implicit, but they have tended to attribute it to vulnerability. Many have claimed that it was the easier North American domination of the backward and vulnerable eastern provinces that caused the North American investors to go to the east more frequently.[3] But careful examination suggests that this characterization of the investors does not accurately depict their motives as participants in international capital markets. While domination of the eastern regional economy may have been a consequence of their actions, the desires of investors looking into the emerging market that Cuba offered for international capital were not domination but, rather, maximization of the returns to their investments. That economic activity was accomplished primarily through the comparison of a wide range of investment options in a number of countries and regions. It is not immediately obvious why they would have chosen the backward region over the developed. One is compelled to ask what the economic incentive was for investing in the east rather than in the west when the west had been the former bastion of Cuban sugar's international competitiveness.

In this chapter I argue that the institutional setting in the west, combined with the influence of preexisting infrastructure, created a disadvantage for western sugar producers in attracting capital to invest in the latest continuous-process technologies.[4] The argument relies on Oliver Williamson's transaction-cost theory of the effects of asset specificity on contractual relations.[5] An examination of the specific assets of the cane transaction shows that the western part of the industry suffered a relative disadvantage in the adoption of new technologies because mills in that region were more likely to suffer holdup problems resulting from the transaction specificity of cane field assets. Accordingly, institutional persistence in the west seems to have caused its relative decline;[6] indeed, it may be said that it was the west's very success with the previous century's technology that was at the root of its difficulties in the early twentieth century.

The Asset-Specificity Argument

How the innovations of mass production were assimilated into sugar production in Cuba is interesting to observe from the point of view of its industrial organization. Although mill capacities grew significantly in all parts of the island, those in the western part grew less rapidly than those in the east. Cubans who lived through these events commonly noticed the difference in average mill capacities that developed between the sugar industries of the east and the west, and they emphasized the coincidence in the east of the largest mills, the greater presence of North American capital, and the greater concentration of land in the hands of mills.[7] Behind these differences, however, must have been economic incentives that made the east more attractive to investors than the west. These incentives need to be explained if we wish to understand why this regional investment pattern formed.

To understand the economic incentives, it must be recognized that cane fields were site-specific assets. First, the working of the cane transaction was dominated by technical attributes that tied the cane production site spatially to the mill. This once again was because of cane's tendency to deteriorate rapidly once it was cut. Deliveries from the harvest to the mill thus had to be made promptly; consequently, the cane railroad became an essential component of sugar production. The mills had to invest in railroads to gain access to the cane supplies, and that investment fixed the site for the long term. The cane railroad was a specific asset to the cane transaction — tied to the site of the particular cane field it was laid for. This created a long-term bilateral trading relationship or collaboration between the colono and the mill. If the proposed bilateral relationship were severed at some point, little of the value of the rail line leading to the colonia could be recuperated. Evidence indicates that the difference between the use value and the salvage value of the cane railroad often put mill management in a vulnerable situation. Given the specificity of the investments made by the mill, theoretically one would expect to find threats of opportunistic behavior on the part of colonos attempting to capture the economic rents created by the investments.[8] This chapter offers an argument and empirical support for the proposition that such holdup threats were effective when renewals of cane contracts were negotiated.

It must also be recognized that the colono was by this time no longer principally a laborer. Some smallholder colonos performed manual labor on their colonias, but during the *zafra* (grinding season) even smallholders were principally involved in hiring and supervising gangs of wage laborers to harvest and haul cane to the mills. Still, many colonos held medium-sized or large plantations and may have managed hundreds of field workers during the zafra. Some colonos were members of aristocratic families; others were men of means who had other businesses as well, as merchants or agriculturalists. Thus many colonos were in a position to bargain effectively with the mills over the terms of their contracts.[9]

To summarize the argument, because of the site specificity of cane field investments made by the mill, dependence on short-term cane supply arrangements was dangerous because of the potential for opportunistic behavior. Once the central mill (or central) and the cane supplier had agreed on a cane price and the central had made the commitment to the site-specific assets, the colono could threaten to withdraw the cane supplies, holding out for a higher price than the one agreed upon. The salvage value of the site-specific investments would be less than its productive value; therefore, the colono's threat to withhold the cane supplies could effectively force the central to accept short-term losses of a magnitude up to the difference between the productive and salvage values of the assets. In this way, the colono could appropriate some of the economic rents generated by the investment in railroads. Further, this appropriation was not limited to a redistribution of the profits between participants; it was feasible for the colono to appropriate as well some of the rents intended for the replacement or updating of equipment.[10]

Explicit contractual stipulations safeguarded against interruptions in cane deliveries during the term of the contract; therefore, the threat of holdup tended to take place during the negotiation for contract renewal. Such holdup threats were most effective if the colono owned the land he cultivated so land ownership increased the relative bargaining position of the colono with respect to the mill. Consequently, the mills' cane costs tended to depend on the initial distribution of property in land, which differed between the two regions.

While the introduction of the new technology and the increase in the optimal scale created incentives to invest in larger scales of production, the effective threats of holdup by landowning colonos, who were more prominent in the west, caused existing mills in that region to confront higher cane costs. The percentage of cane coming from landowning colonos was two to three times higher in the west than in the east (see Table 6.4). The reason for this has to do with the histories of the two regions. The west was the center of the older nineteenth-century plantation industry. Whenever the larger-scale technology was adopted, in the west it took place by consolidation of preexisting plantation properties so that many of the colono contracts were signed with former plantation owners who ceased to grind their own cane. In contrast, the east consisted principally of new lands into which the sugar industry was being introduced. In these lands there was a greater tendency for the mills to own their cane lands and to contract them out to colonos who occupied them only as long as they were under contract. With this arrangement, holdup threats at contract renewal were ineffective.

This initial contractual difference implied a greater disadvantage, from the western mill owners' perspective, in attracting capital for investment. In contrast, in the eastern part of the island—the region into which the Cuban sugar industry was expanding—the institutional and infrastructural landscape was pliable so that contractual relations could be established differently based on the logic of the new technological system. This gave the eastern region a relative advantage in attracting scarce capital for investment in new technology and larger mill capacities. Consequently, the east came to be associated with larger, more technically advanced mills and larger concentrations of landholdings. That the east also came to be associated with the destination of inflowing North American capital was endogenous to this incentive structure.

Regional Variation in Mill Capacities

Given the existence of economies of scale in sugar production in Cuba, there was clearly a contrast in the way the centrales in the various provinces of the island were able to take advantage of the economies of scale. This contrast is evident in Table 6.1 and Figures 6.1 and 6.2, which give summary data for the average mill capacities in 1904–29. In these figures I have included only mills with capacities no less than 100,000 bags under the assumption that any mills smaller than this were employing techniques that were not viable in the long run.[11] Figure 6.1 and Table 6.1 show that the average capacity of sugar mills was much larger in the eastern provinces of Camagüey and Oriente than in the western provinces, most important of which were Havana, Matanzas, and the western part of Santa Clara. Further, Figure 6.2 shows the contrast in the number of viable mills which achieved no less than a 400,000-bag capacity in 1929. The mills in the east were much more successful at taking advantage of the economies of scale than the mills in the west. Why do we find this regional

Table 6.1
Summary Statistics of Mill Capacities by Province, 1929, 1917, 1904

	Pinar del Rio	Havana	Matanzas	Santa Clara	Camagüey	Oriente
			Crop 1929			
Average capacity[a] (000 bags)	178.0 (52.1)	299.5 (167.5)	231.1 (132.7)	197.7 (76.5)	481.2 (241.3)	404.0 (311.4)
Capacity range (000 bags)	100–300	85–600	50–600	75–400	150–1,100	30–1,300
No. mills	10	11	22	47	29	34
No. mills ≥ 400,000-bag capacity	0	3	2	2	18	11
			Crop 1917			
Average capacity[a] (000 bags)	85.7 (42.4)	155.2 (94.1)	140.0 (94.5)	119.1 (52.0)	213.7 (111.0)	176.8 (164.4)
Capacity range (000 bags)	40–150	25–450	30–450	40–250	25–500	15–600
No. mills	7	21	40	70	19	40
No. mills ≥ 400,000-bag capacity	0	1	1	0	1	6
			Crop 1904			
Average capacity[a] (000 bags)	20.3 (9.3)	45.0 (30.5)	45.1 (32.1)	40.3 (34.1)	64.2 (10.1)	43.1 (48.3)
Capacity range (000 bags)	2–34	2–93	1–152	3–201	50–73	9–241
No. mills	7	20	50	66	3	28
No. mills ≥ 400,000-bag capacity	—	—	—	—	—	—

SOURCE: Author's calculations. Data are from Cuba, Secretaría de Agricultura, Comercio, y Trabajo, *Industria azucarera*, 1916/17, 1929; Cuba, Secretaría de Hacienda, *Industria azucarera*, 1903/4, 1916/17, 1929.

[a] Standard deviations are given in parentheses (1 bag = 325 pounds). The figures for 1929 and 1917 are calculated from engineering estimates of mill capacities. For 1904, mill capacities are approximated by sugar production figures at each mill.

disparity in the adoption of large-scale mills? The answer lies in the heightened competition for cane that developed all over the island. The demand for cane was expanding rapidly with the expansion of production on the island. In the west, where the suitable cane lands were already occupied, there was a higher degree of competition among potentially expanding centrales for cane lands located near the centrales. In the east, on the other hand, there was an abundance of lands into which the larger centrales could expand; therefore, the east was more attractive to investors.

One can see that this distinction between the west and the east is not exact. Figure 6.2 would have us include the western province of Havana among those provinces that were relatively successful at adopting the large capacities. But other factors were relevant in Havana that do not appear in this highly aggregated, bivariate diagrammatical analysis. In Havana, many smaller ingenios that had existed for decades were eliminated by urbanization, which had the effect of cutting off the lower tail of the mill size distribution in Havana. Furthermore, those few centrales that achieved large scales in the province of Havana were able to find structural conditions similar to those found more abundantly in the east. It will be convenient for the exposition to think of the structural distinctions initially as distinctions between the west and the east. Aggregating by eastern and western provinces is useful to gain an understanding of the differences mill owners faced in the old versus the new areas of sugar production in Cuba. The propositions put forth in this chapter are, then, supplemented by a more disaggregated statistical analysis in Chapter 7, which completes and confirms the results of this chapter.

One important factor that distinguishes the eastern and the western parts of the island was that the sugar mills in these two regions were constructed at different times in the history of the sugar industry. The ease

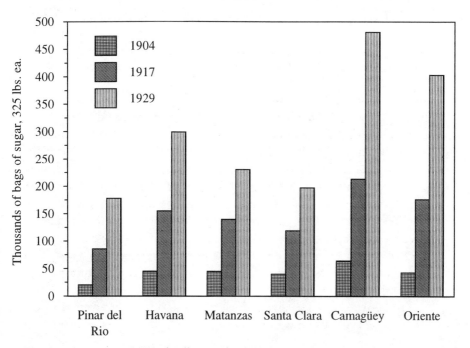

Fig. 6.1. Average capacity of mills in each province in 1904, 1917, and 1929. Source: See Table 6.1.

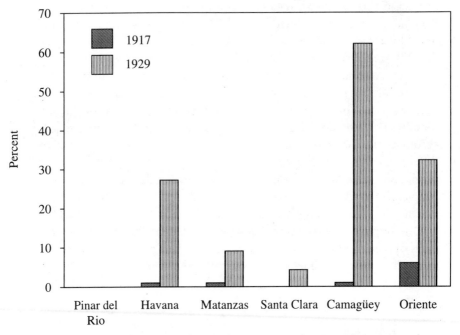

Fig. 6.2. Percent of mills in each province in 1917 and 1929 with capacities greater than 400,000 bags. Source: See Table 6.1.

with which mills could adopt larger scales of operation, therefore, differed between the old and the new regions. The newer areas of expansion in the east had the advantage of being latecomers to sugar production, and they were able to design their cane supply networks to accommodate the greater demands of the new sugar manufacturing technologies. The older sugar mills of the west had established their locations and transportation infrastructure for an older system of production that had required much smaller cane zones. With the infrastructure in place, they could not quickly alter their cane supply networks when cane requirements changed, and their competitiveness was affected detrimentally relative to the east. This had negative implications for their ability to attract capital for the adoption of the large-scale technologies.

The provinces of Havana and Matanzas and the western part of the province of Santa Clara were the centers of the old slave-based plantation system of the nineteenth century. Sugar production in these provinces began under the ingenio system of production, which consisted of a self-contained plantation/mill complex, vertically integrated and centrally managed. The capacities of mills were much smaller than they were in the twentieth century (although Cuban mills, even in the nineteenth century, were generally larger than mills in other parts of the world). Technical changes in the milling machinery and the cane transport systems began to change the optimal size of mills in the late nineteenth century. If the existing mills were to adopt these changes, they would have needed access to much larger areas of cane land to support the larger mills.

Table 6.2 shows the amount of land devoted to cane from 1860 to 1929, and it gives an impression of the change in land requirements of the average mill. These figures are admittedly rough; the amounts of land devoted to cane for 1904, 1916, and 1929 are not available so they are estimated from the amounts of cane ground for each of these years and the average yield of cane per *caballería* for 1913. (52,082 arrobas per caballería, 1 caballería = 33.333 acres, and 1 arroba = 25 pounds. See the explanatory notes in Table 6.2.) The figures for the amount of land devoted to cane in 1860 and 1877 are not reconstructions; they are taken from the agricultural census of Pezuela (1860) and the *Boletín oficial del Círculo de Hacendados de la Isla de Cuba* (1877) reported in Ferrara.[12]

The average mill in 1860 produced about 28,600 arrobas of sugar (1 arroba = 25 pounds) or in bag equivalents, about 2,200 bags of 325 pounds, as reported in Table 1.1. Based on the figures in Table 6.2, in 1860 about 15 caballerías, or about 510 acres, of cane fields were needed to supply the average mill with cane. By 1929, the average mill capacity was

Table 6.2
Inputs of Cane and Cane Fields in Cuba, 1860–1929

Year	No. of mills	Land in cane in Cuba (000s acres)	Cane ground (millions arrobas)	Area in cane per mill (000s acres)	Cane ground per mill (millions arrobas)
1860	1,365	691.9	630.0	0.51	0.5
1877	1,190	590.0	758.6	0.50	0.6
1904	174	606.7	948.0	3.49	5.4
1916	189	1,516.6	2,369.6	8.02	12.5
1929	163	2,409.3	3,764.5	14.78	23.1

SOURCES: Author's estimates based on the following. The figures for 1904, 1916, and 1929 are taken from Cuba, Secretaría de Agricultura, Comercio, y Trabajo, *Industria azucarera*, 1903/4, 1915/16, 1929. The figures for the amount of land in cane in 1904, 1916, and 1929 are estimated from the reported amount of cane ground. The yield of cane per acre is taken to be the average yield in 1913 found in Cuba, Secretaría de Agricultura, Comercio, y Trabajo, *Portfolio azucarero*. The amount of land and the number of mills in 1860 and 1877 are based on Pezuela, 1: 67; and Ferrara, p. 96, respectively. The amount of cane ground is estimated from Moreno Fraginals's estimates for sugar, in *El ingenio*, 3: 35–41, and an assumed yield of 6 arrobas sugar per 100 arrobas cane. The assumed yield is consistent with Bergad's findings of an estimate of 5.91 arrobas in 1840 using a Derosne vacuum evaporator (*Cuban Rural Society*, p. 154). Since yields from Derosne evaporators tended to improve, this may be a downwardly biased estimate of yields (sugar-cane ratios). Consequently, the amounts of cane ground in 1860 and 1877 are likely overestimated here.

2,834,000 arrobas of sugar, or 218,000 bags. Based on my estimates, by 1929 the amount of land required to supply the average mill with cane increased to 443 caballerías, or 14,780 acres. This implies an increase in land requirements per mill of almost 30 times. This change in land requirements was fundamental for the operation of sugar mills that adopted the new, larger-scale technologies. The land needed to support the modern mill, if it was to take advantage of the economies of scale and operate efficiently, grew enormously.

In the older sugar-producing regions, most of the good cane lands were in cultivation by the 1850s; therefore, the ingenios were forced to consolidate if they were to adopt the new large-scale technologies. Consolidation resulted in the vertical disintegration of the self-contained plantation/mill complex, or the ingenio. The central consolidated the processing of the cane supplied conceivably by a multiplicity of former ingenios. The additional cane needed to supply the central was obtained in part through consolidation of ownership of the ingenios. But it was also obtained innovatively through the widespread adoption of cane contracting through the colono system. By 1905, 70 percent of all the cane supplied to mills was supplied through contracts with colonos. And from this time almost all mills obtained at least part of their cane by contracting with colonos.

The institutional change this implied was not a simple task in the west, where the old system was embedded; it required the consolidation of old plantations, either by ownership or by contracting arrangements. Whenever the combination of two plantations was contemplated, it entailed the loss of status of one or more of the owners, either because of the loss of the ingenio or because of the social demotion of one party to the status of colono. But one would expect that the loss of status alone could not have resisted the technological forces at work to consolidate the properties of old plantation owners.

In contrast to the western provinces, the sparsely populated eastern provinces of Oriente and Camagüey had abundant cane land. Before the War of Independence, less than 10 percent of the Cuban sugar crop came from the east, though there was much available land. By 1929 the east produced nearly 60 percent of the Cuban crop.

In the east, consolidation of old plantations was not necessary in general because the large-scale central factories were constructed in areas that were new to the sugar industry. Not only the machinery in the factory but also the transportation network benefited from being built on lands that were uncluttered by the infrastructure of the old system of production.

Table 6.3
Population Density by Province, 1899–1931
(inhabitants per km²)

Province	1899	1907	1919	1931
Pinar del Rio	12.6	17.8	19.3	25.4
Havana	24.6	65.4	84.7	119.7
Matanzas	50.6	28.4	37.0	39.9
Santa Clara	16.7	21.4	30.7	38.1
Camagüey	3.3	4.5	8.7	15.5
Oriente	9.0	12.5	20.0	29.3
TOTAL	13.7	17.9	25.2	34.6

SOURCE: Luzón, pp. 82–83.

The initial layouts of the cane fields, the plantation rail system, the loading and unloading stations, and the location of the factory were designed together and were of the most recent design.[13] Also, based on the technological trend and the fierce competition in the world market, these sugar producers expected the optimal size of the factory to continue to grow, and so the layout included cane lands available for prospective future expansion. As a result, the centrales in the east tended to be situated far apart from each other, to have transportation networks that were independent of other centrales, and to have available expansion sites planned or under consideration.[14]

Designing the cane supply systems according to the scale and logic of the new technology was aided in the east by lower population densities, as is seen in Table 6.3. Lower population density was not the principal factor making land in the east more pliable to the organizational will, though it helped. More important for the systemic logic was the former economic, rather than the human, occupation of the land. Before cultivation of sugar, much of the land was left to open-range grazing; other areas were idle or occupied by smallhold farmers or squatters.[15] The shift into sugar was a shift into an export crop that was much more remunerative than that offered by alternative uses of the land. Coffee, which was the alternative market crop in the province of Oriente cultivable by the poor, declined in production in regions where sugar was developed. But as noted in Chapter 2, coffee exports were not of great significance at this time. The poor had not produced sugar because they could not finance the setup costs. Where the entrance of outside developers was foreseen and expected returns were high, land was bought up in large tracts. For the first time, much of the land in the east was perceived as valuable enough to incur the litigation and surveying costs of establishing title.[16] Even in the later crisis and low prices of 1930s, sugar was more remunerative than any alternative crop.[17] But that income was available only to the colono (with contractual obligations); the small or medium agriculturalist could not undertake sugar production alone.

As a final comment on regional mill differences, the mills in the west were, in general, founded well before the mills in the east; therefore, one might expect that the equipment in western mills was simply of an older vintage and that this would explain the difference between the average capacities of mills in the two regions. But this does not plausibly explain much of the difference. After the devastation of the War of Independence, many of the mills in the west had to be completely rebuilt so that the mills of both west and east needed to purchase large amounts of new equipment. Bergad comments that "by the war's end, only 20 of the 271 rural properties [in Matanzas] classified as ingenios had not been destroyed."[18] Other vestiges of the old ingenio system — the property divisions, the placement of existing railroads, and especially the distribution of land ownership — were less easily altered than the vintages of equipment in the mill. These institutional and structural differences between the west and the east had a much greater impact on the relative attractiveness of the two regions to investors who were interested in rebuilding the Cuban sugar industry after the war.

Competition and the Colono System

The colono system and the central system developed simultaneously. The original motivation for contracting with colonos appears to have been to increase the supply of labor to cultivate cane.[19] Chapter 3 briefly describes the evolution of the colono system over the course of half a century into an institution to support the management and the financial credit needed for the development, maintenance, and harvest of the vast arrays of cane fields upon which the centrales were dependent. Into the twentieth century, the function of colonos, within the organizational structure of the sugar enterprise, came to be principally managerial. Small colonos continued to provide labor on their own colonias, but at peak activity, they hired and supervised labor to complete harvest and planting. In short, by this time, the input of colonos was principally management rather than labor.

Colonos were in no sense homogeneous. Their social status varied from that of poor tenants to locally influential landowners or sometimes absentee (possibly foreign) landowners. The sizes of colonias also varied greatly. Some were smallholds, and some were as large as or larger than the typical plantations of the mid-nineteenth century. The types of contracts they held also varied with their means. There were three types of contracts associated with the colonato (the contract between the central and the colono)—the grinding agreement (*molienda de cañas*), the credit agreement (*refacción agrícola*), and the lease (*arrendamiento*).[20] The colonato always included the grinding agreement, but it did not always include the other two contractual agreements. The grinding contract was a share contract between the colono and the central in which the colono agreed to supply the cane produced from a specified plot of land (the colonia) to the central in return for a share of the sugar produced from that cane.

Whether the lease and credit agreements were included in the colonato depended on the wealth and personal means of the colono. The land on which the colonia was formed was owned sometimes by the central and sometimes by the colono.[21] The colonos who did not own land typically were men of small means. These colonos leased the land from the central, and they generally depended on the central to advance credit each season to finance the expenditures needed to plant, cultivate, and harvest the crop. In this case, the colonato provided for the lease and established a promise on the part of the central to provide a certain amount in credit advances determined proportionately to the tasks assigned to the colono in the contract. These colonos were referred to as *colonos del central* because they were dependent on the central for the capital necessary to run the colonia.

Colonos who owned their land were called *colonos independientes* because they retained a large measure of independence from the central. They were often also men of enough means to obtain credit from outside the central. Their ownership of the land and independent access to credit gave them more control over the bargaining process. The colono contract in their case consisted only of the grinding agreement—the colono agreed to put a certain amount of land in cane to be ground at the central in return for a payment in sugar per pound of cane ground from this property.

The Contractual Arrangements for Cane and Their Distribution

The influence of these institutional and structural legacies worked through the contractual relationships that formed. The contractual arrangements were classified into three categories — colonos independientes, colonos del central, and the administration. Of the cane obtained through contracting, those colonos who owned the land they cultivated were called colonos independientes, and those who occupied land owned or leased by the central were called colonos del central. In both contractual categories, payment was made on the basis of a share of the sugar produced from the cane that the colono delivered to the mill. Cane obtained otherwise through direct management by salaried personnel of the central was referred to as "administration cane."

The distribution of the cane supplies of centrales between these three different types of contracts for the period between 1905 and 1929 can be observed in Table 6.4. The figures for "All Cuba" show that the share of cane in the whole island derived from colonos independientes was declining over the period 1905–29 but also that the share of cane derived from colonos was increasing. The provincial figures show that the proportion of colonos independientes was considerably higher in the west than in the east. Although by 1930 the pattern was becoming much less distinct, in the years of expansion before 1930 it was quite distinct. The geographical distribution of the colonos independientes was related to the different timing of development of the sugar industries of the west and the east. The Commission on Cuban Affairs invited by Cuban President Carlos Mendieta in 1934 came to the conclusion that the distribution of the various contractual arrangements depended on patterns of land organization that were established much earlier in Cuba's history.

The degree to which these different field systems prevail on any given estate seems to depend chiefly on the original conditions of land tenure and the availability of cane. In the older provinces of the island there were a great many holdings, and with the reorganization of the sugar industry after the Ten Years War [1868–78] the owners of many of these planted cane to secure a cash crop. Many *centrales* are the result of a concentration about a single producing unit of a number of old plantations. Many plantation owners thus became *colonos* to large *centrales*. . . . With the rise of sugar production in the eastern end of the island in new areas another situation presented itself. Companies bought land in large tracts and found it convenient to grant much of it on lease to farmers and others with capital who undertook the work of clearing the land and assisted in recruiting the necessary field labor.[22]

Undoubtedly, this is an accurate depiction of the different origins of the colonato in the west and the east. Many of the colonos in the west originated from planter families of the nineteenth century, and many of the estates of colonos in the west were once ingenios of the old technology.

Table 6.4
Shares of Cane Supplied by Each Type of Contractual Arrangement
(percent)

Province	Year[a]	Administration cane	Colonos del central	Colonos independientes	Percentage of crop represented in sample
All Cuba	1905	30.3	33.1	36.5	72.3
	1913	13.4	56.9	29.7	62.4
	1929	18.3	65.9	15.7	92.1
Pinar del Rio	1905	27.8	30.5	41.7	100.0
	1913	18.7	44.3	37.0	52.0
	1929	24.6	46.8	28.6	100.0
Havana	1905	22.6	38.0	39.4	51.4
	1913	8.8	50.3	40.9	55.3
	1929	12.6	74.5	12.9	73.0
Matanzas	1905	27.4	35.2	37.3	76.3
	1913	8.1	46.8	45.1	52.2
	1929	4.5	58.9	36.5	87.6
Santa Clara	1905	24.6	26.4	49.0	73.1
	1913	16.1	50.6	33.3	64.2
	1929	11.5	70.5	18.0	88.9
Camagüey	1905	55.5	43.5	1.1	100.0
	1913	10.6	79.2	10.2	100.0
	1929	14.5	77.1	8.4	94.2
Oriente	1905	41.9	40.4	17.6	71.7
	1913	17.6	72.1	10.3	60.7
	1929	32.7	55.0	12.3	98.5

SOURCES: Author's calculations. Data are from Cuba, Secretaría de Hacienda, *Industria azucarera*, 1904/5; Cuba, Secretaría de Agricultura, Comercio, y Trabajo, *Portfolio azucarero*, and *Industria azucarera*, 1930. See also Dye, "Cane Contracting and Renegotiation," p. 152.

NOTE: In the construction of these averages, the contribution of each mill is weighted by the amount of cane produced by that mill of the total cane produced in each province. The mills included in the sample vary between the three years represented. It is important to allow the sample to vary from year to year; otherwise the mills of the east would be poorly represented because few of them existed in 1905. The expansion of new mills in the east was important for the overall distribution of shares between the tenure arrangements over the island as a whole. Camagüey is the most extreme example. Of the 29 mills grinding in 1929 in Camagüey, only 3 were in operation in 1904. When they entered the industry, the mills of this province tended to have a higher percentage of colonos del central relative to the island's average; likewise in Oriente. For the island as a whole, 243 mills were in operation sometime between 1905 and 1930, but only 95 of those were in operation in both 1905 and 1930. (A mill that changed names or changed hands, of course, is considered only one mill.) But it would be incorrect to consider the decline in the share of cane coming from colonos independientes to be due solely to the entrance of new mills. The decline in the share coming from colonos independientes in the western provinces suggests that the existing mills, as they expanded, tended to reduce their dealings with colonos independientes. Only 39 of the mills for which data are available were in operation from 1905 to 1930. Fixing the sample of mills to these 39 exhibits results which are remarkably similar to the results given in the table and demonstrates that the differences in provincial tendencies are not directly attributable to the newness of mills in the east that entered after 1905.

[a] For 1905 the total number of mills included in the sample is 106 (out of a total of 180 mills grinding); for 1913, 98 (of 172), and for 1929, 136 (of 154).

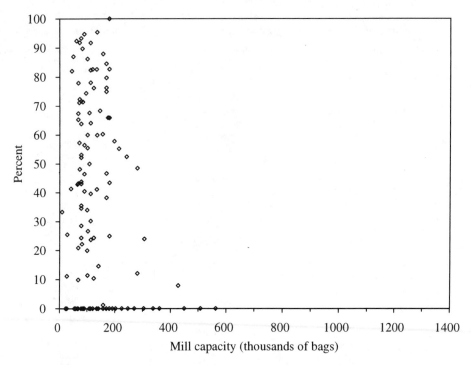

Fig. 6.3. Percent of cane supplied by colonos independientes to each mill in 1913. Source: Secretaría de Agricultura, Comercio, y Trabajo, *Portfolio azucarero*.

The east, being an area of new expansion, did not have this connection with the old sugar industry of the nineteenth century. Another factor was the purchases of land in large tracts in the east in speculation immediately after the War of Independence and during the first U.S. occupation.[23]

Figures 6.3 through 6.8 present scatter diagrams of the shares of cane supplied by each type of tenure arrangement for each mill for the years 1913 and 1930 against the mill capacity of the central. Apparent in these diagrams is the preferences of centrales for different tenure arrangements. Colonias independientes appear to have been less preferred generally to colonias del central because almost none of the centrales obtained all of their cane from colonias independientes while a large number of centrales obtained all their cane from colonias del central. The diagrams also confirm the observation of Table 6.4 that the administration system appears not to have been preferred over the colono system. Guerra y Sánchez seems to have believed that there was a tendency toward a more widespread adoption of the administration system that had simply not worked itself out because of capital constraints, but this appears not to have been the case, given the universal upward trend in colono cane.[24] A final observation is that the employment of colonos independientes was a very uncommon source of cane for the largest centrales. Typically at the mills with larger capacities, the cane coming from colonos independientes was well below 40 percent. On the other hand, the majority of the cane coming to the larger mills did usually come from colonos del central — not from administration cane as some have claimed.[25]

The Centrales and Control over Investments

Foremost in importance was the effect of the site specificity of the central's investments on the interests of both contracting parties. The huge investments in plant and railroad equipment required by the new technology

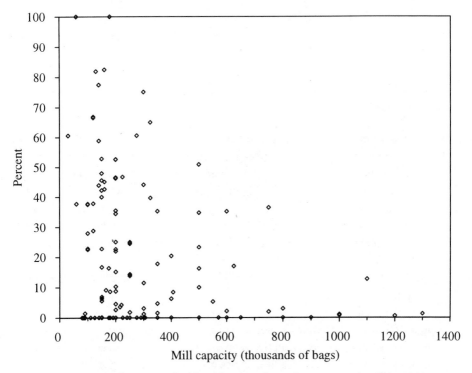

Fig. 6.4. Percent of cane supplied by colonos independientes to each mill in 1930. Source: Secretaría de Agricultura, Comercio, y Trabajo, *Industria azucarera*, 1930.

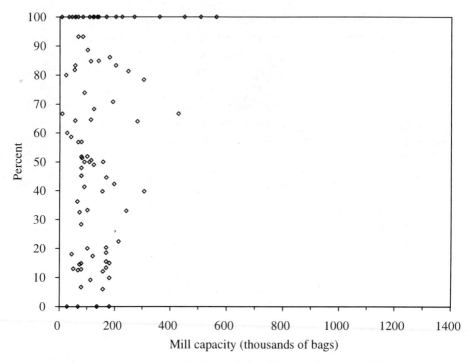

Fig. 6.5. Percent of cane supplied by colonos del central to each mill in 1913.
Source: See Fig. 6.3.

created an incentive for the central to maintain control of the activities in the cane fields and transportation network so that owners could maintain the value of their investments. The profitability of the machinery and the railroad to the central was in question unless the central was assured of sufficient cane supplies for the life of the equipment. Because the railroad network was, for all practical purposes, fixed once it was laid down, the central was committed to the cane lands surrounding the railroad. Given the long-term interests of the mill, the management of the central had an incentive to control the cane production of these lands to ensure its supplies.

One possible reason for the attractiveness of the colono system to sugar manufacturers was that the share contract provided a means to disperse the risks of sugar production between the sugar manufacturer and the cane cultivator. As in agricultural industries in general, sugar prices were unpredictable, subject to changes in international supply conditions and speculation. Furthermore, local weather conditions introduced additional, nonprice or agricultural, risks.[26] Droughts or heavy rains could reduce both the quantity and the quality of cane available to the central each year. Also asymmetric information about the causes of fluctuations of output, whether weather or negligence on the part of the colono, indicates that there were substantial agency (transaction) costs associated with internal governance of cane production. We have seen that these uncertain forces were influential in determining the technology of the delivery of cane to the mills. They also created incentives to reduce the riskiness of these huge capital investments in equipment. Another possible influence might have been the costs of monitoring the cane field management, or the relative costs of organizing and monitoring the field labor by mill or colono management.[27]

The contractual arrangement of the colonato, therefore, seems to have provided a mechanism that served two purposes — it dispersed the risks and reduced the agency costs of production, and it allocated much of the

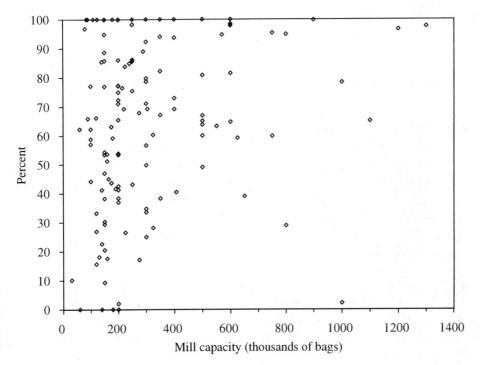

Fig. 6.6. Percent of cane supplied by colonos del central to each mill in 1930. Source: See Fig. 6.4.

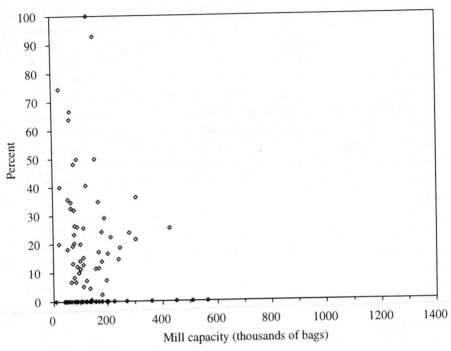

Fig. 6.7. Percent of cane supplied by central administration to each mill in 1913.
Source: See Fig. 6.3.

control of the activities in the cane fields to the central. The dispersion of
risks and the allocation of agency costs was accomplished through a share
payment. In the contract between the colono and the central, the central
agreed to pay so many arrobas[28] of the sugar for every 100 arrobas of cane
delivered by the colono to the mill. In return, the colono agreed not to sell
any of the cane from the plot of land in question to another mill over the
duration of the contract, which generally lasted between six and ten
years.[29]

The colonato also provided a mechanism for the central to maintain
control of its investments. Similar to the findings of Steven Cheung in
Chinese sharecropping arrangements and Joseph Reid in the arrangements of the U.S. post–Civil War South, the management of the central
maintained control of all major decisions by the specific terms of the
agreement.[30] The standard contract established specific requirements of
the colono for the regular delivery of cane assignments to the mill during

the grinding season, and it also set up specific obligations for the development of cane fields and other capital improvements to be made on the colonia. However, the degree of control the central could obtain differed depending on whether the colono was dependent or independent of the central for the provision of land and other capital. To see this, it is useful to summarize some of the terms of the standard contract of the dependent colono, or the colono del central.

In the standard contract of the colono del central — the colono who leased land from the central — the lease agreement gave the colono the right (*usu fructu*) to a plot of land for a specified annual rent, but this right was granted only under limited conditions. The proportion of the lands to be planted in cane and other "minor" crops was strictly specified in the contract. For example, the Central Manati required the colono to plant 90 percent of the lands in cane and the rest were to be devoted to crops and

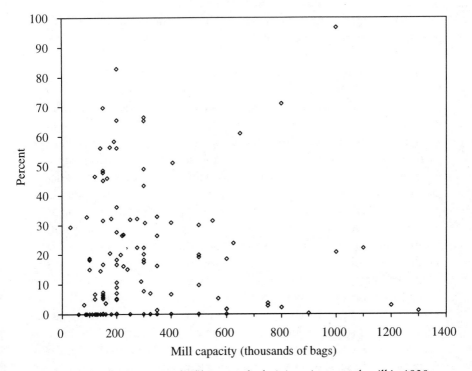

Fig. 6.8. Percent of cane supplied by central administration to each mill in 1930. Source: See Fig. 6.4.

grassland to support inputs into cane production.[31] The colono was pro-hibited from using the land to generate income from any other source than the business of the central. Moreover, the central reserved the discretion to determine how and where the cane plantings were to be laid out in the colonia. Furthermore, as is common in sharecropping arrangements of all sorts, the colono was obliged to construct or maintain other capital goods such as a well, a cane-loading machine to transfer the cane from the oxcarts to the rail cars, scales, housing for laborers, and so on. If the central deemed the colono negligent in these responsibilities, it reserved the right to intervene to fulfill them at the colono's expense. Also very important, all improvements to the land or equipment on the land re-verted to the mill after the term of the lease. As described below, this reversion of property to the mill at the termination of the contract was ensured with the colono del central but not necessarily with the colono independiente. The colono independiente retained the ownership of his land at the end of the contract and was often able to obtain property rights to capital improvements to the land. This depended on the cost of the transfer of ownership and the bargaining position of the colono indepen-diente. The distinction between the bargaining relations of colonos inde-pendientes and of colonos de los centrales is fundamental.

The milling agreement in the standard contract of the colono del cen-tral stipulated that the colono was responsible for delivery of the cane to the mill according to daily quotas set by the central at the beginning of the grinding season. The central also determined where the cane was to be cut within the colonia over the course of the season. The central imposed certain conditions on the freshness and quality of the cut cane upon deliv-ery. In payment, the central agreed to pay the colono so many pounds of sugar (specified in the contract) for every 100 pounds of cane delivered to the mill, but the mill assumed no obligation for the loss of cane resulting from interruptions or termination of grinding. The colono, however, could be penalized for lack of care in the cultivation or delivery of the cane. An implication of this arrangement was that the central often con-tracted for more cane than it would need in an average season to allow for errors in planning or variations in the speed of grinding or the termination of the grinding season, which was determined by the weather. The colonos were not paid for any surpluses left standing in the fields, uncut at the end of the grinding season. The central thus maintained greater control over the continuity of cane supplies given uncertainty in the rate at which the cane could be ground and the length of the grinding season. The surpluses provided insurance to the central against running out of cane at the end of the season, which, if it happened, would increase the unit fixed costs of production at the mill. The costs of this policy were generally incurred by the colono, who paid for the planting and cultivation of the cane.

The central also reserved the right to supervise the colonia and could terminate the contract with penalties if the colono failed to attend to the colonia properly according to the judgment of the central. Under these terms, the central had extensive control over the activities of cane cultivation and harvesting even though it did not manage the colonias directly. The typical colono del central had little control over the major decisions regarding the level of production and investment on the colonia.

This standard contract, which I have described, pertained to the colono del central, who was usually a man with little means to affect the bargaining process. He would likely have been dependent on the central for credit to carry out the terms of the contract, and the colonia would likely have been his only source of income; hence the strictness of the terms of the contract. It was another case for the colonos independientes, who often were successful at obtaining more favorable terms. They often owned large tracts of land and had a number of sources of income. In some cases they would hold contracts to supply cane to more than one central simultaneously. They often managed their colonias in an absentee fashion, contracting with subcolonos. The large colonos were often in much better positions to negotiate to obtain more favorable grinding terms. Most important, as the owners of the land, they retained the property rights to the land at the termination of the contract, and they often obtained the property rights to the capital improvements on the colonia, as well, at the termination of the contract. If the central owned the land, the ownership of the capital improvements, regardless of who had incurred their costs, usually reverted to the central at the termination of the contract. This created a fundamental difference in the relationship of the central with the two types of colonos.

Holdup and Viability

Dependence on short-term cane supply arrangements was subject to potential holdup. The presence of such problems could turn an otherwise sound investment into an unwise one from the investor's point of view. If the outside supplier effectively threatened to withdraw the supplies, holding out for a higher price, the central could be forced to accept short-term losses up to the difference between the productive and salvage value of the specific assets.[32] As Benjamin Klein, Robert Crawford, and Armen Alchian have shown more generally, it was not just that a supplier, such as the colono independiente, could appropriate a greater share of the profits (residual claims) from the mill; he could potentially even appropriate rents needed for the maintenance and replacement of physical capital at the mill. Therefore, if a mill was subject to such holdup problems, the viability of the mill itself or its potential growth might have been threatened.[33] That the colono appeared to be in a weaker social position does not mean that he was always in a weaker bargaining position. It may seem surprising under these circumstances that the cane and milling operations were not vertically integrated (as they had been in the earlier plantation system) to avoid the potential high costs of holdups or interruptions in production. Vertical integration indeed had been the standard form of firm organization in other major sugar-producing regions (e.g., Java, Hawaii, and Peru) for precisely this reason.[34]

Because of the strictness of coordination requirements, such holdup threats would have been particularly acute during the grinding season. Similar to the findings in other studies of share contracting in agriculture, however, explicit contractual stipulations regulating the supplies of inputs of the contracting parties attenuated much of the potential holdup during the contract period.[35] To establish the central's control over the coordination of mill and field activities, the contract gave the central the right to make decisions regarding the direct investment and operating decisions in cane production — the timing, location, and scale of planting, cultivation, and harvest. To facilitate enforcement, the contracts also typically included a clause that gave the central the right to intervene at the colono's expense if the central deemed the colono negligent in his obligations. Although not perfectly, the potential holdups of production during the term of the contract were thus largely reduced provided that the transaction costs of detecting violations and correcting them were not too great. What must be emphasized is the incompleteness of the contracts given the long-term relation between the central and the colono, particularly the colono independiente, and how this led to potential holdup upon contract renewal.[36]

A crucial aspect of the colono contract and the colono system in general was that the desired term of the bilateral relationship between the colono and the mill was generally much longer than the term of the contract. The duration of the contract corresponded with the expected life of the cane planting — six to ten years — but the life of the railroad as well as many other improvements on the land was longer. This made the contractual relationship of the colono independiente with the mill fundamentally different from that of the colono del central. The colono independiente retained the ownership of the land at the termination of the contract; therefore, at renegotiation, he could effectively threaten to hold up production by withdrawing access to his cane fields and other physical assets fixed to them. When the contract of a large independent colonia was up for renegotiation, the central had to negotiate new terms with a colono who could feasibly block access to a significant portion of the central's cane supply. This explains the attractiveness of the colonias de los centrales to the centrales and the rising share of the colonias de los centrales observed in the data of Table 6.4.

A complementary feature of the bargaining relationship between the colono independiente and the central was the access of the colono independiente to the public service railway system. Virtually all of the centrales used private rail lines to transport their cane to their mills; however, the degree of their independence from the public rail systems varied. Some relied exclusively on private rail systems, and others combined the use of public and private service lines. In many cases the large colonia was a tract of land located adjacent to a public railroad. At the establishment of such a colonia, the central would construct a siding or a private feeder line connecting to the public line to obtain access to the cane lands of that colonia. During the harvest, one leg of the shipment of cane from the colonia to the mill was made via the public railroad. This connection with the public railway could be of great advantage to the colono. If the colono owned the land and if the property rights to the private railroad or sidings on his property reverted to him at the termination of the contract, then the bargaining position shifted abruptly in the colono's favor. The access of the colonia to the public rail system opened the colono's land up for bids from nearby mills during contract renegotiation. This, of course, strongly affected the terms of the renegotiation.

Evidence of such holdup threats in contract renegotiations is readily found in the records of negotiations between large colonos independientes and central managers. Observe the following list of occurrences.

(1) *Central Elia, Camagüey.* In 1924, the Central Elia had a contract with Aurelio Portuondo, a large independent colono, which had run for ten years and was scheduled to expire the following year. Portuondo com-

municated to the manager of the Elia that he had received bids from three different nearby centrales that were competing for his land—the Jobabo, which was an established mill in the area that was expanding its capacity, and the Najasa and the Siboney, both of which were newly constructed mills in the area of the Elia. An internal memo of the Elia reported the existence of company railroads, loading stations, and telephone lines whose ownership was to revert to Portuondo at the termination of the contract that was currently in force. The Cuba Railroad (public service) also passed through Portuondo's property giving him easy access to the other local centrales. The management of the Elia was evidently concerned about the potential losses if they should lose access to the railroad and other equipment on Portuondo's property.[37]

(2) *Central Socorro, Matanzas.* Another example is the purchase of the Central Socorro by the Cuba Cane Sugar Corporation from its previous owner, Pedro Arenal, which involved, in addition, purchases of some of the land in Arenal's possession. Arenal refused to sell all the land of the Socorro, reserving the best cane lands for himself. The lands he retained were not only fertile but also well situated because they were traversed by two railroads, one a public service road (United Railways) and the other his own. It turned out that the contractual arrangements established along with the purchase subsequently presented problems of high cane costs for the Central Socorro. After the purchase, the Socorro still depended on Arenal for approximately 60 percent of its cane. Some of this, supplied only indirectly by Arenal, originated from subcolonos who had to contract with Arenal because their access to the Socorro mill depended on Arenal's railroad. Arenal was paid a high liquidation rate of between 7.5 and 8 percent for these supplies.[38]

(3) *Central Tuinucu, Santa Clara.* In this case, the Central Tuinucu had obtained a large part of its cane from lands adjacent to the Cuba Railroad. The lands were leased from a member of the Echemendía family. The Central Tuinucu had constructed a rail line into and through the colonia, accessing the cane lands of the Echemendías as well as some other cane lands that lay beyond the Echemendía property. The lease stipulated that the railroad would revert to the landholders, the Echemendías, at the expiration of the contract, except that the Tuinucu retained the right-of-way for five years after the termination. In 1928, as the lease was about to expire, the Echemendías began to raise their terms for renegotiation of the lease, which involved higher rents and the granting of the right-of-way over the colonia railroad line, to access other lands owned by the Eche-

mendías to the Cuba Railroad. It thus brought into question a large area of the cane supplies of the Central Tuinucu. Regarding the matter, the irate Manuel Rionda wrote to Oliver Doty, the general manager of the Tuinucu, during that difficult year: "It is people like the Echemendías who are getting the blood out of the Company [Tuinucu] and, worse still, out of the poor *colono* and workmen. . . . As for my part, I don't propose that landowners should be the only ones to get the benefits of our work and our investments."[39]

These three examples of renegotiations show how holdup could be threatened through interruption of the access to site-specific assets. They also show how a landowning colono's access to a public service railroad affected the bargaining process to favor the colono. One can also find general comments that indicate that the difficulties in arrangements with colonos independientes noted above were common. For example, the report commissioned from Goethals and Company in Cuba stated that "many colonos grow cane on land not under control of the central, and where favorably located with respect to a number of centrals, they are able, through competition, to receive higher prices than the general average in the locality. The control by centrals of sufficient cane to work the mills to full capacity is, therefore, an important factor."[40]

One might ask why the centrales did not simply purchase the cane lands they wanted. The answer is simple. For the mills already in existence, the purchase of cane lands they were currently using faced similar specificity problems — and potential opportunism — as the purchase of cane. Knowing the central's commitment, colonos who might have sold often held onto their lands to preserve the option of selling them at a future date. Retention was equivalent to the purchase of an option to renegotiate terms in the future.[41] At the rate at which new mills were being constructed, it was not irrational to expect demand conditions to shift in favor of the owner of cane lands.

The Regional Differences in Liquidation Rates

The regional effects of this interaction between public service railroads and colonos independientes on cane costs were different. To see this, the location of the system of public railways that was in existence in the 1920s and the geographical concentrations of mills in the various parts of the island are informative. The maps of Figures 6.9 and 6.10 illustrate the

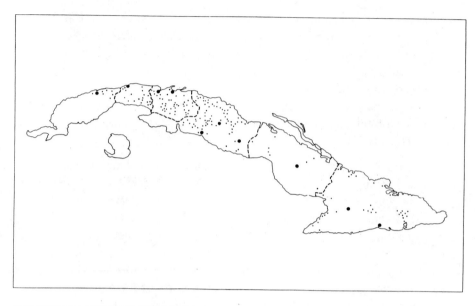

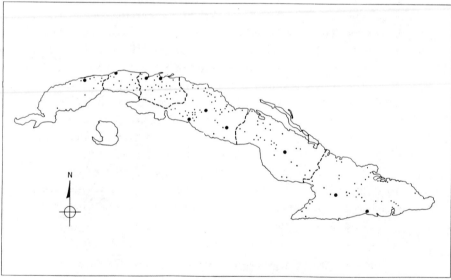

Fig. 6.9. Locations of mills in Cuba in 1913 (top) and 1930 (bottom). Sources: Secretaría de Agricultura, Comercio, y Trabajo, *Industria azucarera*, 1930, and *Portfolio azucarero*.

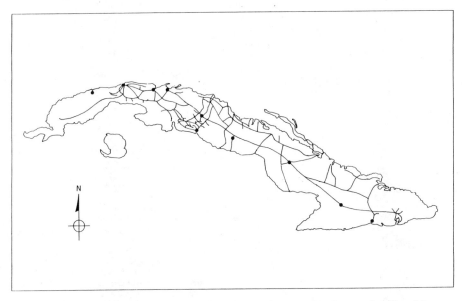

Fig. 6.10. The locations of public railroads in Cuba in 1930. Source: See Fig. 6.9.

distributions of railroads and mills on the island and show the concentrations of public railroads and mills in the west and east. It is easy to see that the heaviest concentration of mills was in the western provinces of Havana and Matanzas and the western part of Santa Clara, especially up to 1913. Table 6.4 shows that the mills in the west also had a higher percentage of colonos independientes. A comparison of Panels A and B of Figure 6.9 reveals that the geographic concentration of mills diminished during the 1920s. The reason was the failures of many unsound mills in the west as prices fell after 1925 and the continued building in the east. Figure 6.10 and Table 6.5 show the relative concentration of public railroads in the west. As is seen in the table, the ratio of kilometers of track per square kilometer of land in the west was three times that of the east in 1915, and it remained twice that of the east by 1930.[42]

The combination of higher concentrations of colonos independientes and the more extensive public railway systems tended to increase the degree of competition for cane that the mills in the west faced. The higher density of sugar mills in a given area of land further heightened the degree of competition. The rates colonos obtained for their cane reflected this difference very sharply. Evidence is seen in the 1919 report of Goethals and Company of the seventeen mills purchased by the Cuba Cane Sugar

Table 6.5
*Extension of Public Railroads in the West and East,
1915, 1930*

	West	East
Length of railroads (000s of km)		
1915	2.45	1.35
1930	2.49	1.88
Density of railroad (km per km² of land)		
1915	0.06	0.02
1930	0.06	0.03
Area of region (thousands of km²)	40.8	72.9

NOTE: The eastern and western geographical areas were defined as follows. The west includes the areas of the provinces of
Pinar del Rio, Havana, Matanzas, and half of the area of Santa
Clara. The east includes the areas of Oriente, Camagüey, and half of
the area of Santa Clara. The provincial areas were obtained from
Marrero, *Elementos de geografía de Cuba*. The estimates of the
length of the railroads include all the major public railroads. The
western public railroads included are United Railways of Havana,
Western Havana Railways, Havana Central, and Cuban Central.
The eastern public railways included are the Cuba Railroad, the
Camagüey and Nuevitas, the Northern Cuba Railway, the Guantánamo and Western, and the Hershey Cuban Railroad. The figures
for their lengths were obtained from Zanetti Lecuona and García
Alvarez, *Caminos para el azúcar*, p. 406.

Corporation in 1917. The newly formed Cuba Cane commissioned,
among other things, a survey of the prevailing cane supply conditions of
each mill, in which the average liquidation rate for the cane at each mill
was reported. (The liquidation rate is the rate of payment in sugar to the
colono for the cane.) The average liquidation rates and standard deviations are reported in Table 6.6. A 95 percent confidence interval for the
average rate in the west still places the estimated western rate well above
that of the east. The interval estimate in the west is 7.1 to 6.7 arrobas for
every 100 arrobas of cane. In the east the rate was 5 arrobas.

Further evidence is provided by a U.S. Department of Commerce report
of 1917, which found that the maximum liquidation rates in the west
in 1916 were around 7.5 while the maximum in the east were around 5.5.
It also found that in Oriente the rates paid to colonos independientes were
between 10 and 20 percent higher than the rates paid to colonos del
central.[43] Additional scattered data on individual mills, collected from
Manuel Rionda's papers, confirm these differences and indicate that they
persisted over time. They also show a tendency of transition in the central part of island (eastern Santa Clara) from low to high liquidation

rates after World War I, as the central cane lands came to incur higher demands.[44]

The best interpretation of this difference in liquidation rates is that the colonos independientes were able to negotiate more favorable terms for themselves, less favorable for the centrales. Holdup was more probable wherever the colonos independientes were prevalent, especially if they could manage to find alternative nearby centrales willing to compete for cane contracts. The higher concentration of colonos independientes made this more likely to occur in the west; therefore, it increased the average liquidation rate paid by mills in the west relative to those in the east.

An alternative hypothesis for the difference in liquidation rates, which has been suggested or alluded to by others, is that regional differences in land productivities might have raised the prices for cane in the west relative to the east.[45] This proposition merits quantitative examination. Before World War I, the average provincial yields per hectare were higher in the east,[46] but data on cane costs are not available to examine the relation between yields and cane costs. This influence cannot be examined properly using the tabular and graphical methods employed in this chapter. In the next chapter, using econometric methods, I show that differences in cane yields per hectare had no significant effect on the expansion behavior of mills, or their ultimate capacities, while the presence of colonos inde-

Table 6.6
Summary Statistics for the Average Liquidation
Rates of Seventeen Mills, 1917

	West	East
Number of mills	13	4
Liquidation rate[a]		
Mean	6.94	5.00
Standard deviation	0.28	0
Sucrose content of cane[b]		
Mean	13.00	13.29
Standard deviation	0.40	0.36

SOURCES: Braga Brothers Collection, Record Group 4, ser. 127; Cuba, Secretaría de Agricultura, Comercio, y Trabajo, *Industria azucarera*, 1916/17–1929. See also Dye, "Avoiding Holdup," p. 648.

[a] A hypothesis test shows that the mean liquidation rate in the west is significantly different from 5.00 at all reasonable significance levels. The small standard deviation for the liquidation rates in the two regions is due to the high degree of integration of the regional markets for colonos.

[b] Hypothesis tests of the mean sucrose content of the cane show that the mean sucrose contents of the cane are insignificantly different between the east and the west for all reasonable levels of significance.

pendientes, regardless of whether they were in the west or the east, had a significant and relatively strong negative effect on the expansion behavior of mills.[47] But we must defer examining this alternative hypothesis until after we have dealt with a number of problems of specifying an appropriate econometric model of the decision to expand the mill capacity in Chapter 7.

Regulation of Private Railroads

In the foregoing investigation, we have seen the importance of the private plantation railroads for the expansion of the centrales in Cuba. The managers of centrales could reduce the competition for cane by building private rail networks to supply the cane that intersected minimally if at all with the public railway system. This strategy was much more effective in the east because there was a much greater expanse of potentially good cane land that was inaccessible by public railroad. The Cuban Railroad Commission, using the body of regulations established by General Wood in 1902 during the U.S. occupation, imposed few restrictions on the construction of private railroads to encourage private railroad construction. This was in stark contrast to the heavy restrictions placed on the public railroads, so there was a huge proliferation of private railroads from the beginning of the century.[48]

There was, however, one restriction on the construction of private railroads that affected the geographical pattern of private railroad construction to the detriment of their proliferation in the west. The regulations of 1902 gave the Railroad Commission considerable authority over the crossing of any two railroads, whether public or private, and a policy of the commission was to require that whenever a private line crossed a public line it become a public railroad, that is, that it provide general services to the public subject to the regulation of the Railroad Commission as a public railroad. Private railroads were thus allowed to connect to, but not to cross, the public lines.[49] This regulation hampered the development of huge plantation rail networks in the west similar to those built in the east. The greater density of public railroads and their long-standing presence in the best cane lands of the west made the likelihood of the crossing of public and private rail lines, or its necessity, much greater in the west than in the east. Operating the cane railroad as a full-service railroad would interfere with the coordination function the railroad performed — the synchronization of the harvest and milling. The alternative of establishing connections with the public railways and combining the use of public and private lines for the shipment of cane greatly increased the costs of production. The coordination of the harvest, transportation, and grinding of cane was already a difficult task for the managerial logistics of the larger centrales. The additional task of coordinating public railway companies with the activities of each colonia along their routes for the transport of cane created more difficulties in coordination. The public railroads were heavily regulated, and furthermore, during this period the public railroads of the west were generally overloaded with traffic. It was, therefore, difficult for mills to obtain the cooperation from the public rail companies to synchronize the transfer of cane over the public line with the grinding activities of the mill, especially given the short distances that were required. Delays, as I have argued, could be very costly because of the effects of the rapid deterioration of the cane on the outcome of the milling process and the fuel costs associated with delays at the mill. This problem simply exacerbated the difference in the attractiveness of the two regions to new capital for investment. In summary, the evidence from observing the geographical location of the mills and public railroads and the differences in liquidation rates demonstrate that the degree of competition for cane lands was much greater in the west and therefore made the west less attractive than the east to investors interested in technical renovation and expansion.

Conclusion

In conclusion, the combination of the greater numbers of colonos independientes, the density of existing mills, and the tighter network of public railways thus increased the degree of competition for cane lands in the west. Since cane costs were the largest component of unit costs in the accounts of the centrales, the stiffer terms that had to be offered to ensure the supplies of cane for the centrales inhibited investment in the west because preferable investment alternatives could be found in the east. I have shown in previous chapters that the adoption of new technologies in Cuba exhibited patterns that can be explained by vintage-capital effects common in capital-embodied technologies such as those being adopted in sugar manufacturing. I would thus conclude that the adoption of new technologies was closely tied to the investment funds that could be attracted to update existing equipment or to expand the existing scale of operation. Any factor that inhibited one region from attracting the needed investment funds would have a detrimental effect on the relative rate of technical change.

It is apparent from the paths of growth of the mills on the island that many mills were constrained from growing to the enormous size of the largest Cuban mills. The scarcity of financial capital was certainly an important influence in these constraints. Much of the physical capital on the island was destroyed during the War of Independence. The reconstruction of the physical equipment and other assets after the war depended greatly on North American financial resources, which could not be attracted with equal abundance to all mills. The pattern of flow of investment funds had a great effect on the abilities of mills to adopt the newest technologies, especially given the large increases in scale which the new technologies implied. But it was the competitive environment of each mill that determined its ability to attract scarce capital. The preexisting patterns of land ownership, the institution of the colonato, and the infrastructure and regulation of the railroads all gave the east a relative advantage in expanding the scale of operation and thus in adopting the more efficient production techniques that the larger scale implied. The channeling of investment funds into the east, as opposed to the west, was a consequence of the differences in the competitive conditions of the two regions of the island.

The institutional environment of each mill existed before the entrance of the new technologies and imposed conditions on the contractual relations that affected the competitiveness of individual mills. The preexisting framework had an important influence on the abilities of mills to adopt larger-scale techniques, and it resulted in granting a form of latecomers' advantages to the eastern provinces. History mattered, therefore, because history was embedded in the pattern of land ownership and the options available to property owners. Ownership patterns did evolve to become more concentrated in the hands of centrales, but they showed considerable resistance to change in the west. The path-dependent process resulted in this case in a latecomer's advantage that accrued to the eastern sugar producers.

Transactions involving investments in site-specific assets often result in vertical integration. Yet empirical studies of specific assets have shown a tendency at times for a substitution of internal organization with long-term contracting when there are specific assets.[50] This was partially the case with Cuban sugar. Central managements perceived other means than complete vertical integration to establish control over the assets. The response of the centrales was to adopt a strategy of obtaining control over those assets by taking possession of the cane fields but not taking over their operation. Further, by the terms of the contract, central management retained control over many day-to-day decisions to enhance their control over the coordination of the mills and fields. The difference between the colono system and an internally organized system of production based on salaried field managers was the incentive structure of the compensation. Contracting out both permitted the colono more control over his income than a salaried manager would have had and imposed the stimulus of market-based incentives on the colono's actions as field manager. Residual gains and losses from fluctuations in the sugar price were shared between the mill and the colono.

As I have shown, the colono system was altered over time to reduce the presence of colonos independientes, who owned their own land, and to increase the presence of the colonos del central, who occupied lands owned by the central. The tendency implied a reduction in the relative bargaining position of colonos, and the reduction had to do precisely with the loss of leverage in negotiating the ownership of assets at the termination of the contract. The central attempted to solve the site-specificity problem by obtaining possession of the site-specific assets, thus obviating the need to take control of the entire cane operation. This organizational construct is consistent with transaction-cost prediction of vertical integration. If management of the assets was not completely internalized, ownership of site-specific assets was unified. It reflects Williamson's observation that the integration tendencies of firms are selective and based on the particular characteristics of the specific assets in each industry or each individual activity in the production process. It also may reflect Paul Joskow's suggestion that choices between unified ownership and alternative long-term contractual options are made by considering the trade-off between the transaction costs of contracting out versus the transaction costs of internal governance.[51]

Much more could be done to examine the contractual relations that developed between the central and the colono, particularly with regard to the structure of risk sharing, the transaction costs associated with the contract, the monitoring of agents, and the effects of sugar technology and the site-specific assets on the relationship. We see here, however, that the persistence of the colono system and the pattern of evolution that the institution took was a rational response to combine the existing Cuban institutions with the new technology. The equity implications of the response for the access or ownership of land was another question. It has been dealt with adequately in other works, so I have not focused on it here.[52] To summarize those findings, concentration of land ownership and industry made land less accessible. Over the course of the early twentieth century, the prospects of land acquisition by smallholders worsened. The fact that land acquisition by large mills was an efficient decision or act on the part of mill owners does not imply that the increased disparity of the distribution of land was a socially desirable outcome. It does suggest that if or when interventions were contemplated to improve the land or wealth distribution, great care needed to be taken to consider both the social benefits that could have been reaped from the improved distribution and the potential social costs that might have resulted because of losses in the efficiency of the mills and their international competitiveness.

Regarding the regional differentiation, in the east the centrales were more successful at obtaining ownership of the land; therefore, the east was more attractive for contractual reasons. The pattern of investment that resulted has been associated with imperialist domination by North American interests; however, the factors that made land concentration attractive to mill owners existed regardless of nationality. They were also independent of persons or class; the heirs of ingenios in the west were both the colonos and the central owners.[53] The twentieth-century attraction to the land-abundant east resulted in the rise of the sugar latifundium, which generated alarm among many interests in Cuba. Yet from the point of view of the central's incentives, the attraction was driven by a concern to maintain control over site-specific investments. The concentration of land came about in an attempt to resolve an economically unviable relationship between the colono independiente and the central. The greater presence of colonos independientes in the west effectively repelled foreign investors; hence, the geographical center of the industry shifted as competing sugar production capacity was built up in the east.

Chapter 7

Impediments to Expansion:
A Fixed-Effects Analysis

CHAPTER SIX ARGUED that regional factors determined by the locations, the infrastructure, and the institutional settings of mills affected the investment behavior of mills and thus affected the rate of adoption of new technology from one Cuban sugar mill to the next. It was hypothesized that such factors were capable of impeding the growth of mills to their optimal scales. The prevalence of colonos independientes, the local densities of competing sugar mills, and the density of public service railroads affected the ease with which a mill could obtain financial resources to build a large scale of production. Regular east-west differences in these factors resulted in a regional distinction in the rate of technical change in sugar mills. One piece of evidence used to support that claim is the relatively higher cost of cane in western provinces. Admittedly, however, there are other possible explanations for the higher costs of western cane which might challenge the use of that observation as evidence for the argument of Chapter 6. For example, cane yields per acre were on average higher in the eastern provinces so a frequently encountered proposition is that greater soil exhaustion in western provinces discouraged investment there. Another proposition is that links to North American sources of credit may have differed between regions. A more complete test of the above hypothesis should account for the influences of these alternative explanatory variables.

In this chapter, these issues are reexamined within a multivariate framework that permits the incorporation and assessment of competing explanations. Using an econometric model of the investment decision, I examine the behavior of mill expansion at the individual mill level. Particular attention is given to the regional differences in infrastructure and institutions (or, more precisely, contractual relations) which were highlighted in the analysis of Chapter 6. The statistical exercise is directed, first, toward isolating these influences on mill investment behavior from market and weather influences and then to comparing the relative influences of these infrastructural and institutional features.

It is often difficult to measure and isolate institutional factors quantitatively. The key to the procedure in this chapter is to consider the influences of location, infrastructure, and institutional setting as relatively fixed or permanent features of each mill, although they varied from one mill to the next. It is convenient to think quantitatively of two polarized kinds of influences on mill expansion behavior — those that varied over time, or "time-variant" factors, and those that were relatively invariant over time, or "time-invariant" factors. The time-invariant factors were the economic "setting" of each mill, which would consist of the existing infrastructure available to the mill, the bounds of existing or potential colono relationships, and other factors related to location. But these belonged to a broader group of factors that included as well the internal organization, managerial ability, and connections to credit and technical services either domestic or from abroad. By contrast, time-variant factors consisted of such variables as weather and market conditions — of both product and factor markets. Both groups of factors were subject to change, but the "time-invariant" factors reflected structural features of each mill that did not change radically over time in the medium term. Decisions invoked by those factors were more long-lasting than the year-to-year responses to expected market conditions. Statistically, we can exploit the distinction between "structural" and "market" factors to isolate the effects of institutional influences in which we are interested. The framework for doing this is to treat the relatively fixed, structural features of mills as "fixed effects" and to isolate and estimate them using a fixed-effects regression model.

A two-step procedure is used to perform the statistical analysis. First, we isolate the fixed effects. The resulting estimated fixed effects provide a summary statistic of the composite influence of structural features of the individual mills — or a composite index of structural influences for each mill, which includes both directly observable and unobservable influences. Second, having estimated this composite index, we examine its composition. To do this, we consider the correlations of the fixed effects with a cross section of various *observable* structural features, such as the public service railroad layout, the proximity of competing mills, and the prevalence of colonos independientes. Also included are variables to account for links of individual mills to North American institutions and cane yields per acre — to incorporate the principal alternative explanations for the expansion behavior of individual mills.

The outcome of the estimation shows that the expansion of individual mills was strongly correlated with two principal observable variables — the prevalence of colonos independientes and the mill's orientation toward North America. These correlations support the hypothesis presented in Chapter 6 that regional variations in mill capacities were largely a result of differences in the relative weights and bargaining positions of the colonos independientes, via potential holdup. Equally important, we find no significant correlation of mill expansion with the cane productivities, measured by yields per acre. There is also no significant correlation with the related factor of cane quality, measured as the sucrose content of the cane juice. As a consequence, the results do not corroborate relative soil exhaustion as a principal factor in the decision to expand. Rather, they provide independently derived support for the conclusions reached in Chapter 6. Additionally, a strong association of expansion with the mill's orientation toward North America is detected. This statistical result supports the proposition that company links to North America made a difference. This may imply differential access to foreign capital or to other services that mills required — technical or managerial. One is led to conclude that mills were affected both by internal institutional factors and external factors related in some sense to business connections in the United States. At the end of the chapter, I will discuss how these results should be interpreted within the broader picture.

Given the importance of the treatment of structural factors as fixed, it is warranted at the outset to discuss the merits of this simplification. The characterization of these features as permanent, of course, is not strictly correct. Soil qualities, the existing network of public service railroads, and the prevailing colono relationships were not fixed. They could change over time. But they were fixed in a relative sense. Soil qualities and the network of public service railroads could change only incrementally and in such a way that the differences between mills would be preserved for some time. Likewise, the colono contracts were of six- to ten-year duration, and they expired in a staggered manner at each central so that the central could not immediately alter its contractual arrangements for cane supplies. Furthermore, as we have seen, the regional differences in the patterns of colono landholding were clearly a holdover and a persistent feature handed down from the ingenio system. Although the east-west distinctions show a pattern of convergence, there was a considerable degree of inertia in those relations. Within the frame of a few years' time, the differences between mills as regards their contractual arrangements were likely to be preserved. This permits our treating them, as a first approximation and in a relative sense, as fixed.

For the reader unfamiliar with fixed-effects estimation, it will be useful at this point to discuss briefly the advantages of the procedure to be used. The use of estimated fixed effects as summary statistics of structural influences offers several advantages over the regional or provincial aggregates used in the previous chapter. Unlike the provincial aggregates, they capture differences between mills within provinces or regions, which permits a release from the straitjacket of long-standing province-wide generalizations. The fixed-effects regression model depends on a sample of individual mill data that permits observation of the production records of each mill over regular intervals of time. The observations required represent a matrix of pooled cross-section and time series data, referred to as a panel. Through differencing procedures, the panel permits statistical isolation of fixed and variable influences on mill expansion. Individual fixed effects in this exercise are analogous to the assignment of a dummy variable to each mill, although the degrees of freedom are not reduced as they would be with a multitude of dummy variables. Further, fixed effects in this case are superior to the direct inclusion of explicit variables to account for each of the observable structural features, such as the percentage of cane coming from colonos independientes or a dummy variable to account for North American orientation, for the following reason. The differencing procedure used to estimate fixed effects permits incorporation both of observable factors, such as the presence of colonos independientes, and unobservable factors, such as the quality of the managers or organizations of individual mills. Estimation biases caused in ordinary least squares regressions by omitting unobserved explanatory variables can thus be eliminated using a covariance regression procedure and the fixed-effects approach.[1]

The chapter proceeds as follows. The first section will discuss a few issues regarding the specification of the econometric model of the investment decision. It is followed by a discussion of the data to be used. Then the two-step estimation procedure is performed and interpreted. The final section summarizes the results of the chapter and draws some comparisons between these results and the findings of other studies regarding the economics of cane farming systems.

Econometric Specification of the Investment Decision

In estimating economic decisions such as the mill owners' decision to expand capacity, it is advisable to begin with a choice-theoretic framework in order to determine a proper specification of the econometric model. The analysis presented here is based on such an approach. The model to be estimated, equation (7.1), is a relationship between the annual rate of expansion of the capacities of individual mills and various structural and market factors to be outlined below. The derivation of the econometric model represented in equation (7.1) is not presented here, but the interested reader will find a discussion of it elsewhere.[2]

The dependent variable is the year-by-year expansion of each mill in the sample.[3] The panel of data to be used is a series of thirteen annual observations of a large number of the mills operating in Cuba from 1917 to 1929. These data record the expansion and production behavior of mills for a period of twelve years (lagging one year). Using these data, the estimated fixed effects are controlled for time-variant influences, such as changes in weather, market conditions, or the vintage of the mill's equipment. Once these time-variant effects are controlled for, the statistical information remaining includes the influence only of time-invariant factors, including the infrastructural and institutional features we are interested in isolating.

Careful examination of the decision to invest in larger capacity suggests that individual mill expansion behavior depended on the following explanatory variables: the market price of sugar, the prices of variable factors of production such as fuel and labor services, and the purchase prices for mill equipment. Also important were technical characteristics of existing equipment at individual mills. The relevant characteristics include the vintage of the existing equipment and the degree to which economies of scale had been reaped. The best quantitative proxies for these equipment characteristics are the unit cane requirement of the mill and the existing capacity of the mill. Because they should represent ex ante influences on the mill owners' decisions, these two indicators are lagged one year to act as explanatory variables on the mill prior to the act of expansion.

Expressed in general form, the regression equation used to estimate the fixed effects is

$$\Delta x_{it} = f(\rho_{i,t-1}, x_{i,t-1}, q_t, m_{it}, z_i) \qquad (7.1)$$

where the dependent variable, Δx_{it}, is the annual increase in the log-capacity of mill i. The right-hand side indicates that the dependent variable is a function, f, of the logarithmic forms of $\rho_{i,t-1}$, the unit cane requirement of mill i in year $t-1$; $x_{i,t-1}$, the mill capacity of mill i in year $t-1$; and q_t, a vector of market prices (of sugar and both variable and fixed inputs) that were the same for all mills. The m_{it} is a vector of cane qualities — the sucrose and water contents of the cane juice. Besides the completely random influences of weather, these also capture the soil qualities at each mill that may have influenced investment decisions. The z_i are the individual fixed effects, to be treated initially as unobserved. Not all the individual structural effects are unobservable; however, there were many individual structural characteristics that cannot be observed. These would include the effectiveness or experience of managerial personnel and many site-specific influences. The regression equation is log-linear in the form expressed by equation (7.1). The precise form is specified in the appendix to this chapter.

Once this regression equation is estimated, the fixed effects can be examined separately to identify their composition.

The Data

The data needed for estimating equation (7.1) include mill capacities, yields, cane qualities, and market prices. The data for the mill capacities, yields, and cane qualities are taken from a panel (a set of pooled cross-section and time series data) which includes almost all the mills operating in Cuba for a period of thirteen years, 1917–29.[4] They provide a sample of 130 mills for thirteen years. Because the model includes lagged variables, the complete panel would have the dimension 12×130, but the actual number of observations is only 1,473 (which is less than 12×130) because some of the mills failed to file complete reports of their factory to the Secretaría de Agricultura, Comercio, y Trabajo for all thirteen years. The panel is referred to as an "incomplete panel" because it includes some missing values — some incompletely observed individual mills. It may be preferable to work with a complete panel of reduced size, in which mills with missing values are deleted so that all individual mills are observed each year. The possible advantage of the complete panel is that equal amounts of information are provided from each mill in the sample and each year. A disadvantage is that the complete panel restricts the number of observations considerably. The complete panel reduces the sample of 130 mills down to 71 mills in a panel of 852 observations. We obtain estimates of equation (7.1) using both the larger, incomplete sample of 130 mills and the smaller, complete sample of 71 mills. The larger sample is referred to as the "full sample" and the smaller sample as the "limited sample." As long as the missing observations are randomly missing, the statistical properties are the same for both the incomplete and the complete panel because the error terms are distributed independently between mills.[5]

The factory data are useful for measuring the quality of equipment in the mill and the quality of cane being ground in the mill each year. The unit cane requirement is employed to capture the vintage effects of equipment on the process of expanding mill capacity. The proxy for the unit cane requirement, ρ_{it}, is the yield, or the ratio of the amount of sugar produced to the amount of cane ground where both are measured by weight. If the mill operated at full capacity, then this is essentially the inverse of the unit cane requirement, except that the unit cane requirement was a characteristic of the machinery. The yield, on the other hand, was affected not only by the vintage of the machinery but also by the stochastic influences of weather and soil qualities. The additional influences may compromise the usefulness of the lagged yield as a measure of the vintage of equipment in the mill; however, no better measure is available.

The influences of natural conditions such as the soil quality and the weather will affect the investment decision through the quality of the cane. The quality of the cane at each mill is measured by the sucrose content and the water content of the cane each year. These variables were derived and discussed using a chemical components model discussed in the appendix to Chapter 4. The mill productivity regressions reported in Table 4.3 show that they perform well as measures of the qualities of the cane.

Price data employed are in constant U.S. dollars, terms, scaled for changes in the price level using the U.S. Bureau of Labor Statistics wholesale price index. Given the ties of Cuban sugar producers to U.S. markets for imports of many factors of production — machinery, fuel, and capital — this is the best available measure of general fluctuations in prices.

The Cuban peso was tied one-to-one to the dollar; no distinction was made between U.S. dollars and Cuban pesos in domestic circulation in Cuba during this period.[6]

The price data used in the regression estimates are taken from various sources: wages for cane cutting are taken from the Braga Brothers Collection,[7] and prices of equipment for sugar mills are taken from the import statistics of the Cuban Secretaría de Hacienda, *Comercio exterior*.[8] Prices for bituminous coal and steel rails are taken from U.S. Bureau of Labor Statistics publications.[9] The wholesale prices given in the Bureau of Labor reports are applicable to Cuban imports of these products, which came primarily from the United States.

Price expectations play an important role in the investment decision. One of the results of the comparative statics of the decision model behind the econometric analysis is that responses to the prices that enter the equation through the operating profits are dominated by the managers' expectations of future prices.[10] Price expectations are tricky, however. Sugar prices went through periods of price controls and price speculation during which the sugar price was extremely volatile. Producers understood that the high sugar prices of World War I were abnormal. For the purposes of their long-term investment plans, they would not have formed expectations of future sugar prices solely on the basis of the current or recent prices, which were clearly unsustainable in peacetime. What their expectations were is hard to know, but given that, apart from the wartime prices, the sugar price had a relatively stable recent history, it is not difficult to come up with a plausible pattern of expectations.

As observed in Figure 2.5, from 1903, when Cuban sugar production began to pick up again, to 1914, the world sugar price had remained stable, fluctuating between two and three cents per pound. The high sugar prices of World War I until 1920 would not have entered into the managers' calculations of long-term price expectations. Given the stability of prices for the decade and a half before the war and the lack of any other information about sugar price expectations, it is plausible to assume that during the period of high wartime prices managers believed that in the long run the sugar price would return to its prewar level. After the war, there is evidence of belief among Cuban sugar producers that the price would fluctuate throughout the rest of the decade around a level not too much different from the prewar levels. Manuel Rionda, who was the president of the sugar agency Czarnikow-Rionda, which at one time handled over 60 percent of Cuban sugar sales in New York, wrote in personal correspondence as late as 1929 that he expected a recovery in the price of sugar.[11] Therefore, the best approximation is to assume a constant level for the expected long-term price of sugar over the period, and there is no need to specify what level. This assumption can account for an aspect of price expectations that is commonly overlooked in econometric models. Different managers may have been more or less optimistic in their assessments of the future sugar price. The fixed effects will pick up any differences in expectations between individual mill managers. Though we cannot observe the differences, there is no danger of bias entering the estimated coefficients through not having controlled for them explicitly.[12]

We must also consider structural changes in the expectations for the sugar market during and after World War I. The price controls in 1918 and 1919 and the years of high prices immediately after must still be accounted for because they could have had an influence on investment behavior. As noted in Chapter 4, the rate of construction of new mills increased substantially during the war. The adjustment cost effects that were introduced are picked up in the model by the inclusion of lagged capacity as an explanatory variable. But World War I would have affected investment behavior during the war in other ways. It is possible that investors would wish to take advantage of this period of high prices to make investments because the fixed costs could have been quickly written off. If so, we might expect expansion in mill capacities to have been stimulated during the war. It is also possible, however, that the uncertainty introduced in the long-run price originating in wartime pricing policies and the general disruptive effects of the war on the market may have had a stronger influence that offset the former. The higher level of uncertainty would have had the effect of reducing the level of investment as producers postponed improvements in their mills until conditions in the market settled down.[13]

As Figure 2.5 displays, the price of sugar fluctuated greatly. It was subject to greater uncertainty both during and after World War I. It rose sharply at the beginning of the war, then toward the end (1918–19) it was set by price controls at a historically high level, though at a lower level than would have been determined by the existing market conditions. During the price controls of 1918–19, it was difficult for producers to judge the outcome of the international sugar price negotiations, but worse was that no one knew how long the price controls would be in effect, nor did they know how destabilizing their removal would be. When they were lifted, unrealistic expectations of what the market price would be led to the speculative bubble, known as "the dance of the millions," in which the price of Cuban sugars in New York rose as high as 22.5 cents per pound, then fell to 3.75 cents in the same season. The average nominal price of sugar for the year 1920 was 400 percent higher than the prewar level.[14] Many sugar producers were ruined at the end of the speculation because they had taken on debt to invest in sugar based on a double-digit price expectation. Stocks were being kept off the market, in anticipation of higher prices, when the price plummeted. A crisis was created in the banking industry in Cuba that led to the failure of Cuban and Spanish banks on the island.[15] All the major domestic banks were closed, including the three leading banks at the time in Cuba, the Banco Español, the Banco Nacional, and the Banco Internacional. As a consequence of the crisis, North American banks—the National City Bank, the Royal Bank of Canada, Chase National, and Guaranty Trust—abruptly replaced these Cuban and Spanish banks as the leading banks in the country. In the historiography, it is widely claimed that the investment regime was altered significantly by all these events.[16] In an attempt to capture these effects, I include a dummy variable, which I refer to as the "war dummy," defined such that it is equal to 1 during the years 1917–20.

Regarding the input prices that figure into operating costs, expectations of future prices are treated in the same manner as expectations of the price of sugar. Current variable input prices are very important, however, especially the cost of labor in the fields, because these prices also affected the costs of investment. There was a large labor input in the construction of railroads and the preparation and planting of cane fields. Therefore, current variable input prices are included as explanatory variables in the regression. Labor costs were dominated by the labor in the fields, where labor-saving technologies had not been adopted. The tasks that were required in the fields were largely unskilled, including labor for planting cane and building railroads and bridges. I use the wage of cane cutters to represent the cost of unskilled labor in the fields—the most complete series of wages available for field labor.[17]

The price of bituminous coal for fueling the boilers is included to represent the cost of fuel at the mill. The mills generally were fueled by bagasse (cane trash) supplemented with coal, wood, or fuel oil. The bagasse was a by-product of sugar production. The cost of wood was simply the labor cost of gathering it so that fluctuations of this internal cost are captured with the wage variable. The price of coal most accurately reflects the changes in relative costs of using each of the supplementary fuels. The sales price of oil in Cuba was out of line with international oil prices. The use of fuel oil in sugar mills in Cuba was first introduced in the midst of our sample period. One observes that the prices of fuel oil imported from the United States reported in *Comercio exterior* were much lower than the price of fuel oil in the United States in the first few years after it began to be reported in Cuban trade statistics. The apparent reason for the lower price is that a portion of the payment for fuel oil by those innovators who first adopted it was made in other forms. Those who first used fuel oil in the mill were involved in the establishment of oil distribution facilities at Cuban ports through subsidiaries of major U.S. oil companies. The agreements they made with mother companies to establish distribution facilities in the country very likely included remuneration through discounts on oil purchases in exchange for capital investments designed to open the Cuban fuel oil market. As a consequence, oil prices were not representative of the long-run cost of adopting oil as a fuel. The price of coal, its closest substitute, was more representative.[18] The price of steel rails is included in the regression to represent the cost of railroad construction. As mentioned, factor prices are deflated using the U.S. Bureau of Labor Statistics wholesale price index; no better proxy for the producer price level in Cuba is available. The ties of Cuban sugar producers to the U.S. markets for producers' goods were very close. Mills depended on imports of machinery, fuel, and capital. The Cuban peso was tied to the dollar, and U.S. currency circulated in Cuba. The cost accounts of sugar companies in Cuba were generally kept in U.S. dollars. Because of these intimate ties to U.S. markets, this is the best available measure of general fluctuations in prices.

The liquidation rates of colonos for deliveries of cane — the payment to the colonos in sugar for each 100 arrobas of cane delivered to the mill — have been examined but are not included among the explanatory variables in the regression for two reasons. Unfortunately, liquidation rates are available for only a few mills. I have been able to construct a time series of liquidation rates that would apply reasonably well to mills in eastern Camagüey province and western Oriente. These might conceivably serve as a time-specific series of liquidation rates. Liquidation rates would have differed considerably from mill to mill, however, depending on the age and expiration dates of their contracts with their colonos. The liquidation rates were fixed in the contracts, which were of six to ten years' duration; therefore, the fluctuation of the rates was restricted by the expiration and renewal of contracts. The average liquidation rates paid by mills could not generally respond immediately to fluctuations in the market for sugar or for cane. Mill managers employed other means to provide incentives for short-run responses in cane supply, but these expenses were determined by the cost of labor. The primary means was the use of credit advances both for planting and for maintenance of cane fields. When managers wished to stimulate cane production in the short run, they intensified the maintenance of the cane fields to increase the yields per acre of cane. Advances of this sort were typically tied to a specific cultivation or planting task; to intensify maintenance, they simply increased the number of tasks they financed. The amount of each advance was determined by the cost of performing the particular task required. Since these tasks were labor-intensive, changes in these costs are reflected in the wages of field labor.[19]

There was a rising trend in the liquidation rates in the area around eastern Camagüey and western Oriente. This trend would need to be accounted for in the investment decision. The trend very likely was general on the island so the available data for liquidation rates, though limited, might be useful for representing the general trend. The series of liquidation rates is severely collinear with the war dummy and the wage for cutting cane, however, and its inclusion tends to confuse the influence of the other variables. Therefore, I have excluded the liquidation rates from the regression, understanding that any influence of their rising trend is picked up by the field wages and the war dummy.

The Regression Estimates

The regression estimates are presented in Table 7.1. The overall fit of the regression model is very good for the full-sample estimates and relatively good for the limited-sample estimates. The F-ratio for both is significant at all reasonable levels of significance.

Multicollinearity is present among the input prices so it is inaccurate to draw conclusions about their significance using the individual tests. High degrees of multicollinearity between some of the variables inflate the standard errors and bias the t-ratios. The t-ratios reported for any of the explanatory variables involved in multicollinearity give test results that are biased against significance because they do not account for the correlations between explanatory variables. Wages are independently significant in both regressions. Joint tests of significance based on comparison of restricted and unrestricted models validate the significance of the other

Table 7.1
Estimated Regression of Mill Expansion

A. Dependent variable: increase in mill capacity as a proportion of existing capacity

	Full sample			Limited sample		
N	1,473			852		
F	89.245**			49.524**		
Adj. R^2	0.324			0.313		
MSE	0.154			0.176		
DW	2.007			1.987		
Explanatory variables:	Estimated coefficient	*t*-ratio	Prob > |t|	Estimated coefficient	*t*-ratio	Prob > |t|
Capacity lagged one year	−0.509	−25.679	0.000**	−0.474	−17.930	0.000**
Yield lagged one year	0.105	1.763	0.078	−0.100	−1.116	0.682
War dummy	−0.026	−2.174	0.030*	−0.024	−1.645	0.082
Wages for cutting cane	−0.260	−9.080	0.000**	−0.247	−6.914	0.014*
Price of coal	−0.009	−0.352	0.725	−0.008	−0.234	0.815
Price of steel rails	0.087	1.415	0.157	0.055	0.725	0.468
Price of equipment	−0.018	−0.899	0.369	0.010	0.395	0.693
Sucrose content of cane juice	0.483	3.672	0.000**	1.035	5.539	0.000**
Water content of cane juice	3.601	4.795	0.000**	6.495	6.191	0.000**

B. Tests of joint significance

Zero restrictions imposed on:	F	F
Wages for cane cutting, war dummy	95.229**	57.888**
Price of steel rails, war dummy	10.928**	5.263**
Price of steel rails, wages for cane cutting	92.393**	54.268**
Price of coal, wages for cane cutting	90.830**	55.058**
Price of equipment, wages for cane cutting	91.500**	52.029**
Prices of coal, steel rails, and equipment	2.379	0.965
Prices of steel rails and coal	2.899	1.184
Prices of steel rails and equipment	2.676	1.447
Prices of coal and equipment	1.784	0.526
Sucrose content, water content	24.309**	41.311**

SOURCES: Author's calculations. Data are from Cuba, Secretaría de Hacienda, *Industria azucarera*, 1916/17–29; *Comercio exterior*, 1917–29; Cuba, Secretaría de Agricultura, Comercio, y Trabajo, *Industria azucarera*, 1916/17–29; U.S. Bureau of Labor Statistics; Braga Brothers Collection, Record Group 2, ser. 10a, box 7, f. 1; ser. 10c, box 27, ff. 27, 38; Record Group 4, ser. 96. See also Dye, "Cane Contracting and Renegotiation," pp. 162–63.

NOTE: ** indicates significance at 0.01 and * at 0.05. Panel B gives maximum likelihood tests of the compatibilities of the unrestricted model of Panel A and the indicated zero-restricted models.

factor price variables for both regressions. Presented in Panel B of Table 7.1, they show that input prices paired either with cane cutting wages or with the war dummy are significant. The presence of multicollinearity, of course, presents no problem because I am not attempting to separate the influences of these prices.

The statistical insignificance of the prices of nonlabor investment in-puts — on prices of coal, steel rails, and equipment — (and even the positive signs on the coefficients) is not unexpected theoretically given the pattern of complementarity between the inputs in investment. Investment in cane fields required primarily labor input, but investment in railroads and mill equipment required the combination of material inputs with labor (steel rails or equipment). Given the presence of this complementary relation-ship, the estimated coefficients absorb the influence of cross-price effects. If the prices of steel rails and wages moved in opposite directions, the own-price effect of steel rails on investment would have been offset by the cross-price effect of wages on railroad construction. Meanwhile, at the same time, the own-price effect of wages on cane field development was not offset by the movement in the cost of steel rails.[20]

The sign on the coefficient of the war dummy is negative. This result suggests that the uncertainties of World War I and its aftermath tended to discourage mill expansion, and/or the new banking environment of Cuba in the 1920s, with greater North American presence, stimulated the growth in mill capacities. It turned out that after the speculative bubble of 1920, sugar properties fell into the hands of the North American banks because of foreclosures on bad debt. In many cases, they decided to main-tain possession and continue to make investments in these properties at least for the short run hoping that the demand for sugar properties, af-fected adversely by the uncertainty in the sugar price, would improve in the near future.[21]

The lagged mill capacity is highly significant. The expected sign is nega-tive because the smaller the existing capacity of the mill, the greater were the potential economies of scale. This result may provide some corrobora-tion that mills pursued larger scales as the constraint of costs of adjust-ment was relaxed to reap economies of scale. This result should be ob-tained regardless, however, because $\Delta x_{it} = x_{it} - x_{i,t-1}$ and $x_{i,t-1}$ are not independently constructed. The lagged yield is mildly significant at the 0.1 level in the full sample and insignificant in the limited sample, and, as well, the signs of the coefficients alternate between the two sample estimates. One would expect the yield offered by the existing equipment to be smaller the older the vintage of the mill; therefore, there would be a greater incentive for updating the equipment. But the use of the lagged yield as a proxy for the vintage of the equipment is not reliable because of other factors that influence the yield, particularly weather conditions, which are highly stochastic and had a very strong influence on the yield. So the insignificance of the lagged yield probably arises because it is a poor proxy of the vintage of equipment at the mill. Finally, the sucrose and water contents of the cane are highly significant and exhibit the expected signs because for a given weight of cane, higher contents of sucrose and water in the cane juice indicated a lower impurity content and better factory results.

The Fixed Effects

The object of this statistical exercise is to examine within a multivariate framework competing structural effects on the rate of mill expansion at individual mills. A regression procedure with estimates of the fixed effects established as the dependent variable is employed to permit a multivariate examination of the statistical influences of various structural factors. The results of this second regression may be thought of as a procedure to examine the correlations of the manager's propensity to expand the mill capacity with the structural features in which particular attention is given to the factors highlighted in Chapter 6.

The estimates of the fixed effects are obtained from the estimated coefficients of the covariance regression and the individual-mill sample means of the explanatory variables in the regression as described in the appendix to this chapter. To establish notation, $\hat{\mu}_i$ represents the estimated fixed effects. As a composite index, they embody information about the structural effects on each mill's rate of expansion. To analyze their composition, we observe conditional correlations by regressing them on the following observable structural features that are derived from the analysis of Chapter 6: the percentage of cane at each mill supplied by colonos independientes, the percentage of cane supplied by the administration, the number of active nearby mills that served as potential competitors for a colono's cane, and the accessibility of the public service railroad system to each mill. Other structural features of interest, also included in the regression, are the cane yields per acre and mean sucrose contents (both of which are measures of cane productivity) and a dummy variable to account for a mill's orientation toward North America.

Explicitly, the regression is a log-linear form of the following:

$$\hat{\mu}_i = g(CI_i, CA_i, MA_i, RB_i, \bar{s}_i, YC_i, OR_i) \tag{7.2}$$

where CI_i is the percentage of cane supplied to mill i by colonos independientes, CA_i is the percentage of cane supplied by the mill i administra-

Table 7.2

Regression to Examine Correlations Between Fixed Effects and Structural Features of Mills

Dependent variable:	A. Fixed effects (full sample)			B. Fixed effects (limited sample)			C. Mill capacity		
N	82			82			82		
F	5.865**			5.422**			5.025**		
R²	0.357			0.339			0.322		
MSE	0.236			0.239			0.569		
Explanatory variables:	Estimated coefficients	t-ratio	Prob > |t|	Estimated coefficients	t-ratio	Prob > |t|	Estimated coefficients	t-ratio	Prob > |t|
Constant	−7.812	−3.517	0.001**	−21.609	−9.587	0.000**	−16.274	−5.350	0.003**
Orientation toward North America	0.176	3.258	0.002**	0.190	3.453	0.001**	0.383	2.933	0.005**
Percent cane supplied by colonos independientes	−0.005	−3.791	0.000**	−0.005	−3.768	0.000**	−0.012	−4.247	0.000**
Percent cane supplied by administration	−0.000	−0.012	0.990	−0.000	−0.043	0.996	−0.001	−0.228	0.820
Mean sucrose content in cane juice	−2.554	−3.193	0.002**	−1.901	−2.342	0.022*	−3.846	−1.996	0.050*
Cane yields per acre	−0.001	−0.338	0.736	0.001	0.250	0.803	−0.003	−0.332	0.741
No. of competing mills within 10 km radius	−0.014	−0.490	0.626	0.012	−0.416	0.679	−0.009	−0.138	0.891
No. of branches of public railroad within 15 km radius	−0.024	−0.790	0.434	−0.032	−0.622	0.536	−0.027	−0.356	0.723

SOURCES: Author's calculations. Data are from Table 7.1; Braga Brothers Collection, Record Group 2, ser. 10c, box 61, f. 11; Cuba, Secretaría de Agricultura, Comercio, y Trabajo, *Industria azucarera*, 1930; and Cuba, Secretaría de Hacienda, *Industria azucarera*, 1905. See also Dye, "Cane Contracting and Renegotiation," p. 166.

NOTE: ** indicates significance at the 0.01 level and * at 0.05. The estimated fixed effects, $\hat{\mu}_i$, for the full-sample regression are calculated as described in the appendix to Chapter 7; one fixed effect estimate for each mill is calculated. The estimation of fixed effects for the limited-sample regression has been altered to increase the number of observations. The 71 observations of mills from the limited sample do not provide a sufficient number of degrees of freedom. In fact, the degrees of freedom are reduced further because of the lack of data of structural effects for some of the 21 mills in the sample. Therefore, the estimated fixed effects from the full and limited sample regressions used to obtain these results are calculated using the sample means of the full sample and the estimated coefficients of the limited sample. So the two sets of estimates have the same number of observations (mills); the only difference between them is that they employ different estimates of the coefficients, γ_i, $i = 0, 1, 2, 3, 4$. This is a reasonable procedure since the purpose for using the second set of fixed effects estimates is to observe the sensitivity of the results to plausible variations in the estimated coefficients of Table 7.1 due to the effects of multicollinearity between the factor price variables.

tion, MA_i is the number of other mills within a ten-kilometer radius of mill i, RB_i is the number of branches of public railroads within fifteen kilometers of mill i, $\bar{s}_i$ is the mean sucrose content in the cane juice of mill i for the seasons from 1917 to 1929, YC_i is the yield of cane per acre of mill i in 1930, and OR_i is a dummy whose value is 1 when the mill has an orientation toward North America and 0 otherwise.

The estimated fixed effects depend on the estimated coefficients of Table 7.1. (See the appendix to this chapter for details.) Because of the multicollinearity among the input prices, the estimated coefficients of factor prices in Table 7.1 have high standard errors and are sensitive to sampling. The two sets of results based on the full and limited samples provide different results for the estimated coefficients based on different samples. Under the assumptions of the regression model both give unbiased estimates of the regression coefficients. There is reason to prefer the full-sample regression of Table 7.1, however, because of the larger sample size and greater explanatory power of the regression. Yet because of our concern over the variation in the estimated coefficients, I have estimated and analyzed the fixed effects of both sets of regression estimates. It turns out that the results are very similar using either set of fixed effects estimates. This lends confidence to the inferences drawn from the results.

The fits of the estimated regressions, presented in Table 7.2, columns A and B, are good in both cases; the F-ratio for each is significant at 0.01; and the signs of all the coefficients correspond with a priori expectations. Multicollinearity between explanatory variables is not a problem; all pairwise correlation coefficients between explanatory variables are less than 0.3. Examination using the characteristic roots test reveals no significant other linear combinations between explanatory variables.

To interpret the results, we focus initially on two variables which are statistically significant. (1) First is the percent share of cane supplied by colonos independientes, which is highly significant. The greater the percentage of cane supplied by colonos independientes, the smaller was the long-run expected yearly rate of expansion of the capacity of the mill. This result corroborates my hypothesis that colonos independientes indeed occupied bargaining positions that hampered the expansion of mills. The percent share of cane supplied by the central administration is also included but is found to be insignificant. The data for both these variables are for the 1930 crop.[22]

(2) A dummy variable included to represent each mill's orientation toward North America is also highly significant. It attempts to capture

any differences between mills resulting from their access to North American credit markets, access to managerial and technical information and support, or as well, any differences in the quality of management stemming from association with the North American business environment. Orientation toward North America is proxied by a list compiled in 1928 by the Sugar Club of Cuba (a mill owners' business and technical organization), which categorized mills by the national orientation of their business connections.[23] The significance of this variable indicates that the connections with the United States were important for obtaining the resources needed for expanding to large-scale techniques. Whether the difference was in terms of credit access or management or technical skills or something else cannot be determined from these results.

To compare the relative strengths of these two influences, we must consider the dimensions of the coefficients. From the estimates of the coefficient of OR_i, we infer that the capacities of mills that had an orientation toward North America increased at an average annual rate that was 18 to 19 percent higher than those without such orientation (0.18–0.19 in the units given in Table 7.2). A comparable degree of variation must be considered for the influence of colonos independientes. If, for example, the shares of cane supplied by colonos independientes at two mills should differ by two sample standard deviations, the difference in the average annual rates of increase of these two mills, according to our estimates of the coefficient of CI_i (0.005), would differ by 22 percent (0.005 × 44.2 = 0.22, in the units given in Table 7.2). The sample mean and standard deviation of the share of cane supplied by colonos independientes are 19.4 and 22.1 percent respectively. Therefore, these two separate influences were indeed of comparable magnitude.

A few comments should be made, to interpret the estimated coefficients of the other explanatory variables included in the regression of Table 7.2. (3) Two variables are included to account for the other mills in close proximity that provided feasible alternatives to the local colonos for establishing cane supply contracts. To proxy the potential competition from nearby mills, the number of mills within a ten-kilometer radius of the mill in question is included to represent the presence of alternative mills in close proximity. To proxy the availability of public rail transportation to the colono, the number of branches of public service railroad lines that passed within fifteen kilometers of the mill is included to represent the access of the colonos to public railroads.[24] The number of railroad branches was entered as 0, 1, 2, or 3. If more than three branches were near the mill, that observation of the variable was assigned a value of 3 so as not to place extremely high weights on mill sites in the neighborhoods of seaports. The variables are insignificant. Their signs are as expected and suggest that the proposed influence may have existed, though it is difficult to capture statistically.

(4) The mean sucrose content of each mill over the period 1917–29 and cane yields per acre for 1930 are included to control for cane lands and cane quality and fertility of the cane lands. Cane yields per acre also control for differences between mills in the costs of cultivating cane, particularly through an influence on unit requirements of labor and other inputs in cane cultivation and delivery. Colonias with less productive land and a low elasticity of substitution between land and labor would have had higher unit labor costs and might have been willing to supply cane only if better terms were offered. Investors may have thus chosen to invest in mills that had higher cane yields.[25] Cane yields, however, turn out to have an insignificant effect on mill expansion behavior. Sucrose content is significant but is inversely related to the rate of mill expansion. Though it is an unexpected result, differential rents with vintage effects may provide a possible explanation. All else constant, higher cane yields have had the effect of prolonging the relative advantages of operating with existing outmoded equipment instead of incurring the fixed costs of investing in new equipment. Mills in some areas of extraordinarily rich land, perhaps by chance, continued to use equipment obtained in the first few years after independence.

(5) In addition, we have observed that the coefficient of the share of the cane supplied by the central administration is insignificant. This corresponds with our observation elsewhere that the larger centrales in Cuba seem to reveal a preference against integrating cane cultivation vertically with sugar manufacturing activities. Although I have not explained why this was the case, these results confirm that there was no significant statistical relationship between the vertical integration of cultivation and milling and the tendencies of mills to expand their capacities.[26]

Because adjustment costs prevent the immediate adoption of the desired mill capacity, mill owners made investment decisions regarding their rate of growth to the desired long-run capacity. The relative unattractiveness, from the investor's point of view, of mills with a large presence of colonos independientes, therefore, directly affected the rate of increase in the capacities of mills. For this reason, I have examined the variation in the rate of increase of the capacities between individual mills. The rate of increase is also dependent on the initial capacities of the mills, and it might appear that this has not been taken into consideration. This influence is incorporated in the fixed effects because the fixed effects are controlled for the initial (or preexisting) capacities through the inclusion of the lagged capacity in their construction. Nonetheless, the influences I have found in the rate of increase of mill capacities should show up as well in the end-year distribution of mill capacities. And it is useful for the sake of comparison to estimate a more parsimonious variant of equation (7.2) using the same independent variables but replacing the fixed effects with the log of mill capacity in 1930 as the dependent variable. The results of this latter regression are presented in column C of Table 7.2. The results in column C corroborate the earlier results, virtually the same in statistical significance as columns A and B. Less of the total variation in the dependent variable is explained in column C because the investment decision is less carefully modeled, and also the magnitudes of the coefficients are larger than those of columns A and B. The estimated coefficients obtained from the fixed effects model are preferable because they are obtained from more careful modeling of the investment decision and their magnitudes have clearer behavioral interpretations. But as is seen, the support for my hypothesis holds up when the empirical test is altered.

Summary

The results of these regressions suggest that the correlations of the estimated fixed effects with the observable structural features of mills conform to the pattern I have proposed. They show that there was an association between the expansion of mills and the prevalence of colonos independientes, thus they provide evidence to support the proposition that the superior bargaining positions of colonos independientes could discourage managers from expanding their mill capacities.

The influence of the orientation of mills toward North America appears to be very strong and merits further attention. From this analysis, it is difficult to say exactly what causal factors contributed to the influence of mill orientation. It may indicate informational factors relating to markets for credit or skills or it may reflect barriers to access of those same factors. Credit was important; however, this orientation variable may be picking up numerous other sources of influence. For example, mill orientation is correlated with the horizontal integration of mills. Therefore, the significance of mill orientation may indicate the influence of organizational factors at the firm level. Though ambiguous, the result does strongly reflect the influences Chandler emphasizes, and it suggests that the forces behind the growth, the technical change, and the structural change in the Cuban sugar industry were related to the general developments in modern technology and business in the industrial countries in the early twentieth century. The results are also consistent with the claims by Oscar Pino Santos and others that larger North American sugar companies had advantages over smaller domestic companies. Further examination is needed to sort out these influences.[27]

On the other hand, the influence of colonos independientes was not only significant with a magnitude comparable to that of mill orientation; it was also independent of the orientation of the mill. The percent of cane coming from colonos independientes and mill orientation were not significantly correlated. Therefore, in addition to the external influence of the North American presence, the regional differences between the east and the west that affected the internal institutional settings created relative differences in the attractiveness of different sugar mills from the points of view of prospective investors. The foreign capital that flowed into Cuba was scarce and tended to flow to those areas of the island where the centrales found themselves in a better position to maintain the capital invested in the cane supply networks with as little threat from local colonos independientes as possible.

Some International Comparisons

The existence of this institutional mechanism clearly depended on technical factors related to the handling of cane that created the site specificity of cane field assets. Internationally, the sensitivity of cane imposed similar technical restrictions to production, but these did not always translate into the same institutional relationship. In fact, international comparisons must be made with care because climate, labor markets, the degree of vertical integration, and the extent of government intervention varied greatly from one sugar-producing country to another. In some countries, mills integrated the cultivation and milling of cane vertically; examples are Java, Hawaii, and Peru. The use of market versus internal organization of transactions was likely related to differences in the costs of cane transactions relative to the efficiency costs of internal governance.[28] Given the focus on institutions, the experience of other former Spanish colonies is of interest. In Puerto Rico, the institutional relationship between colonos and centrales was similar to that in Cuba. In the Philippines, however, legal restrictions imposed in 1903 limited the amount of land that could be possessed by individuals or corporations. Farmers typically owned their own land, but farms were small to meet the regulation.[29]

Finally, the case of Queensland makes an interesting comparison with Cuba because the development of its cane farming system has been studied thoroughly.[30] In Queensland, a unique system was developed that combined the permanent labor of small cane farmers and the seasonal labor of nonhierarchical worker peer groups for the harvest. Mills were larger in the north than in the south, but Ralph Shlomowitz does not find regional variation in the cane farming institution. The cane farming system consisted primarily of small, owner-operated farm units. Its formation came about when the Australian government imposed legal restrictions on labor imported from nearby islands. Institutional change was stimulated when mills subdivided their cane lands and promoted the settlement of whites as cane farmers as a means of increasing labor input. The process of settlement continued until 1913. Then after World War I, regulation of cane transactions overrode private contracting mechanisms. At that point, the Australian government began to fix cane prices and even determined the mills to which farmers were to send their cane each season.[31]

An interesting question arises when comparing Cuba and Queensland. Why did Queensland mill owners tend to offer the settlers ownership of the land whereas in Cuba mill owners tended to prefer retaining ownership? Shlomowitz emphasizes that ownership in Queensland was an additional incentive to settle. In Cuba, by contrast, labor was not as scarce or as restricted, and settlement of the land was not a principal objective of mill owners. Labor was provided by seasonal workers who migrated from the densely populated regions within Cuba as well as from Jamaica, Haiti, the Canary Islands, and elsewhere.[32] Accordingly, the function of colonos in the production process, rather than to provide labor itself, was, in large part, to recruit and to manage the masses of seasonal labor. Regarding the hazard of the cane farmers withdrawing assets from the mill's access, one should ask whether other conditions existed in Queensland before the war that could have reduced the threat of farmers severing their long-term relations with the mill.[33] One important difference apparently had to do with the structure of farm ownership in Cuba and Queensland. In Cuba, many of the landowning cane farmers (colonos independientes) were not smallhold owner-operators as they were in Queensland. Many were large landholders, sometimes absentee, and it was the large landholder who presented the effective hazard to the mill's investments in the fields because he could threaten a significant portion of the mill's cane supplies. Smallholders could have posed effective threats only through concerted efforts, which were not as easily accomplished.[34]

In sum, the colono independiente's history as former plantation owner differentiated Cuba from countries where sugar production under traditional methods had not been so important, such as Queensland or Hawaii or even the Philippines. Our findings regarding the influence of the colono independiente on investment behavior demonstrate that his history mattered in the contractual relations, and consequently, it affected the organizational structure of sugar production regionally. This might be regarded as institutional persistence, or a path-dependent effect on organizational structure à la David.[35] The industrial or technical development of certain sugar-producing regions was affected not only by the availability of resources but also by historically established institutional factors.

Appendix: The Fixed-Effects Econometric Model

The precise estimated equation is in the log-linear form:

$$x_{it} - x_{i,t-1} = \gamma_0 + \gamma_1 \rho_{i,t-1} + \gamma_2 x_{i,t-1} + \gamma_3 q_t + \gamma_4 m_{it} + \gamma_5 z_i + \epsilon \quad (A.7.1)$$

where $x_{i,t-1}$ is the mill capacity of mill i in year $t-1$; $\rho_{i,t-1}$ is the unit cane requirement of mill i in year $t-1$; and q_t is a vector of market prices — time variant but individual invariant. The m_{it} is a vector of cane qualities — the sucrose and cane contents of the cane juice. Besides completely random influences of weather, they also capture the soil qualities at each mill that may have influenced investment decisions. Also there were some systematic time variant changes. For example, the incidence of mosaic disease rose during the 1920s, and infected canes suffered in their sucrose contents. The z_i are the individual time-invariant factors, which are treated as unobserved in the first step of the procedure. Not all the individual structural effects are unobservable; some were indeed observed in Chapter 6. But there were many influential individual characteristics that cannot be observed. These would include the effects of managerial experience and the access of each mill to credit markets in North America.

When there are unobservable influences, estimated regression coefficients often suffer from specification bias. Panel data offer a welcome advantage in this regard because panel techniques can resolve problems of specification bias resulting from the omission of unknown explanatory variables. The effects of unobserved variables are eliminated by taking differences of the observed variables from their individual or cross-section means (the means of each individual mill taken by averaging yearly observations across time). In other words, we obtain a sample mean of all variables in equation (A.7.1) for each of the mills to obtain

$$\overline{\Delta x_i} = \gamma_0 + \gamma_1 \overline{p_i} + \gamma_2 \overline{x_i} + \gamma_3 \overline{q} + \gamma_4 \overline{m_i} + \gamma_5 z_i + \epsilon \qquad \text{(A.7.2)}$$

where $\overline{x_i}$ is the mean over time of x_i, etc. Then we subtract equation (A.7.2) from equation (A.7.1). The individual fixed effects, $\gamma_5 z_i$, are canceled and drop from the equation. We can then estimate all the coefficients except γ_5 using the unbiased covariance estimator (CVE).[36] After these coefficients are estimated we recursively obtain estimates of the fixed individual effects, $\gamma_5 z_i$, which are interpreted, similarly to dummy variables, as shift factors in the constant term. The first step, then, is to obtain the covariance regression estimates of the coefficients of equation (A.7.1) except for γ_5.

Estimates of the fixed effects are obtained from the estimated coefficients of the covariance regression and the individual-mill sample means of the explanatory variables in the regression. Define μ_i to be the fixed, individual mill effects, $\mu_i = \gamma_5 z_i$. (See notation in equation [A.7.1].) We estimate μ_i with

$$\hat{\mu}_i = \overline{\Delta x_i} - \hat{\gamma}_0 - \hat{\gamma}_1 \overline{x_i} - \hat{\gamma}_2 \overline{p_i} - \hat{\gamma}_3 \overline{q} - \hat{\gamma}_4 \overline{m_i} \qquad \text{(A.7.3)}$$

where $\hat{\gamma}_i$ are the estimated coefficients of Table 7.1 and $\overline{x_i}$, etc. are the sample means for each mill i across time. The following regression is estimated.

$$\mu_i = \delta_0 + \delta_1 CI_i + \delta_2 CA_i + \delta_3 MA_i + \delta_4 RB_i$$
$$+ \delta_5 \overline{s_i} + \delta_6 YC_i + \delta_7 OR_i + v_i \qquad \text{(A.7.4)}$$

where CI_i is the percentage of cane supplied to mill i by colonos independientes, CA_i is the percentage of cane supplied by the mill i administration, MA_i is the number of other mills within a ten-kilometer radius of mill i, RB_i is the number of branches of public railroads within fifteen kilometers of mill i, $\overline{s_i}$ is the mean sucrose content in the cane juice of mill i for the seasons from 1917 to 1929, YC_i is the yield of cane per acre of mill i in 1930, and OR_i is a dummy representing the orientation of the mill toward North America.

Chapter 8

The Choice of Technique
and the Modernization of Sugar

WE SAW IN CHAPTERS SIX AND SEVEN that the choice of technique in Cuban sugar mills was determined by the institutional and infrastructural settings of the mills. It gave certain geographical conditions an advantage over others, and these advantages were determined largely by the profit-making conditions of the mill at its own site as they had existed in the distant past. The legacy of the sugar industry of the nineteenth century left its imprint on the institutions and the infrastructure, and this imprint affected economic opportunities, even the propensity to adopt further innovations.

The link between investment and technical adoption suggests that studies of the technical diffusion of continuous processing in sugar manufacturing technology in Cuba needs to incorporate a theory of investment behavior to give a sense of the mechanism by which new technical incentives affected the decisions of mill owners and investors. Primary in this is the need to account for the effects of relative factor prices in the decision-making process. The vintage-capital model demonstrates the effect of relative factor prices of capital and operating inputs on the rate of physical capital formation employing new techniques and the range of coexisting techniques at a given period of time. Factor prices also affected the rate of investment in new technologies through their effects on the economic value of complementary resources. We have seen that the technical inter-relatedness of the activities between the cane fields and the mill imposed very strong complementarities between the capital inputs for cane supply and sugar manufacture.[1] This resembles the arguments of Paul David about the mechanization of reaping and its interactions with the land-scape in the midwestern United States and Britain.[2]

David explains that the slow adoption of the mechanical reaper in Britain despite its relatively rapid diffusion in the midwestern United States was a result of complementarities between specific characteristics of the design of the mechanical reapers and the design of fields. His study emphasizes the importance of what may be termed the environmental endowment, which in his context refers to the preexisting state of the landscape as it had been shaped by premechanical agricultural methods. David shows that the previous practices of using hedges and drainage ditches in Britain had partitioned British fields into irregular units and acted as obstructions for handling the machinery. Farmers found it diffi-cult and time-consuming to maneuver the relatively cumbersome mechan-ical reaper within the preexisting field layout. Hence the field layout seems to have delayed the adoption of mechanization there. In the midwestern United States, by contrast, fields had not been sculpted as much by the history of preparation for older techniques of production. They tended to be contiguous, square, and unobstructed, and the reaper had space for maneuvering.[3]

The institutional endowment has also been shown to have had an im-portant influence on the adoption of new technology. For example, War-ren Whatley has argued that existing institutions in the southern United States impeded the adoption of the mechanical cotton picker. The prevail-ing use of share tenancy arrangements for cotton production had the effect of discouraging the adoption of mechanical harvesting of cotton even while it was rapidly being adopted in the nascent California cotton indus-try of the 1950s. In California, where sharecropping had not been estab-lished, high harvest-time wages induced cotton farmers to switch to less labor-intensive mechanical pickers. In the South, by contrast, the preexist-ing share tenancy institutions, in which tenants did not receive their an-nual income until the crop was made, discouraged workers from leaving the cotton plantations during the harvest, lured away by high peak-time harvest wages. Consequently, the preexisting tenancy arrangements had created an institutional environment in the South in which it was uneconomical to mechanize. In a study of the California cotton industry, Moses Musoke and Alan Olmstead have shown that there was likely an interaction between environmental and institutional endowments that caused the differential rates of adoption in California and the South.[4] In these studies, a lesson has been brought home. Producers' choices regarding whether a new technology is adopted differ depending on factor endowments and the natural or institutional environment.

Similar to the studies of David, Whatley, and Musoke and Olmstead, we found in Chapters 6 and 7 that the adoption of large-scale continuous-processing technology in Cuban raw sugar manufacture was affected by an interaction of environmental and institutional endowments. Differential rates of adoption of the new technology in the western and eastern parts of the island were related both to the layout of railroads and preexisting ingenios and colonias and to the institutional setting inherent in preexisting patterns of land use and ownership.

In one respect, however, the studies of the adoption of mechanical harvesters in wheat and cotton differ from this study of technical adoption in Cuban sugar. The reaper and the picker were clearly defined devices that were either being adopted outright or not. The act of adoption of continuous-process technology in Cuban sugar was not so explicit. It was accomplished through the purchase of a range of new machines; but nonetheless, it also involved many modifications to machines with which sugar producers were already familiar and changes in their combined use with other machines. It also often involved a rearrangement of the factory design and reconfiguration of the speed, continuity, and precision of processing. In general, the process of adoption of new sugar manufacturing technology was not represented by the highly discrete changes exemplified by the purchase of a mechanical reaper for the first time. Rather, the process tended to give the appearance of continuity as producers incrementally adapted and modified their plant and equipment to accommodate improvements to technological processes in use.[5] Nevertheless, where these modifications progressed more quickly and had a more profound impact on local economies depended on the infrastructural and institutional environments that were in place prior to their development.

Technical Interrelatedness: Field and Factory

To understand the pattern of expansion of the sugar mills in Cuba it is necessary to understand the technical interrelatedness between the central factory and its cane supply network. The difference in the ease of expansion of sugar mill capacities was determined by the relative costs of establishing and maintaining a complementary cane supply network to ensure sufficient supplies of cane to the mill. The difference in the relative costs of cane in the east and the west was truly a consequence of the different histories of the two parts of the island. The association of the west with the older, well-established nineteenth-century sugar industry offered a different setting for the investor than was present in the east. The previous occupation of cane lands in the west with the smaller, self-contained plantations had created a different institutional environment, with long-lasting economic and social consequences.

In the case of the western provinces, an obstacle was imposed by the preexisting technical system and the existing structure of land ownership. The legacy of influential colonos independientes in the west was connected to the association of the western provinces with the old ingenio (self-contained plantation) system. The layout of the western public service railroad system also played a crucial role. It allowed colonos independientes to negotiate with more than one central. Without access to railroads to haul cane quickly, it was not feasible for colonos to obtain an alternative buyer for their cane.

Contrasts were great in the opportunities the western and eastern regions offered investors. In the east, the abundance of land of sparse economic occupation was important. It would have been difficult for investors to alter the layout of the public railroad system to change effectively the competitive positions of the west. In contrast, in the east, because they were building the infrastructure for the first time, investors were better able to design the layout of their private rail lines in such a way that the colonos were constrained to negotiate solely with their central as a local monopsony. The centrales were also more able to avoid establishing cane supply arrangements in the communities where the colonos were more likely to achieve stronger bargaining positions. For the centrales, a greater range of options was available in the east. Therefore, investors who considered the option of building a mill in the west or building anew in the east more often chose the east. This meant that, in the vintage-capital framework, the western mills were not able to update their technologies as frequently because the investment capital was lured away to the east; hence mills in the west tended to be more outmoded. The consequence for the structure of the Cuban industry was great. It shifted the geographical concentration of the sugar industry in Cuba from its traditional location in the west to the east, and it thus redirected the flows of capital away from the old centers of industry and population toward the new.

The regional transition points to the importance of path-dependent or persistent processes in Cuba's regional development.[6] A small historical event in the distant past had a persistent effect on the regional pattern of development of the island. The early establishment of Havana as the major port led to the selection of the provinces of Havana and Matanzas as the major sites of the nineteenth-century sugar industry. As the development of the industry progressed, railroads were extended, and ingenios proliferated and filled the landscape. By the twentieth century, the new parameters of the best-practice technology changed the preferred layout for railroads, other infrastructure, and land distribution. The preestablished economic environment had an irreversible effect on the available options for further investment. Although it could not have been foreseen, once the new technology had arrived, the persistent impact of the existing railroad layout and relative colono bargaining power discouraged investment in western mills when otherwise comparable eastern options were available.

The concentration of the nineteenth-century industry in the west seems to have been attributed to economies of agglomeration, related perhaps to advantages of pooling distribution services and to minimizing the amount of railroad construction necessary for shipping sugar to port. The arrival of the new technology reversed those economies, giving the untouched eastern region a latecomer's advantage under the new technological regime.[7] The opportunity costs of investing in the two regions differed based on these historically established factors. The technical and institutional persistence in the west was highly instrumental in both the geographical shift of the dynamic center of sugar production and in the association of the east with North American capital.

Technical Choice in Cuba, Hawaii, and Java

The abundance of land in Cuba undoubtedly had an enormous and pervasive influence on the techniques adopted there. In turn, the choice of technique affected the progression or development of new techniques employed in Cuba in comparison with the techniques employed in sugar manufacturing in other parts of the world. A comparison of the sugar industries of Cuba, Hawaii, and Java is interesting because it presents contrasting examples of the availability of land relative to other factors of production. We have seen that the mills in Cuba were considerably larger than those in either Java or Hawaii. The difference in size, of course, represents a difference in the choice of technique. The choice of technique in Cuba, reflected in the larger average capacity of mills, was a result of the relative abundance of naturally fertile cane land, determined by both the soil and the climate. Dissimilar conditions resulted in different choices of technique.

In the standard epidemic model of technical diffusion the mechanism by which a technical innovation diffuses is the spread of information from one firm to the next. In other words, the flows of information about the new technology are considered key to the process of diffusion. A superior conceptualization, in many cases, is one in which the mechanism of diffusion is conceived to be a threshold, internal to each firm, determined by the opportunity costs of the old versus the new technique.[8] The vintage-capital model offers this kind of conceptual framework for the process of diffusion, in which the criterion for adoption of an innovation depends on relative profitabilities dependent on the vintage of the existing equipment and the fixed cost of replacing it. Such an approach has been useful for understanding the structural differences between the east and the west in the Cuban sugar industry. Meanwhile, in the foregoing arguments I have dismissed, for the most part, the influence of information flows.

The historical record shows that the dissimilarity of techniques in use was clearly not a problem of information flows. The best-known sugar technologists had a global perspective of the industry and did a considerable amount of traveling. The more innovative sugar producers in these three places were closely connected both through professional and trade associations and through personal correspondence and contact. There is much evidence of this contact in the sugar trade journals that proliferated during the period. It is also clear that there were economic incentives as well as disincentives for exchanging new technical discoveries, but the channels of communication were open, and there were incentives. The relationships between the producers and users of sugar manufacturing equipment were also instrumental in this respect. So were the activities of engineering consultants and the circulation of skilled personnel throughout the different major sugar-producing countries of the world.[9]

Comparison of the dissimilar conditions in different producing areas and their choice of techniques is interesting. Land abundance prompted Cuban sugar producers to adopt techniques of production that were relatively more land-intensive than in Java or Hawaii. The most important comparison is the use of ratoons. The cultivation of ratoons in Cuba reduced the labor component per ton of cane, but it also greatly reduced the yield of cane per acre. Neither Java nor Hawaii cultivated ratoons, and their yields per acre were twice as high as Cuba's even though Cuban soils were known to be far superior to the soils of either Java or Hawaii.[10]

A number of contemporaries and historians have concluded that Cuban cane agriculture was backward and inefficient because of its lower cane yields relative to its major competitors. Moreno Fraginals argues that the unbalanced nature of the technical advances in the Cuban sugar industry — the coupling of advanced manufacturing technologies with traditional agricultural methods of cultivating cane — created an obstacle to the modernization of the sugar industry. He argues that the adherence to traditional agricultural methods in Cuba was obsolete and that the failure to adopt modern labor-intensive methods in the fields was the reason for the separation of the management of the mill and the fields which the colono system represented. But one contemporary expert who looked directly into the question did not concur. Noel Deerr, one of the most well-known sugar technologists of the time, was commissioned by the Cuban government in 1914 to assess the technology in use in cane cultivation operations in Cuba, widely criticized as being backward relative to the sophisticated agricultural operations of Hawaii and Java. After investigating cane cultivation, Deerr concluded that because of the abundance and fertility of the land in Cuba, the techniques in use in Cuba were more cost-efficient than the more capital- and labor-intensive techniques used in Hawaii and Java.[11] Cuban cane yields per acre were not lower because of inefficiencies but rather because of a choice of technique in cane cultivation based on a greater abundance of land. The diversification of cane fields to coordinate deliveries of cane to the mill was another land-intensive technique. As I have argued, the practice of cane field diversification introduced scale economies into sugar manufacture in Cuba, but this practice required abundant land. It could not have been adopted to the same degree in either Java or Hawaii because of the relative unavailability of suitable land.

Factor endowments are key to understanding the intercountry differences. To compare, the climate in Java is very similar to that of Cuba, but the population density of the island was much greater in Java. This difference had two important consequences for relative availabilities of resources. Food was not generally imported so a much larger proportion of the land in Java was devoted to growing food for the population. The colonial government of Java had imposed a regulatory system that restricted the amount of land that could be used each year for cane cultivation. It also established a mandatory system of rotating cane with food crops. This cane regulation replaced an earlier institution, and it was imposed to prevent abuses that had characterized the previous system. This earlier institution, known as the *cultuur* system, had used coerced labor to cultivate cane and had led to widespread malnourishment in the population because insufficient supplies of food were being produced on the island.[12]

Because of the abundant labor in Java and the scarcity of land authorized for growing cane, sugar producers were led to adopt more labor-intensive and less land-intensive practices. Among the differences between Java and Cuba was a contrast in the practice of ratooning. In Java the entire crop was planted each year; or in other words, ratooning was not practiced in Java as it was in Cuba. In both places, planting was done by hand with simple tools so the practice in Java of planting the entire crop every year raised the labor requirements considerably relative to Cuba. In contrast, because a planting yielded up to six to ten annual crops, only 10–17 percent of the crop was planted each year in Cuba. Also, more skilled resources and effort were put into cane cultivation in Java. In the late nineteenth and early twentieth centuries many resources in Java were put into the development of new cane varieties, and specialized varieties were developed for the various altitudes and soil types on Java. In Cuba before 1927 virtually all the cane grown on the island was of a single natural variety.[13]

The differences in the method of cane cultivation in the Hawaiian Islands were imposed by differences in land availability, as in Java, but also in climate. The lands in Hawaii suited to cane cultivation were scarce, hilly, and rugged. Limited amounts of land induced more intensive use of labor to obtain greater yields per acre. But also the ruggedness of the terrain made railroads more costly to build so that they could not offer the same flexibility in transportation for Hawaiian as they had for Cuban producers.[14] In a similar circumstance, David Denslow found the costliness of railroad construction because of the ruggedness of the terrain to be a major reason for the decline of the sugar industry in northeastern Brazil. This decline is seen in the steady fall of Brazil's share of the world market in the nineteenth century, shown in Table 2.1. The hilly terrain obstructed the expansion of mill capacities with the introduction of the new industrial technologies because of the costliness of establishing the cane supply network. The location of the Brazilian sugar industry in hilly regions was a rational consequence under an older technological regime. Brazil's industry was built at a time when the scale of production could be handled very efficiently by water power. In earlier centuries the existence of abundant and relatively cheap water power in the Brazilian northeast had caused the sugar industry to be located in the hilly regions along the coast. With the increase in the optimal scale of production and cane field requirements, it was difficult for Brazilian sugar producers to adjust to the new large-scale technologies that created centralized milling in Cuba.[15] It is interesting that Hawaii solved a similar problem by adopting a system of flumes to transport cane to the large sugar mills. This transport innovation aided Hawaii's adoption of large-scale milling, but fluming did not offer the potential for long-distance transportation that the railroads in Cuba did so the expansion of the cane acreage per mill in Hawaii was limited relative to Cuba.

Because of the direction of surrounding ocean currents, Hawaii's climate was both cooler and drier than that of either Cuba or Java. The lower average temperature caused the cane to mature much more slowly in Hawaii. The growing season is between 18 and 24 months in duration, whereas in Cuba it is 12 to 15 months; therefore, a given plot of land in Hawaii had to be occupied for roughly two years to yield a single crop of cane. In Cuba, the crop matured in a year or a few months more. A further contrast is that ratooning was not practiced in Hawaii as it was in Cuba. On a given plot of land in Cuba, a single planting was made once to yield a new crop every year for several years. In Hawaii, only one crop was obtained per planting, and it took up to two years to mature. In addition to the temperature, the rainfall patterns in the Hawaiian cane fields were not favorable to cane cultivation as they were in Cuba. The Hawaiian cane fields were dependent on irrigation. The capital-intensiveness of irrigation in Hawaii tended to encourage intensive methods of land use. Because of the higher yield per acre required to support the mills, almost all cane grown in Hawaii was plant cane, that is, ratoons were not used. Consequently, similar to the comparison between Java and Cuba, the labor costs of planting were much higher in Hawaii.

Hawaiian sugar producers received two major benefits from their dependence on irrigation. First, the grinding season was not bounded by the end and beginning of the wet season; it could extend over the larger part of the year, unlike in Cuba, where it lasted for about six months.[16] Second, irrigation gave the producers control over the amount and timing of moisture the canes received. This allowed them to control the timing of the growing season of each field. Application of moisture during critical periods of the growing season was used to maintain greater control over the quality (sucrose content) of the cane. It also meant that the problem of coordinating the harvest with the incidence of heavy rains did not exist in Hawaii as it did in Cuba.[17]

The technological achievements in cane cultivation elsewhere were developed primarily through private agricultural experiment stations which were offshoots of the sugar producers' organizations of various countries. Agricultural innovation would by nature have required local input. As Nathan Rosenberg observes, agricultural technology does not transfer as easily as industrial technology from one region to another because agricultural systems are systemically not as closed. It depends on knowledge of specific details of the biology, genetics, and other characteristics of the particular geographic region.[18] The benefits of agricultural innovation might have been great if technical linkages to other local agricultural products had existed. Promotion of the development of new agricultural technology in cane cultivation may, therefore, have generated external benefits.

The most successful experimental research stations for developing new cane cultivation methods in the twentieth century were in Java and the Hawaiian Islands.[19] Why Cuba had not developed a strong agricultural research agenda is an interesting question, given its otherwise very strong position in the industry. There is no reason why technological improvements could not have been developed for the land-intensive techniques of Cuba, but any achievements would have needed to be substantial to compete with the already very fertile conditions in Cuba. To put the question in perspective, the experiment stations in Java got their impetus from the incidence of the sereh disease around 1884 which did severe damage to the cane fields of Java. The sugar producers of that island first organized themselves to breed new varieties that were resistant to the sereh.[20] In comparison, the mosaic disease in Cuba had reached epidemic proportions and was doing severe damage to the cane crops in 1928 and 1929. Cuban sugar producers, in similar fashion, began to organize in response to the threat of ruination of the cane crops by infection. They imported various high-yielding varieties from other parts of the world, including the famed POJ 2878 from Java. They found that none of the varieties gave as high a yield as the cristalina, which was the variety of cane commonly

Table 8.1
Comparative Unit Costs of Sugar Production, 1913–14, 1921–22

	1913–14			1921–22		
	Cuba	Hawaii	Java	Cuba	Hawaii	Java
Cane costs	1.01	1.78	—	1.16	2.69	1.44
Manufacturing expenses	0.30	0.22	—	0.27	0.32	0.30
Repairs and maintenance	0.09	0.06	—	0.15	0.14	0.23
Fixed expenses	−0.04	0.62	—	0.92	1.51	0.40
Unit cost (total)	1.36	2.69	—	2.51	4.66	2.37
U.S. duty paid	1.35	0.00	—	1.78	0.00	—
Unit cost, incl. duty	2.71	2.69	—	4.28	4.66	—

SOURCES: Dye, "Producción en masa del azúcar cubano," p. 586. The data are from U.S. Tariff Commission; Prinsen Geerligs, F. O. Licht, and Mikusch; *Czarnikow-Rionda Annual Sugar Review*.

in use in Cuba—that is, if the cristalina was uninfected. Some of the imported varieties, however, showed signs of being more resistant to the mosaic. The Sugar Club of Cuba, an organization consisting of most of the larger producers, began to organize and support some existing private experiment stations in Cuba to arrive at a solution to the problem.[21] They might have succeeded in establishing an experiment station of the stature of those in Java and Hawaii if the bottom had not fallen out of Cuba's sugar market in the 1930s.

In summary, the above comments indicate some of the sources of diversity in the techniques used in different parts of the world. In each major sugar-producing island there was a strong interaction between the technology and the environment—the geographical factors of climate, soil, and terrain. In addition, the interaction between the tropical technology and historical factors had affected the density of the population, the shape of the infrastructure, and the institutional structure. One can see these differences as well in the relative unit costs of sugar production of these countries. Table 8.1 gives unit costs for Cuba, Hawaii, and Java for 1913–14 and 1921–22. It is noteworthy that unit cane costs in Cuba were lower than in either of the other countries. This reflects the lower opportunity cost of land in Cuba. This cost differential, however, was not great between Cuba and Java because of factor substitution in which the low cost of land in Cuba was offset by lower field labor costs in Java. According to Maxwell's comparison, unskilled labor was paid $0.20 U.S. per day in Java, $1.25 in Cuba, and $1.50 in Hawaii. Maxwell's comparison of seven sugar-producing countries showed that Java paid the lowest wages and Hawaii and Cuba paid the second and third highest.[22] Total costs, not including duties, were similar in Cuba and Java but considerably higher in Hawaii. In the case of Hawaii, higher cane costs were offset by free access to the U.S. market. Duties imposed on Cuban imports brought the unit cost including the duty roughly in line with Hawaiian unit costs of production once they had entered the United States.

Chapter 9

Conclusion

THE GROUND COVERED in the foregoing pages touches on issues that are at the heart of the history of early republican Cuba. It was a period of landmark economic change. The sugar industry, as the dominant industry in the Cuban economy, was in the forefront of the social and economic transformations taking place after the demise of colonial rule. As in this work, large-scale centrales play a key role in conventional views about Cuban socioeconomic development in this and subsequent periods; however, their rise is usually depicted with a different emphasis and tone. Much of the social transformation has been attributed to the forces of politics and imperialism, whereas less attention has been given to the economics of the central.

The most influential history of the rise of the central and the colono is the classic work of Ramiro Guerra y Sánchez, *Azúcar y población en las Antillas*. Guerra was a vocal opponent of the large sugar interests of his day in the 1920s and 1930s. His account, rather than a story of technical change and Cuban reintegration into the global sugar economy, is one of Cuban decadence, U.S. imperialism, and the rise of the sugar latifundia. Guerra characterizes this crucial period of Cuban economic history as the time when the sugar latifundia "flourished." With inordinate financial backing, large sugar companies extended their control and took over much of the land of the country. He established the image of the large twentieth-century central that has become conventional. One may wish to ask how the conclusions of this book fit into the existing vision of the role of the central in early republican Cuban history, as established by Guerra's classic work. Do they support or revise the current historiographical perception? The answer is mixed. In large part, the findings here are a complement to Guerra's study of the central. A feature that stands out as unique here is the focus on the incentives of sugar mill owners and investors—to ask what caused the decision makers to take the steps they did. From this standpoint we identify economic forces that caused the sugar enterprise to take the form it did. To place these findings within Cuban economic historiography, it is useful to compare them directly with Guerra's analysis of the same historical events. The following two sections summarize key features of Guerra's arguments and discuss how my conclusions complement or challenge Guerra's views.

The Rise of the Sugar Latifundium

Guerra proposed that the sugar latifundium arose in Cuba as result of the combination of two factors: the introduction of the railroad for cane transportation and the unequal financial power of foreign investors who were able to turn the railroad into a tool for capturing land and subjecting its occupants.[1] The railroad permitted extension of the borders of the traditional plantation and the emergence of the central and the colono. Unequal financial power created the latifundium. It permitted the central owners who had access to foreign capital to accumulate the lands surrounding their mills until they rather than the colonos controlled their cane zones. The two factors did not enter the story simultaneously. The first sugar centrales and extensive use of the colono system emerged in the late 1870s or 1880s. Guerra argues that this was a socially healthy and progressive development that implied both greater economic efficiency and the development of a rural middle class. The rise of the latifundium, he argues, came after 1899 as large centrales absorbed the lands of colonias and increased economic power over them. These developments were a threat to the further development of the nation because they led to the demise of the rural middle class of colonos, displaced Cuban control of the leading industry, and led Cuba to intensify monoculture and dependence on the U.S. sugar market.

In Guerra's story, the one *essential* technical innovation behind the transformation of the sugar industry was the application of the railroad to cane hauling. Similar to this study, he found that the high costs of cane transport prohibited cane from being hauled over long distances and, consequently, it was not until the arrival of the cane-hauling railroad that the latifundium became possible.[2] In his words, its introduction permitted the "unlimited extension" of a mill's cane lands. When this took place, it amounted to a revolution in the sugar enterprise. It revolutionized not only the relationship between the mill and its cane lands but also the relationship with neighboring mills. Once introduced, the railroad made it possible for one mill to extend its borders and to invade the cane zones of a neighboring mill.[3]

Initially, the consolidation of cane lands and the formation of colono and central was advantageous to both parties. As the capacities of mills expanded, they would arrange with adjacent farmers to grow cane under contract. The aftermath of the Ten Years' War made social conditions favorable to the reorganization as many planters in financial arrears found it in their advantage to become colonos. Remarkably, this break with the tradition of the self-contained plantation/mill complex did not meet with the opposition that often accompanies a technical reorganization of such magnitude.

The harmoniousness of the contractual agreements began to break down, according to Guerra, when the existing mills began to compete on the perimeters of their respective cane zones. Rivalry led to the demise of the economic independence of the colono and opened the way to the latifundium. To keep cane costs low, Guerra says, mill owners took over ownership of the cane lands and either grew cane themselves or leased the land out to colonos. The degree of control awarded to the central in the standard colono contract created frictions, and it eventually led to what he interpreted as a set of feudal obligations on the colono.[4] But he argues that the feudal "subjugation" of the colono could not have come about until the entrance of foreign capital after the turn of the century. Before that, mill owners and colonos confronted each other in relatively equal bargaining positions. The arrival of the foreign capitalists with inordinate financial backing altered the balance. Unlike the domestic sugar aristocracy, the foreign capitalists had at their fingertips resources sufficient to stretch railroads into undeveloped areas to dominate local transportation and monopolize access to cane fields. Capital created the sugar latifundium, and colonos became victims dependent on it to sell their cane.

The Rise of Continuous Processing

Complementary to Guerra's view of the rise of the central as technologically motivated, this book has examined the economic implications of the technology of the central more carefully. Riding on the wave of the second industrial revolution, continuous-processing technologies adopted in Cuban sugar introduced economies of scale into raw sugar manufacture that resulted in a huge growth in the capacities of mills. New transportation technology, in the form of the plantation railroad, was key to the adoption of the new technology. Just as Guerra argued, without it or some other inexpensive and rapid means of hauling cane, the large scale would never have been adopted. The costs in lost sucrose would have been too great. Other scholars have traced the origins of these changes to the middle of the nineteenth century.[5] This study has demonstrated the continued trajectory that these technological developments followed after the turn of the century.

The role that economies of scale play in Guerra's analysis and mine differs considerably. But the contrast might be considered as counterpoint reflecting the alternative economic interests of colonos and efficiency concerns of mill owners. Economies of scale play only a minor explicit role in Guerra's story. He notes the existence of economies of scale as the economic motive for the initial formation of centrales, but he does not recognize the continuation of the increase in the optimal scale of production throughout the first decades of the twentieth century. In contrast to Guerra, we have seen that the role of the increasing optimal scale was of great significance for the international competitiveness of the sugar enterprise. Economies of scale were inherent in the high and increasing fixed costs of production. Improved coordination increased both technical efficiency and the volume of production. Cane field diversification was also found to be an important organizational feature that reduced interruptions in cane deliveries, but it also had significant implications for the scale of production. It is apparent in his writings that Guerra understood the negative efficiency implications of doing away with large-scale production. He expressly understood that, in policy questions, any attempt to obstruct or limit the size of the mills by regulation would have serious detrimental consequences for the industry.[6] In his analysis, however, he downplayed the efficiency issue presumably because it did not support his political program of seeking regulatory protection for the colono class.[7]

With regard to the role of the railroad, the conclusions of this book are revisionary. Guerra, along with many adherents to his views, depicted the plantation railroad as an instrument to capture land rather than a tool to permit mills to reap economies of scale. If land capture were the principal objective of private railroad investments, however, there would have been no need for the other investments in plant and equipment that converted the sugar mill into the vast agroindustrial complex it became. A strategy dominated by the objective of land capture could have been accomplished solely by monopolizing the transportation network. Without the motive of improved efficiency, there would have been no need to consolidate mills, increase the scale of production, or change the location of the cane-processing sites. All of those changes reveal a set of organizational and technical incentives for the transformation of the mill itself. Empirical examination of the cost structure of mills supports this conclusion.

The historical process that took precedence in Guerra's analysis is the rise of the sugar latifundium. What do the results of this study have to say about the process of land concentration or the rise of the sugar latifundium? First, economies of scale in milling were an important factor, but alone they were not enough to cause the concentration of land ownership. Hypothetically, cane could have been supplied by small farmers, or colonos, independent of the control of the centrales. In practice, this was a complicated issue. The problem of rapid cane deterioration, the biological factor that imposed the necessity of strict coordination between field and mill, was solved by the creation of specific assets. The presence of specific assets implied a contractual problem for the organizational independence of colonos. There were actually two problems. One was that costs of the coordination were considerably higher if there was no central decision maker to determine when and how much to plant and harvest. This problem was solved by the use of long-term contractual arrangements that granted the central mill legal control over many of the planting and harvest decisions. It did not require the accumulation of land ownership to solve the problem.

The other problem was that the asset specificity made the central vulnerable to holdup when its cane lands were owned by the colonos. Land-owning colonos could, at a strategic time, refuse to deliver the cane on which the mill depended for its own viability. Such actions might have been profitable for some colonos, but they could also discourage investors from committing funds to mills where this was likely to happen. In principle, without a solution to this problem, investment in mills was not viable in the long run. It should be emphasized that the effectiveness of the holdup threat that colonos could make was not due to any power of force that they had over mill owners. It was because mill owners, if they were to realize the returns to any sugar investment, had to sink a substantial but irreversible financial commitment into the assets of the mill, the railroad, and the cane fields. Key to the threat's effectiveness was the fact that the investment took a form that was not readily salvageable if market conditions should change the expected value of the investment.

Centrales found a solution to this problem in land acquisition. By taking ownership of the lands on which their cane supplies were located, they could effectively eliminate the threat of holdup. The consequence was that over time cane lands became more and more concentrated in the hands of the sugar companies. This is apparent in the data in Table 6.4 showing the sources of cane supplies from different contractual or land tenure arrangements. The share of cane coming from landowning colonos independientes diminished between 1905 and 1930 from 37 to 16 percent. By 1930, 84 percent of cane supplies were obtained from lands controlled (owned or leased) by the centrales. Most of this cane was supplied by colono tenants, as 66 percent of all cane supplied came from that type of contractual arrangement. These figures are indicative of two social outcomes. As is often emphasized, they show the expropriation of an important nationalist class — the colonos. But they also reflect a solution to a real problem of firm organization that needed to be resolved if substantial investments in modern milling equipment were to be made.

This solution was more easily accomplished in the eastern provinces, where well-established planter families were largely absent and did not have to be bargained with, and where there were fewer comparable economic claims to land for purchase or lower opportunity costs, so that land was relatively inexpensive. Other factors of great importance were related to the relative expected costs that holdup might impose on centrales from one region to the next. The percentage of the central's cane supplies that was dependent on the cooperation of colonos independientes was important. Additionally, the accessibility of the colono independiente's land to other competing mills was also important. This meant that the density of mills in the provinces of Havana, Matanzas, and western Santa Clara as well as the greater access to public service railroads was a problem as it pertained to potential holdup. As a consequence of these factors, the eastern provinces of Camagüey and Oriente were more attractive from an investor's viewpoint. And these provinces received a greater proportion of the inflowing international capital.

The use of the railroad as a tool to monopsonize local cane supplies was at times an additional means by which centrales gained control of their cane supply zones. Because of certain regulations of railroad construction, it was difficult to accomplish in the western provinces. Conditions in the east at the beginning of the century, however, offered considerable opportunity for the construction of extensive isolated private rail networks with few outlets to public service systems. To view the strength of centrales and colonos in a proper balance, we note that on the sites of the traditional western sugar estates, it was more likely that the colonos held strong bargaining positions and a relative degree of independence by maintaining the threat of holdup and by having the options of contracting elsewhere at the termination of their contracts.

As Guerra suggested, the superior financial backing of the North American sugar companies made land acquisition easier. But the analysis presented in Chapters 6 and 7 indicates that the incentive for mills to acquire cane lands was the same regardless of the nationality of the sugar company. The empirical analysis in Chapter 7 is consistent with this aspect of Guerra's analysis, although there are other plausible explanations for the statistical pattern we observe. Besides access to credit, access to technical institutions or advantages inherent in large, hierarchical business organizations, as Chandler has demonstrated in other contexts, offer alternative explanations.

Finally, what implications do the results of this study have for the so-called demise of the colono class? Guerra argued that the rise of the latifundia resulted in the undoing of the colonos as the basis for the Cuban agrarian middle class. Juan Martínez Alier has taken issue with Guerra's image of the colonos as a farmer class with uniform interests. He has shown that, in the 1930s and 1940s, the political activities of colonos reflecting their economic interests were divided depending on whether they were large landholders, medium-sized, or smallholders.[8] His analysis fits well with the picture of the bargaining positions of large colonos presented in Chapter 6.

Furthermore, the statistical trends in the cane supply arrangements of mills do not follow exactly the patterns that would be expected given Guerra's claims about the demise of colonos. Guerra and other scholars have claimed that centrales were doing away with the colono system, replacing it with administration cane.[9] If this were true, there should have been a long-term rise in the share of administration cane relative to colono cane. But the data in Table 6.4 on the sources of cane supplies show the reverse pattern—a rise in the relative amount of cane supplied by colonos. The share of cane coming from tenant colonos rose at the expense of the shares of both colonos independientes and administration cane. This suggests, from the economic standpoint, that the colono system offered efficiency gains over administration cane in most instances. It implies from the social standpoint that the structural changes in the sugar industry were not threatening the disappearance either of the colono system or of the colonos as a class. It does imply the shift in the distribution of land from the colono to the mill, with negative implications for the overall distribution of land in the island.

For this argument, however, the trends in the absolute levels of cane from each class are more relevant because they are the best indicator of the intertemporal demands of cane from each class. In absolute terms, the amount of cane sold by colonos independientes to mills increased by about two-thirds between 1905 and 1930. Overall for colonos of both contractual types, the amount of cane supplied increased more than fourfold in those 25 years. This increase was driven by the growth in the industry. The point is that the growth in sugar production was responsible for the creation of additional demands for cane and for the rise of the colono class. The increased demands for cane created the opportunities on which the proliferation of colono contracts depended. These opportunities for colonos would not have arisen if the industry had not been competitive—if it had not adopted continuous-process technologies with the accompanying features of economies of scale and the built-in incentives for land concentration. Despite all their ramifications for the social landscape, the colonos, along with the Cuban sugar industry, were more prosperous because of the adoption of mass production.

The rise of mass production during Cuba's transition from colony to republic transformed the cane sugar industry. The adoption of continuous-process, high-throughput technologies introduced economies of scale into milling that resulted in a huge growth in the capacities of sugar mills. The sugar enterprise passed from being the traditional self-contained plantation into a modern business that managed an enormous industrial complex and a multitude of contractual arrangements for cane supplies. Underlying the organizational changes were many qualitative changes in the technology embodied in the physical capital. The sugar mill and its surroundings were now composed of highly sophisticated equipment, a plantation railroad network, and extensive investments in land and cane fields.

The transformation of the industrial plant and the organization of sugar enterprises mirrored the technical and managerial revolution taking place in the industrial world at the same time. It took place so thoroughly in Cuba because of Cuba's proximity to the growing U.S. market for sugar and because cane grew well there. But more than this, it took place because of a technical reason—cane had to be processed immediately. If it were not for that constraint, North American investors would have considered it much less risky to build their massive industrial plants at home.

Vintage-Capital Effects and Monoculture

Some economists have pointed to monoculture and the degree of export concentration as the most critical problem in the twentieth-century Cuban economy. A common viewpoint is that structural changes in the sugar industry after the turn of the century were responsible for the intensification of monoculture in Cuba. In particular, the intensive construction of new capacity during World War I, followed by the continued expansion in the capacities of those mills after the war, caused a substantial increase in the aggregate sugar production capacity of the island. Meanwhile, the sugar market conditions after the war did not seem favorable to expansion so that many questioned the rationality of the creation of additional capacity from the standpoint of the aggregate social welfare.

The influences I have identified of vintage-capital and adjustment costs on the process of mill capacity expansion have important implications for understanding these events. Underlying the formation of aggregate sugar production capacity was a range of mills of varying degrees of technical advance and two fronts or boundaries at which decisions were made that affected any changes in it. The two fronts were the innovation front, or the margin of innovation, and the obsolescence front, or the margin of obsolescence. There are two ways to perceive the pattern of aggregate capacity increase depending on which front or margin one focuses on. Sugar producers on the innovative front entered and built new mills during the profitable years of World War I. Once the war was over, they continued to expand in accordance with the adjustment-cost effect described in Chapter 4. Sugar producers on the margin of obsolescence remained in operation during the unusually high prices of World War I. Under normal circumstances, their mills would have been retired or renovated, but in these years they more often found it advantageous to remain in operation without upgrading their techniques of production. When prices fell, many inframarginal mills found themselves suddenly on the verge of having to shut down. Recalling the arguments of Chapter 4, it was natural, according to the vintage process of obsolescence and retirement, that as the price of sugar fell a contraction at the obsolescence margin should take place. But since it was largely Cuban and Spanish sugar producers who faced the adjustment, it generated alarm and opposition when the Cuban sugar industry passed into North American hands.

It has been argued that the producers who had to shut down were victims of the overzealous expansion of modern mills with enormous capacities. An implication of the vintage-capital model, however, is that the decision of producers to shut down was made independently of the decision to enter. When the sugar price returned to normal levels after the war, the outmoded mills that were faced with shutting down did so because the market price no longer covered their unit operating costs. Even if the additional mill capacity at the innovational margin had not been built, these producers at the obsolescence margin would have faced the same problem. They fell into difficulties because the shutdown margin was shrinking as the price declined. The level of prices was not determined by Cuban capacity but by worldwide capacity. It had been adversely affected by the reentrance of European beet sugar producers onto the scene. The price of Cuban sugars would not move independently of those events. This fact was learned the hard way by the failure of the Verdeja Act quotas to have an impact.

The occurrence of the Verdeja Act is very instructive. Eventually a political response to the nationalist outcry came about when President Machado passed this law, effective in 1927 and 1928, in which a quota for each mill was imposed to reduce the overall Cuban crop by 10 percent in an attempt to support the market price for sugar. A secondary objective was to protect the inefficient mills by fixing levels of production to prevent a further reduction of their industry shares. This regulation, which blocked the attrition of mills at the obsolescence margin, had a secondary consequence. It impeded the natural process by which older, less efficient mills were replaced by modern, more efficient ones. The first objective of the act failed, however. Supplies of other producers on the world market increased in response to Cuba's reduction. It soon became very clear that Cuba did not control the world price. Indeed, a rise in the price of sugar under those market conditions was not plausible. The argument of W. Arthur Lewis, summarized below, is applicable here.

Monoculture and Market Instability

That Cuba's exports were concentrated in a single crop subject to extreme natural price fluctuations was important, but it was not the most important source of instability associated with Cuban monoculture. The more threatening source was the ever-present potential closure of its markets through antitrade action. The attitudes of the United States Congress toward trade policy were critical for maintaining the openness of the Cuban market. Monoculture and export concentration made Cuba extremely vulnerable to adverse political action from abroad.

The investment in the sugar industry in the first decades of the twentieth century stimulated the Cuban economy. It attracted foreign capital and stimulated growth in the production capacity and the infrastructure of the island. Even though North Americans had in many cases taken control of the resources, it would still not seem fitting to suggest that either North American dominance or the Spanish colonial heritage had not increased the material wealth of the island. Both Cubans and North Americans were beneficiaries. The large influx of foreign capital gave Cuban businessmen experience in dealing with the international economy. It also apparently had positive effects in a relative sense on the island. Life expectancy in Cuba by 1930 was 41.5 per thousand, equal to that of Costa Rica and higher than in any other Latin American country except Argentina. Estimates of gross domestic product per capita also place Cuba third among Latin American countries. Estimates by Angus Maddison of 1929 for Cuba are $238 in current U.S. dollars, relative to $415 for Argentina and $250 for Chile. By contrast, estimates for Mexico and Brazil are around $85.[10] A later comment from the U.S. Department of Commerce compares Cuba favorably with other Latin American countries. "Cuba is not an underdeveloped country in the sense usually associated with that term. The industrial segment of the sugar industry is a highly mechanized and efficient operation, national networks of railways and highways blanket the country, and numerous well-equipped ports provide easy access and egress for a flourishing foreign trade. . . . The people have one of the highest standards of living in Latin America, an indication of the intrinsic worth of the country's development assets."[11] Although annexation was of much less interest to the United States than it had been in the mid-nineteenth century, many Americans felt that there were closer bonds between the United States and Cuba than with other Latin American countries.[12] Cubans also had closer family ties to the United States than did people of other Latin American nations. Contemporaries considered the economic status and growth potential of Cuba to be comparable with certain regions in the United States. They also considered the investment opportunities comparable. Cuba was described at times as a land of progress and opportunity for settlement, a "new California."[13] Leland Jenks pointed out that Cuba was politically more stable than Alabama and could in general obtain credit more cheaply than Florida. For its railroad construction, Cuba was able to borrow at the same rate as railroads in the United States.[14]

The problem that export monoculture created for sustained economic development in Cuba was not that it did not generate income. Arthur Lewis's distinction between stability of trade in tropical and temperate crops is useful for sorting out the problems in understanding Cuba's development situation.[15] To Lewis, the problem was not only the vulnerability of basing development on a single commodity; it was also the potentially limitless supplies of the crop on the world market. This argument has some validity. It suggests that there could have been no significant rise in the market price of sugar under alternative plausible scenarios for the world market. Numerous locations in the tropics could have offered low wages, were searching for entry into international markets, and could have developed their own domestic sugar industries. Indeed, prices since the mid-nineteenth century had declined greatly. But during this first quarter of the twentieth century, the demand for sugar was rising so rapidly that it provided many opportunities for tropical countries to expand into the sugar industry.

The United States's overtures of reciprocity were not as secure as they might have seemed in 1903. The U.S. State Department actively promoted increased investment activity in Cuba as a means to its own strategic ends. But the political intervention was probably of less consequence to the level of investment than private interests' perception of profit-making opportunities. Capital flowed into Cuba to seize economic opportunities that had been recognized by investors in North America for some time but had not been exploited because they had been blocked by Spanish policy. On the other side of this interaction, the Spanish government for some time had attempted to block the creation of these economic ties.[16]

Domestic sugar interests in the United States were also opposed to the establishment of these ties. They repeatedly attempted to restrict the trade with protective policies. Indeed, intervention in the sugar market had been the rule for centuries in all European countries. The very existence of the beet sugar industry had depended in its infancy on the system of subsidies that protected it. The era of the complex system of bounties to protect the beet sugar interests in western Europe ended with the Brussels Convention of 1902, but it did not do away with the general practice of protecting domestic sugar industries. Great Britain was the only major market with no protective policies, and even Britain imposed them after 1914 to protect British colonial sugar interests and to encourage the development of a domestic beet sugar industry even though the growing conditions in Britain were not favorable to beets.[17] The consequence of these policies was that the global market for sugar was protected and segmented, and sugar countries had to form bilateral trade relationships with the countries where markets for sugar existed if they were to survive.

The major market for Cuban sugar was the United States, which gave Cuba a preferential discount on the full tariff of 20 percent. At the end of the War of Independence — or the Spanish-Cuban-American War — the U.S. government undertook a commitment to strengthen ties with Cuba. From the viewpoint of the United States, the motivation in 1903 to give preferential tariff treatment to Cuba was a concession given in return for Cuba's acceptance of the Platt Amendment. Still, Cuba had to overcome 80 percent of the U.S. tariff wall to compete with duty-free suppliers, Hawaii, Puerto Rico, the Philippines, and domestic beet and cane sugar producers. Many sugar producers in Cuba expected or hoped eventually to obtain duty-free status or at least a more favorable treaty of reciprocity similar to the treaty with the Hawaiian Islands of 1876.[18] But also at this time, the alliances of the sugar interests within the United States were changing. The east coast sugar refiners, who had the strongest vested interests in the open trade policies with Cuba, became more heavily involved in west coast beet sugar as well.[19] Furthermore, beet producers became allied politically with western farming interests. The upshot was that tendencies toward trade reciprocity with Cuba came under stiff opposition from the beet lobby. As Jenks put it, "It became speedily apparent that it was not so much the American government with whom the Cubans had to deal with as it was the beet-sugar producers of the American West."[20]

The end of the Cuban sugar boom came with the imposition of the Hawley-Smoot Tariff in 1930, which raised the duty on Cuban sugars to two cents per pound. It reduced the price received by Cuban producers to less than half the price domestic producers received. Given the plummeting price on the market, it was a deliberate act of closing the majority of

Cuban producers out of the U.S. market to reduce the impact of the declining price on domestic producers. Although Arthur Lewis is correct in emphasizing the peripheral location and the monoculture as introducing a high degree of instability in the market, the source of the instability was not the availability on the supply side of unlimited competitors. It was the restricted possibilities for selling the product on the demand side and, in particular, the high degree of adverse intervention during times of crisis.

Reference Matter

A p p e n d i x

Data Sources

The data employed in the study come from two primary sources: data contained in the business and personal papers of Manuel Rionda found in Record Groups 2 and 4 of the Braga Brothers Collection in the University Archives of the University of Florida, Gainesville, and Cuban government publications of the Secretaría de Agricultura, Comercio, y Trabajo and the Secretaría de Hacienda on the sugar trade.

The Braga Brothers Collection

The Braga Brothers Collection is business archives whose principal holdings are related to the Czarnikow-Rionda Company of New York, one of the leading sugar brokerage houses of the twentieth century, founded in 1909. Through its affiliate, the Cuban Trading Company, this company handled a large proportion of the exports of sugar from Cuba. It contains the personal and financial papers of Manuel Rionda y Polledo, 1895–1943, who was the founder and president of Czarnikow-Rionda. Many of his papers are related to the management of sugar estates that he and his family owned in Cuba. Also included are papers relating to subsidiaries of Czarnikow-Rionda located in Cuba. These materials became accessible only in 1985, and many of them still remain virtually untouched.

Record Group 2 contains 122 linear shelf feet of materials — one of four record groups in the collection which together contain 729 linear feet of material. It is a collection of correspondence and business papers of Manuel Rionda. The collection contains business files from Rionda's Wall Street office that include reports and letters of persons related to the business of Czarnikow-Rionda and more than 150 bound volumes of private letters of Manuel Rionda. The Rionda family owned a number of centrales, and numerous papers are concerned with the day-to-day operation of sugar mills, the harvests, and managers' dealings with colonos. For numerical data, some of the most valuable material is the reporting of prices paid for various factors of production at the mills. From these letters and internal reports, primarily in series 1, 2, 5, 10a, and 10c, I was able to glean prices of wages for various occupations, salaries paid to skilled personnel, liquidation rates paid to colonos, freight rates, prices of mill and railroad equipment, and other information. The reports of prices are scattered throughout the collection in letters between managers and owners. I have collected and compiled annual price series for some wages and factor prices for the years 1917–29. Given their source, in private letters dealing with day-to-day business, the prices they report are very reliable. From the contexts of the letters, it can be determined for what population the report is representative. Notes were made in this regard to assure the utmost reliability of the data.

Also contained in series 10a are cost reports of many of the centrales in Cuba that Rionda collected to prepare reports of sugar production cost estimates to be presented to the United States Sugar Equalization Board for the purposes of the wartime sugar price controls of 1918 and 1919. Rionda was the Cuban representative on the board. These reports provide itemized unit costs of a cross section of mills in Cuba between 1916 and 1918. These reports were solicited by Rionda from mill owners in Cuba. Participation was voluntary. The reports available in most cases are the cost worksheets sent to Rionda by the mill managers who chose to participate. The mills represented cover a broad range of capacities, age, and performance. These data have been useful to gain a picture of unit costs of a cross section of mills.

Besides the price and cost data, the collection has been invaluable for understanding many aspects of the operation of sugar mills in Cuba. Box after box of letters and reports describe the issues that sugar managers deemed important to the operation of their mills. Especially interesting are the letters concerning their affairs with the colonos. Topics include problems of indebtedness of the colonos, quality of work, supervision and monitoring, and negotiation of contracts. Also, files of letters exist which were exchanged between managers and some of the more important colonos. There also is much material describing the competition between mills in various regions in Cuba for cane lands. This material describes the strategies they used to attempt to obtain control of a piece of land they were planning to expand into before a neighboring mill did so. There is also considerable material that describes the problems of dealing with public railroads (railroads offering public services) versus private railroads (railroads owned and operated by the sugar company solely for its own use) and compliance with the Railroad Commission.

Record Group 4 is a collection of reports and corporate files of 24 companies that were subsidiaries of, or affiliated with, the Czarnikow-Rionda Company. The materials I found most useful were from the company files of the Francisco Sugar Company and the Cuba Cane Sugar Corporation. Record Group 4 contains 140 linear shelf feet of materials.

One of the richer bodies of material is the collection of reports and correspondence from the Francisco Sugar Company, which controlled the Centrales Francisco and Elia. In series 95, a set of annual reports to the stockholders provide data about these mills from 1911 to 1930. In series 96, for certain years, reports offer very complete knowledge of the operation of the factory, including itemized cost accounting records and reports of the performance of the mill at the Central Francisco. Especially useful for this study is a series of reports related to a major renovation of the Central Francisco that lasted from 1918 to 1922. This series of reports begins with a report by the engineering consulting firm of Griggs and Myers which analyzes the performance and technical problems encountered at the Central Francisco and makes recommendations for improvements involving replacement of machinery in the mill and reorganizing the labor at certain stations to achieve more efficient operation of the machinery. The report is interesting because its principal concern is the irregularity of the power being generated to drive the mill. Much of the discussion in the report is a detailed analysis of the power plant and prescriptions for obtaining continuity of power to run the mill at a constant speed. Achieving this would have reduced the frequency of breakdowns, and it would have allowed the rollers in the grinding mill to be set to obtain better extraction rates. Following this report are a series of five very detailed annual manager's reports regarding the performance of the mill. It is from these reports that I obtained data regarding the mill stops,

presented in Chapter 4, and the details on the proportion of cane in ratoons, presented in Chapter 5. In 1922, at the end of the renovation
period, a descriptive inventory of the physical assets of the Central Francisco was made. Although little of the numerical data of this inventory
was used directly in the exercises in this study, careful reading of it has
been very useful because it includes the specifications of every piece of
equipment in the factory, and for the major pieces of machinery it includes
the purchase date and cost.

Also useful was the report of the organizers of the Cuba Cane Sugar
Corporation, found in series 125 and 127. One report is a survey of the
seventeen mills that the company being founded made of the mills it was
interested in acquiring. The survey contains much information about the
economic conditions of each mill and the surrounding area, including
descriptions of the mill and railroad equipment for the mill, the cane
supplies, costs, and projected difficulties in negotiating or renegotiating
contracts for acquiring cane.

I would stress that the value of this collection for the quantitative
economic historian is not only in the available quantitative material but its
use in combination with the huge volume of letters between persons involved with the Cuban sugar industry that reveal their attitudes, percep-
tions, and strategies at different events in the history of the Cuban sugar
industry. There is no question that much material remains to be discovered in this collection.

Cuban Government Publications

Extensive use has been made of reports from the Cuban Secretaría de
Agricultura, Comercio, y Trabajo, and the Secretaría de Hacienda. These
reports provide a very complete quantitative picture of the sugar industry
in Cuba because they contain production figures of all the mills operating
in Cuba for the years of interest here.

Secretaría de Hacienda, *Industria azucarera y sus derivados*, reports
production figures for each of the mills grinding each year beginning in the
1903/4 crop and extending past 1930. Between 1917 and 1929 up to 198
mills were grinding at a time. Over this period, these reports give data for
243 different centrales that were in operation at some time during the
period. Included in the reports are figures of the 96° pol. and 89° pol.
sugars, molasses, and the amount of cane ground.

Secretaría de Agricultura, Comercio, y Trabajo, *Industria azucarera:*

Memoria de la zafra, reports production statistics along with factory control and performance data. These reports are a rich source of information about the workings of the sugar mills. The reports were published annually from 1916 until after 1929. The manner of reporting changed in 1929. These reports are the source of the data on mill capacities, which were given independent of yearly levels of production, based on the engineering capacity specification of the mill each year. They also are the source of the data used to obtain the sucrose and water contents of the cane, used for measuring the quality of the cane entering each mill each year, the yields (sugar-to-cane-ratios), and the extraction rates of mills.

The reliability of these government statistics can be examined by comparing data for the same series collected by the two agencies. Production of 96° pol. and 89° pol. sugars and molasses and the cane ground at each mill were collected separately and reported by both agencies. Comparisons reveal that the production data are consistent and discrepancies are of negligible orders of magnitude. They have also been compared with the production reports of various mills found in the internal reports in the Braga Brothers Collection, showing similar negligible discrepancies. Therefore, the production and yield series have been shown to be reliable. Extraction rates, sucrose contents, and other factory data reported have been compared with data found in the Braga Brothers Collection in internal reports of various mills and were also found to be reliable.

Notes

Chapter 1

1. For world sugar production figures, see references to FAO, and Deerr, *History of Sugar*, 2: 490–91. For figures on the U.S. market, see U.S. Congressional Committee on Agriculture. For information on relative costs of production, see Prinsen Geerligs, F. O. Licht, and Mikusch, pp. 4–16; and U.S. Department of Commerce, *Cane Sugar Industry*. For Cuban sugar production, see Moreno Fraginals, *El ingenio*, 3: 35–40.

2. U.S. Department of Commerce, *Foreign Commerce and Navigation*, 1910–26; Winkler, pp. 183–84; Maddison, "Economic and Social Conditions in Latin America," p. 5. On Cuban railroad expansion, see Zanetti Lecuona and García Alvarez, *Caminos para el azúcar*.

3. Pérez, *Cuba and the United States*, p. xiii.

4. Benjamin, *Origins of the Cuban Revolution*, p. 5.

5. See Moreno Fraginals, *El ingenio*, 1: chaps. 4, 5; 2: chap. 2; and *La historia como arma*, pp. 56–144; Iglesias García, "Development of Capitalism in Cuban Sugar Production," and "Azúcar, esclavitud y tecnología." See also Bergad, *Cuban Rural Society*, chaps. 15, 16; and García Alvarez, *La gran burguesía comercial en Cuba*, chap. 2.

6. Provocative arguments in this framework are found in Pino Santos, *El asalto a Cuba*, and Benjamin, *The United States and Cuba*, pp. 13–33. Cardoso and Faletto, p. 19, place Cuba within the general context of their classic discussion of economic dependency and underdevelopment.

7. Benjamin, *Origins of the Cuban Revolution*, p. 7.

8. See U.S. Department of Commerce, *Cane Sugar Industry*; U.S. Tariff Commission, *Costs of Production in the Sugar Industry*; and Prinsen Geerligs, F. O. Licht, and Mikusch, pp. 4–16.

9. Bergad, *Cuban Rural Society*, chap. 17.

10. Jenks, pp. 128–40; Taussig, *Tariff History of the United States*, pp. 399–401; Ballinger, pp. 16–19. The Philippines were in a situation similar to Cuba between 1902 and 1909, when they received a 25 percent reduction on the full sugar duty. The Philippines were granted the same treatment as Puerto Rico in the Tariff Act of 1909. A thorough examination of the history of trade policies between Cuba, Spain, and the United States is found in Zanetti Lecuona, *Cautivos de la reciprocidad*.

11. Maluquer de Motes, "El mercado colonial antillano"; Taussig, *Tariff History of the United States*, pp. 457–58; Wright, *Sugar in Relation to the Tariff*, pp. 78–81; Zanetti Lecuona, "1929." An excellent history of this period is Pérez, *Cuba Under the Platt Amendment*, chaps. 2, 3. For a summary of early U.S. sugar policy, see U.S. Congressional Committee on Agriculture, *History and Operations of the U.S. Sugar Program.*

12. Maddison's figures, admittedly weak, give a GDP per capita of U.S. $415 for Argentina, $250 for Chile, and $238 for Cuba. In contrast, both Mexico's and Brazil's were around $85 per capita, all according to Maddison's estimates expressed in terms of 1929 U.S. dollars in *Two Crises*, Table A.1, and "Economic and Social Conditions in Latin America," Table 1.7c. These compare with Maddison's estimates for the United States and Canada using U.S. relative prices of 1929 of $1,035 and $698, respectively, according to figures in Maddison, *Dynamic Forces in Capitalist Development*, Appendixes A, B, and E, Tables A.2, B.2, and E.2.

13. Wallich, p. 3.

14. See, for examples, comments by Halperin, p. 65; and U.S. Department of Commerce, *Investment in Cuba*, pp. 5–6.

15. Díaz-Briquets, pp. 19, 22; CERP, p. 208.

16. Numerous studies have traced the origins of the Cuban Revolution of 1959 to monoculture in the sugar industry or to the sugar latifundium. For more recent studies, see Pérez-Stable, p. 7; and Benjamin, *Origins of the Cuban Revolution*, pp. 20–23. There are also a number of insightful studies that appeared shortly after the revolution. See Huberman and Sweezy, pp. 1–22; Seers, pp. 3–19; Bianchi, pp. 65–99; Zeitlin and Scheer, pp. 11–29; Ruiz, pp. 40–58; Dumont, pp. 7–20.

17. The estimate of the area of land controlled by mills is taken from Bianchi, p. 76, or U.S. Department of Commerce, *Investment in Cuba*, p. 32. The estimate of the amount of land in cane is based on my own calculations, presented in Chapter 6, Table 6.2. "Controlled" lands refer to explicit legal control—lands owned plus lands leased by the mills. For the estimates of lands planted in cane, see Table 6.2.

18. Moreno Fraginals, *La historia como arma*, p. 90; Clark, pp. 694–701, 737–44; Hoernel, pp. 234–38.

19. Jenks, pp. 164–65, 300. See also estimates by Winkler, pp. 183–84, and Lewis, *America's Stake in International Investment*, p. 606.

20. Benjamin, *The United States and Cuba*, pp. 14–27; Pérez, *Cuba and the United States*, pp. 113–81.

21. Jenks, p. 284. Determining the nationality of ownership was not always completely straightforward; therefore, these estimates would differ depending on the definition. Some of those heavily involved in the sugar industry, such as Manuel Rionda, clearly had multiple national ties. Also many sugar enterprises combined national and foreign sources of capital. For further discussion, see García Alvarez, "Una saga azucarera," pp. 45–47.

22. Jenks, pp. 284–86, 290–91; Zanetti Lecuona and García Alvarez, *Caminos para el azúcar*, p. 402. The figure of 4,300 kilometers does not take into account the private railroads owned by sugar companies. If they were counted, the

total trackage would probably be more than double the figure for public service railroads. Direct U.S. investments peaked in sugar at $543 million and in railroads at $62.3 million, both around 1924, according to the estimates of Cleona Lewis, taken from book-value estimates, *America's Stake in International Investment*, pp. 592–94, 602.

23. Wallich, pp. 68–69; Jenks, pp. 206–45; Benjamin, *The United States and Cuba*, pp. 14–17.

24. The principal works developing this thesis are Chandler, *Visible Hand* and *Scale and Scope*.

25. Pino Santos, *El asalto a Cuba*, pp. 73–135; Moreno Fraginals, *El ingenio*, 3: 18–32, and *La historia como arma*, p. 70; Guerra y Sánchez, p. 83. Considerable emphasis is placed on the role of the cartel of sugar refiners in controlling raw sugar prices and access to the American market, notoriously known as the Sugar Trust, organized by Henry Havemeyer under the American Sugar Refining Company. The trust began to break up after 1907, and the buying market for Cuban raw sugars passed into an oligopolistic structure. See Eichner, pp. 291–331.

26. See Chandler and Daems, eds.; Lazonick.

27. See Table 1.1; Charadán López, p. 76; and Ayala, pp. 98–99.

28. Moreno Fraginals, *El ingenio*, 1: chap. 5; Iglesias García, *De El Ingenio al central*; Deerr, *History of Sugar*, 2: chap. 23.

29. The most thorough micro-level case study of the transformation of a single firm is Zanetti Lecuona and García Alvarez, *United Fruit Company*, pp. 98–113.

30. See Lewis, *Growth and Fluctuations*, p. 209.

31. Hoernel, p. 217.

32. Hoernel, p. 225; Ayala, p. 103; Commission on Cuban Affairs, pp. 269–70.

33. Ayala, pp. 111–14.

34. Hoernel, pp. 225–26; Pérez, *Cuba Under the Platt Amendment*, pp. 68–72; Jenks, pp. 129–32.

35. Guerra y Sánchez, pp. 73–96.

36. Ayala, pp. 112–13.

37. From a report by Goethals and Company for the Cuba Cane Sugar Corporation, Braga Brothers Collection, University Archives, University of Florida, Gainesville, Record Group 4, series 127.

38. Ayala, p. 112.

39. See Table 6.4.

40. CERP, pp. 241–42; Martínez Alier, pp. 5–7.

41. Bianchi, pp. 75–78.

42. Pino Santos, *El asalto a Cuba*, pp. 161–62; Bergad, *Cuban Rural Society*, p. 153.

43. Guerra y Sánchez, pp. 76–77, 91–112.

44. The seminal work was Coase, "The Nature of the Firm." Williamson's principal contributions have been *The Economic Institutions of Capitalism* and *Markets and Hierarchies*. Also important have been the contributions of Douglass North. See for example, *Institutions, Institutional Change, and Economic Performance*. For surveys of this literature, see Eggertsson, *Economic Behavior and*

Institutions, and Williamson and Winter, eds., *The Nature of the Firm*. There is a growing application of these theoretical ideas to questions of development and underdevelopment. See, for example, Haber, "Industrial Concentration and the Capital Markets" and *Industry and Underdevelopment*; Bates, *Beyond the Miracle of the Market*; LaCroix and Roumasset, "The Evolution of Private Property in Nineteenth-Century Hawaii"; and Feeny, "The Development of Property Rights in Land."

45. See Williamson, *Economic Institutions of Capitalism*; Chandler, *Visible Hand* and *Scale and Scope*; Teece; Rosenberg, *Inside the Black Box* and *Exploring the Black Box*; Mowery and Rosenberg; and David, *Technical Choice, Innovation and Economic Growth*.

Chapter 2

1. On the Caribbean sugar industry, see Galloway, pp. 77–83; Knight, *The Caribbean*, chap. 4; Sheridan, pp. 14–16; Richardson, *The Caribbean in the Wider World*, pp. 28–34; on Cuba, see Moreno Fraginals, *El ingenio*, 2: 93–174; Pérez, *Cuba: Between Reform and Revolution*, chaps. 3, 4.

2. Summerhill, p. 23.

3. Moreno Fraginals, *El ingenio*, 1: 15–21.

4. Maluquer de Motes, "El mercado colonial antillano," pp. 322–57; Zanetti Lecuona, *Cautivos de la reciprocidad*, pp. 26–42.

5. Ballinger, pp. 34–35; Zanetti Lecuona, *Cautivos de la reciprocidad*, pp. 103–7; CERP, pp. 241–42.

6. Moreno Fraginals, *El ingenio*, 2: 104–5; Corbitt, "Immigration in Cuba," p. 280. For discussions of the general policy orientation of imperial Spain, see Lockhart and Schwartz; and Engerman and Sokoloff.

7. CERP, pp. 81–82; Goizueta-Mimo, p. 6; Moreno Fraginals, *El ingenio*, 2: 98–101; Deerr, *History of Sugar*, 1: 240, 2: 490–91. Not only was St. Domingue the world's largest producer of sugar at the time of the collapse, it also supplied about 50 percent of the world's unprotected markets.

8. In 1792, Spain adopted a wartime policy of permitting neutral ships to enter the harbor at Havana. Since regular traffic from the Caribbean to the continent was disrupted, North American carriers found Cuba a convenient source of sugar for reshipment to Europe, hence the high levels of imports of sugar into (and reexports from) the United States during these years. The Spanish wartime policy was suspended in 1812, but the colony continued to enjoy legal authorization to carry out trade directly with foreign ports. See Moreno Fraginals, *El ingenio*, 2: 100–109, 120–25, 130.

9. Eltis, *Economic Growth*, pp. 46, 86–88, 237, 249; Klein, *African Slavery in Latin America*, pp. 247–49; Emmer, "Abolition of the Abolished," p. 179; Laurence, pp. 40–41.

10. Moreno Fraginals, *El ingenio*, 1: 15–18; Robertson, pp. 10–11; Deerr, *Cane Sugar*, pp. 45–54; Maxwell, p. 13.

11. Deerr, *History of Sugar*, 1: 130, 2: 552, 565; Moreno Fraginals, *El ingenio*, 1: 173; CERP, p. 91.

12. Moreno Fraginals, Klein, and Engerman, p. 1207; Bergad, "Economic Viability of Sugar Production," pp. 100–101; Eltis, *Economic Growth*, pp. 119–22.

13. Corbitt, "Immigration in Cuba," p. 282.

14. Absolute decline in the population of color occurred in 1862–77 and 1887–99. Both were periods of war in which the black and mulatto populations fought in pursuit of their freedom (Eltis, *Economic Growth*, p. 245). The fall in the population of color in 1877 was probably less than indicated in the census data reported in the table. The 1877 census, taken during the Ten Years' War, was unreliable. Many slaves had fled their estates during the war, and census takers likely failed to enumerate them (Pérez de la Riva, *El barracón*, pp. 57–59).

15. Pérez, *Cuba: Between Reform and Revolution*, pp. 133–44. Although the rates of growth are similar for the two racial groups between 1817 and 1841, they reflect different demographic experiences and rates of immigration. Rates of natural increase were much lower for the black population than for the white. Death rates were high among the African population, and Moreno Fraginals argues that birth rates were low in the early years of the nineteenth century but that they rose by around 1860. A higher rate of increase in the population, then, implies a higher rate of immigration of Africans (Moreno Fraginals, "Africa in Cuba," p. 196).

16. This is consistent with the early treatment of Chinese when initially they were imported officially under a program to promote white immigration. Separate enumerations of Chinese were made in the 1861, 1877, 1899, and later censuses, in which 34,054 and 46,835 were counted, respectively (Pérez de la Riva, *El barracón*, p. 61; Corbitt, "Immigration in Cuba," pp. 285, 301). On the Chinese in Cuba, see also Corbitt, *Study of the Chinese in Cuba*, and Pérez de la Riva, *El barracón*, pp. 469–507.

17. Chinese contract workers were often assigned to tasks in the mill, and slaves were redistributed into field work (Bergad, *Cuban Rural Society*, p. 252; Scott, *Slave Emancipation in Cuba*, pp. 29–41, and "Explaining Abolition," p. 35).

18. Pérez de la Riva, "Cuba y la migración antillana," pp. 34–39; Sánchez Alonso, *Las causas de la emigración española*, chaps. 3, 4.

19. Using the census dates to define these periods gives misleading estimates for the sugar production growth rates because of the inappropriate end periods determined by the censuses. Both 1899 and 1931 are in the troughs of wide swings in production during those years. A more meaningful indicator of medium-term growth is obtained by using peak-to-peak growth rates. These are given in Table 2.2.

20. See Pino Santos, *El asalto a Cuba*, p. 140: "The second stage was initiated approximately a century later with the penetration in Cuba of Yankee capital. Its characteristic trait consisted in adopting the monocultural and monoexporting pattern inherited from the previous stage, but it developed and consolidated it such that this structural deformation was converted into a phenomenon even more negative." See also Charadán López, p. 81.

21. Marrero, *Cuba*, 11: 120–21.

22. Although many Latin American economies exhibited similar patterns of

concentration of production during their export-led growth periods, Cuba's degree of concentration in a single commodity was extreme in the Latin American context. To compare, in 1913 the ratio of sugar to total exports in Cuba was 72 percent whereas the concentration ratios of the principal export commodity of other countries of comparable size (in terms of population or surface area) were between 40 and 60 percent (Bulmer-Thomas, p. 59). True to its geographical location, however, the degree of concentration was similar to that of other Caribbean sugar islands.

23. As was common in Britain and many other countries, a differential tariff was charged on refined sugars to encourage and protect local refineries. There may have been other cost-related reasons for locating the refineries, at least in the early years, in industrially developed areas (Deerr, *History of Sugar*, 2: 467–68).

24. The counterpart to this incomplementarity was the metropolis's inability to restrict Cubans from trading directly with other nations. Although attempts were made, Spanish officials could not restore the mercantilist practice of requiring shipments of Cuban merchandise in Spanish vessels (Moreno Fraginals, *El ingenio*, 2: 122–25, 174–86, 210, 218–19). On the Spanish lag relative to other European powers, see Prados de la Escosura, *De imperio a nación*, pp. 50–64, and "Spain's Gross Domestic Product," pp. 58–61; and Tortella, *El desarrollo de la España contemporánea*, pp. 1–4.

25. Chalmin, pp. 11–14; Perkins, pp. 31–38; Deerr, *History of Sugar*, 2: 475–87.

26. Henry O. Havemeyer consolidated the trust by 1887. On the operations of the Sugar Trust, see Eichner, pp. 93–119; Heitmann, pp. 34–35.

27. In the 1870s, Cuba's share was about 70 percent; it declined to about 45 percent by the 1890s (Ballinger, pp. 9–10, 16–17).

28. This movement was supported by a broad base of business and industrial interests, set off by a meeting of the Círculo de Hacendados; Junta General de Comercio; Junta General de Agricultura, Industria y Comercio; and the Sociedad Económica (Zanetti Lecuona, *Cautivos de la reciprocidad*, pp. 28–34).

29. Resistance to abolition in the peninsula remained strong as Spain continued to struggle to retain this portion of its empire. Abolitionism penetrated Spanish political thought along with liberalist ideas. But in this age of decolonization, abolitionism and liberalism in Cuba were associated with the pursuit of political and economic autonomy. Spanish officials recognized that abolition could break up the empire and cost Spain indispensable public revenues. The shift of economic power in the North Atlantic did not aid matters. Cuban pursuit of greater economic autonomy was a natural outcome of the relative economic developments in Spain and the United States. Before the Civil War in the United States, slaveholders in Cuba might have considered the permanence of slavery to have been a possibility through some sort of fraternity between slaveholding states. But after the war no major slaveholding market remained, and diplomatic opposition to Cuban slavery came from the United States as well (Corwin, pp. 173–237; Eltis, *Economic Growth*, chap. 6). For a recent intellectual history of liberalism in Spain and Cuba in this period, see Schmidt-Nowara.

30. Mokyr, pp. 113–41; Mowery and Rosenberg, pp. 21–34; Chandler, *Vis-*

ible Hand, pp. 240–83, 315–29; Wilkins, *Emergence of Multinational Enterprise*, pp. 80–109.

31. Moreno Fraginals, *La historia como arma*, pp. 50–54, 75–80, *El ingenio*, 1: 221, and "Plantation Economies," 18–19; Scott, "Explaining Abolition"; Bergad, "Economic Viability of Sugar Production."

32. Scott, *Slave Emancipation in Cuba*, p. 7. By 1862 the census indicates that the slave population was 27.1 percent of the total. Another 16.3 percent were free people of color and 0.3 percent were *emancipados* — Africans confiscated from captured slave ships and contracted out under government authority.

33. Guerra y Sánchez, pp. 74–75; Martínez Alier, p. 5.

34. The first years of the Ten Years' War did not disrupt the pattern of growth in the sugar industry. Although at a slower rate than in earlier years, it continued along a path of growth until 1875. Until then, the war was confined to the eastern provinces, and the sugar industry, which was largely located in the western provinces, remained unscathed. After 1875, when the rebel army crossed into the west, several sugar zones were damaged. Bergad remarks that the decline in production in these years was probably due more to adverse weather than to war damages (*Cuban Rural Society*, p. 184 and n. 2, p. 377). Nonetheless, by the end of the war large numbers of mills had shut down, particularly in the east (Pérez, *Cuba: Between Reform and Revolution*, p. 127).

35. The essential feature of the Moret Law was that it freed all children born of slaves after 1868 and the elderly, with the implication that the current working-age generation would be the last under bondage. But the legal actions were not the only cause. Before emancipation legislation had been passed, manumission of slaves seemed to take on a momentum of its own, operating both within and outside of the framework of legislation for emancipation. The decline in the availability of slaves had begun well before legal action was taken. Spanish slavery was unique in that from early on it had incorporated a relatively liberal mechanism by which slaves could purchase their own freedom. *Coartación*, a provision in the imperial slave code that guaranteed slaves the right of self-purchase on an installment basis, provided a vehicle through which Afro-Cubans could obtain their freedom, and the free Afro-Cuban community existed and grew. The number of slaves relative to the total population of color peaked sometime before 1846. In absolute terms, the number of slaves continued to rise before the enactment of the Moret Law; but between 1846 and 1862, when sugar production had more than doubled, the increase in the number of slaves was only 14 percent. After the Moret Law, the absolute as well as the relative number of slaves fell more quickly, and sugar production stagnated. See CERP, pp. 10–11; Scott, *Slave Emancipation in Cuba*, pp. 7, 65, 87–88, 123–29, 193–94; Klein, *Slavery in the Americas*, pp. 75–76, 196–99; Knight, *Slave Society in Cuba*, pp. 121–36.

36. Scott, *Slave Emancipation in Cuba*, pp. 239, 244–50; Bergad, *Cuban Rural Society*, p. 265; Engerman, "Contract Labor, Sugar, and Technology in the Nineteenth Century," p. 652, and "Servants to Slaves to Servants," p. 266; Knight, *Slave Society in Cuba*, pp. 68–77.

37. Engerman, "Economic Change and Contract Labor," pp. 141–45; Scott, *Slave Emancipation in Cuba*, p. 120; Sitterson, pp. 234–46, 390; Wright, *Old*

South, New South, pp. 47–50. For data that show these trends, see Deerr, *History of Sugar*, 1: 193–205, 250; and Moreno Fraginals, *El ingenio*, 3: 35–40.

38. Engerman, "Economic Change and Contract Labor," pp. 143–47, "Contract Labor, Sugar, and Technology," pp. 636–49, and "Servants to Slaves to Servants," pp. 263–86. See also the collection by Emmer, *Colonialism and Migration*, for an excellent survey of issues regarding the contract labor migration to the Caribbean.

39. Engerman shows an association between the land-labor ratios of the British West Indian colonies and their medium-run postemancipation declines. Those that enjoyed the smoothest adjustments had low land-labor ratios. Examples were Barbados and Antigua with 4.4 and 8.1 square kilometers per thousand slaves, respectively, in 1834. British Guiana, Trinidad, and Jamaica, which faced rougher adjustments, had ratios of 2200, 120 and 32, respectively ("Economic Change and Contract Labor," Table 2, p. 142). Since Cuba's labor force was more racially and institutionally heterogeneous, the labor force basis is not appropriate. Cuba's land-labor ratio in 1877 was 230 square kilometers per thousand inhabitants of color, or 75 per thousand inhabitants of all races. See Luzón, pp. 82–83.

40. Scott, *Slave Emancipation in Cuba*, p. 239.

41. Corwin, p. 248; Pérez, *Cuba: Between Reform and Revolution*, pp. 121–22; Scott, *Slave Emancipation in Cuba*, pp. 67–68. Scott notes that slaveholders succeeded in delaying implementation and attenuating certain aspects of its enforcement. Slaveholders may have intended to preserve a coerced labor regime under a new guise, but the new language of emancipation changed slaves' expectations. The inevitable emancipation became imminent.

42. Corbitt, "Immigration in Cuba," pp. 296–300; CERP, pp. 91–92; Guerra y Sánchez, p. 74; Marrero, *Cuba*, 10: 252–56. By mid-century, the Spanish government impeded the efforts toward white immigration. Spanish officials associated the advocacy of white immigration with the independence movement. They discerned that a reduction of the slave population would reduce the threat of a slave revolt and eliminate one of the services the metropolis offered the creole population—a strong military to defend property against such threats (Corbitt, "Immigration in Cuba," p. 298).

43. Scott, "Transformation of Sugar Production," pp. 112–13, and *Slave Emancipation in Cuba*, pp. 240–42; Bergad, *Cuban Rural Society*, pp. 257–59.

44. Corbitt, "Immigration in Cuba," pp. 301–2; Scott, *Slave Emancipation in Cuba*, pp. 29–34; Bergad, *Cuban Rural Society*, pp. 248–54. The trade in Chinese indentured laborers ended abruptly in 1874 because of accusations that the Chinese laborers were receiving harsh treatment, little different than that given slaves, and forced to renew their contracts against their will. After an investigation, Chinese authorities decided to prohibit continuation of the trade.

45. The contractor would distribute earnings and meals according to an agreement with the workmen, retaining a commission for himself. How democratic or authoritarian these gangs were is unknown. In the United States and Australia, similar gangs formed which exhibited some form of internal democracy (Scott, *Slave Emancipation in Cuba*, pp. 99, 229; Corbitt, *Study of the Chinese in Cuba*,

p. 91). Similar collective contractual arrangements for cane plantation work existed in other sugar-producing countries. An interesting study of the economics of this kind of group contracting in the Australian context is Shlomowitz, "Team Work and Incentives."

46. Sánchez Alonso, *Las causas de la emigración española*, pp. 116, 142–51; Corbitt, "Immigration in Cuba," p. 303; Carmagnani, pp. 96–106. In assessing the impact of Spanish immigrants both before and after independence, the historiography pays relatively more attention to their dominance in commerce, the professions, and urban industries, in which it is often argued that they displaced Cubans from the best jobs and strategic positions in the economy. See Pérez, *Cuba Under the Platt Amendment*, pp. 60–61, and *Cuba: Between Reform and Revolution*, pp. 117–19, 200–201; CERP, p. 180; Clark, p. 739; and Wright, *Cuba*, pp. 134–42. Nonetheless, the positive economic impact of Spanish immigrants to the agricultural sector was no less important. Maluquer de Motes notes that the only group that gave positive rates of net immigration were those who declared themselves "agriculturalists," which included both farmers and rural wage laborers. The ratio between entrants from and returns to Spain was high. Between 1882 and 1894, there were two-thirds as many returns as entrants. After the turn of the century, this ratio tended to be even higher (Maluquer de Motes, *Nación e inmigración*, pp. 49–54, 118, 135–37; Iglesias García, "Características de la inmigración española en Cuba," pp. 277–92). These white immigrant agricultural workers worked alongside slaves or former slaves on cane plantations. Unlike the experiences in the southern United States or Australia, where whites in general were not willing to work alongside blacks, it was not uncommon to find Afro-Cubans and Spaniards working for wages in the same fields (Porter, pp. 79–85).

47. The timing of seasonal migratory streams of both arrivals and departures was highly correlated with the beginning and end of the grinding season. Arrivals of immigrants peaked in November just before the beginning of the grinding season. Departures of returnees peaked in May as the harvest ended (Bergad, *Cuban Rural Society*, pp. 286–88). Much of this transient population was employed directly in the sugar sector; however, even the large circulation of merchants and employees in the commercial sector contributed to the seasonal labor demands of the sugar crop. Higher demands were placed on all sectors of the economy during the six months of harvest and grinding as intermediate demands of the sugar industry (on other sectors) were greater and consumption was higher (Maluquer de Motes, *Nación e inmigración*, pp. 54–55, 116–18; see also Pérez de la Riva, "Los recursos humanos de Cuba").

48. Pérez de la Riva, "Cuba y la migración antillana," pp. 30–32, 60–63; Helg, pp. 246–47; Ayala, p. 118; Guerra y Sánchez, pp. 179–88; Zanetti Lecuona and García Alvarez, *United Fruit Company*, pp. 212–23. Zanetti and García suggest that the West Indians had a significant multiplier effect on the economy that could have been even stronger had the government not required the deportation of West Indian workers after the grinding season ended (p. 219). In addition, to the extent that mills were constrained from investing in new technology or expanding mill

capacity because of the scarcity of field workers, the rate of adoption of new technology would have been impeded. This argument follows from the analysis of Chapters 6 and 7.

49. Bergad, *Cuban Rural Society*, p. 284. There was still considerable discrimination against blacks and mulattoes in the workplace. Although the newly acquired right to exit the workplace represented a substantial improvement in welfare, many barriers to equal treatment remained (Helg, chap. 3).

50. Chalmin, pp. 10–14; Deerr, *History of Sugar*, 2: 501–8; Timoshenko and Swerling, p. 237.

51. Prinsen Geerligs, *Cane Sugar and Its Manufacture*, pp. 111–12; *Revista de Agricultura* 10, edición extraordinaria, Oct. 15, 1890.

52. See Heitmann, pp. 49–67, 169–87.

53. A large wartime issue of paper money had been used to finance the war, which was withdrawn by decrees of 1875 and a law of July 7, 1882. This action reduced the availability of funds for credit, raised interest costs, and had a general contractionary effect on the economy (CERP, pp. 35–36; Iglesias García, "Azúcar y crédito," pp. 134–37; see also Roldán de Montaud).

54. Planters had previously stored their capital in slave property; therefore, with emancipation, the retained earnings plowed back for decades into investments in slaves had dissipated by legislation.

55. Bergad, *Cuban Rural Society*, p. 275; Pérez, *Cuba Between Empires*, p. 20; CERP, p. 93.

56. Maluquer de Motes, "El mercado colonial antillano," pp. 346–49; CERP, pp. 48–52; Pérez, *Cuba Between Empires*, pp. 20, 27–38, and "Toward Dependency and Revolution," pp. 128–30; Roldán de Montaud, pp. 242–45. The wall of protection was raised higher against Cuban sugar through tariff increases and tax exemptions to the peninsular sugar industry to promote the peninsular beet sugar industry at the expense of the colony (Martín Rodríguez, pp. 81–93).

57. An amendment to the McKinley bill had required the president of the United States to impose retaliatory measures against the exports of any country that did not offer reciprocal tariff concessions in exchange for those granted under the McKinley bill. Against the opposition of strong manufacturing interests, Cubans succeeded in persuading Spanish authorities to grant preferential tariff concessions to exports from the United States in exchange for the full enjoyment of the McKinley tariff. In the Foster-Cánovas agreement Spain conceded preferential treatment to certain exports of the United States but otherwise retained the high tariffs currently in effect to protect peninsular industries (Zanetti Lecuona, *Cautivos de la reciprocidad*, pp. 33–37; Pérez, *Cuba Between Empires*, pp. 29–30; Tortella, "El desarrollo de la industria azucarera," pp. 143–45; Taussig, *Tariff History of the United States*, pp. 305–16).

58. Pérez, *Cuba Between Empires*, pp. 26–27. Jenks describes the situation: "Then came the blow. . . . In the face of falling prices for sugar, the effects of the tariff change struck with full force at the Cuban producers. Prices fell for them below two cents a pound for the first time in the history of the sugar industry. At the same time the restored duties of the colonial system meant higher prices for everything Cubans purchased abroad. The Autonomista movement swept the

more conservative members of the community. . . . The Cuban revolution drew strength from the economic catastrophe of the Wilson tariff" (p. 40).

59. Independence from Spain was achieved, but it was not an unconditional independence. Frustrated by the inability of Spain to end the conflict, the United States intervened in July 1898 to pacify the island. In one month Spain had capitulated and the U.S. military occupation of Cuba began. The outcome came about in a much different way than was hoped in Cuba. Various interests in Cuba sought a *Cuba libre*, a continuation of colonial rule, or annexation to the United States. None of these happened. Spain was out, and the United States was unwilling to recognize the revolutionary government, but to obtain authorization from Congress for the intervention, U.S. president William McKinley had to give up the possibility of annexing Cuba. The Teller Amendment to the Joint Resolution of Congress added a disclaimer of "any disposition of intention to exercise sovereignty, jurisdiction, or control over said island except for pacification thereof, and asserts its determination, when that is accomplished, to leave the government and control of the island to its people." In the compromise, the United States established itself as a tutor. A U.S. military government was set up and kept in occupation from January 1, 1899, until May 20, 1902. Under the direction of General Leonard Wood, the U.S. occupational government enacted a sweeping set of reforms in these few years to dismantle many of the mercantilist regulations of Spanish rule and to establish democratic institutions patterned after an American model. On the War of Independence and the role of U.S. involvement, see Pérez, *Cuba Between Empires* and *Cuba and the United States*, chap. 4.

60. Díaz-Briquets, pp. 19, 22; CERP, p. 208.

61. On the troubled period between the world wars, see Santamaría García, "La industria azucarera."

62. Quoted from CERP, pp. 150–51.

63. Jenks, pp. 75–84; Pérez, *Cuba Between Empires*, pp. 322–27, and *Cuba Under the Platt Amendment*, pp. 44–55; Zanetti Lecuona, *Cautivos de la reciprocidad*, pp. 58–61.

64. On the context of these interventions, see Pérez, *Cuba Under the Platt Amendment*, pp. 32–55, 98–107, 168–81; and Jenks, pp. 85–127.

65. The Cuban Constitutional Convention had sought reciprocity as a condition of acceptance of the Platt Amendment, but they were forced to accept on good faith that such an agreement would be implemented. As the negotiations in Congress got under way, the treaty was not passed without considerable opposition from protectionist interests in the United States. The domestic sugar lobby and, in particular, the nascent North American beet sugar industry almost succeeded in suppressing it. But advocates of reciprocity insisted that the United States was obliged to promote economic recovery and insisted that the revival of the sugar industry was a condition of political stability in Cuba. General Wood insisted that reciprocity was indispensable as a means of strengthening the links between the United States and those Cubans most in support of the U.S. efforts to establish political and economic stability. Meanwhile, the private American economic interests in opposition to reciprocity were realigned as, in 1902, Henry Havemeyer and related refining interests associated with the Sugar Trust invested heavily in shares

in the beet sugar industry to placate some of the opposition (Zanetti Lecuona, *Cautivos de la reciprocidad*, pp. 62, 69–78; Jenks, pp. 133–38; Pérez, *Cuba Between Empires*, pp. 351–52; CERP, pp. 279–82; Wright, *The Cuban Situation and Our Treaty Relations*, pp. 23–31; Stubbs, p. 31; see Eichner on the activities of Havemeyer and the Sugar Trust).

66. For example, Victor Clark, of the U.S. Department of Labor, commented that "the real labor supply of Cuba . . . is inadequate to the needs of the island. It does not permit the exploitation of resources already in sight, much less does it afford a social motive for developing new industries. The intelligent people of the island appreciate this condition. They have tried to remedy it by encouraging the importation of labor from abroad" (pp. 684–85). See also Porter, p. 89.

67. This policy was also consistent with current U.S. immigration policy and reinforced by the vision the U.S. military government had for the island. Early republican immigration law was established by military order of General Wood, and like all other military orders, it was reinforced by Article IV of the Platt Amendment. Military Order No. 155 of 1902 set the policy for the next few years, essentially putting the immigration laws of the United States in force in Cuba. The explicit provision that precluded immigrants of color restricted the importation of laborers under contract. It has been argued that this provision was aimed specifically at the exclusion of potential black West Indian immigration. Thus it represented a continuation of policy inherited from Spain. Spanish colonial legislation had prohibited the entrance of any free person of African origin who was not accompanied by a white person as a domestic servant. Also, besides the general prohibition of the entrance of migrant contract labor, there was an explicit prohibition of Chinese immigration, reflecting a similar U.S. policy. See Corbitt, "Immigration in Cuba," pp. 304–5; Maluquer de Motes, *Nación e inmigración*, p. 99; Zanetti Lecuona and García Alvarez, *United Fruit Company*, p. 207; Pérez de la Riva, "Cuba y la migración antillana," p. 28.

68. Hoernel, p. 228.

69. The Nipe Bay Company operated two sugar mills on behalf of the United Fruit Company — Centrales Boston and Preston. These first steps were taken when pressure was exerted by the manager of the Nipe Bay Company, who repeatedly approached Presidents Tomás Estrada Palma and José Miguel Gómez insisting that the existing legal immigration channels provided inadequate supplies of labor for his company (Zanetti Lecuona and García Alvarez, *United Fruit Company*, pp. 207–12).

70. In June 1921, two years after the proclamation of peace, the migrant workers imported under the law of 1917 were to be repatriated. From that year forward, a special government permit was required for legal importation of Antillean workers (Zanetti Lecuona and García Alvarez, *United Fruit Company*, pp. 211–25).

71. Sánchez Alonso, *Las causas de la emigración española*, p. 120; Maluquer de Motes, *Nación e inmigración*, p. 118; Pérez de la Riva, "Cuba y la migración antillana," pp. 38–39. The magnitudes of the two major labor streams can provide some indication of their relative effects on labor supplies and wages. Customs records indicate that about 740,000 Spanish immigrants entered between 1902

and 1929, whereas about 300,000 Haitians and Jamaicans entered (the overwhelming majority of West Indian immigrants). Seasonal migrants who entered only for the harvest season were an important component in both of these migratory streams. The figures of gross entrants do not take account of returnees for which data are less abundant and less reliable (Sánchez Alonso, "Una nueva serie anual de la emigración española," pp. 165–66; Pérez de la Riva, "Cuba y la migración antillana," pp. 34–39). Net immigration is reflected in the census figures for foreign-born residents. The censuses of 1899, 1907, and 1919 show that roughly 8 to 9 percent of the population on the island had been born in Spain. By 1931, that percentage had fallen to 6.5 percent. By contrast, the West Indian population (not including Spanish West Indians) was 0.1 percent of the population in 1899. By 1919, it had risen to 1.4 percent of the population, and by 1931 that figure had reached 2.7 percent. The numbers of residents born in Spain reported in the censuses of 1899, 1907, 1919, and 1931 were 129,240, 185,393, 245,644, and 257,596 respectively. The censuses for 1899, 1907, 1919, and 1931 reported the number of West Indian residents on the island as 1,712, 6,713, 31,159, and 105,741 respectively. See U.S. Department of War, *Report of the Census of Cuba, 1899,* pp. 98; U.S. Oficina del Censo, *Censo de la República de Cuba, 1907,* p. 211; Cuba, Dirección General del Censo, *Census of the Republic of Cuba, 1919,* p. 310; *Memorias inéditas de censo de 1931,* p. 74. See also Luzón, p. 68. Migrants who did not establish permanent residence were not enumerated in the censuses, but they did contribute to the labor force. Since seasonal migration was such an important component of labor supplies, the presence of nonresidents in most years would have been substantial.

72. Ayala, pp. 116–17; Zanetti Lecuona and García Alvarez, *United Fruit Company,* pp. 206–12; Braga Brothers Collection, Record Group 2, ser. 10a, box 5, f. 2.

73. For the data see Sánchez Alonso, "Una nueva serie anual de la emigración española," pp. 165–66, *Las causas de la emigración española* p. 120; and Pérez de la Riva, "Cuba y la migración antillana," pp. 38–39. Maluquer de Motes suggests, for example, that the 1917–18 drop in Spanish immigration may have been a response to the February Revolution of 1917 in Cuba (*Nación e inmigración,* pp. 116–17).

74. García Alvarez, *La gran burguesía comercial en Cuba,* pp. 73–77; Jenks, pp. 33–36, 161–62.

75. Benjamin, *The United States and Cuba,* pp. 25–27.

76. All estimates of foreign assets in this section are given in 1926 constant dollars, based on the U.S. Bureau of Labor Statistics wholesale price index.

77. Jenks, pp. 161–65. Jenks reports an estimate by Antonio S. de Bustamante of Cuban holdings in American securities of $50 million and holdings of French, German, and British securities of $20 million. (All dollar figures given in this note are evaluated in 1926 U.S. prices.) The World Bank reports that estimates of Cuban-held U.S. securities before World War I were around $45 million. In 1941, Cuban-held U.S. securities amounted to about $60 million, in 1926 prices. Deposits of Cubans in U.S. banks amounted to $48 million, and in 1950 Cuban-owned real estate in the United States amounted to no less than $62 million. See

International Bank for Reconstruction and Development, pp. 519–20; and U.S. Department of Commerce, *Investment in Cuba*, p. 15.

78. Jenks, pp. 33–37; Bergad, *Cuban Rural Society*, pp. 170–71, 295–99. Investments in mining included interests of two Pennsylvania companies, Pennsylvania Steel Company and Bethlehem Iron Works.

79. Zanetti Lecuona and García Alvarez, *United Fruit Company*, pp. 49–52, 63–65; García Alvarez, "Una saga azucarera," p. 47; Atkins.

80. Pino Santos, *El asalto a Cuba*, pp. 44–50.

81. See García Alvarez, "Una saga azucarera," pp. 45–47; Atkins; Pino Santos, *El asalto a Cuba*, pp. 44–50; Moreno Fraginals, "Plantations in the Caribbean," p. 19.

82. On the merger wave, see Lamoreaux; and Chandler, *Visible Hand*, chap. 10. See also García Alvarez, "Una saga azucarera," pp. 49–51; Ayala, p. 111; Braga Brothers Collection, Record Group 4, ser. 127; Jenks, pp. 176–81; Lewis, *America's Stake in International Investment*, pp. 264–70; Pino Santos, *El asalto a Cuba*, pp. 101–22. See also Santamaría García, "La crisis financiera de 1920–1921," pp. 138–40.

83. Zanetti Lecuona and García Alvarez, *Caminos para el azúcar*, pp. 200–201, 219–27, 233–44, 402, 406–7; Jenks, pp. 150–54; Pino Santos, *El asalto a Cuba*, pp. 40–41, 50–55; U.S. Department of Commerce, *Investment in Cuba*, p. 11.

84. These are descriptions of the nominal price of sugar. The rise in the real price of sugar, deflated, for example, using the U.S. Bureau of Labor Statistics wholesale price index, is not so dramatic. It was somewhat high in relative terms in 1915 and 1916 but fell after that. Deflation using the general price index does not reflect the relative prices that sugar producers faced, however. The prices of many other commodities and inputs into sugar manufacture rose dramatically during the war. Wages also rose, but in Cuba, producers were successful at keeping the wages paid to sugar workers from growing at the same rate as the price of sugar. Therefore, the price of sugar relative to unit wage costs increased considerably, and it provided a strong incentive for sugar producers to expand their operations. Wages from 1914 to 1919, according to estimates of Zanetti and García, increased only 35 percent, whereas the price of sugar increased by 110 percent. The real wage, deflated by the Bureau of Labor Statistics wholesale price index, fell by 34 percent. See Zanetti Lecuona and García Alvarez, *United Fruit Company*, p. 441; *Czarnikow-Rionda Annual Sugar Review*; U.S. Bureau of Labor Statistics.

85. Jenks, pp. 178–82; Lewis, *America's Stake in International Investment*, pp. 270–71.

86. Lewis, *America's Stake in International Investment*, p. 268.

87. Wallich, pp. 52–68; Jenks, pp. 206–45; Wright, *The Cuban Situation and Our Treaty Relations*, pp. 53–58. Canadian banks had a larger weight in the Caribbean than might be expected because until 1914 U.S. banks were prohibited from establishing foreign branches. Canadian banks, the Bank of Nova Scotia, and the Royal Bank of Canada, which initially was the Merchants' Bank of Halifax, took advantage of more liberal regulations permitting them to set up branches both in the Caribbean and in New York; therefore, especially before 1914, Cana-

dian banks served as a link between Caribbean countries and the rising New York financial center. See Quigley, pp. 800–808; and Cleveland and Huertas, pp. 105–10.

88. Pino Santos, *El asalto a Cuba*, p. 128. It was reported that National City Bank had made loans that amounted to $100 million, although bank officials denied it (Lewis, *America's Stake in International Investment*, pp. 272–75). Cleveland and Huertas, in their study of National City Bank, note that this was a critical time for the leading North American international bank. The bank's decision to go into the sugar business was fateful both for the bank and for Cuba. If the bank had decided to write off the Cuban loans, the losses were so great that they would have substantially reduced the bank's capital and limited its aggressive expansionary policy. The decision was made in 1922 to hold onto the Cuban sugar properties, betting on an improvement in the sugar market. It did not pay off — eventually the bank had to incur substantial losses for its gamble in 1922 — but the postponement of the revision to the bank's capital permitted National City Bank to continue with its ambitious goals for expansion (Cleveland and Huertas, pp. 108–10).

89. Jenks, pp. 262, 291–96; Pino Santos, *El asalto a Cuba*, pp. 127–30. On the political economy of the adjustment, see Santamaría García, "La crisis financiera de 1920–1921."

90. Albert and Graves, *The World Sugar Economy in War and Depression*, pp. 1–9.

91. The exceptional quantity of Cuban sugar going to the United Kingdom during the war reflects the cooperation between the United States and Britain. It does not reflect a permanent increase in the demand for Cuban sugar in the United Kingdom but rather the redirection of resources destined for the United States toward Europe. After the war, the sugar supplies once again were directed toward the United States, as is seen in Figure 2.7.

92. Taussig, *Tariff History of the United States*, pp. 457–58, 501–4. The beet interests were defeated only temporarily with the treaty of reciprocity. The special interest battle over the effect of reciprocity on the domestic industry was resolved only when Henry Havemeyer, president of the American Sugar Refining Company (the Sugar Trust), invested heavily in the stocks of beet sugar companies. This maneuver had the effect of encouraging the beet interests to lower their objections in favor of the refiners' interests. Philip Wright points out that later it had the opposite effect. When beet interests began to clamor for tariff adjustments after World War I, Havemeyer had hedged his interests in cane properties in Cuba with beet properties in the American West. The proposed tariff adjustments would have hurt his Cuban interests but benefited his beet interests (Wright, *Sugar in Relation to the Tariff*, p. 59; Jenks, pp. 132–38).

93. Such comments are found in the private letterbooks of Manuel Rionda, Braga Brothers Collection, Record Group 2, ser. 2.

Chapter 3

1. Prinsen Geerligs, *Cane Sugar and Its Manufacture*, pp. 111–12.
2. *Revista de Agricultura* 10, edición extraordinaria, Oct. 15, 1890.

3. Aguilar, p. 30.

4. Zanetti Lecuona, *Cautivos de la reciprocidad*, pp. 25, 28–30, 54–59.

5. Lewis, *Growth and Fluctuations*, p. 191.

6. Rosenberg points out that agricultural technology is less self-contained. It is more closely enmeshed with the natural environment and, therefore, dependent on local conditions. An implication is that it is likely not as easily transferable (*Perspectives on Technology*, p. 168).

7. Lewis, *Growth and Fluctuations*, pp. 181–223, "Economic Development with Unlimited Supplies of Labour," pp. 139–91, and *Evolution of the International Economic Order*.

8. Corbitt, *Study of the Chinese in Cuba*, pp. 1–26; Tinker, pp. 112–15, 274.

9. Ayala has found that highest yields reported declined from more than 100,000 *arrobas* per *caballería* in the 1870s to 84,000 in 1913 (p. 105). (An arroba equals 25 pounds and a caballería equals 33.33 acres.) Besides maximum yields on the island, average yields probably also fell. Soil exhaustion is often claimed; however, another likely influence was lower field-to-mill transportation costs, which reduced the relative costs to the mill of using more land to obtain the same volume of cane. A survey of the techniques used in the agricultural sector of the sugar enterprise is found in Moreno Fraginals, *El ingenio*, 1: 175–203.

10. Sugar technicians often commented on Cuba's backwardness in cane cultivation techniques and its need to adopt "scientific methods" in cane cultivation. See Maxwell, pp. 7–14, and Ayala, p. 113. The well-known cane sugar expert Noel Deerr was hired by the Cuban government as a consultant to investigate this matter. He concluded that Cuba's apparent backwardness in cane cultivation was cost efficient given the abundance and quality of Cuba's soils and climate. Critical of the substitution effects of the abundance of land, Moreno Fraginals has argued that the low-cost method of cultivation both inhibited innovation in the agricultural processes and exacerbated the latifundium structure of Cuban sugar enterprises. Moreno does not question what cane costs might have been in Cuba under alternative circumstances and whether Cuba would have lost its competitive advantage. See U.S. Department of Commerce, *Cane Sugar Industry*, pp. 375–81; Moreno Fraginals, *La historia como arma*, p. 91.

11. Deerr, *History of Sugar*, 2: 560–89; Heitmann, pp. 25–67, 208–43.

12. Mowery and Rosenberg, pp. 76–77; Rosenberg, *Inside the Black Box*, pp. 73–80, "Technological Change in the Machine Tool Industry," pp. 414–46, *Exploring the Black Box*, p. 191.

13. Deerr, *History of Sugar*, 2: 560–89, *Cane Sugar*, chap. 16; Heitmann. Although Guerra y Sánchez emphasized the importance of this technical development for the costs of railroad construction, the overall impact was much broader and of greater significance (pp. 76–77).

14. Sugar manufacturing innovations were also labor-saving, and this was another benefit. Even though immigrant supplies of labor from Spain and the West Indies were relatively elastic, there were costs to obtaining it because the importation of immigrant laborers often had to be financed privately by the recipients.

15. There were three product divisions in the world sugar industry of the early twentieth century. Beet sugar producers produced a finished, refined sugar prod-

uct. The cane sugar industry consisted of raw sugar producers and refiners. The refiners were geographically located in industrial cities near the major markets for sugar. The raw sugar producers located their manufacturing equipment on the site of the plantation because of the necessity of rapid cane processing. There was no technical constraint which required cane sugar to be made in two separate stages, processing and refining, but most major markets for cane sugar had established differential tariffs to protect their refining industries.

16. The first attempt at applying steam power to sugar production was made by John Stewart in 1768 in Jamaica. The first steam engine reported in Cuba was at the Ingenio Seibabo of the Conde de Mopox y Jaruco in 1769. The early attempts at employing steam power were not successful. According to Deerr, the first profitable application of the steam engine in sugar production occurred in Cuba in 1797. By the third decade of the nineteenth century, steam power was commonly used in Cuba. Cuba was the seventh country in the world to have a railroad (Deerr, *History of Sugar*, 2: 551–53; Zanetti Lecuona and García Alvarez, *Caminos para el azúcar*, pp. 5, 32–39).

17. Moreno Fraginals, *El ingenio*, 1: 170–71; Iglesias García, "Azúcar, esclavitud y tecnología," pp. 127–29; Deerr, *History of Sugar*, 2: 556–72.

18. On the concept of learning by using, see Rosenberg, *Inside the Black Box*, chap. 6.

19. Cuba and Brazil were the last two countries in the Western world to complete emancipation, in 1886 and 1888 respectively.

20. Moreno Fraginals, *La historia como arma*, pp. 80–81, "Plantations in the Caribbean," pp. 18–19; *El ingenio*, 1: 220–21.

21. On abolition movements in the Spanish Empire, see Corwin.

22. Bergad, "Economic Viability of Sugar Production," pp. 105–9. Bergad does not consider the added unreliability that dependence on wage labor in a thin market might have created. Nonetheless, the costs of an unreliable labor force might have been substantial and might have added to the attractions that producers continued to see in slave labor. The price patterns for the 1850s and 1860s from Moreno Fraginals, Klein, and Engerman likewise do not suggest a collapse of the slave system. See also the cost analysis of sugar production for 1844 by Turu.

23. Scott, "Explaining Abolition." pp. 28–39. Proponents of the incompatibility literature presume that a rise in the number of rented slaves on plantations represented evidence of the breakdown of the economic relations of slavery before legal acknowledgment. Scott rightly points out that the slave rentals do not necessarily indicate any such breakdown of relations. They were an arrangement by which slaves could flexibly be shifted from less to more profitable regions or sectors of the economy.

24. That is, as the final emancipation approached, the prices of slaves declined as the expected duration of ownership declined. Consequently, planters incurred capital losses as the lifetime use or resale value of assets in slaves dissipated (Scott, "Explaining Abolition," p. 45; Bergad, "Economic Viability of Sugar Production," pp. 104–5).

25. See Galloway, chap. 7.

26. This figure is relative to all the sugar produced for the international mar-

kets, both cane and beet. The figures are based on estimates of world supply made by Deerr in *History of Sugar*, 2: 490–91.

27. None of these had independent political status. Java was a Dutch colony, the Hawaiian Islands was a territory of the United States, and Cuba, although a new republic, was a protectorate of the United States.

28. See Deerr, *International Sugar Journal* (1920): 216, quoted by Maxwell, p. 108.

29. Braga Brothers Collection, Record Group 2, ser. 1, box 11, and ser. 2, box 25.

30. Maxwell, p. 22; Deerr, *Cane Sugar*, p. 124; Hawaiian Sugar Planters' Association, pp. 12–13.

31. Deerr, *History of Sugar*, 1: 218–25. This regulatory system was developed as a response to the abuses of the earlier *cultuur* system, which existed in Java from 1831 to 1870. The cultuur system was established by the Dutch colonial government to require or coerce the native population to produce and deliver cane to the sugar mills. Besides the objection that the system was a covert form of slavery, the main criticism of the system was that it tended to create food shortages (Campbell, 1: 425).

32. Chandler, *Visible Hand*, pp. 240–44; Mokyr, pp. 113–41; Mowery and Rosenberg, pp. 38–42.

33. Hunter, 2: 252–53, 334–39, 430; Deerr, *History of Sugar*, 2: chap. 23.

34. Compare David, "Computer and Dynamo."

35. Atkins, p. 94; Braga Brothers Collection, Record Group 2, ser. 5, box 1, f. 10; Chandler, *Visible Hand*, p. 282. The trend in the employment of chemists with the chemicals-based innovations parallels the employment of mechanics with the introduction of the steam engine into the Cuban sugar industry in the early nineteenth century (Deerr, *History of Sugar*, 2: chap. 33; Heitmann, chap. 2; Moreno Fraginals, *El ingenio*, 1: chap. 5). The chemists were employed primarily to do laboratory work and acted as assistants to the sugarmaster. The sugarmasters of the new mills also had much more technical training than in the old industry; it was needed to operate the new machinery more efficiently. Cuba, Secretaría de Agricultura, Comercio, y Trabajo, *Portfolio azucarero*, reports that 236 chemists, 101 of whom were classified as foreign, were working on some 140 mills. These numbers are probably too small because of underreporting.

36. Chandler, *Scale and Scope*, pp. 23–24, and *Visible Hand*, pp. 244, 281.

37. According to the figures of Moreno Fraginals, in 1860, 72.3 percent of all mills in Cuba used steam power for grinding cane, and these mills represented 91.4 percent of the cane ground in Cuba (Moreno Fraginals, *El ingenio*, 1: 173). An excellent survey of the technology used in Cuban sugar mills in 1860 and before is found in this work of Moreno Fraginals, 1: 167–255. A survey of technological developments in the sugar industry is found in Deerr, *History of Sugar*, 2: chap. 23. See also Deerr, *Cane Sugar*, chap. 16; and Leon.

38. Deerr, *History of Sugar*, 2: 584. One of the first mills to operate entirely on bagasse was the Central Hormiguero in Cuba. Chandler, "Anthracite Coal and the Beginnings of the Industrial Revolution," pp. 141–81.

39. Deerr, *Cane Sugar*, pp. 89–95, and *History of Sugar*, 2: 540–43.

40. See Deerr, *History of Sugar*, 2: 556–72; Moreno Fraginals, *El ingenio*, 1: 214–29; Iglesias García, "Azúcar, esclavitud y tecnología," p. 129; Heitmann, pp. 31–40.

41. Moreno Fraginals, *El ingenio*, 1: 234.

42. The packaging of the hogshead weighed 10 to 14 percent of the gross weight, whereas the bag weighed less than 1 percent of the gross weight (Moreno Fraginals, "Plantation Economies," p. 193).

43. The polariscope previously used for chemical research was modified by Jean Baptiste Biot in 1840 for use in the sugar house. The polariscope whose use was diffused after mid-century incorporated a further innovation to Biot's instrument by Henri Soleil of 1846. It permitted both greater control quality and greater control of chemical processes performed in defecation. Another important instrument by Henri Soleil in 1846. It permitted both greater quality control and greater juice, which also became a basic instrument of factory control (Heitmann, pp. 26–31; see also *Willett and Gray's Weekly Statistical Sugar Trade Journal*).

44. The 89° pol. sugars were sometimes referred to as "muscovado"; however, this product was completely different from the muscovadoes of the mid-nineteenth century. The 89° pol. sugars were obtained as well from centrifugal machines.

45. Cuba, Secretaría de Hacienda, *Industria azucarera*, 1916/17.

46. This is inferred from the tariff equivalents for Dutch Standard and polariscopic tests established in 1897 by the United States. No. 16, Dutch Standard was treated for tariff purposes equivalent to 75° pol. The standard muscovadoes in Cuba generally were rated at No. 16, Dutch Standard (Wright, *Sugar in Relation to the Tariff*, p. 93; Moreno Fraginals, *El ingenio*, 1: 253).

47. Moreno Fraginals, *El ingenio*, 3: 21–22, *La historia como arma*, pp. 63–64, "Plantations in the Caribbean," p. 11.

48. Physical destruction was not the only avenue by which the war persuaded mill owners to shut down their mills. If, at the end of the war, a mill owner had to make some capital outlays to put the mill back into production, the mill owner might have decided not to do it. Using a conclusion of the vintage-capital model presented in Chapter 4, one could reason that many of the owners of smaller mills would have chosen not to resume grinding after the war because sinking further investments either into repairing the existing outmoded equipment or into other complementary investments necessary to resume grinding could not be justified.

49. For a detailed history of the events of the war, see Pérez, *Cuba Between Empires*. See also Pérez, *Cuba: Between Reform and Revolution*, pp. 156–75, and "Insurrection, Intervention, and the Transformation of Land Tenure." For an excellent description of the economic and social impact of the war on the province of Matanzas, see Bergad, *Cuban Rural Society*, chap. 17.

50. Bergad, *Cuban Rural Society*, pp. 307–12, 401 n. 2. For a description of these events, see Pérez, *Cuba Between Empires*, pp. 50–56. See also Pérez de la Riva, "Los recursos humanos de Cuba al comenzar el siglo," pp. 22–23, 28.

51. Bergad, *Cuban Rural Society*, p. 314. Estimates of the number of horned cattle in Matanzas fell from 298,391 in 1894 to 8,800 in 1899, the number of horses fell from 102,268 to 3,700, and the number of mules from 7,725 to 803. Since Matanzas was the center of the sugar industry, this destruction directly

affected the sugar industry (Bergad, *Cuban Rural Society*, pp. 313–14; Ayala, p. 98; Maxwell, p. 13).

52. In 1902, stocks of cattle, horses, and mules were, respectively, 999,862, 167,933, and 30,950, according to CERP, p. 256. These figures indicate either massive importation of livestock after the war, or gross undercounting of the livestock at the end of the war, or both.

53. The process of retirement of nonrenovating ingenios that began after the Ten Years' War may be thought of as an enactment in the Cuban sugar industry of the process, identified by Joseph Schumpeter, as creative destruction. "The history of the productive apparatus . . . is a history of revolutions. The opening up of new markets, foreign or domestic, and the organizational development from the craft shop to the factory . . . illustrate the same process of industrial mutation . . . that incessantly revolutionizes the economic structure *from within*, incessantly destroying the old one, incessantly creating a new one. This process of Creative Destruction is the essential fact about capitalism" (Schumpeter, p. 83).

54. Bergad, *Cuban Rural Society*, p. 314; Moreno Fraginals, "Plantations in the Caribbean," pp. 20–21.

55. Some authors have argued that the smaller mills disappeared because of their inability to pay for protection during the war. The more modern mills were owned by people with greater means for incurring such expenditures during the war. Both this effect and the outmodedness of smaller mills were likely important. See Pérez, "Insurrection, Intervention, and the Transformation of Land Tenure," p. 232; and Bergad, *Cuban Rural Society*, p. 314.

56. The occupational government undertook various measures to improve the situation, falling short of offering direct financial assistance to planters or other agriculturalists. The tax system was reformed to remove the great fiscal burden of the Spanish regime, a two-year moratorium on debt was declared, and a policy of trade reciprocity was actively pursued (accomplished in 1903). Given the shortage of credit on the island, various economic interests in Cuba sought direct aid from the occupational government, but General Wood chose to rely on private incentives to rebuild the economy. For a discussion of these policies, see Bergad, *Cuban Rural Society*, pp. 320–27; Pérez, *Cuba: Between Reform and Revolution*, pp. 189–90, and "Insurrection, Intervention, and the Transformation of Land Tenure," pp. 233–42.

57. *Colono* literally means "settler," but in Cuba, besides the general usage, it has taken on the specialized meaning as "outside cane grower," with many connotations fixed to it based on the peculiarities of the cane farming institution in Cuba. There were two distinct meanings in Cuba in the late nineteenth century. One referred to a group of immigrant settlers brought in to populate unsettled areas by establishing colonias, not necessarily having to do with the sugar industry. The other meaning referred to outside growers who had contracts to supply cane to a central. These could be either tenants of the central or independent landowners with their own sources of credit. The colono arrangements of this sort became standardized and identified as one of the basic institutions underlying and supporting the Cuban sugar industry. In the 1920s, the term was further fixed by

legislation that defined the colono as a legal category (Usategui y Lezama, pp. 19–30; see also Bergad, *Cuban Rural Society*, pp. 277–78).

58. On Australia see, for example, Shlomowitz, "The Search for Institutional Equilibrium," and "Melanesian Labor and the Development of the Queensland Sugar Industry," and Graves, pp. 23–48; on Natal, Richardson, "Natal Sugar Industry," pp. 243–47; on Puerto Rico, Martínez-Vergne, pp. 11–37, and Ramos Mattei, *La sociedad del azúcar*; on the Philippines, Larkin, pp. 54–60, and Nagano, pp. 176–78; on Trinidad, Haraksingh, pp. 133–35.

59. Moreno Fraginals, *La historia como arma*, p. 73, and "Plantations in the Caribbean," p. 4; Iglesias García, "Development of Capitalism in Cuban Sugar Production," pp. 69–70; Charadán López, p. 75; Deerr, *History of Sugar*, 1: 130.

60. Reports and related discussions are scattered throughout the issues of the *Revista de Agricultura* and the *Revista Económica* in the 1880s and 1890s. See also Friedlaender, 2: 541–48; and Charadán López, pp. 76–77.

61. Moreno Fraginals, *El ingenio*, 1: 173. Simply counting mills, 28 percent still had not adopted steam power; however, those mills were smaller on average, and given their scale of production it is likely that the fixed cost of installing a steam engine was not economically justified. On the concept of the threshold in agricultural mechanization, see David, *Technical Choice, Innovation and Economic Growth*, pp. 195–232; Atack and Bateman, pp. 186–200; Olmstead, pp. 327–52.

62. Noel Deerr notes that a number of the earlier applications of the vacuum apparatus, or its introduction into functioning mills, were by Cuban producers (*History of Sugar*, 2: 556, 565).

63. Moreno Fraginals comments that while the Jamaica train was being diffused in the Cuban sugar industry in the mid-nineteenth century, it was not a recent invention. Rather, it had been used in the British West Indies since the early eighteenth century. Its adoption in Cuba was an indication of factor substitution as fuel wood reserves became more scarce and producers shifted to a fuel-saving technique (*El ingenio*, 1: 173, 216, 221–22). It is natural in the early stages of development of a new technical insight, such as vacuum evaporation, that an older technology would continue to develop and undergo improvements stimulated by the competition between the two coexisting techniques. See Rosenberg, *Perspectives on Technology*, pp. 202–6.

64. Moreno Fraginals, *El ingenio*, 1: 230–34.

65. Iglesias García, "Azúcar, esclavitud y tecnología," pp. 121, 123, 129, and "Development of Capitalism in Cuban Sugar Production," p. 57.

66. Moreno Fraginals, *El ingenio*, 1: 215.

67. Ibid., p. 234.

68. Iglesias García, "Azúcar, esclavitud y tecnología," p. 129.

69. Compare Chandler, *Scale and Scope*, pp. 23–24, and *Visible Hand*, pp. 244, 281. Note also the relationship between these developments and Hirschman's notion that more mechanically intensive "process-centered" production can be conducive to economic development because of a narrower scope for poor performance on the part of labor, which may be less socialized industrially or

unskilled (pp. 146–47). See Scott's comments regarding Hirschman's ideas in relation to the issue of compatibility of modern technology and slave labor ("Explaining Abolition," p. 35).

70. Venegas Delgado, pp. 72–74. The classification of the sugar produced is identified by how it was packaged. Roughly, centrifugal sugars were packed in bags and conventional sugars were packaged in hogsheads or boxes. Iglesias has noted that the correspondence was not perfect and, therefore, the packaging is not an accurate indicator of sugar type. Until the 1890s, centrifuged sugars of less than 92° pol. were sometimes packaged in hogsheads. This would lend a possible downward bias to Venegas's estimates of the percentage of centrifugal sugar in the 1880s and 1890s in Remedios. The transformation of sugar type may have been even more abrupt. See Iglesias García, "Development of Capitalism in Cuban Sugar Production," p. 72.

71. Venegas Delgado, p. 74; Cuba, Secretaría de Agricultura, Comercio, y Trabajo, *Industria azucarera*, 1924/25.

72. Estimates come from Charadán López, p. 76; Commission on Cuban Affairs, p. 219; and sources for Table 1.1.

73. See Chapter 3, n. 53.

74. Guerra y Sánchez, pp. 8, 86–87. Explicit characterization of these stages is found in Pino Santos, *El asalto a Cuba*, and Moreno Fraginals, *El ingenio*, 2: 94–97.

75. Deerr, *History of Sugar*, 2: 546; Jenks, p. 131; García Alvarez, *La gran burguesía comercial en Cuba*, p. 38. The Gómez Mena was a well-established Havana merchant family. J. B. Hawley was a congressman from Texas involved also in sugar properties in Louisiana, and Mario Menocal was a Cornell engineer who managed the estate mentioned, the Chaparra, until he became president of Cuba in 1912.

76. Ayala, p. 106.

77. Deerr, *History of Sugar*, 2: 543–46.

78. Iglesias García shows that the technical trajectories for these various devices originated after 1880. See "Azúcar, esclavitud y tecnología," pp. 128–29; "Development of Capitalism in Cuban Sugar Production," p. 70.

79. Compare Venegas Delgado, Anexo 4, pp. 109–10, which includes an inventory of the Ingenio Central Narcisa in 1890, and Braga Brothers Collection, Record Group 4, ser. 96, which includes a detailed 1922 inventory including equipment specifications of the Central Francisco.

80. These lands were not all in cane, but for an impression of the distances cane traveled, the cane lands available to the centrales are what mattered. The distances to the perimeters implied by the acreages discussed would be between 8 and 43 kilometers. Because of the abundance of land for sugar production, centrales tended to use about twice as much land as they had in cane at any one time. Besides cane, land was kept in pasture for the large herds of oxen used to haul cane out of the fields to the railroad loading stations, for roads, firelanes, *bateyes*. In addition, some land was often kept in fallow (Commission on Cuban Affairs, pp. 268–69). See Table 6.2. On the acreage owned by the largest centrales, see Pino Santos, *El asalto a Cuba*, pp. 160–61; and Guerra y Sánchez, p. 95.

81. The object was to obtain high volumes of sucrose in the cane, which would be extracted and crystallized in the milling process. Sucrose, glucose, and fructose are all present in cane, but only the sucrose was useful to the producer. The other sugars, commonly referred to by sugar manufacturers as invert sugars, did not crystallize or provide the desired taste so the economic value of the cane was directly related to the sucrose content of the cane. When the cane was cut, the sucrose in the cane began the process of inversion of the sucrose into the other sugar forms—glucose and fructose (Deerr, *Cane Sugar*, pp. 11–12; Robertson, chaps. 2, 4).

82. "Public" railroads had been privately owned since 1842. See Cok Márquez, p. 138; Zanetti Lecuona and García Alvarez, *Caminos para el azúcar*, pp. 42–46.

83. Zanetti Lecuona and García Alvarez, *Caminos para el azúcar*, pp. 153, 207–8. See also Guerra y Sánchez, chaps. 8–10.

84. Guerra y Sánchez, p. 122.

85. Cok Márquez, pp. 143–44; Iglesias García, "Development of Capitalism in Cuban Sugar Production," pp. 67–68.

86. Guerra y Sánchez, pp. 84, 125–27; Charadán López, p. 109; Zanetti Lecuona and García Alvarez, *Caminos para el azúcar*, pp. 153, 202–4.

87. Guerra y Sánchez, pp. 125–26.

88. The classic work on the colono system by Guerra y Sánchez has since been complemented by other works. See Bergad, *Cuban Rural Society*, pp. 257–59, 277–83; Scott, *Slave Emancipation in Cuba*, pp. 240–42, and "Transformation of Sugar Production in Cuba," pp. 112–14; Zanetti Lecuona and García Alvarez, *United Fruit Company*, pp. 223–28.

89. See Scott, "Transformation of Sugar Production in Cuba," pp. 112–14; and Iglesias García, "Development of Capitalism in Cuban Sugar Production," p. 65.

90. Bergad, *Cuban Rural Society*, pp. 277–78; Iglesias García, "Azúcar y crédito," pp. 135–44; Guerra y Sánchez, pp. 73–74.

91. *Revista de Agricultura* 8 (June 17, 1888), 8 (July 15, 1888), 10 (Mar. 2, 1890), 10 (Mar. 9, 1890); Bergad, *Cuban Rural Society*, p. 280.

92. Thomas, p. 275; CERP, pp. 91–92; Corbitt, "Immigration in Cuba," pp. 296–97.

93. See Jenks, p. 33; Cuba, Secretaría de Hacienda, *Industria azucarera*, 1905/4. See Table 6.4.

94. Bergad, *Cuban Rural Society*, p. 279.

95. Dye, "Factor Endowments and Contract Choice."

96. The Commission on Cuban Affairs, p. 69, reports on a "well-to-do *colono*" who lived in the city of Santiago de Cuba, who in 1933 received an income of $9,100 to be shared between fifteen persons—$600 per person. This, according to the study, compares to an aggregate income of less than $90 per person. The range of colonia sizes is illustrated in Bergad's data on the distribution of colonos in selected jurisdictions of Matanzas (*Cuban Rural Society*, pp. 278–79).

97. Such a tenor in the debates is found perusing the articles in the 1880s and

1890s of the *Revista de Agricultura*. See for examples, 2 (Mar. 31, 1880): 73–79; 8 (June 17, 1888); 9 (May 26, 1889); 9 (Aug. 18, 1889): 394; 10 (Feb. 17, 1890): 76; 10 (Mar. 16, 1890): 125; 10 (Apr. 6, 1890): 159–60; 10 (Apr. 15, 1890): 172. Similar attitudes regarding the nature of the colonato are found by Martínez Alier, apparent in the proceedings of the Association of Colonos in the 1930s and 1940s ("Cuban Sugar Cane Planters," p. 17).

98. Introduction to J. B. Jiménez, *La colonia*, published in the *Revista de Agricultura* 8 (July 15, 1888). He published a pamphlet criticizing the abuses in the mill-colono relationship entitled *Los esclavos blancos: Por un colono de las Villas* (Havana: Imprenta de A. Alvarez y comp., 1893). He later recanted his militancy, but others continued to inveigh against abuses related to the bargaining power of the mills. See Scott, "Transformation of Sugar Production in Cuba," p. 114.

99. Discussions of the most beneficial form of the contract were being carried out between participants and reflected in articles of the *Revista de Agricultura* between 1880 and 1890. See also Scott, "Transformation of Sugar Production in Cuba," p. 113 and n. 13, p. 320.

100. Dye, "Factor Endowments and Contract Choice"; U.S. Department of Commerce, *Cane Sugar Industry*, pp. 364–65.

101. Chandler, *Visible Hand*, p. 281.

102. Chandler describes the origins of the line and staff form in *Visible Hand*, pp. 272–79. This form of management is reflected in salary and wage records, hierarchical personnel charts, and correspondence in the Braga Brothers Collection.

The comments made here are about the organization within the factory, that is, at the plant level, not the firm level. To this point, I have said little about the organization of the Cuban sugar company or firm. To understand the organization of the Cuban sugar company, as much as the activities at the mill, the activities associated with sales and marketing must be analyzed, and these activities are outside the scope of this study.

103. Albert and Graves, *The World Sugar Economy in War and Depression*, p. 12.

104. U.S. Department of Commerce, *Cane Sugar Industry*, p. 375; Dye, "Producción en masa del azúcar cubano," p. 586.

105. During labor strife cane fields were often set afire. Burned cane was easier to harvest, so cane cutters could attempt to increase their wages by burning the cane. Burning the cane presented problems for the manufacturing because, although burned cane could be ground, the costs of grinding were increased. Hawaiian producers had found that a technique that incorporated intentional burning of the cane at harvest was a preferred approach for them, but Cuban producers found the limits in which burned cane could be ground to be restrictive and less efficient for their operations. If they had other sources of cane, mill managers would refuse to grind burned cane. So the colono was left bearing the cost and the incentive to keep the burnings under control. See Dye, "Factor Endowments and Contract Choice."

106. More study of the institutional and organizational characteristics of the

systems of cane farming that developed in other places is needed to understand how much they differed and why. On Cuba and Puerto Rico, see Ramos Mattei, "Growth of the Puerto Rican Sugar Industry;" and Moreno Fraginals, "Plantation Economies and Societies." On the Dominican industry, see Castillo and Plant. On a similar cane farming system in the Philippines, also referred to as a colono system, see Nagano. Other cane farming systems developed in Trinidad, Mauritius, and Queensland. See Johnson, Blouet, Haraksingh, North-Coombes, and references for Shlomowitz.

107. Moreno Fraginals, "Plantation Economies and Societies," p. 5, and *La historia como arma*, p. 91.

Chapter 4

1. Jenks, pp. 282–83; Ballinger, p. 31; Pino Santos, *El asalto a Cuba*, pp. 96–97.

2. Jenks, pp. 282–83.

3. Salter, chaps. 4, 5. For comments on Salter's model, see Davies, pp. 29–30.

4. Deerr, *History of Sugar*, 2: 546–48; Zanetti Lecuona and García Alvarez, *United Fruit Company*, p. 135. *La doble presión* — "double milling" — had been practiced in some mills in the 1880s. See Iglesias García, "Azúcar, esclavitud y tecnología," p. 128.

5. The design of the three-roll mill was modified and improved over time.

6. Deerr, *History of Sugar*, 2: chap. 23, and *Cane Sugar*, chap. 11.

Maceration is historically related to the process of diffusion, which was important in the beet sugar industry. Diffusion is a process that replaced the grinding (crushing) process in the beet sugar industry in the nineteenth century. To extract the juice containing sucrose, diffusion involves slicing the material (beets or cane) into small pieces and immersing them in a sucrose solution. The sucrose contained in the (cane or beet) cells diffuses through the woody, porous cell walls into the solution.

The success of sucrose diffusion in the beet sugar industry, an alternative industrial process for extracting the sucrose from the raw material — a substitute for the grinding process — caused it to receive much attention from cane sugar producers in the 1880s in Louisiana and Cuba, but it was never as successful as crushing primarily because, with diffusion of cane, the bagasse was rendered useless as fuel. Attempts to apply diffusion to cane in Cuba were made. The Central San José in Santa Clara province was constructed as a diffusion mill. It was abandoned before 1911; the Central Washington — with a grinding mill — was built in its place (Braga Brothers Collection, Record Group 2, ser. 1, box 9; ser. 5, box 1, ff. 6–8, and box 2, ff. 11, 12). On the experimentation with the diffusion process in Louisiana, see Heitmann, pp. 59–67. The application of maceration, which works on a similar principle, was so successful that in the twentieth century attempts to adapt diffusion to cane sugar were abandoned (Prinsen Geerligs, *Cane Sugar and Its Manufacture*, p. 112).

Problems of water supply can be read about in the correspondence of Manuel Rionda with the managers of the Centrales Francisco and Tuinucu. Innovations in other departments also strained the existing water supply infrastructure. High mineral contents created problems for the condensers and vacuum pan apparatus (Braga Brothers Collection, Record Group 2, ser. 10c, box 26, f. 46).

7. Chandler, *Visible Hand*, chap. 8.

8. Because sugar manufacturing was one of the oldest of these related industries, technological discoveries in sugar manufacturing made important contributions to developments of techniques in other industries. An important example is the development of vacuum distillation in petroleum refining. Modern methods of petroleum cracking owe their existence to four major advances of the nineteenth century, one of which was vacuum distillation. The original devices used for vacuum distillation were adapted from the multiple-effect vacuum apparatus being developed in the sugar industry in the mid-nineteenth century (Williamson and Daum, p. 218). There are some interesting recent articles on the technologies of some of the related industries. See references for Cohen and Nuwer.

9. See Braga Brothers Collection, various mill records, Record Group 2, ser. 1, 5, 10a, and 10c.

10. Some recent works discuss how this principle of bottlenecks has been fundamental in determining the optimal scale of production, the organization of the plant, and the boundaries of the firm. See references for Langlois and Leijonhufvud. See Braga Brothers Collection, various mill records, Record Group 2, ser. 1, 5, 10a, and 10c.

11. See Shlomowitz, "Plantations and Smallholdings," p. 7. Agricultural researchers at the time were attempting to determine a precise relationship between the inversion of sucrose with the passage of time after the cane was cut. A discussion of the research is found in Deerr, *Cane Sugar*, p. 168.

12. Two things hindered the prolongation of the grinding season beyond the beginning of the wet season. The wet season made the fields muddy and made the harvest more difficult, at times impossible, to continue. But also there is an annual cycle in sucrose content in the cane based on seasonal variation of rain, heat, and sunshine, as the sugars in the cane inverted from sucrose to uncrystallizable glucose and fructose. The months of peak sucrose in Cuba were February through April. The arrival of the rains initiated a new growing period in the canes, causing the inversion of the sucrose in the cane to noncrystallizable fructose and glucose. This, of course, would reduce the yield of sucrose from the cane if grinding continued.

13. Zanetti Lecuona and García Alvarez, *United Fruit Company*, p. 137.

14. Braga Brothers Collection, Record Group 4, ser. 96. Unusual occurrences, such as train derailments, were excluded from the hours stopped as a result of delays in cane deliveries.

15. The benefits of avoiding the public railroads wherever possible should not be underestimated. Reams of pages can be read in the correspondences of producers concerning this problem in the Braga Brothers Collection. A discussion of the problems of using public railroads for cane delivery is found in Chapter 6. "Public railroad" is used here to refer not to a publicly owned or operated enterprise but to the type of traffic that it carried. The railroads in Cuba that offered

public services were owned and operated by private companies, but they were closely regulated by the government body, the Cuban Railroad Commission.

16. Braga Brothers Collection, Record Group 2, ser. 10c, box 17, f. 9.

17. A single cartload generally weighed about 3,000 pounds, net of the weight of the cart. Additionally, because of the ruggedness of the fields, the oxcarts were very heavy. Although plowing was practiced in some fields, many of the fields were never plowed, and stones and stumps had not been removed from them; therefore, lightweight carts generally could not handle the work (Moreno Fraginals, *El ingenio*, 1: 198). Zanetti Lecuona and García Alvarez also found that the rains were the principal cause of delays at the Centrales Boston and Preston (*United Fruit Company*, p. 137).

18. The area controlled by the largest centrales ranged around 150,000 acres of cultivated and uncultivated land, in cane, pasture, and fallow. Guerra y Sánchez comments about the enormity of the largest of the landholdings of sugar companies in Cuba, but the landholdings of the mills were only a part of the lands from which they drew cane. Further inquiry into the proportions of plantations that were owned or not owned by the central and their geographic location relative to the location of the mill would be useful. See Braga Brothers Collection, Record Group 4, ser. 127. See also Pino Santos, *El asalto a Cuba*, pp. 160–61. Diversification to reduce the effects of weather and other natural stochastic influences on agricultural production has been recognized in other contexts. For the seminal contribution on this agricultural phenomenon, see McCloskey on the scattering of plots in the English open fields.

19. The importance of the soil quality for the outcome of the grinding season in Cuba should not be underestimated. The sugar technician Francis Maxwell remarked that the extraordinary soil quality of the island was the most important feature responsible for making Cuba an outstanding sugar region (p. 13). See also similar comments by Robertson, pp. 6–7. For a discussion of the permeability of the soils in Cuba and how they affected cane cultivation, see Deerr, *Cane Sugar*, pp. 45–54.

20. This is one of the themes of Chandler's work in *Scale and Scope*, chaps. 4, 5.

21. Guerra y Sánchez, p. 64; Moreno Fraginals, *La historia como arma*, pp. 73–117; Venegas Delgado; Iglesias García, "Development of Capitalism in Cuban Sugar Production," and "Azúcar, esclavitud y tecnología." This bias is most obvious in the neglect in the historiography of technical change after 1894.

22. Rosenberg, *Inside the Black Box*, chap. 1; Mokyr, chap. 7. One of the contributions of the so-called New Economic History has been the greater attention given to the role of technical diffusion and technical choice in long-term economic development.

23. Mansfield, "Technical Change and the Rate of Imitation," and *Economics of Technological Change*.

24. See Temin and comment by Rosenberg, *Inside the Black Box*, p. 23.

25. David, *Technical Choice, Innovation and Economic Growth*, pp. 195–232.

26. See references for Sahal, Mihajan and Peterson, Davies, and Stoneman.

27. Salter, chaps. 4, 5.

28. Ibid.

29. This can vary with the prices of the factors of production, but it is well-defined when factor prices or factor proportions are stable over time.

30. If the following condition held, the decision to build a new plant was made:

$$E \left(\int_{t_0}^{t_1} [p(t) - v_n(t)]y_n(t)e^{-rt} \, | \, J_n(t_0)dt \right) - G_n(t_0) \geq 0$$

where $G_n(t_0)$ is the investment cost of the construction of the mill of the latest vintage, n, in year t_0, $p(t)$ is the market price of sugar, $v_n(t)$ is the unit operating costs of the mill, and $y_n(t)$ is the sugar output of mill n. The rate of discount is r. The first term is the expected stream of operating profits, which is conditional on the available information, $J_n(t_0)$.

Any owner of an existing mill would have the option of adopting the new technology by updating the existing equipment at the mill. The decision would be made if the expected stream of operating profits using the new technology exceeded the expected stream under the old technology enough to cover the additional fixed costs of purchasing the new equipment. That is, if

$$E \left(\int_{t_0}^{t_1} [p(t) - v_i^N(t)]y_i^N(t)e^{-rt} \, | \, J_i(t_0)dt \right) - G_i^N(t_0)$$

$$\geq E \left(\int_{t_0}^{t_1} [p(t) - v_i^o(t)]y_i^o(t)e^{-rt} \, | \, J_i(t_0)dt \right) \geq 0$$

where $G_i^N(t_0)$ is the capital cost of updating mill i in year t_0, v_i^N is the unit operating costs and y_i^N is the output that would be associated with the new vintage, and v_i^o is the unit operating costs and y_i^o is the output associated with the vintage of the existing equipment. In general, the new vintage, N, from the perspective of any mill i need not be the latest technology.

31. The new vintage from the perspective of any particular mill need not be the latest, or overall best-practice, technology. Complementarities or technical interrelatedness between different machines in the mill might affect profit opportunities in such a way that the next best alternative to some mills would be to make partial rather than complete improvements to the existing machinery (see Frankel). In his theoretical work, Salter found it useful to simplify the number of alternatives by assuming that the production plant is indivisible. This restriction artificially forces all investors to purchase an entire plant each time they invest, and therefore, they would upgrade with the latest technology every time they invest. It simplifies the exposition of the theory (in fact, I find it useful for expository purposes below), but there are no problems in relaxing the assumption to allow a more realistic investment behavior of partial or incomplete updating of equipment.

32. Evaporation consisted of defecation, clarification, and concentration of the juices into the massacuite, and curing involved the separation of the massacuite into crystallized sugar and molasses, as described in Chapter 3.

33. The report of Griggs and Myers, engineering consulting firm to the Francisco Sugar Co., 1917, in the Braga Brothers Collection, Record Group 4, ser. 96.

34. The models involve only identities describing the cane constituents commonly found in cane sugar manufacturers' manuals published after the turn of the century. Two useful references from which I have drawn heavily are Prinsen Geerligs, *Chemical Control in Cane Sugar Factories* and *Cane Sugar and Its Manufacture*. Prinsen Geerligs was perhaps the most well-known expert of his time in the chemistry of the sugarcane, and he was the director of the cane sugar experiment station in Java, which was the most successful research institution in the industry involved in developing new cane hybrids.

35. Le Riverend, 2: 578.

36. A good example is Zanetti and García's examination of the installation of large mills at the Centrales Boston and Preston. See *United Fruit Company*, chap. 6.

37. See Griliches.

38. In Chapter 5, I present a model derived from a simple cost-theoretic framework which demonstrates the economies of scale in the long-run cost curve. Here, it is instructive to examine the correlations of productivity measures with the mill capacities.

39. The models to be estimated are simple log-linear regressions of the form

$$\ln\sigma = \delta\beta_0 + \delta\beta_1\ln x_1 + \delta\beta_2\ln x_1^2 + \beta_3\ln x_2 + \beta_4 t + \epsilon$$
$$\ln\xi = \delta\beta_0 + \delta\beta_1\ln x_1 + \delta\beta_2\ln x_1^2 + \beta_3\ln x_2 + \beta_4 t + \epsilon$$

where σ is the yield (the ratio of the weight of the sugar produced to the weight of the cane); ξ is the extraction rate (the ratio of the weight of the cane juice to the weight of the cane); x_1 is capacity of the mill (according to engineering specifications), x_2 is a vector of cane qualities S/J, W/J, W/C; and t is the year of each observation. The variable, δ, is a set of dummy variables for the six provinces in Cuba, which interact with β_0, β_1, and β_2. The dummy variables are included to account for regional geographical and institutional differences related to cost differences between the newer (eastern) and older (western) sugar-producing regions within Cuba. These differences are the subject of Chapters 6 and 7. The data are pooled without differencing, and the observations are of each mill that ground cane for each season from 1917 to 1929. There are missing values, but they do not affect the consistency of the results. The estimates for the respective equations are presented in Table 4.3.

40. The creditors were primarily banks, merchants, sugar brokerages, and refining companies. The brokerages and refining companies were located in the United States, but the banks were Cuban, Spanish, or North American. Until 1921, the dominant banks in Cuba were the Cuban bank, Banco Nacional, and the Spanish bank, Banco Español de la Isla de Cuba. In 1921, a banking crisis in Cuba resulted in a number of bank failures, including that of the Banco Nacional. The Banco Español was also severely weakened, and at that point, the North American banks — the National City Bank, the Chase National Bank, and the Royal Bank of Canada — first achieved dominant positions among the banks operating in Cuba. See Jenks, and the Braga Brothers Collection.

41. "New mills," as before, are the mills newly established between 1917 and 1929.

42. Santamaría García, "La industria azucarera," Appendix 6.

43. Kindleberger, pp. 86–100; Guerra y Sánchez, p. 143.

44. Taussig, *Tariff History of the United States*, pp. 451–57; Ballinger, pp. 31–33.

45. A multivariate regression, presented in Chapter 7, indicates that, controlling for relative factor prices and other influences, the rate of mill expansion among existing mills was higher after the war, in 1921–29, than it was in the 1917–20 period.

46. Jenks, pp. 282–83.

47. Cleveland and Huertas, p. 109.

48. Santamaría García, "La crisis financiera de 1920–1921," p. 134, discusses a political economy dimension to this effect. Santamaría's arguments suggest that opportunities arose after 1921 for a collusive agreement between Cuban sugar and North American beet sugar interests to restrict production, which he suggests might have been beneficial to domestic Cuban interests. But he argues that a policy of crop restriction would have hurt those mills that were still in process of adjustment to their optimal capacities.

49. Two useful references from which I have drawn heavily are Prinsen Geerligs, *Chemical Control in Cane Sugar Factories* and *Cane Sugar and Its Manufacture*.

50. "The specific gravity is the ratio of mass of the substance and the mass *in vacuo* of an equal volume of water at the standard temperature [20° C]." It was actually the apparent specific gravity that was used in practice because measurements at the mill were not taken *in vacuo*. The Brix was actually only the apparent specific gravity of a solution of pure sucrose; however, it was the practice to consider it the specific gravity of all solids dissolved in the cane juice (Meade and Chen, pp. 569–70).

Chapter 5

1. Jenks, p. 262.

2. Pino Santos, *El asalto a Cuba*, pp. 91–95.

3. Ballinger, p. 31; Cleveland and Huertas, pp. 107–10; Santamaría García, "La crisis financiera de 1920–1921," p. 134.

4. Some of the principal contributions are Jorgenson; Tobin; Eisner and Strotz; Lucas, "Optimal Investment Policy and the Flexible Accelerator"; Arrow, "Optimal Capital Policy with Irreversible Investment"; and Treadway. See Takayama, pp. 688–701, for a survey of the debate.

5. More recent theoretical work that incorporates adjustment costs includes Abel, "Optimal Investment Under Uncertainty" and "A Unified Model of Investment Under Uncertainty"; Caballero; Lucas and Prescott; and Pindyck, "Adjustment Costs, Uncertainty and the Behavior of the Firm." Empirical work that has incorporated the adjustment cost concept includes Morrison and Berndt; Morrison; Dorfman and Heien; and Lichtenberg.

6. The same pattern was seen in the founding of the centrales owned by the United Fruit Company (Zanetti Lecuona and García Alvarez, *United Fruit Company*, pp. 135, 138–40).

7. Braga Brothers Collection, Record Group 4, ser. 96. Zanetti Lecuona and García Alvarez find a similar pattern of adjustment of mills over time in the Centrales Boston and Preston (*United Fruit Company*, pp. 135–39).

8. The Audubon Sugar School closed soon afterward, in 1896, for various reasons. William Stubbs, who was Louisiana's leading sugar specialist on the faculty, was disappointed with the results of the program. He did not feel that the students were proper sugar specialists after completing the program. The Audubon School was incorporated into Louisiana State University in 1897 (Heitmann, pp. 218–26).

9. Ibid., p. 234.

10. Ibid., pp. 241–43.

11. Braga Brothers Collection, Record Group 2, esp. ser. 10c, box 40, f. 33; but also ser. 2, box 25; ser. 5, box 1, f. 8; ser. 5, box 2, f. 10; ser. 10a, box 5 f. 2; ser. 10c, box 72, f. 19. The references range from 1909 to 1924. One such recruitee was a Mr. Hart from the University of Wisconsin (ser. 10a, box 5, f. 2). This confirms Stubbs's complaint about the Audubon School. See note 8.

12. See Dye, "Tropical Technology and Mass Production," pp. 86–87.

13. There were variables that could, in principle, be varied to alter the cane requirement marginally. The length of the grinding season could, from a technical viewpoint, be varied; but there were economic reasons that would limit the degree of variation that producers were willing to make under competitive conditions. The grinding season was marked both at its commencement and termination by the favorable weather conditions brought by the dry season. The average product was considerably smaller before the rainy season had ended or after it had begun again. The speed of operation of the mill could also be altered, but it could be done only marginally. The machinery would have operated efficiently only within a limited range of speeds so that in practice it is unlikely that altering the speed of grinding would have affected the cane requirement greatly.

14. See Dye, "Tropical Technology and Mass Production," pp. 88–91. Even with fixed production coefficients between capital and cane inputs, factor substitution is present in the vintage-capital model. It enters the model through the process of investment in new equipment with a different technique embodied. That is, a given vintage of technique would require an X:Y ratio between mill capacity and cane field capacity. A different vintage could have a different required ratio, say X:Y'. Substitution of factor intensities can take place through selection of existing vintages or the introduction of a new one. Also, as in standard models of factor substitution, the rate of substitution is governed by relative factor prices. The lower the costs of equipment relative to cane, the greater is the rate of investment in new equipment. If the new equipment has a lower cane requirement per unit of capacity, then the capital-cane ratio is increased.

In the context of sugar production, this appears to be a very natural way to describe the capital intensification of a mill. Suppose that the mill has incurred an increase in the price of labor, and the management has decided to substitute capital for labor. It cannot be accomplished in the current grinding season because the installation would interrupt the harvest/grinding, but afterward, during the dead season, new relatively cane-saving equipment can be purchased and installed to be ready for the next grinding season. Not all mills would have been willing to make this substitution at the same time, even if they all faced the same cane costs. Whether the mill would be willing to make this substitution would have depended on the "outmodedness" — to use Salter's term — of the existing equipment at each mill. Mills would have been more willing to make the substitution the higher the operating costs of the existing equipment, and this would depend on the age, or vintage, of the existing equipment. Zanetti Lecuona and García Alvarez describe behavior similar to this at the Centrales Boston and Preston (*United Fruit Company*, p. 137).

15. Although sugar technologist Francis Maxwell's comments about Cuba were often derogatory and exaggerated, his comments about the care given to cultivating cane in Cuba and the longevity of ratoons are instructive. "The extraordinary fertility of the natural cane lands in [Cuba] is a well known fact. Cane once planted . . . continue[s] to yield annual crops for decades. Cases are met with where cane has been ratooned for a generation and over. Largely due, no doubt, to this boon, very little and often no care is bestowed by the 'colonos' . . . upon the tillage and manuring of their fields" (p. 13). The records of mills show that the claim that "no care was bestowed" was, of course, an exaggeration, or at least that he was not accounting for the costs of cane field maintenance not directly related to the activity of cultivation. Nonetheless, the longevity of the ratoons in Cuba was surprising to one, such as he, who was accustomed to the relatively more intensive cane cultivation techniques of most other parts of the world.

16. Also, regulatory costs could intervene and create planning problems. Regulations in Cuba prohibited private railroads from crossing public railroads. If a company wished to extend its private rail lines over an existing public line, it had to convert the private to a public line, under which conditions it was subject to much stricter state regulation and much more costly to operate. Such crossings were generally avoided. See Chapter 6.

17. Not only were its cane operations managed by its private railroads, but shipments of sugar were carried on the Francisco private line to its own remote private port at Guayabal, on the south side of the island. It was known for the efficiency of its railroad.

18. Also uncertainty in the sugar market may have affected investment patterns. Sugar prices were very unpredictable during the speculative bubble of 1920 and its aftermath. The degree of uncertainty may have postponed intended investment at the Francisco. The large amount of construction during 1918 and 1919 may as well have been in part caused by reduced uncertainty. In these years the price of sugar was being controlled as part of U.S. war policy. Manuel Rionda, who was the representative for Cuba in the price control negotiations, was also the president and a major stockholder of the Central Francisco.

19. An excellent study of the experience of the field laborer is Mintz, *Worker in the Cane*, which is an examination of the life of a field laborer who lived in Puerto Rico during the 1920s and 1930s. The experiences of laborers in Puerto Rico and

Cuba would have been very much the same, with the exception that trends that were changing the organization of labor in the fields in Cuba and Puerto Rico were likely to have occurred with a lag in Puerto Rico. See also Mintz, *Caribbean Transformations*, pp. 116, 122–23. Commission on Cuban Affairs, pp. 77–78, describes the opportunities and options that were available to the field laborer. These sources offer evidence that decisions affecting the worker were being made on the basis of the personal ties of the worker to the employer.

20. Zanetti Lecuona and García Alvarez, *United Fruit Company*, p. 139, find evidence of this in the investment programs of the Central Preston. On learning by using, see Rosenberg, *Inside the Black Box*, chap. 6. For further discussion, see Dye, "Tropical Technology and Mass Production," pp. 96–102.

21. The unit of analysis has been the plant and not the firm. There was concentration of firms in the Cuban industry, but it was generally less than in other major sugar-producing countries. Many sugar companies (firms) owned more than one central. The largest company, the Cuba Cane Sugar Corporation, established in 1919, owned seventeen centrales. Still, there were a large number of companies that owned a single central. The observation regarding the entry of mills at small capacities applies both to new mills in new firms and new mills in already existing firms.

22. If three or more prices are included, the matrix of explanatory variables is linear dependent.

23. This assumes that the proportional increase in expenditures in response to factor price increases is the same for all mills. This seems to be a reasonable approximation to control for the influence of short-run market conditions on average costs of production in sugar mills.

24. In the meantime, if a new vintage had been introduced establishing a larger best-practice optimal capacity, the mill owners may have altered their desired capacity to the new best-practice optimum, or they may have preferred not to change their target capacity, in accordance with the decision criteria of vintage-capital theory discussed in Chapter 4.

25. A major reason for the difficulty in ascertaining the desired scale is that managers of centrales were uncertain about how large the scale of production could get before the costs of maintaining the organization offset the economies associated with high volume and rapid throughput. The advance in the technical frontier caused maximum mill sizes to grow throughout the first three decades of the twentieth century. The largest mill in 1917 could produce 600,000 bags of sugar at capacity. The first mill that could produce 800,000 or more bags was built in 1919. It is probable that these large-scale mills encountered numerous organizational problems as they were established, and a certain amount of experimentation was required. Initially only a few firms would have been willing to absorb the risks of attempting the large-scale organization. Therefore, the long-range investment plans for new mills may often have been relatively conservative in that their objective long-run capacities may have been considerably smaller than the maximum capacity in Cuba at the time. It is, nonetheless, unlikely that the desired scale was less than 400,000 bags, as long as there were no constraints to the firm gaining the best available equipment and the technical personnel necessary to operate the

equipment efficiently and the firm faced no constraints in obtaining credit for expansion of the mill facilities.

26. Imperfections in capital markets would be conditions for credit access that were unrelated to the real profitability or risk of the investments for which the credit would be used. Information asymmetries would be responsible for some of it. Personal linkages and common interests between banking houses and sugar companies might be another source. But competition would have limited the extent to which highly profitable investments would be barred from access to credit; therefore, one cannot infer imperfections simply from identification of interlinked economic interests.

Chapter 6

1. Hoernel, pp. 219–20, 232–36.
2. Ibid., pp. 225–34.
3. On this issue, many authors reflect the views of Guerra y Sánchez, pp. 108–11, 123–24. See Hoernel, p. 217; Pino Santos, *El asalto a Cuba*, p. 153; Charadán López, p. 85.
4. The contents of this chapter are taken largely from Dye, "Avoiding Holdup."
5. Williamson, *Economic Institutions of Capitalism*, chs. 3–7.
6. Persistence or path dependence arises because the formation of institutions in the past had a long-lasting effect on current economic constraints. This aspect of the analysis is reminiscent of a study by David, *Technical Choice, Innovation and Economic Growth*, pp. 233–90, in which the incompatibility of preexisting infrastructure hindered the adoption in Britain of innovations that had been successfully implemented elsewhere. In this case, however, the preexisting institutional framework, as well as the infrastructural layout, is seen to have affected current contractual relations. Comparisons of the U.S. South and California have revealed a similar interaction between institutional and technical factors. See Musoke and Olmstead; and Whatley.
7. Guerra y Sánchez, chap. 10; Pérez, *Cuba Under the Platt Amendment*, pp. 62–72, and *Cuba: Between Reform and Revolution*, pp. 195–99.
8. See Williamson, "Credible Commitments," and *Economic Institutions of Capitalism*; and Klein, Crawford, and Alchian.
9. Recall the discussion of the evolution of the colono system in Chapter 3.
10. Williamson, "Credible Commitments," and *Economic Institutions of Capitalism*, pp. 90–95; and Klein, Crawford, and Alchian, pp. 298–99.
11. Because of low capital costs, many small, obsolete mills that had shut down could keep the option of reentering production in years of high sugar prices or low labor costs. Therefore, some years there would be a number of mills that were not "viable" — i.e., they were not using techniques that could be profitable in more ordinary market conditions. A discussion of the activities of these "primitive" sugar mills is found in the technical sugar journal, *Sugar*, Jan. 23, 1921, pp. 1–2.

One technique for estimating the minimum viable scale (also referred to in the literature as the "minimum efficient scale") is the survival technique developed by

George Stigler and Leonard Weiss (Stigler, pp. 61–67; Weiss, pp. 246–61). The technique is based on the premise that, if the proportion of plants in a given size class diminishes in the distribution of plants in an industry, then that size class is not viable. (See Table 2.1 to verify the conclusion.) The conclusion we come to with this approach—that the minimum viable scale of sugar mills in Cuba is 100,000-bag capacity—is confirmed in Table 2.4, which shows that new mills entering the industry in this period were built at 100,000-bag capacities and greater but not at smaller capacities.

12. For the data sources, see the citations in Table 6.2. Moreno Fraginals suggests that the data of Pezuela are unreliable, and this may be of some concern (Moreno Fraginals, *El ingenio*, 1: 81–82). Yet to take an alternative route, if we use Moreno Fraginals's estimates of Cuban sugar production, the average yields of sugar from the cane, and the average yields of cane per caballería for 1860 we arrive at an estimate which is similar to the one obtained more directly from the Pezuela data. Because of the similarity and the consistency between the estimates based on Pezuela's data and data of the Círculo de Hacendados, it seems unlikely that the conclusions drawn from these data are misleading.

13. David, *Technical Choice, Innovation and Economic Growth*, pp. 233–75.

14. Braga Brothers Collection, Record Group 2, ser. 10a, 10c; Zanetti Lecuona and García Alvarez, *United Fruit Company*, p. 135.

15. Oriente was the province into which many freed slaves had migrated either before or after general emancipation (1886) to avoid working in the sugar industry. How disruptive the expansion was to local population settlements is open to question. In some cases, particularly in Oriente, local inhabitants may have been uprooted and moved into the hill country. In other cases, settlers had to be brought in to be established as colonos whenever a new mill was established. The local disruption or stimulus notwithstanding, employment opportunities on the island as a whole grew as a consequence. The expansion of the eastern sugar industry offered growth in seasonal wage labor demands for the growing population that the west did not offer, and voluntary seasonal migration from the west to the east to take advantage of these opportunities became common. See Guerra y Sánchez, chap. 8; and Scott, *Slave Emancipation in Cuba*, pp. 247–54 and chap. 11.

16. See Hoernel, pp. 223–26, 230; Nelson, pp. 79–90, 111. When colonial land grants were initially made, the Laws of the Indies provided that they be handed down to their heirs as communal property (*haciendas comuneras*). A royal order of 1819 had provided for the shift in Cuban landholding from communal to fee simple property. Over the course of the nineteenth century titles to most of the land in the west had been established. Nonetheless, throughout the nineteenth century the property in the east remained largely unaffected by the land reform, keeping its traditional communal form. Litigation and surveying costs to establish the title to a piece of land were very high while, before sugar, the land in the east was of low commercial value.

17. Guerra y Sánchez, p. 268.

18. Bergad, *Cuban Rural Society*, p. 313 and Table 17.3; CERP, pp. 96, 233.

19. Scott, "Transformation of Sugar Production in Cuba," pp. 111–19; Bergad, *Cuban Rural Society*, pp. 277–80; CERP, p. 92.

20. In some cases, the agreement was referred to legally as the colonato.

21. There were also cases when either the central management or the colono leased land from a third party which was then used to form a colonia. The bargaining position of the lessee in these cases was almost as if he owned the land. Therefore, to simplify the exposition, I disregard this complication in the contractual arrangements discussed in the text.

22. Commission on Cuban Affairs, pp. 269–70.

23. See Pérez, *Cuba: Between Reform and Revolution*, pp. 195–96, and *Cuba Under the Platt Amendment*, pp. 69–72; Zanetti Lecuona and García Alvarez, *United Fruit Company*, pp. 43–79, 119–24.

24. Guerra y Sánchez, pp. 102–4.

25. Hoernel, p. 239.

26. Price fluctuations could be quite large. Recall the "dance of the millions," discussed in Chapter 2.

27. Several studies have found risks to be an important mutually beneficial aspect of share contracts to landlords and tenants. On risk sharing, see, for example, Stiglitz, Cheung, and Reid. On agency costs and monitoring, see, for example, Alston and Higgs; Hoffman; and Bardhan.

28. An arroba is equal to 25 pounds.

29. The number of ratoons tended to be between six and ten years so that a single planting of cane would be harvested once a year for six to ten years. The duration of the contract corresponded, therefore, with the life of the investment in cane planting.

30. See Reid and Cheung.

31. The contract I used as a model here is the standard contract of the Central Manati, in western Oriente. These contracts were printed in forms that left a few blanks to be filled to give the names of the parties, dates, and other details. The basic contract does not seem to have varied greatly from central to central, although, as we shall see, variations according to the capital inputs and bargaining power of the colono were common. Managers of different centrales regularly compared their contracts and advertised clauses that had proven to be successful (Braga Brothers Collection, Record Group 2, ser. 10c, box 17, f. 9; and ser. 10c, box 27, f. 20; see also Appendix 4 in Guerra y Sánchez, pp. 265–80).

32. Williamson, in *Economic Institutions of Capitalism*, has given the most thorough treatment of the problem of transacting when specific assets are involved. The key to the argument, as stated earlier, is the difference in the use value and the secondary sales value of the transaction-specific asset. There is a tendency in the historiography to treat bargaining power as if it were determined by the size or net worth of the agent. Colonos' operations were smaller than those of the mills; therefore, their bargaining positions are seen as weaker. Size was clearly a factor, but clearly not the only determinant. At times, colonos' bargaining positions vis-à-vis the centrales fared well. Moreno Fraginals mentions that bargaining positions tended to favor the colonos at the beginning of period of study (*La historia como arma*, p. 90; or "Plantation Economies," pp. 212–13). Juan and Verena Martínez Alier argue that they again had the upper hand in the 1930s largely

through unionization and corporatist legislation ("Cuban Sugar Cane Planters," and *Cuba*, chap. 4).

33. On these points, see Klein, Crawford, and Alchian, p. 289; and Williamson, *Economic Institutions of Capitalism*, p. 522.

34. An explanation of the tendency for vertical integration in cane sugar production is found in Shlomowitz, "Plantations and Smallholdings." Williamson has argued that site specificity of assets encourages vertical integration, or unified ownership, because site specificity is an extreme form of transaction specificity of assets. But the theory depends on the interplay of holdup costs and offsetting costs of internal governance (*Economic Institutions of Capitalism*, pp. 85–96, 118–19). The reason that vertical integration is not realized in Cuba appears to be related to relatively high monitoring costs in the cane fields. Here I assume for reasons that must be elaborated elsewhere that the choice to contract with colonos rather than to integrate vertically was based on profit-making incentives on the part of mill owners. See Dye, "Factor Endowments and Contract Choice."

35. For example, the contracts also stipulated the parties' obligations in supplying capital inputs (Braga Brothers Collection, Record Group 2, ser. 10c, box 17, f. 19; ser. 10c, box, 27, f. 20; Guerra y Sánchez, Appendix 4). See also Reid; Alston and Higgs; and Cheung.

36. On the implications of contracting incompleteness, see Williamson, *Economic Institutions of Capitalism*, pp. 45–46, 79–83.

37. The loading stations on Portuondo's colonia (Finca Borbollón) had a joint capacity to load 42 cane cars. These loading stations, the corresponding railroad sidings, scales, telephone lines, and other capital improvements all reverted to Portuondo at the termination of the contract (Letter of May 19, 1924, by Leandro Rionda, general manager of the Central Elia, Braga Brothers Collection, Record Group 2, ser. 10c, box 23, f. 62).

38. The liquidation rate is the rate of payment in sugar for the cane delivered (in pounds sugar per 100 pounds cane). For comparison of rates, see the discussion of liquidation rates below. See "Report by George W. Goethals and Company, Inc. on the Cuba Cane Sugar Corporation," Braga Brothers Collection, Record Group 4, ser. 127.

39. Braga Brothers Collection, Record Group 2, ser. 10c, box 69, f. 25. Several exchanges between Manuel Rionda and Oliver Doty regarding this incident are found in letters of June 6, 25, and 28, 1928, and February 15 and 22, 1929.

40. "Controlled land" was the common internal language used to refer to land either owned or leased by the company or surrounded by the company-owned railroad. See Goethals and Company Report, Braga Brothers Collection, Record Group 4, ser. 127. A 1915 stockholders' report of the Washington Sugar Company (Central Washington, Santa Clara) further corroborates the high cost of cane obtained from colonos independientes. See Braga Brothers Collection, Record Group 2, ser. 10a, box 7, f. 34.

41. See Pindyck, "Irreversibility, Uncertainty, and Investment," pp. 1110–48.

42. In 1913, the density of public service Cuban railroads (km per km^2) was

almost as great as that of the United States. See Maddison, "Economic and Social Conditions in Latin America," p. 5.

43. U.S. Department of Commerce, *Cane Sugar Industry*, pp. 359–62. Goethals and Company also reported that higher rates were paid to the colonos independientes (Braga Brothers Collection, Record Group 4, ser. 127).

44. For example, average liquidation rates paid at the Central Washington, in western Santa Clara, fluctuated between 6.2 and 6.5 during 1911–17. Meanwhile, at the Central Francisco, in eastern Camagüey, the average rate was 5 during the same period, and rates at the centrally located Tuinucu in eastern Santa Clara rose from 5.25 to about 6.

45. Le Riverend, 2: 578. This was also suggested by the surveyors of the U.S. Department of Commerce, *Cane Sugar Industry*, p. 359; however, no direct evidence is given to support their suggestion. Moreno Fraginals also discusses the historical importance of soil exhaustion in Cuba on cane yields (*La historia como arma*, p. 59).

46. Cuba, Secretaría de Agricultura, Comercio, y Trabajo, *Portfolio azucarero*.

47. Dye, "Cane Contracting and Renegotiation."

48. The use of railroads to reduce competition is described in Guerra y Sánchez; see chaps. 11–14, especially chap. 14. The regulations for both public service and private railroads are recorded in the U.S. Department of War, *Civil Report of Major General Leonard Wood*. The regulations imposed by General Wood during the military occupancy were not easy to alter. The Platt Amendment to the constitution of the new republic, known for giving the United States the right to intervene militarily in Cuban affairs for "the maintenance of a stable Government adequately protecting the life, property and individual liberty," also provided that all "Acts of the United States in Cuba [ratified] during its military occupancy" would be "maintained and protected." See Pérez, *Cuba and the United States*, pp. 109–10. See also in this context Van Ness.

49. Braga Brothers Collection, Record Group 2, ser. 10c, boxes 67–73, contain numerous references to this regulation.

50. Joskow, "Vertical Integration and Long-Term Contracts," pp. 33–80, and "Asset Specificity and the Structure of Vertical Relationships," pp. 95–117. An analogous situation is found in Fishback's study of company towns in U.S. coal mining, *Soft Coal, Hard Choices*, pp. 155–59, "Economics of Company Housing," pp. 346–65. Also compare Stuckey's study of long-term arm's-length contracts in the alumina market (Stuckey, chap. 3).

51. Williamson, *Economic Institutions of Capitalism*, pp. 95–98. "Unified ownership is the preponderant response to an asset specificity condition that arises when successive stages are located in close proximity to one another. Such specificity is explained by an asset immobility condition, which is to say that the setup and/or relocation costs are great. Once such assets are located, therefore, the parties are thereafter operating in a bilateral exchange relation for the useful life of the assets" (ibid., p. 95). Joskow, "Asset Specificity and the Structure of Vertical Relationships," p. 105.

52. Chonchol, pp. 69–143; Bianchi, pp. 65–99. For post-1959 developments, see references for Mesa Lago; Rodríguez; and Zimbalist and Brundenius.

53. It evokes Platt's observations regarding foreign business in Latin America: "Business would have been conducted in the same way irrespective of nationality" because "each of the parties was subject to market forces over which they had no control" (p. 6).

Chapter 7

1. Hsiao, chap. 2.

2. The empirical analysis presented in this chapter is taken from Dye, "Cane Contracting and Renegotiation." Presentation of the choice-theoretic derivation of the econometric model is also found there. Results of Chapter 4 indicate the importance of incorporating the influences of vintage-capital effects and adjustment costs into the conceptual framework behind the estimation. These are also considered explicitly in the derivation of the model.

3. As a concern for the proper specification of the econometric model, one might raise the question of simultaneity bias from the treatment of colono arrangements as exogenous when they were likely endogenously influenced by factor endowments and technical conditions. Similar to arguments made at the beginning of the chapter, however, inasmuch as the distribution of colono land ownership could be altered, it could be altered only at a much slower rate than that at which mill capacities were increased. The decision regarding whether to expand capacity in a given year would be based on a given distribution of land ownership. Mills would have been forward-looking; therefore, when planning for future expansion into new lands, they would form realistic expectations of how much of those lands they could, or were willing, to acquire. Over the medium term, it is a reasonable assumption to treat these expectations as fixed, and as will be seen below, I do attempt to proxy the forward-looking nature of the expectations in estimating the model.

4. The number of mills operating in Cuba ranged between 163 and 198 in the 1917–29 period.

5. Hsiao, pp. 194–97.

6. Wallich, pp. 32–38.

7. See note 17.

8. Cuba, Secretaría de Hacienda, *Comercio exterior*, 1917–29.

9. See U.S. Bureau of Labor Statistics.

10. See Dye, "Cane Contracting and Renegotiation," p. 156.

11. Such comments are found in the private letterbooks of Manual Rionda. See the Braga Brothers Collection, Record Group 2, ser. 2.

12. Keeping the specification of price expectations simple is very important for the specification of the econometric model because there is a strict upper limit to the number of variables included that are time-variant but individually invariant in the model. Given that there are only twelve years of observations for the time-specific, individually invariant variables, twelve or more time-variant, individual-invariant variables will create strict multicollinearity in the matrix of explanatory variables, which would prevent the inversion of the cross-products matrix.

13. In a standard microeconomic treatment of firm behavior under risk-

uncertainty, when uncertainty in the price of sugar, utility maximization, and risk aversion are introduced into the investment decision model, they have the effect of reducing the level of investment relative to when there is no uncertainty. See references to McKenna and Hey.

14. In real terms, using the U.S. Bureau of Labor Statistics wholesale price index, the price was almost double. See Figure 2.5.

15. Jenks, chaps. 11, 12.

16. Pérez, *Cuba Under the Platt Amendment*, pp. 182–89; Jenks, pp. 242–45; Cleveland and Huertas, pp. 105–7.

17. The data were collected from Manuel Rionda's papers (see Data Appendix). Data for field labor are found in the Braga Brothers Collection, Record Group 2, ser. 10a, box 7, f. 1; ser. 10c, box 27, ff. 27, 38; and Record Group 4, ser. 96.

18. Braga Brothers Collection, Record Group 2, ser. 10c.

19. Braga Brothers Collection, Record Group 2, ser. 10 a and 10c.

20. This result follows directly from the cost structure developed in Dye, "Cane Contracting and Renegotiation," pp. 154–58. Consider the function of net returns to investment, $F = \pi[x_1, z(x_2)] - w_1(x_1 + x_2) - w_2 z(x_2)$, where π is a function of returns to investment which is convex in order to exhibit diminishing returns to investment, and x_i and z are the labor and materials inputs (steel rails, etc.) obtained at prices w_i $(i = 1, 2)$. Because of complementarity, the labor input, x_i $(i = 1, 2)$, enters both directly in the function, π, and indirectly through the material inputs, $z = z(x_2)$, since the materials must be combined with labor to be useful. Necessary conditions for maximizing net returns to investment are

$$\pi_2 z' = w_1 + w_2, \text{ and } \pi_1 = w_1$$

where $\pi_2 z' \equiv (\partial \pi / \partial z) (dz/dx_2)$, and $\pi_1 \equiv \partial \pi / \partial x_1$. Because of diminishing returns, the derivatives of $\pi_2 z'$ and π_1 with respect to x_2 are negative. If w_1 and w_2 move in opposite directions, the own-price effect of w_2 on z is offset by the complementary effect of w_1 on z. However, w_1 has an own-price effect, through x_1, which is not offset. Consequently, we detect statistically the inverse relationship between w_1 and x_1 but not that of w_2 and z.

21. The crisis that left the Banco Nacional and the Banco Internacional bankrupt also left these North American branches in insecure positions because they also were heavily exposed to Cuban sugar when the bubble burst. They continued to meet depositors' demands to withdraw funds by tapping the funds of their head offices (Cleveland and Huertas, pp. 105–7).

22. The data for these shares are of the 1930 crop obtained from the Cuba, Secretaría de Agricultura, Comercio, y Trabajo, *Industria azucarera*, 1930. Data for other years within the period are not available. In any case, the end-period observation may be the preferred one. The reason is that some mills that depended heavily on colonos independientes before World War I tended to reduce their dependence on colonos independientes as time progressed. If these mills could foresee their opportunities for reducing their dependence on colonos independientes, the end-period observation better represents their expectations. Of course, they

could not have achieved significant reductions in the dependence on colonos independientes instantaneously because of contract duration, but they could, and in fact did, negotiate cane contracts in advance or concurrently with plans to expand mill capacity.

23. Braga Brothers Collection, Record Group 2, ser. 10c, box 61, f. 11. The list does not correspond to the nationalities of the owners of the mills. Most mills were incorporated, and their shareholders as well as their boards of directors consisted of people of different nationalities. Instead, the list classifies the nationalities of mills according to their connections to the business communities of either Cuba or the United States, as assessed by the members of the Sugar Club. A handful of the mills in the sample are not included in this list. The orientation of these mills is determined by the country in which the sugar company was incorporated, which is obtained from Cuba, Secretaría de Hacienda, *Industria azucarera*, 1928.

24. These data were obtained using maps of the Cuban sugar industry in 1920 published in Cuba, Secretaría de Agricultura, Comercio, y Trabajo, *Industria azucarera*, 1919/20.

25. The data used are the yields of cane per acre reported by Cuba, Secretaría de Agricultura, Comercio, y Trabajo, *Industria azucarera*, in 1930. It is unfortunate that it is necessary to use cane yields from 1930 rather than from the middle of our period. Cane yields were not collected on an annual basis, and the year 1930 is the first year in which cane yield data are available after 1913.

26. For a comparison of this decision in Cuba with the alternative decision of vertical integration in Hawaii, see Dye, "Factor Endowments and Contract Choice."

27. Chandler, *Scale and Scope*; Pino Santos, *El asalto a Cuba*, pp. 140–46. The findings, nonetheless, contradict other aspects of Pino Santos's arguments. He claims that North American companies simply absorbed domestic properties without making additional investments to increase their productive efficiency. These findings suggest that mills with greater connections to North American institutions tended to renovate and improve their factories at a faster rate than did mills with a more domestic orientation.

28. Examination of the incentive structure of cane transactions which affected decisions to internalize transaction is found in Dye, "Factor Endowments and Contract Choice," and Shlomowitz, "Plantations and Smallholdings." Dye compares the incentives for the vertically integrated Hawaiian sugar industry with the vertically disintegrated structure in Cuba represented by the use of the colono system. Based on this comparison, the decision hinges on issues of the relative economies of scope in cane field management and the monitoring costs, which differ in the two places because of differing factor endowments. Shlomowitz examines the differences in incentive structures between sugar and cotton cultivation and processing to show why cotton has tended to become a smallhold, or sharecropping, crop whereas sugar more often preserved the vertically integrated structure of plantation cultivation. In other studies he has analyzed the incentives for the rise of cane farming in Queensland, cited below. His explanation is based on conditions specific to Queensland. Whether his explanation for Queensland has more general application is not clear.

29. In the Philippines, individuals were limited to 40 acres and corporations to 2,500 acres. See Ramos Mattei, *La sociedad del azúcar en Puerto Rico*, pp. 105–8; and Nagano.

30. Shlomowitz, "The Search for Institutional Equilibrium," "Team Work and Incentives," and "Melanesian Labor and the Development of the Queensland Sugar Industry."

31. The domestic sugar market had been protected since 1901. See Graves.

32. Although immigration of Jamaicans and Haitians was restricted, they nonetheless represented a large part of the labor force in the east.

33. After World War I, the hazard question was solved by the Australian government's intervention allocating cane supplies among mills. Interestingly, in the 1930s when Cuba's market was protected by international agreement, similar regulation was adopted in Cuba.

34. Richardson cites cases in South Africa where large mills acquired lands formerly owned by smallhold cane farmers stimulated by cooperative actions by the farmers to raise the prices paid for cane.

35. David, "Path-Dependence."

36. Hsiao, chap. 2.

Chapter 8

1. On technical interrelatedness, see Frankel.

2. David, *Technical Choice, Innovation and Economic Growth*, pp. 233–88.

3. Ibid.

4. Whatley, pp. 47–50; Musoke and Olmstead, pp. 405–11.

5. Rosenberg, *Inside the Black Box*, pp. 63–70; Mokyr, p. 289; Sahal, p. 37; Salter, chap. 4; Mansfield et al., pp. 17–18.

6. A path-dependent effect is one in which a small historical event can have a cumulative and irreversible effect on the path of economic development, applied often to technical and regional change. On path-dependent effects in economics, see David, "Path-Dependence."

7. On agglomeration effects, see Arthur; on the latecomer's advantage, see Gerschenkron.

8. For a general argument for this type of diffusion model, see David, "A Contribution to the Theory of Diffusion."

9. Recall Chapter 3.

10. See Maxwell; Cuba, Secretaría de Agricultura, Comercio, y Trabajo, *Portfolio azucarero*; and Robertson.

11. U.S. Department of Commerce, *Cane Sugar Industry*, pp. 375–81; Moreno Fraginals, *La historia como arma*, p. 91.

12. Campbell, pp. 421–25, 928–30; Knight, *Colonial Production in Provincial Java*, pp. 26–34.

13. The variety of cane used in Cuba in this period was called cristalina. See Cuba, Secretaría de Agricultura, Comercio, y Trabajo, *Portfolio azucarero*. For those who are familiar with the varieties of cane used in Cuba in the nineteenth

century, it was a variety adopted widely in the latter half of the nineteenth century. In the early part of the century there was much experimentation with new varieties (Moreno Fraginals, *El ingenio*, 1: 175–79). The activity of breeding new cane varieties in Java began in the 1880s with the occurrence of the sereh disease in Java which devastated the varieties in use there. Interestingly, in Cuba the occurrence of the mosaic disease prompted sizable investments in experimenting with varieties that had been developed in Java and elsewhere as well as experimentation to develop new varieties. Braga Brothers Collection, Record Group 2, ser. 10c.

14. Hawaiian Sugar Planters' Association.

15. Denslow, pp. 75–132.

16. The grinding season in Cuba lasted from six to seven months between the months of December and June. In Hawaii, the grinding season lasted from ten to eleven months, between December and September. In Java, the grinding season was as long as Cuba's, but it fell in the months between May and November (Maxwell, p. 22; and Deerr, *Cane Sugar*, p. 124).

17. Those places where the crops depended almost wholly on irrigation in 1911 were Hawaii, Peru, and parts of Mauritius. Irrigation was also extensive in Java but used only partially. In Cuba, irrigation had been introduced on some estates, but its application was rare. See Deerr, *Cane Sugar*, pp. 91–96.

18. Rosenberg, *Perspectives on Technology*, p. 168.

19. There were also locally important experiment stations in Louisiana, Peru, and South Africa.

20. Boomgaard, pp. 160–63; Campbell, pp. 921–23.

21. Braga Brothers Collection, Record Group 2, ser. 10c.

22. Maxwell estimated unskilled wages at $4.10 in the Queensland sugar industry. Cane cutters in both Cuba and Hawaii were compensated according to the volume of cane handled each day, and in general their wages earned per day were likely somewhat greater than the daily unskilled rate given by Maxwell. Australia paid the highest wages of all the countries in Maxwell's comparison. Because of the protectionist policies and government regulation of that market, they were well out of line with wages paid in other countries (Maxwell, pp. 81–90).

Chapter 9

1. Guerra y Sánchez, pp. 76–79.

2. Ibid., p. 64.

3. Ibid., pp. 76–77.

4. Initially, it was favorable to the colonos because competition for cane raised the rates paid for cane, but ultimately higher cane costs drove the central owners to search for alternative arrangements.

5. Other excellent studies have contributed to our understanding of the technological changes. Substantial contributions to the study of the nineteenth-century technology have been made by Moreno Fraginals, *El ingenio*; Iglesias García, "Azúcar, esclavitud y tecnología"; and Venegas Delgado. Likewise, on organizational and institutional changes, see Bergad, *Cuban Rural Society*. Our under-

standing of both the technical and organizational changes in the twentieth-century sugar industry have been extended considerably by Zanetti Lecuona and García Alvarez, *United Fruit Company.*

6. Guerra y Sánchez, pp. 159–68.

7. Ibid., pp. 189–98; Martínez Alier, p. 5.

8. Martínez Alier, pp. 12–13, 17. See also Pollitt, pp. 5–28.

9. Guerra y Sánchez, pp. 103–4; Hoernel, p. 239. The tendency may have changed when the regulatory policies after 1930 were instated, which likely altered the efficient functioning of the colono system from the mill's viewpoint and changed the relationship between colono and central. See Pollitt, p. 12.

10. See Díaz-Briquets, pp. 19, 22; Maddison, *Two Crises*, Table A.1, and "Economic and Social Conditions in Latin America," Table 1.7c. See also Fraile, Salvucci, and Salvucci, pp. 92–93.

11. U.S. Department of Commerce, *Investment in Cuba*, pp. 5–6.

12. The Cuban people had been developing a strong sense of nationalism for some time. The support among Cubans for annexation to the United States had been much stronger in the middle of the nineteenth century (Pérez, *Cuba and the United States*). By the 1920s, the sentiment had become more strongly in favor of developing its own national culture. Furthermore, with the rise of the beet sugar industry in the United States since the turn of the century and its strong political support, any thought of annexation met with strong opposition in the United States Congress (Jenks, p. 305).

13. Pérez, *Cuba and the United States*, p. 123.

14. Jenks, pp. 130–31, 304, 309.

15. Lewis, *Growth and Fluctuations*, pp. 188–91, 199–224, and *Evolution of the International Economic Order*. Lewis would argue that income per capita could not have risen in Cuba on the basis of sugar industry development because of the existence worldwide of virtually unlimited supplies of land and labor for a limited number of internationally marketable tropical crops with inelastic demands with respect to world income.

16. Jenks claimed that the political intervention had mixed effects on the level of investment in Cuba; the threat of intervention often tended to disturb rather than raise the confidence of investors. As time progressed, the U.S. right to intervene became increasingly detrimental to the stability of business conditions on the island. Pérez gives more weight to the implicit promise that the U.S. government would intervene to protect North American investments in Cuba (Pérez, *Cuba Under the Platt Amendment*, pp. 112–16; Jenks, chaps. 9, 24).

17. Albert and Graves, *The World Sugar Economy in War and Depression*, p. 19; Deerr, *History of Sugar*, 2: chap. 29.

18. For example, Manuel Rionda believed that Cubans would finally receive the long-sought treaty of reciprocity for their cooperation in the price controls during World War I (Braga Brothers Collection, Record Group 2, ser. 2). The Reciprocity Treaty of 1903 between the United States and Cuba established the preferential discount on the full tariff of 20 percent (Jenks, pp. 132–40).

19. By 1907, the end had come to the Sugar Trust. The Havemeyers' and other east coast refinery interests began to spread their interests into the western beet

sugar industry. This meant that the political alliance between the east coast refiners and those with interests in the Cuban sugar industry in the United States was breaking up. See Eichner.

20. Jenks, pp. 128–40, 254–58, 305. Taussig, *Tariff History of the United States*, pp. 501–4. Taussig comments that the beet sugar producers enlisted support from farmers "posing as a representative of the farmers when in fact the great bulk of the farmers were affected only as consumers" (p. 501). See Wright, *Sugar in Relation to the Tariff*, chap. 8. See also Albert and Graves, *The World Sugar Economy in War and Depression*, pp. 5–12; Pollitt, pp. 5–25.

Bibliography

For information on archival sources, see the Appendix, pp. 263–67.

Abad, L. V. de. *Azúcar y caña de azúcar.* Havana: Editora Mercantil Cubana, S.A., 1945.

Abel, Andrew B. "Optimal Investment Under Uncertainty." *American Economic Review* 73 (1983): 228–33.

———. "A Unified Model of Investment Under Uncertainty." *American Economic Review* 84 (1994): 1369–84.

Aguilar, Luis E. *Cuba 1933: Prologue to Revolution.* Ithaca: Cornell University Press, 1972.

Albert, Bill, and Adrian Graves, eds. *Crisis and Change in the International Sugar Economy, 1860–1914.* Norwich: ISC Press, 1984.

———. *The World Sugar Economy in War and Depression.* London: Routledge, 1988.

Alienes-Urosa, Julian. *Características fundamentales de la economía cubana.* Havana: Biblioteca de Economía Cubana, Banco Nacional de Cuba, 1950.

Alston, Lee, and Robert Higgs. "Contractual Mix in Southern Agriculture Since the Civil War." *Journal of Economic History* 42 (1982): 327–52.

Arrow, Kenneth. "The Economic Implications of Learning by Doing." *Review of Economic Studies* 24 (1962): 155–73.

———. "Optimal Capital Policy with Irreversible Investment." In J. N. Wolfe, ed., *Value, Capital and Growth*, pp. 1–19. Edinburgh: Edinburgh University Press, 1968.

Arthur, Brian. "Path-Dependent Processes and the Emergence of Macro-Structure." *European Journal of Operational Research* 30 (1987): 294–303.

Atack, Jeremy, and Fred Bateman. *To Their Own Soil: Agriculture in the Antebellum North.* Ames: Iowa State University Press, 1987.

Atkins, Edwin. *Sixty Years in Cuba.* Cambridge, Mass.: Riverside Press, 1926.

Ayala, César. "Social and Economic Aspects of Sugar Production in Cuba, 1880–1930." *Latin American Research Review* 30 (1995): 95–124.

Ballinger, Roy A. *A History of Sugar Marketing.* U.S. Department of Agriculture, Economic Research Service, Agricultural Economic Report 197, Feb. 1971.

Bardhan, Pranab. *The Economic Theory of Agrarian Institutions.* Oxford: Clarendon Press, 1989.

Bates, Robert. *Beyond the Miracle of the Market: The Political Economy of Agrarian Development in Kenya.* New York: Cambridge University Press, 1989.

Beechert, Ed. "Labour Relations in the Hawaiian Sugar Industry, 1850–1937." In Bill Albert and Adrian Graves, eds., *Crisis and Change in the International Sugar Economy, 1860–1914*, pp. 281–92. Norwich: ISC Press, 1984.

Benjamin, Jules. *The United States and Cuba: Hegemony and Dependent Development, 1880–1934*. Pittsburgh: University of Pittsburgh Press, 1974.

——. *The United States and the Origins of the Cuban Revolution: An Empire of Liberty in an Age of National Liberation*. Princeton: Princeton University Press, 1990.

Bergad, Laird W. *Cuban Rural Society in the Nineteenth Century: The Social and Economic History of Monoculture in Matanzas*. Princeton: Princeton University Press, 1990.

——. "The Economic Viability of Sugar Production Based on Slave Labor in Cuba, 1859–1878." *Latin American Research Review* 24 (1989): 95–113.

Bianchi, Andrés. "Agriculture — The Pre-Revolutionary Background." In Dudley Seers et al., eds., *Cuba: The Economic and Social Revolution*, pp. 65–99. Chapel Hill: University of North Carolina Press, 1964.

Blouet, Brian W. "The Post-Emancipation Origins of the Relationships Between Estates and the Peasantry in Trinidad." In Kenneth Duncan and Ian Rutledge, eds., *Land and Labour in Latin America*, pp. 435–52. London: Cambridge University Press, 1977.

Boomgaard, Peter. "Treacherous Cane: The Java Sugar Industry Between 1914 and 1940." In Bill Albert and Adrian Graves, eds., *The World Sugar Economy in War and Depression*, pp. 157–69. London: Routledge, 1988.

Boorstein, Edward. *The Economic Transformation of Cuba*. New York: Monthly Review Press, 1968.

Bulmer-Thomas, Victor. *The Economic History of Latin America*. Cambridge, England: Cambridge University Press, 1994.

CERP (Cuban Economic Research Project). *A Study on Cuba*. Miami: University of Miami Press, 1965.

Caballero, Ricardo. "On the Sign of the Investment-Uncertainty Relationship." *American Economic Review* 81 (1991): 279–88.

Campbell, Donald MacLaine. *Java: Past and Present*. 2 vols. London: William Heinemann, 1915.

Cardoso, Eliana, and Ann Helwege. *Cuba After Communism*. Cambridge, Mass.: MIT Press, 1992.

Cardoso, Fernando Enrique, and Enzo Faletto. *Dependency and Development in Latin America*. Translated by Marjory Mattingly Urquidi. Berkeley: University of California Press, 1979. Originally *Dependencia y desarrollo en América latina*. Mexico: Siglo Veintiuno S.A., 1971.

Carmagnani, Marcello. *Emigración mediterránea y América. Formas y transformaciones, 1860–1930*. Colombres, Asturias, Spain: Fundación Archivo de Indianos, 1994.

Castillo, del, J. "The Formation of the Dominican Sugar Industry: From Competition to Monopoly, from National Semiproletariat to Foreign Proletariat." In Manuel Moreno Fraginals, Frank Moya Pons, and Stanley Engerman, eds., *Between Slavery and Free Labor: The Spanish-Speaking Caribbean in the Nineteenth Century*, pp. 215–34. Baltimore: Johns Hopkins University Press, 1985.

Chalmin, P. G. "The Important Trends in Sugar Diplomacy Before 1914." In Bill Albert and Adrian Graves, eds., *Crisis and Change in the International Sugar Economy, 1860–1914*, pp. 9–20. Norwich: ISC Press, 1984.

Chandler, Alfred D., Jr. "Anthracite Coal and the Beginnings of the Industrial Revolution in the United States." *Business History Review* 46 (1972): 141–81.

———. *Scale and Scope: The Dynamics of Industrial Capitalism*. Cambridge, Mass.: Belknap Press of Harvard University Press, 1990.

———. *The Visible Hand: The Managerial Revolution in American Business*. Cambridge, Mass.: Belknap Press of Harvard University Press, 1977.

Chandler, Alfred D., Jr., and Hermann Daems, eds. *Managerial Hierarchies: Comparative Perspectives on the Rise of the Modern Industrial Enterprise*. Cambridge, Mass.: Harvard University Press, 1980.

Charadán López, Fernando. *Industria azucarera en Cuba*. Havana: Editorial de Ciencias Sociales, 1982.

Chetty, V. K., and J. J. Heckman. "A Dynamic Model of Aggregate Output Supply, Factor Demand and Entry and Exit for a Competitive Industry with Heterogeneous Plants." *Journal of Econometrics* 33 (1986): 237–62.

Cheung, Steven. "Transaction Costs, Risk Aversion, and the Choice of Contractual Arrangements." *Journal of Law and Economics* 12 (1969): 23–42.

Chonchol, Jacques. "Analisis crítico de la reforma agraria cubana." *Revista Trimestre Económico* 30, no. 117 (1963): 69–143.

Clark, Victor S. "Labor Conditions in Cuba." *Bulletin of the Department of Labor*, 41 (July 1902): 663–793.

Cleveland, Harold van B., and Thomas F. Huertas. *Citibank: 1812–1970*. Cambridge, Mass.: Harvard University Press, 1985.

Coase, Ronald. "The Nature of the Firm." *Economica* 4 (1937): 386–405.

Cohen, Avi. "Technological Change as Historical Process: The Case of the U.S. Pulp and Paper Industry, 1915–1940." *Explorations in Economic History* 24 (1987): 197–219.

Cok Márquez, Patria. "La introducción de los ferrocarriles portátiles en la industria azucarera, 1870–1880." *Santiago* 41 (1981): 137–47.

Collazo Pérez, Enrique. *Una pelea cubana contra los monopolios (Un estudio sobre el crac bancario de 1920)*. Oviedo, Asturias, Spain: Vicerrectorado de Relaciones Internacionales, Universidad de Oviedo, 1994.

Commission on Cuban Affairs. *Problems of the New Cuba*. New York: Foreign Policy Association, J. J. Little and Ives, 1935.

Corbitt, Duvon. "Immigration in Cuba." *Hispanic American Historical Review* 22 (1942): 280–308.

———. *A Study of the Chinese in Cuba, 1847–1947*. Wilmore, Ky.: Ashbury College, 1971.

Corwin, Arthur F. *Spain and the Abolition of Slavery in Cuba, 1817–1886*. Austin: University of Texas Press, 1967.

Cuba, República de, Dirección General del Censo. *Census of the Republic of Cuba, 1919*. Havana: Maza, Arroyo y Caso, 1922.

Cuba, República de, Secretaría de Agricultura, Comercio, y Trabajo, Oficina de Estadística. *Industria azucarera: Memoria de la zafra*. Havana: Imprenta y Papelería de Rambla, Bouza y Ca., Zafras de 1916/17–1930.

———. *Portfolio azucarero, Industria azucarera de Cuba, 1912–14.* Havana: Lib. e Imprenta "La Moderna Poesía," 1914.

Cuba, República de, Secretaría de Hacienda, Sección de Estadística. *Comercio exterior.* Havana: Imprenta, "La Propangandista," 1917–29.

———. *Industria azucarera y sus derivados.* Havana: Imprenta Mercantil; P. Fernandez y Ca.; Imp. y Lit. "Habanera"; Imprenta y Papelería "La Propagandista"; Montalvo y Cárdenas; Imp. Carasa y Ca.; Fernández Solana y Cia.; Tipos Molina y Cia., Zafras de 1903/4–1929.

Czarnikow-Rionda Annual Sugar Review. Czarnikow-Rionda, 1930.

David, Paul. "Computer and Dynamo: The Modern Productivity Paradox in a Not-Too Distant-Mirror." Stanford University, CEPR Publication 172, 1989.

———. "A Contribution to the Theory of Diffusion." Stanford University, Center for Research in Economic Growth Research, Memorandum 71, 1969.

———. "Path-Dependence: Putting the Past into the Future of Economics." Paper presented at the Social Sciences Summer Workshop of the Institute for Mathematical Studies, Stanford University, 1988.

———. *Technical Choice, Innovation and Economic Growth: Essays on American and British Experience in the Nineteenth Century.* London: Cambridge University Press, 1975.

David, Paul, and Julie Ann Braun. " 'The Battle of the Systems' and the Evolutionary Dynamics of Network Technology Rivalries." Center for Economic Policy Research, Working Paper 15, 1987.

Davies, Stephen. *The Diffusion of Process Innovations.* Cambridge, England: Cambridge University Press, 1979.

Deerr, Noel. *Cane Sugar: A Textbook on the Agriculture of the Sugar Cane, the Manufacture of Cane Sugar, and the Analysis of Sugar House Products.* Manchester: Norman Rodger, 1911.

———. *The History of Sugar.* 2 vols. London: Chapman and Hall, 1949–50.

Denslow, David. *Sugar Production in Northeastern Brazil and Cuba, 1858–1908.* New York: Garland, 1987.

Díaz-Briquets, Sergio. *The Health Revolution in Cuba.* Austin: University of Texas Press, 1983.

Dorfman, Jeffery, and Dale Heien. "The Effects of Uncertainty and Adjustment Costs on Investment in the Almond Industry." *Review of Economics and Statistics* 71 (1989): 263–74.

Dosi, Giovanni. "Sources, Procedures, and Microeconomic Effects of Innovation." *Journal of Economic Literature* 26 (1988): 1120–71.

Dumont, René. *Cuba: Socialism and Development.* Translated by Helen R. Lane. New York: Grove Press, 1970.

Dye, Alan. "Avoiding Holdup: Asset Specificity and Technical Change in the Cuban Sugar Industry, 1899–1929." *Journal of Economic History* 54 (1994): 628–53.

———. "Cane Contracting and Renegotiation: A Fixed Effects Analysis of the Adoption of New Technologies in the Cuban Sugar Industry, 1899–1929." *Explorations in Economic History* 31 (1994): 141–75.

———. "Factor Endowments and Contract Choice: Why Were Sugar Cane Supply Contracts Different in Cuba and Hawaii? 1899–1925." Mimeo, Oct. 1995.

———. "Producción en masa del azúcar cubano, 1899–1929: Economías de escala y elección de técnicas." *Revista de Historia Económica* 11 (1993): 563–93.

———. "Tropical Technology and Mass Production: The Expansion of Cuban Sugar Mills, 1899–1929." Ph.D. diss., University of Illinois, 1991.

Eggertsson, Thráinn. *Economic Behavior and Institutions.* Cambridge, England: Cambridge University Press, 1990.

Eichner, Alfred S. *The Emergence of Oligopoly: Sugar Refining as a Case Study.* Baltimore: Johns Hopkins Press, 1969.

Eisner, R., and R. H. Strotz. "Determinants of Business Investment." In D. B. Suits, ed., *Impacts of Monetary Policy*, pp. 117–335. Englewood Cliffs, N.J.: Prentice-Hall, 1963.

Eltis, David. *Economic Growth and the Ending of the Transatlantic Slave Trade.* New York: Oxford University Press, 1987.

———. "Free and Coerced Transatlantic Migration." *American Historical Review* 88 (1983): 251–80.

Emmer, P. C. "The Abolition of the Abolished: Illegal Dutch Slave Trade and the Mixed Courts." In David Eltis and James Walvin, eds., *The Abolition of the Atlantic Slave Trade.* Madison: University of Wisconsin Press, 1981.

———, ed. *Colonialism and Migration: Indentured Labour Before and After Slavery.* Dordrecht: Martinus Nijhoff, 1986.

Engerman, Stanley L. "Contract Labor, Sugar, and Technology in the Nineteenth Century." *Journal of Economic History* 43 (1983): 635–60.

———. "Economic Change and Contract Labor in the British Caribbean: The End of Slavery and the Adjustment to Emancipation." *Explorations in Economic History* 21 (1984): 133–54.

———. "Servants to Slaves to Servants." In Pieter C. Emmer, ed., *Colonialism and Migration: Indentured Labour Before and After Slavery*, pp. 263–94. Dordrecht: Martinus Nijhoff, 1986.

Engerman, Stanley, and Kenneth Sokoloff. "Factor Endowments, Institutions, and Differential Paths of Growth Among New World Economies: A View from Economic Historians of the United States." NBER Working Paper Series on Historical Factors in Long Run Growth, Historical Paper 66, 1994.

Enos, John. *The Rate and Direction of Inventive Activity.* Princeton: Princeton University Press, 1962.

FAO. *The World Sugar Economy in Figures, 1880–1959.* Rome: United Nations, Food and Agriculture Organization, Commodity Reference Series, No. 1, 1971.

Feeny, David. "The Development of Property Rights in Land: A Comparative Study." In Robert Bates, ed., *Toward a Political Economy of Development*, pp. 272–99. Berkeley: University of California Press, 1988.

Fernández, Susan. "The Money and Credit Crisis in Late Colonial Cuba." *Cuban Studies* 21 (1991): 3–18.

Ferrara, Orestes. *Anuario estadístico de la República de Cuba.* Havana: Imprenta "El Siglo XX," 1915.

Fishback, Price V. "The Economics of Company Housing: Historical Perspectives from the Coal Fields." *Journal of Law, Economics, and Organization* 8 (1992): 346–65.

——. *Soft Coal, Hard Choices: The Economic Welfare of Bituminous Coal Miners, 1890–1930*. New York: Oxford University Press, 1992.

Fraile Balbín, Pedro, Richard Salvucci, and Linda Salvucci. "El caso cubano: Exportación e independencia." In Leandro Prados de la Escosura and Samuel Amaral, eds., *La independencia americana: Consecuencias económicas*. Madrid: Editorial Alianza, 1993.

Frankel, Marvin. "Obsolescence and Technological Change in a Maturing Economy." *American Economic Review* 45 (1955): 296–319.

Friedlaender, Heinrich. *Historia económica de Cuba*. Vol. 2. Havana: Editorial de Ciencias Sociales, 1978.

Furtado, Celso. *The Economic Development of Latin America: Historical Background and Contemporary Problems*. 2d ed. Translated by Suzette Macedo. Cambridge, England: Cambridge University Press, 1976.

Galloway, J. H. *The Sugar Cane Industry: An Historical Geography from Its Origins to 1914*. Cambridge, England: Cambridge University Press, 1989.

García Alvarez, Alejandro. *La gran burguesía comercial en Cuba, 1899–1920*. Havana: Editorial de Ciencias Sociales, 1990.

——. "Una saga azucarera entre dos siglos." In Jorge Uría, ed., *Asturias y Cuba en torno al 98*, pp. 43–55. Barcelona: Universidad de Oviedo, Editorial Labor, 1994.

Gerschenkron, Alexander. *Economic Backwardness in Historical Perspective*. Cambridge, Mass.: Belknap Press of Harvard University Press, 1979.

Goizueta-Mimo, Felix. *Bitter Cuban Sugar: Monoculture and Economic Dependence from 1825–1899*. New York: Garland, 1987.

Gould, J. P. "Adjustment Costs in the Theory of Investment of the Firm." *Review of Economic Studies* 35 (1968): 47–56.

Graves, Adrian. *Cane and Labour: The Political Economy of the Queensland Sugar Industry, 1862–1906*. Edinburgh: Edinburgh University Press, 1993.

Griliches, Zvi. "Issues in Assessing the Contribution of Research and Development to Productivity Growth." *Journal of Economics* 10 (1979): 92–116.

Guerra y Sánchez, Ramiro. *Azúcar y población en las Antillas*. 3d ed. Havana: Cultural, S.A., 1944.

Guggenheim, Harry F. *The United States and Cuba: A Study in International Relations*. New York: Macmillan, 1934.

Haber, Stephen. "Industrial Concentration and the Capital Markets: A Comparative Study of Brazil, Mexico, and the United States." *Journal of Economic History* 51 (1993): 559–80.

——. *Industry and Underdevelopment: The Industrialization of Mexico, 1890–1940*. Stanford: Stanford University Press, 1989.

Halperin, Maurice. *Return to Havana*. Nashville: Vanderbilt University Press, 1994.

Haraksingh, K. "Labour, Technology and the Sugar Estates in Trinidad, 1882–1906." In Bill Albert and Adrian Graves, eds., *Crisis and Change in the International Sugar Economy, 1860–1914*, pp. 133–46. Norwich: ISC Press, 1979.

Harley, Knick. "Ocean Freight Rates and Productivity, 1740–1913: The Primacy of Mechanical Invention Reaffirmed." *Journal of Economic History* 48 (1988): 851–76.

Hawaiian Sugar Planters' Association. *The Sugar Industry of Hawaii and the Labor Shortage.* Compiled by the Hawaiian Sugar Planters' Association, 1921.

Heitmann, John Alfred. *The Modernization of the Louisiana Sugar Industry, 1830–1910.* Baton Rouge: Louisiana State University Press, 1987.

Helg, Aline. *Our Rightful Share: The Afro-Cuban Struggle for Equality, 1886– 1912.* Chapel Hill: University of North Carolina Press, 1995.

Hernández, Jesús. "Estudios sobre economías de escala en ingenios de crudos." *Economía y desarrollo* 23 (1974): 95–111.

Hey, John D. "Decision Under Uncertainty." In Frederick van der Ploeg, ed., *Mathematical Methods in Economics*, pp. 433–56. New York: Wiley, 1984.

Hirschman, Albert O. *The Strategy of Economic Development.* New Haven: Yale University Press, 1958.

Hoernel, Robert. "Sugar and Social Change in Oriente, Cuba, 1898–1946." *Journal of Latin American Studies* 8 (1976): 215–49.

Hoffman, Philip. "The Economic Theory of Sharecropping in Early Modern France." *Journal of Economic History* 44 (1984): 309–20.

Hsiao, Cheng. *Analysis of Panel Data.* Cambridge, England: Cambridge University Press, 1986.

Huberman, Leo, and Paul Sweezy. *Cuba: Anatomy of a Revolution.* New York: Monthly Review Press, 1960.

Hunter, Louis C. *A History of Industrial Power in the United States, 1780–1930.* 2 vols. Charlottesville: University Press of Virginia, 1985.

Iglesias García, Fe. "Azúcar, esclavitud y tecnología (Segunda mitad del siglo XIX)." *Santiago* 61 (1986): 113–31.

———. "Azúcar y crédito durante la segunda mitad del siglo XIX en Cuba." *Santiago* 52 (1983): 119–44.

———. "Características de la inmigración española en Cuba." In Nicolás Sánchez Albornoz, ed., *Españoles hacia América: La emigración en masa, 1880–1930*, pp. 270–95. Madrid: Alianza Editorial, 1988.

———. *De El Ingenio al central.* Havana: Instituto de Historia Cubano, forthcoming.

———. "The Development of Capitalism in Cuban Sugar Production, 1860– 1900." In Manuel Moreno Fraginals, Frank Moya Pons, and Stanley Engerman, eds., *Between Slavery and Free Labor: The Spanish-Speaking Caribbean in the Nineteenth Century*, pp. 54–76. Baltimore: Johns Hopkins University Press, 1985.

International Bank for Reconstruction and Development. *Report on Cuba.* Baltimore: Johns Hopkins Press, 1951.

Jenks, Leland Hamilton. *Our Cuban Colony.* New York: Vanguard Press, 1928.

Johnson, Howard. "The Origins and Early Development of Cane Farming in Trinidad." *Journal of Caribbean History* 5 (1972): 46–73.

Jorgenson, Dale. "The Theory of Investment Behavior." In Robert Ferber, ed., *Determinants of Investment Behavior.* New York: National Bureau of Economic Research, 1967.

Joskow, Paul. "Asset Specificity and the Structure of Vertical Relationships: Empirical Evidence." *Journal of Law, Economics, and Organization* 4 (1988): 95– 117.

———. "Vertical Integration and Long-Term Contracts: The Case of Coal-Burning Electric Plants." *Journal of Law, Economics, and Organization* 1 (1985): 33–80.

Kamien, Morton, and Nancy Schwartz. *Market Structure and Innovation.* Cambridge, England: Cambridge University Press, 1982.

Kindleberger, Charles P. *The World in Depression, 1929–1939.* Berkeley: University of California Press, 1973.

Klein, Benjamin, Robert Crawford, and Armen Alchian. "Vertical Integration, Appropriable Rents, and the Competitive Contracting Process." *Journal of Law and Economics* 21 (1978): 297–326.

Klein, Herbert S. *African Slavery in Latin America and the Caribbean.* New York: Oxford University Press, 1986.

———. *Slavery in the Americas: A Comparative Study of Virginia and Cuba.* 1967. Reprint. Chicago: Elephant Paperbacks, Ivan R. Dee, 1989.

Knight, Franklin W. *The Caribbean.* 2d ed. New York: Oxford University Press, 1990.

———. *Slave Society in Cuba During the Nineteenth Century.* Madison: University of Wisconsin Press, 1970.

Knight, G. R. *Colonial Production in Provincial Java: The Sugar Industry in Pekalongan Tegal, 1800–1942.* Series in Comparative Asian Studies. Amsterdam: VU University Press, 1993.

LaCroix, Sumner J., and J. Roumasset. "The Evolution of Private Property in Nineteenth-Century Hawaii." *Journal of Economic History* 50 (1991): 829–51.

Lamoreaux, Naomi R. *The Great Merger Movement in American Business, 1895–1904.* Cambridge, England: Cambridge University Press, 1985.

Langlois, Richard. "Economic Change and the Boundaries of the Firm." *Journal of Institutional and Theoretical Economics* 144 (1988): 635–57.

Larkin, John A. *Sugar and the Origins of Modern Philippine Society.* Berkeley: University of California Press, 1993.

Laurence, K. O. *Immigration into the West Indies in the 19th Century.* Aylesbury, Bucks, U.K.: Caribbean Universities Press, Ginn and Co., 1971.

Lazonick, William. *Business Organization and the Myth of the Market Economy.* Cambridge, England: Cambridge University Press, 1991.

Leijonhufvud, Axel. "Capitalism and the Factory System." In Richard Langlois, ed., *Economics as a Process: Essays in the New Institutional Economics,* pp. 203–23. Cambridge, England: Cambridge University Press, 1986.

Leon, John A. *On Sugar Cultivation in Louisiana, Cuba, &c, and the British Possessions.* London: P. Oliver, 1848.

Le Riverend, Julio. *Historia económica de Cuba.* Vol. 2. Edición revolucionaria. Havana: Instituto del Libro, 1971.

Lewis, Cleona. *America's Stake in International Investment.* Washington, D.C.: Brookings Institution, 1938.

Lewis, W. Arthur. "Economic Development with Unlimited Supplies of Labour." *Manchester School of Economics and Social Studies* 22 (1954): 139–91.

———. *The Evolution of the International Economic Order.* Princeton: Princeton University Press, 1978.

———. *Growth and Fluctuations, 1870–1913*. London: George Allen and Unwin, 1978.

Lichtenberg, Frank R. "Estimation of the Internal Adjustment Costs Model Using Longitudinal Establishment Data." *Review of Economics and Statistics* 70 (1988): 421–35.

Lockhart, James, and Stuart Schwartz. *Early Latin America: History of Colonial Spanish America and Brazil*. Cambridge, England: Cambridge University Press, 1983.

Lucas, Robert E. "Adjustment Costs and the Theory of Supply." *Journal of Political Economy* 75 (1967): 321–34.

———. "Optimal Investment Policy and the Flexible Accelerator." *International Economic Review* 8 (1967): 78–85.

Lucas, Robert E., and Edward C. Prescott. "Investment Under Uncertainty." *Econometrica* 39 (1971): 659–81.

Lundahl, Mats. "A Note on Haitian Migration to Cuba, 1890–1934." *Cuban Studies* 12 (1982): 21–36.

Luzón, José Luís. *Economía, población y territorio en Cuba (1899–1983)*. Madrid: Instituto de Cooperación Iberoamericana, 1987.

McCloskey, Donald N. "The Open Fields of England: Rent, Risk, and the Rate of Interest, 1300–1815." In David W. Galenson, ed., *Markets in History: Economic Studies of the Past*, pp. 5–51. Cambridge, England: Cambridge University Press, 1989.

MacEwan, Arthur. *Revolution and Economic Development in Cuba*. New York: St. Martin's Press, 1981.

McGreevey, William. *An Economic History of Colombia, 1845–1930*. Cambridge, England: Cambridge University Press, 1971.

McKenna, C. J. *The Economics of Uncertainty*. New York: Oxford University Press, 1986.

Maddison, Angus. *Dynamic Forces in Capitalist Development: A Long-Run Comparative View*. Oxford: Oxford University Press, 1991.

———. "Economic and Social Conditions in Latin America, 1913–1950." In Miguel Urrutia, ed., *Long-Term Trends in Latin American Economic Development*, pp. 1–22. Washington, D.C.: Inter-American Development Bank, 1991.

———. *Two Crises: Latin America and Asia, 1929–38 and 1973–83*. Paris: OECD, 1985.

Mak, James, and Gary Walton. "Steamboats and the Great Productivity Surge in River Transportation." *Journal of Economic History* 32 (1972): 619–40.

Maluquer de Motes Bernet, Jordi. "El mercado colonial antillano en el siglo XIX." In Jordi Nadal and Gabriel Tortella, eds., *Agricultura, comercio colonial y crecimiento económico en la España comtemporánea*, pp. 322–57. Actas del Primer Coloquio de Historia Económico de España. Barcelona: Editorial Ariel, 1972.

———. *Nación e inmigración: Los españoles en Cuba (ss. XIX y XX)*. Colombres, Asturias, Spain: Ediciones Jucar, 1992.

Mañach, Jorge. "The Revolution in Cuba." *Foreign Affairs* 12 (1933): 46–56.

Mansfield, Edwin. *The Economics of Technological Change*. New York: Norton, 1968.

———. "Technical Change and the Rate of Imitation." *Econometrica* 29 (1961): 741–66.

Mansfield, Edwin, et al. *The Production and Application of New Industrial Technology*. New York: Norton, 1977.

Marrero, Levi. *Cuba: Economía y sociedad*. Vols. 10, 11. Madrid: Editorial Playor, 1984.

———. *Elementos de geografía de Cuba*. 2d ed. Havana: Editorial Minerva, 1946.

Martín Rodríguez, Manuel. *Azúcar y descolonización: Orígen y desenlace de una crisis agraria en la vega de Granada. El "Ingenio de San Juan," 1882–1904*. Granada, Spain: Instituto de Desarrollo Regional, Universidad de Granada, 1982.

Martínez Alier, Juan. "The Cuban Sugar Cane Planters, 1934." *Oxford Agrarian Studies* 2 (1974): 3–29.

Martínez Alier, Juan, and Verena Martínez. *Cuba: Economía y sociedad*. Paris: Ruedo Ibérico, 1972.

Martínez-Vergne, Teresita. *Capitalism in Colonial Puerto Rico: Central San Vicente in the Late Nineteenth Century*. Gainesville: University Press of Florida, 1992.

Maxwell, Francis. *Economic Aspects of Cane Sugar Production*. London: Norman Rodger, 1927.

Meade, George P., and James P. Chen. *Cane Sugar Handbook*. 10th ed. New York: Wiley, 1977.

Memorias inéditas de censo de 1931. Havana: Editorial de Ciencias Sociales, 1978.

Mesa-Lago, Carmelo. *The Economy of Socialist Cuba: A Two Decade Appraisal*. Albuquerque: University of New Mexico Press, 1981.

———, ed. *Cuba After the Cold War*. Pittsburgh: University of Pittsburgh Press, 1993.

Mihajan, Vijay, and Robert A. Peterson. *Models for Innovation Diffusion*. Beverly Hills: Sage, 1985.

Mintz, Sidney W. *Caribbean Transformations*. New York: Columbia University Press, 1989.

———. *Sweetness and Power: The Place of Sugar in Modern History*. New York: Penguin, 1985.

———. *Worker in the Cane: A Puerto Rican Life History*. New York: Norton, 1974.

Mokyr, Joel. *The Lever of Riches: Technological Creativity and Economic Progress*. New York: Oxford University Press, 1990.

Moreno Fraginals, Manuel. "Africa in Cuba." In Vera Rubin and Arthur Tuden, eds., *Comparative Perspectives on Slavery in New World Plantation Societies*, pp. 191–205. New York: New York Academy of Sciences, 1977.

———. *La historia como arma, y otros estudios sobre esclavos, ingenios y plantaciones*. Barcelona: Editorial Crítica, Grupo Editorial Grajalbo, 1983.

———. *El ingenio: El complejo económico social cubano del azúcar*. 3 vols. Havana: Editorial de Ciencias Sociales, 1978. The first volume also appeared in an older edition as *El ingenio: El complejo económico social cubano del azúcar*. Havana: Comisión Nacional Cubana de la UNESCO, 1964. It has been revised and translated as *The Sugarmill: The Socioeconomic Complex of Sugar in Cuba, 1760–1860*. Translated by Cedric Belfrage. New York: Monthly Review Press, 1976.

———. "Plantation Economies and Societies in the Spanish Caribbean, 1860–1930." In Leslie Bethell, ed., *The Cambridge History of Latin America*, 4: 187–231. Cambridge, England: Cambridge University Press, 1986.

———. "Plantations in the Caribbean: Cuba, Puerto Rico, and the Dominican Republic in the Late Nineteenth Century." In Manuel Moreno Fraginals, Frank Moya Pons, and Stanley Engerman, eds., *Between Slavery and Free Labor: The Spanish-Speaking Caribbean in the Nineteenth Century*, pp. 3–24. Baltimore: Johns Hopkins University Press, 1985.

Moreno Fraginals, Manuel, Herbert Klein, and Stanley Engerman. "The Level and Structure of Slave Prices on Cuban Plantations in the Mid-Nineteenth Century: Some Comparative Perspectives." *American Historical Review* 88 (1983): 1201–18.

Moreno Fraginals, Manuel, Frank Moya Pons, and Stanley Engerman, eds. *Between Slavery and Free Labor: The Spanish-Speaking Caribbean in the Nineteenth Century*. Baltimore: Johns Hopkins University Press, 1985.

Morrison, C. J. "Quasi-Fixed Inputs in U.S. and Japanese Manufacturing: A Generalized Leontief Restricted Cost Function Approach." *Review of Economics and Statistics* 70 (1988): 275–87.

Morrison, C. J., and E. R. Berndt. "Short-Run Labor Productivity in a Dynamic Model." *Journal of Econometrics* 16 (1981): 339–65.

Mowery, David C., and Nathan Rosenberg. *Technology and the Pursuit of Economic Growth*. Cambridge, England: Cambridge University Press, 1989.

Musoke, Moses S., and Alan Olmstead. "The Cotton Industry in California: A Comparative Perspective." *Journal of Economic History* 42 (1982): 385–412.

Nagano, Yoshiko. "The Oligopolistic Structure of the Philippine Sugar Industry During the Great Depression." In Bill Albert and Adrian Graves, eds., *The World Sugar Economy in War and Depression*, pp. 170–81. London: Routledge, 1988.

Nelson, Lowry. *Rural Cuba*. Minneapolis: University of Minnesota Press, 1950.

Nelson, Richard, and Sidney Winter. *An Evolutionary Theory of Economic Change*. Cambridge, Mass.: Belknap Press of Harvard University Press, 1982.

North, Douglass. *Institutions, Institutional Change, and Economic Performance*. Cambridge, England: Cambridge University Press, 1990.

North-Coombes, M. D. "Struggles in the Canefields: Small Growers in Mauritius, 1921–1937." In Bill Albert and Adrian Graves, eds., *The World Sugar Economy in War and Depression*, pp. 194–208. London: Routledge, 1988.

Nuwer, Michael. "From Batch to Flow: Production Technology and Work-Force Skills in the Steel Industry, 1880–1920." *Technology and Culture* 29 (1988): 808–38.

Olmstead, Alan L. "The Mechanization of Reaping and Mowing in American Agriculture, 1833–1870." *Journal of Economic History* 35 (1975): 327–52.

Ortiz, Fernando. *Cuban Counterpoint: Tobacco and Sugar*. Translated by Harriet de Onís. New York: A. A. Knopf, 1947.

Pérez, Louis A. *Cuba and the United States: Ties of Singular Intimacy.* Athens: University of Georgia Press, 1990.

———. *Cuba Between Empires, 1878–1902.* Pittsburgh: University of Pittsburgh Press, 1983.

———. *Cuba: Between Reform and Revolution.* New York: Oxford University Press, 1988.

———. *Cuba Under the Platt Amendment, 1902–1934.* Pittsburgh: University of Pittsburgh Press, 1986.

———. "Insurrection, Intervention, and the Transformation of Land Tenure Systems in Cuba, 1895–1902." *Hispanic American Historical Review* 65 (1985): 229–54.

———. "Toward Dependency and Revolution: The Political Economy of Cuba Between Wars, 1878–1895." *Latin American Research Review* 18 (1983): 127–42.

Pérez de la Riva, Juan. *El barracón: Esclavitud y capitalismo en Cuba.* Barcelona: Editorial Crítica, 1975.

———. "Cuba y la migración antillana, 1900–1931." *Anuario de estudios cubanos* 2 (1979): 1–75.

———. "Los recursos humanos de Cuba al comenzar el siglo: Inmigración, economía y nacionalidad (1899–1906)." *Anuario de estudios cubanos* 2 (1975): 7–44.

Pérez-López, Jorge. *The Economics of Cuban Sugar.* Pittsburgh: University of Pittsburgh Press, 1991.

Pérez-Stable, Marifeli. *The Cuban Revolution: Origins, Course, and Legacy.* New York: Oxford University Press, 1993.

Perkins, John. "The Political Economy of Sugar Beet in Imperial Germany." In Bill Albert and Adrian Graves, eds., *Crisis and Change in the International Sugar Economy, 1860–1914,* pp. 31–46. Norwich: ISC Press, 1984.

Pezuela, Jacobo de la. *Diccionario geográfico, estadístico, y histórico de la isla de Cuba.* 4 vols. Madrid: Imprenta del Establecimiento de Mellado, 1863.

Pindyck, Robert S. "Adjustment Costs, Uncertainty and the Behavior of the Firm." *American Economic Review* 72 (1982): 415–27.

———. "Irreversibility, Uncertainty, and Investment." *Journal of Economic Literature* 29 (1991): 1110–48.

Pino Santos, Oscar. *El asalto a Cuba por la oligarquía financiera yanqui.* Havana: Casa de las Américas, 1973.

———. *Cuba: Historia y economía.* Havana: Editorial de Ciencias Sociales, 1983.

Plant, Robert. *Sugar and Modern Slavery.* London: Zed Books, 1987.

Platt, D. C. M. *Business Imperialism, 1840–1930: An Inquiry Based on British Experience in Latin America.* Oxford: Oxford University Press, 1977.

Pollitt, Brian. "The Cuban Sugar Economy and the Great Depression." *Bulletin of Latin American Studies* 2 (1982): 5–28.

Porter, Robert P. *Industrial Cuba.* New York: G. P. Putnam's Sons, 1899.

Prados de la Escosura, Leandro. *De imperio a nación: Crecimiento y atraso en España (1780–1930).* Madrid: Alianza Editorial, 1988.

———. "Spain's Gross Domestic Product, 1850–1993: Quantitative Conjectures."

Universidad Carlos III de Madrid, Working Paper 95–05, Economic Series 01, 1995.

Prinsen Geerligs, H. C. *Cane Sugar and Its Manufacture*. 2d ed. London: Norman Rodger, 1924.

——. *Chemical Control in Cane Sugar Factories*. London: Norman Rodger, 1917.

Prinsen Geerligs, H. C., F. O. Licht, and Gustav Mikusch. *Sugar: Memoranda Prepared for the Economic Committee*. Geneva: Series of League of Nations Publications, No. C.148.M.57; Economic and Financial, 1929.II.20.

Quigley, Neil C. "The Bank of Nova Scotia in the Caribbean, 1889–1940." *Business History Review* 63 (1989): 797–838.

Ramos Mattei, Andrés A. "The Growth of the Puerto Rican Sugar Industry Under North American Domination, 1899–1910." In Bill Albert and Adrian Graves, eds., *Crisis and Change in the International Sugar Economy, 1860–1914*, pp. 121–32. Norwich: ISC Press, 1984.

——. *La sociedad del azúcar en Puerto Rico, 1870–1910*. Dominican Republic: Recinto de Rio Piedras, Universidad de Puerto Rico, 1988.

Reid, Joseph D. "Sharecropping as an Understandable Market Response: The Post-Bellum South." *Journal of Economic History* 33 (1973): 106–30.

Revista de Agricultura 10, edición extraordinaria, Oct. 15, 1890.

Reynoso, Alvaro. *Ensayo sobre el cultivo de caña de azúcar*. 1862. Reprint. Havana: Josefina Tarafa y Govín, 1954.

Richardson, Bonham C. *The Caribbean in the Wider World, 1492–1992: A Regional Geography*. Cambridge, England: Cambridge University Press, 1992.

Richardson, Peter. "The Natal Sugar Industry in the Nineteenth Century." In Bill Albert and Adrian Graves, eds., *Crisis and Change in the International Sugar Economy, 1860–1914*, pp. 237–60. Norwich: ISC Press, 1984.

Robertson, C. J. *World Sugar Production and Consumption: An Economic-Geographical Survey*. London: John Bale, Sons and Danielson, 1934.

Rodríguez, José Luís. "Agricultural Policy and Development in Cuba." In Andrew Zimbalist, ed., *Cuba's Socialist Economy Toward the 1990s*, pp. 25–41. Boulder: Lynne Reinner, 1987.

Roldán de Montaud, Inés. *La hacienda en Cuba durante la guerra de los diez años (1868–80)*. Madrid: Instituto de Cooperación Iberoamericana, 1990.

Rosenberg, Nathan. *Exploring the Black Box: Technology, Economics, and History*. Cambridge, England: Cambridge University Press, 1994.

——. *Inside the Black Box: Technology and Economics*. Cambridge, England: Cambridge University Press, 1982.

——. *Perspectives on Technology*. Cambridge, England: Cambridge University Press, 1976.

——. "Technological Change in the Machine Tool Industry, 1840–1910." *Journal of Economic History* (1963): 414–46.

Ruiz, Ramon Eduardo. *Cuba: The Making of a Revolution*. Amherst: University of Massachusetts Press, 1968.

Sahal, Devendra. *Patterns of Technological Innovation*. Reading, Mass.: Addison Wesley, 1981.

Salter, W. E. G. *Productivity and Technical Change*. Cambridge, England: Cambridge University Press, 1966.

Sánchez Alonso, Blanca. *Las causas de la emigración española, 1880–1930*. Madrid: Alianza Editorial, 1995.

———. "Una nueva serie anual de la emigración española, 1882–1930." *Revista de Historia Económica* 8 (1990): 133–70.

Santamaría García, Antonio. "Caña de azúcar y producción de azúcar en Cuba: Crecimiento y organización de la industria azucarera cubana desde mediados del siglo XIX hasta la finalización de la Primera Guerra Mundial." In Consuelo Naranjo and Miguel A. Puig-Samper, eds., *La nación soñada: Cuba, Puerto Rico y Filipinas ante el 98*. Madrid: Editorial Doce Calles, 1995.

———. "La crisis financiera de 1920–1921 y el ajuste al alza de la industria azucarera cubana." *Revista de Historia Industrial* 5 (1994): 121–47.

———. "La industria azucarera y la economía cubana durante los años viente y treinta: La crisis del sector exportador, comercial y azucarero y su incidencia en la sociedad y en la economía insular." Doctoral thesis, Universidad Complutense de Madrid and Instituto Ortega y Gasset, 1995.

Schmidt-Nowara, Christopher. "The Problem of Slavery in the Age of Capital: Abolitionism, Liberalism and Counter-Hegemony in Spain, Cuba and Puerto Rico, 1833–1886." Ph.D. diss., University of Michigan, 1995.

Schumpeter, Joseph. *Capitalism, Socialism and Democracy*. 1942. Reprint. New York: Harper Torchbooks, 1976.

Scott, Rebecca. "Explaining Abolition: Contradiction, Adaptation, and Challenge in Cuban Slave Society, 1860–1886." In Manuel Moreno Fraginals, Frank Moya Pons, and Stanley Engerman, eds., *Between Slavery and Free Labor: The Spanish-Speaking Caribbean in the Nineteenth Century*, pp. 25–53. Baltimore: Johns Hopkins University Press, 1985.

———. *Slave Emancipation in Cuba: The Transition to Free Labor, 1860–1899*. Princeton: Princeton University Press, 1985.

———. "The Transformation of Sugar Production in Cuba After Emancipation." In Bill Albert and Adrian Graves, eds., *Crisis and Change in the International Sugar Economy, 1860–1914*, pp. 111–20. Norwich: ISC Press, 1984.

Seers, Dudley. "The Economic and Social Background." In Dudley Seers et al., eds., *Cuba: The Economic and Social Revolution*, pp. 1–64. Chapel Hill: University of North Carolina Press, 1964.

Sheridan, Richard B. *Sugar and Slavery: An Economic History of the British West Indies, 1623–1775*. Baltimore: Johns Hopkins University Press, 1973.

Shlomowitz, Ralph. "Melanesian Labor and the Development of the Queensland Sugar Industry, 1863–1906." In P. Uselding, ed., *Research in Economic History*, pp. 327–61. Vol. 7. Greenwich, Conn.: JAI Press, 1982.

———. "Plantations and Smallholdings: Comparative Perspectives from the World Cotton and Sugar Cane Economies, 1865–1939." *Agricultural History* 58 (1984): 1–16.

———. "The Search for Institutional Equilibrium in Queensland's Sugar Industry, 1884–1913." *Australian Economic History Review* 19 (1979): 91–122.

———. "Team Work and Incentives: The Origins and Development of the Butty

Gang System in Queensland's Sugar Industry, 1891–1913." *Journal of Comparative Economics* 3 (1979): 41–55.

Sitterson, Carlyle. *Sugar Country: The Cane Sugar Industry in the South, 1753–1950.* Lexington: University of Kentucky Press, 1953.

Smith, Robert F. *The United States and Cuba: Business and Diplomacy, 1917–1960.* New York: Bookman Associates, 1960.

Solow, Barbara, and Stanley Engerman, eds. *British Capitalism and Caribbean Slavery: The Legacy of Eric Williams.* New York: Cambridge University Press, 1987.

Stigler, George. "The Economies of Scale." *Journal of Law and Economics* 1 (1958): 61–67.

Stiglitz, Joseph. "Incentives in Risk-sharing in Sharecropping." *Review of Economic Studies* 41 (1983): 219–55.

Stoneman, Paul. *The Economic Analysis of Technical Change.* Oxford: Oxford University Press, 1983.

Stubbs, Jean. *Tobacco on the Periphery: A Case Study in Cuban Labour History, 1860–1958.* Cambridge, England: Cambridge University Press, 1985. Spanish edition: *Tabaco en la periferia: El complejo agro-industrial cubano y su movimiento obrero, 1860–1959.* Havana: Editorial de Ciencias Sociales, 1989.

Stuckey, John A. *Vertical Integration and Joint Ventures in the Aluminum Industry.* Cambridge, Mass.: Harvard University Press, 1983.

Sugar, Jan. 23, 1921, pp. 1–2.

Summerhill, William. "The Cuban Agricultural Economy Before the Ten Years' War." Paper presented at the Annual Meeting of the Economic History Association, October 1994, Cincinnati.

Sunkel, Osvaldo. "Capitalismo transnacional y desintegración nacional en la América Latina." *El Trimestre Económico* 38 (1971): 571–628.

Takayama, Akira. *Mathematical Economics.* 2d ed. Cambridge, England: Cambridge University Press, 1985.

Taussig, F. W. *Some Aspects of the Tariff Question: An Examination of the Development of American Industries Under Protection.* Cambridge, Mass.: Harvard University Press, 1931.

———. *The Tariff History of the United States.* 8th ed. Reprints in Economics Classics. New York: Augustus M. Kelley Publishers, 1967.

Teece, David. "Economics of Scope and the Scope of the Enterprise." *Journal of Economic Behavior and Organization* 1 (1980): 223–47.

Temin, Peter. *Iron and Steel in Nineteenth-Century America.* Cambridge, Mass.: MIT Press, 1964.

Thomas, Hugh. *Cuba: The Pursuit of Freedom.* London: Eyre and Spottiswoode, 1971.

Timoshenko, Vladimir, and Boris Swerling. *The World's Sugar: Progress and Policy.* Stanford: Stanford University Press, 1957.

Tinker, Hugh. *A New System of Slavery: The Export of Indian Labour Overseas, 1830–1970.* London: Oxford University Press, 1974.

Tobin, James. "Comment." In Robert Ferber, ed., *Determinants of Investment Behavior.* New York: National Bureau of Economic Research, 1967.

Tortella, Gabriel Casares. *El desarrollo de la España contemporánea: Historia económica de los siglos XIX y XX*. Madrid: Alianza Editorial, 1994.

———. "El desarrollo de la industria azucarera y la guerra de Cuba." *Moneda y Crédito* 91 (1964): 131–63.

Treadway, Arthur B. "The Rational Multivariate Flexible Accelerator." *Econometrica* 39 (1971): 845–55.

Turu, Danielle. "En torno a los costos de producción azucarera en Cuba a mediados del siglo XIX." *Cuban Studies* 11 (1981): 65–86.

U.S. Bureau of Labor Statistics. *Wholesale Prices and Price Indexes*. Washington, D.C.: Bureau of Labor Statistics, 1890–1930.

U.S. Congressional Committee on Agriculture. *History and Operations of the U.S. Sugar Program*. Washington, D.C.: U.S. Government Printing Office, 1962.

U.S. Department of Commerce. *The Cane Sugar Industry: Agricultural, Manufacturing, and Marketing Costs in Hawaii, Porto Rico, Louisiana, and Cuba*. Washington, D.C.: U.S. Government Printing Office, 1917.

———. *Investment in Cuba: Basic Information for the United States Businessman*. Washington, D.C.: U.S. Government Printing Office, 1956.

U.S. Department of Commerce, Bureau of the Census. *Historical Statistics of the United States from Colonial Times to the Present*. Part 1. Washington, D.C.: U.S. Government Printing Office, 1975.

U.S. Department of Commerce, Bureau of Foreign and Domestic Commerce. *Foreign Commerce and Navigation of the United States*. Washington, D.C.: U.S. Government Printing Office, annual series.

U.S. Department of War. *Civil Report of Major General Leonard Wood: Civil Orders and Circulars*. Vol. 2, no. 34, Feb. 7, 1902. Baltimore: Guggenheimer, Weil, 1902.

———. *Report of the Census of Cuba, 1899*. Washington, D.C.: U.S. Government Printing Office, 1900.

U.S. Oficina del Censo. *Censo de la República de Cuba, 1907*. Washington, D.C.: Oficina del Censo, 1908.

U.S. Tariff Commission. *Costs of Production in the Sugar Industry*. Tariff Information Series, no. 9. Washington, D.C.: U.S. Government Printing Office, 1919.

Usátegui y Lezama, Angel. *El colono cubano*. Havana: Jesus Montero, Editor, 1938.

Van Ness, Carl. "Sugar, Railroads, and Dollar Diplomats: Railroad Construction in Eastern Cuba, 1891–1923." Master's thesis, University of Florida, Gainesville, 1985.

Venegas Delgado, Hernán, "Acerca del proceso de concentración y centralización de la industria azucarera en la región remediana a fines del siglo XIX." *Islas* 86 (1987): 63–121.

Wallich, Henry. *Monetary Problems of an Export Economy: The Cuban Experience, 1914–1947*. Cambridge, Mass.: Harvard University Press, 1960.

Waterson, Michael. *Economic Theory of the Industry*. Cambridge, England: Cambridge University Press, 1984.

Weiss, Leonard. "The Survival Technique and the Extent of Suboptimal Capacity." *Journal of Political Economy* 71 (1963): 246–61.

Whatley, Warren. "Southern Agrarian Labor Contracts as Impediments to Cotton Mechanization." *Journal of Economic History* 48 (1987): 45–70.

Wilkins, Mira. *The Emergence of Multinational Enterprise: American Business Abroad from the Colonial Era to 1914*. Cambridge, Mass.: Harvard University Press, 1970.

———. *The Maturing of Multinational Enterprise: American Business Abroad from the Colonial Era to 1914*. Cambridge, Mass.: Harvard University Press, 1974.

Willett and Gray's Weekly Statistical Sugar Trade Journal. New York: Willett and Gray.

Williamson, Harold, and Arnold Daum. *The American Petroleum Industry*. Evanston: Northwestern University Press, 1959.

Williamson, Oliver E. "Credible Commitments: Using Hostages to Support Exchange." *American Economic Review* 73 (1983): 519–40.

———. *The Economic Institutions of Capitalism*. New York: Free Press, Macmillan, 1985.

———. *Markets and Hierarchies: Analysis and Antitrust Implications*. New York: Free Press, 1975.

Williamson, Oliver E., and Sidney G. Winter, eds. *The Nature of the Firm: Origins, Evolution, and Development*. New York: Oxford University Press, 1993.

Winkler, Max. *Investments of United States Capital in Latin America*. Boston: World Peace Foundation, 1929.

Wright, Gavin. *Old South, New South*. New York: Basic Books, Harper Collins, 1986.

Wright, Irene A. *Cuba*. New York: Macmillan, 1910.

Wright, Philip G. *The Cuban Situation and Our Treaty Relations*. Washington, D.C.: Brookings Institution, 1931.

———. *Sugar in Relation to the Tariff*. New York: McGraw-Hill, 1924.

Zanetti Lecuona, Oscar. *Cautivos de la reciprocidad*. Havana: Editorial ENPES, 1989.

———. "1929: La crisis mundial y la crisis cubana." *Santiago* 49 (1983): 173–94.

Zanetti Lecuona, Oscar, and Alejandro García Alvarez. *Caminos para el azúcar*. Havana: Editorial de Ciencias Sociales, 1987.

———. *United Fruit Company: Un caso del dominio imperialista en Cuba*. Havana: Editorial de Ciencias Sociales, 1976.

Zeitlin, Maurice, and Robert Scheer. *Cuba: Tragedy in Our Hemisphere*. New York: Grove Press, 1963.

Zimbalist, Andrew, ed. *The Cuban Socialist Economy Toward the 1990s*. Boulder: Lynne Reinner, 1987.

Zimbalist, Andrew, and Claes Brundenius. *The Cuban Economy: Measurement and Analysis of Socialist Performance*. Baltimore: Johns Hopkins University Press, 1989.

I n d e x

In this index an "f" after a number indicates a separate reference on the next page, and an "ff" indicates separate references on the next two pages. A continuous discussion over two or more pages is indicated by a span of page numbers, e.g., "57–59." *Passim* is used for a cluster of references in close but not consecutive sequence.

Library of Congress Cataloging-in-Publication Data

Dye, Alan.
  Cuban sugar in the age of mass production : technology and the
economics of the sugar central, 1899–1929 / Alan Dye.
    p. cm.
  Includes bibliographical references and index.
  ISBN 0-8047-2819-4
  1. Sugar trade — Cuba — History — 20th century.   2. Sugar trade —
Cuba — Technological innovations — History — 20th century.   3. Sugar
factories — Cuba — History — 20th century.   I. Title.
HD9114.C89D79   1998
338.1'7361'097291 — dc21   97-6657
                                                      CIP

This book is printed on acid-free, recycled paper.

Original printing 1998
Last figure below indicates year of this printing:
07 06 05 04 03 02 01 00 99 98